# TEXTURES OF THE ORDINARY

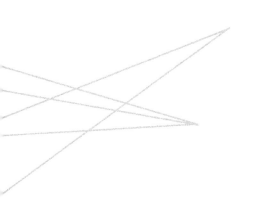

# Thinking from Elsewhere

FORDHAM UNIVERSITY PRESS    NEW YORK 2020

# TEXTURES OF THE ORDINARY

## Doing Anthropology after Wittgenstein

VEENA DAS

Fordham University Press has no responsibility for the persistence or accuracy of URLs for external or third-party internet websites referred to in this publication and does not guarantee that any content on such websites is, or will remain, accurate or appropriate.

Fordham University Press also publishes its books in a variety of electronic formats. Some content that appears in print may not be available in electronic books.

Visit us online at www.fordhampress.com.

Library of Congress Control Number: 2020901894

Printed in the United States of America

22 21 20    5 4 3 2 1

First edition

*For—Stanley Cavell*
*In your writing I am existed.*

*And, connecting generations above and beyond me,*

*For—Nayan, Lucas, Uma, Ayla, Lola, Kiran, and Nathaniel*
*In your gifts and your dadu's too, I am taken afar and brought back home.*

# CONTENTS

# PREFACE

Either we are able to rethink a thought that comes our way, to own and access it as it occurs, or we must let it pass, it is not ours.

—RALPH WALDO EMERSON

This book is composed in the nature of a collection, not only in the sense that it is a collection of essays, many of which had earlier incarnations, but also because it involved a task best described as raking the leaves of memory: collecting pieces of an ethnographic past, recollecting a life lived with texts—literary and philosophical—and in the process allowing myself to be educated, as it were, in public. I dared myself to return to questions that had baffled me or on which I had settled too quickly. In the following essays, readers familiar with my earlier work will see how new aspects of a biography, or of a relationship, or of a neighborhood, dawn upon me as I go back to earlier accounts; or they will see how the passage of time has made certain figures reappear, made to carry a different kind of weight in my thinking now. Readers encountering my work for the first time will, I hope, see that the persons, scenes, events seem to have had past lives to which some may be attracted and some may even feel like befriending them. There are some relations I made with people, places, and texts that are marked by a much greater intensity than others—but there were also those with whom I did not have the mental fortitude to stay with or who faded from my life and work because of accidents of fate.[1]

It is not easy to retell something. In the famous play, *Uttararamacharita* (Rama's Last Act) the eighth-century playwright, Bhava-bhuti (2007), builds the entire action as a story that is not unfolding before us but that is being created in the retelling.[2] In some ways, this is the fate of epic stories in

India as they are constantly retold, reinterpreted, reinvented—the past never dies. As Girish Karnad, in his foreword to Sheldon Pollock's excellent translation, describes the play:

> In the "Final chapter" (*Uttarakāṇḍa*) of the "Ramayana," however—a later addition to Valmiki's poem—a single act of Rama's sets the entire action rolling, and it is an act the ethical justification of which has always been ambiguous. Rama here is responsible for inflicting humiliation and pain on the queen he knows to be innocent. . . . Bhava-bhuti in "Rama's Last Act" exploits the enormous potential and ethical complexity of this situation but instead of a straightforward dramatization of a fairly simple original narrative, he takes breath-taking risks with his material by refracting the narrative and projecting it from different and often conflicting angles. (Karnad 2007, 19–20)

I evoke one poignant moment in the play at the end of Act 1. The prologue has already established the fact that we are in the middle of a performance. Here Lakshmana, Rama's younger brother, is showing Rama and Sita the story of Rama's life as depicted by a skilled painter "just as we depicted it to him." Rama asks, "How far does the story go?" Lakshmana replies, "Up to sister-in-law's purification by fire." Rama immediately exhorts him to stop. "Silence," adding that "neither holy water nor fire requires cleansing from some secondary source." Here the word with which Rama stops Lakshmana's depiction is *shāntam* (lit. "peace"). The word's more luminous shades indicate an end to turbulence, but in its darker shades it refers to death as in someone becoming *shānta*. The reader will see that there are many places in the text when I too find it impossible to go on. Chapter 1 concludes with the words: "The love of anthropology may yet turn out to be an affair in which when I reach bedrock I do not break through the resistance of the other. But in this gesture of waiting, I allow the knowledge of the other to mark me." Chapter 4 ends with: "At one point in *Endgame*, Clove says, 'The end is terrific,' to which Hamm responds: 'I prefer the middle.' And Cavell has much of importance to say on being an eschatologist versus being just in the middle in this scene when finding a cure for being on earth is not the issue, perhaps enduring this condition is. I stop at this point." Chapter 9, in which I read Wittgenstein's *Remarks on Frazer's "Golden Bough,"* ends with something like the idea of stopping in the middle: "For now, I leave this chapter with the idea . . ."[3]

From one perspective, leaving things in the middle indicates a kind of fragility in my writing—that I am unable to come up with forceful, compelling conclusions. My thought seems to proceed in crab-like movements, forward and sideways, rather than being able to run for the finishing line. I forgo the big story but there is a lattice of small stories—perhaps an album of sorts.

In that spirit, I take several small steps in order to build an edifice of concepts and descriptions that emerge simultaneously from a reading of Wittgenstein and from events and characters I delineate from my fieldwork experiences in several low-income localities and slums in Delhi, where my work for the last two decades has been located.[4] I would caution here that concepts emerge out of the engagement with practices of everyday life: they are humble, everyday, and not magisterial even when, and especially because, I attach the names Wittgenstein and Cavell to them.[5] In each of the following chapters I engage with one or another notion that is a part of the lexicon made available in Wittgenstein's writings—our life *in* language (not just *with* language); forms of life; philosophical grammar; grammatical illusion; private language; primitive reactions; pain; doubt; skepticism; pictures that hold us captive; language games; interiority; depth; taking words home; physiognomy of words; builder's language; error; superstition; ordinary; everyday; concepts; human; bedrock; learning (see also Chauviré and Sackur 2003). Yet these words do not function as specialized concepts that can simply be applied to a region of reality that they parse out for themselves. In putting these words on a mobile trajectory occasioned by an ethnographic event, or scene, or snips of dialogue, or gestures and not only with regard to plots and characters, I find a way to shed some light on and make intelligible the elusiveness of the ordinary. Together they show the many facets of everyday life—questions about politics, ethics, kinship, friendship, labor, landscape arise, as do references to happiness, sorrow, anger, violence, death—but these are built together through descriptions, examples from literary texts, and sometimes confrontations with vocabularies from Sanskrit texts or words honed by the residents of these areas within the flux of everyday experiences. I do not use the astonishing variety of terms from Wittgenstein as some kind of magic words that will open up a region of thought and illuminate empirical observations as with the touch of a button. Instead, I think of my work in this book as a sifting of field notes, books, memories of encounters in the field and with fellow thinkers—it is a picture of thinking that does not rest on flashing illuminations but almost begs for the cover of darkness within which thought can take shape.

# TEXTURES OF THE ORDINARY

# INTRODUCTION

An early thought in Wittgenstein's *Philosophical Investigations* comes in the form of a warning, by pointing to examples that show thought to be sometimes conceived in a gaseous medium. Wittgenstein then declares, "The problems are solved, not by giving new information, but by arranging what we have always known. Philosophy is a battle against the bewitchment of our intelligence by means of language" (Wittgenstein [1953] 1968, §109).[1] This book, the one before you, comes not from any desire to establish or contribute to something like a field of study called "philosophical anthropology" but from the desire for an education (call it an education for grownups) by working with texts of Wittgenstein and their iteration in the writings of Stanley Cavell, on the one hand, and learning through a deep immersion in the lives of families and neighborhoods in Delhi with whom I have worked for more than three decades, on the other. I call my mode of reading Wittgenstein and Cavell a striving for an education, an apprenticeship, in part to show the work I did to quieten somewhat the fear of my thought becoming gaseous and in part to acknowledge that I read these texts not as a Wittgenstein scholar in philosophy but as one for whom the problems these philosophers discern in their work arise equally in the weave of actual lives in which I have participated as an anthropologist. I hope that as the following chapters unfold they will reveal that the axis of need on which my thinking revolves is the sense of puzzlement arising in my ethnographic work and the concern that I will fall into the trap of covering up what I do not understand by using a lattice of terms that I understand even less.[2]

Because I have imagined my reader in this book as a "you" and not as part of an anonymous third-person public, I have allowed autobiographical moments to seep into the scenes I construct out of my ethnography and out of my life. This means that I am not presenting this book as an authoritative account of how philosophy enters anthropological discussions, not even as an authoritative account of the social institutions, interpersonal relations, or modes of thought revealed through fieldwork in a bounded community. Yet, as I said, I have immersed myself resolutely in the books from which I draw in the discussions that follow. I have also spent decades with families in low-income neighborhoods in Delhi just as I spent years when I was young, researching family and kinship matters among those displaced by the Partition of India, and later, in communities made destitute by the horrendous violence perpetrated against Sikhs living in the peripheral areas of Delhi (Das 2007).[3] I have eschewed neither method nor the attraction of the concrete—indeed, I contend that the ethnographic impulse to render the texture of the ordinary depends upon close attention to detail. But how much detail and what kind of detail?

During fieldwork I have collected genealogies, conducted surveys, elicited life histories, made time charts, drawn maps, held focus group discussions at my field sites, with the help of the staff at ISERDD in Delhi who have also acted as my interlocutors (for more detail, see Das 2014).[4] But most of all what I have treasured is the opportunity to have been able to place myself in proximity to quotidian flows of conversations within these neighborhoods, participating in things that happened when I was there, or listening to what people in these places wanted to tell me. Part of the impulse of this book is to see how different routes to knowing—through tracing microhistories and microgeographies of neighborhoods, through attentiveness to words that suddenly swell up without any warning, and through quotidian forms of revelation and concealment—are all braided into each other as I try to understand the texture of the ordinary. In his lectures delivered at the Collège de France in 1973–1974, and later compiled in the book *Psychiatric Power*, Foucault makes a distinction between two different conceptions of truth (see Foucault 2003). The first is demonstrative truth that underlies the contemporary scientific understanding of demonstrating through marshalling of evidence whether a hypothesis is true or false, and thus, in theory, allowing anyone with the right qualifications to judge its truth or falsity. The second is a notion of truth that only some people by virtue of their position or by some special dispensation are allowed to pronounce (e.g., oracles, prophets).[5] It was Foucault's careful attention to detail

*Foucault's notion of truth*

that allowed him to show that even though the first notion of truth had become dominant, the second continued to hide in the nooks and crannies of the first. He famously compared the first to the sky—such truth was supposed to be discoverable everywhere by everyone—while the second kind of truth he called the truth-thunderbolt that bursts upon us not by following any method but by virtue of an uncommon insight or a vision that was available only through charisma of one sort or another (Foucault 2003, 235–40).

One way that I can describe the method I follow is to incorporate both notions of truth within the ethnography rather than elevating one above the other. Thus, for some purposes it matters to me that I have carefully collected information on how an authorized map of a neighborhood was made and what consequences it had for securing electricity meters; or the number of households that had access to municipal water through taps within the house; or why houses had several addresses inscribed on the wall (see Chapter 2). On the other side, an allusive sentence—"I refer to my husband by his name"—said in the context of a discussion on reproductive histories signaled something that I would need to hold, to wait, to receive as a kind of grace, for its significance to dawn—slowly or in a flash (Chapter 4). Meanwhile, in my mind, I would be garnering all the little bits of knowledge I had imbibed about women in the conjugal family, about naming, and about the elusive ways in which anger or love is expressed. That is to say, in interpreting such a statement for which no narrative was offered—there were many times when asked to explain further an opaque statement as this one, the person would respond by saying *"ab aap hi samajh lo"* (now you decipher it)—I would need to gather in my mind all I could about what constituted context within which I could take forward the invitation to try and understand without being explicitly told. This is a question that will be expanded in the chapters that follow, but let me state that context here cannot be restricted to what can be carved out from a flux of experiences by the linguistic apparatus of indexical statements; nor is it simply the information about location and chronology. Rather, it is oriented to questions such as how boundaries between sense and nonsense emerge in a particular life world and how philosophical grammar and its associative criteria create broader understandings of what is a statement, what a request, what a command, and what an appeal for deferral. Said otherwise, we might say that what is at stake is not simply the meaning of a word but what gives words life. Consider the following two remarks from *Philosophical Investigations*:

There is a gulf between an order and its execution. It has to be filled by the act of understanding. (§412)

Only in the act of understanding, is it meant that we are to do THIS. The *order*—why, that is nothing but sounds, ink marks. (§431)

Every sign *by itself* seems dead. *What* gives it life?—In use it is *alive*. Is life breathed into it there?—Or, is the *use* its life? (§432)

I read the two questions—is life *breathed* into the sign when we use it, or is the use its life—to relate to two moments in the life of words: How are they given life? And how might they also be drained of life? Language in either case is internal to forms of life rather than standing outside a reality that it then seeks to represent. When signs are alive—the use is just what is its life—words are at home. But words can be drained of life, become frozen slides, as I showed earlier with reference to the speech of women who could "relate" stories about sexual violence done to them during the Partition of India in 1947 but with what I described as the third-person voice (Das 2007), or what Cavell, in a deeply insightful discussion of what happens to the woman's voice in the film *Gaslight*, calls "negation of voice" (Cavell 1996).[6] Cavell deciphers the cruelty being inflicted on Paula (the protagonist) by her husband: "the mode of torture that is systematically driving Paula out of her mind is to note that she is being deprived of words, of her right to words, of her own voice" (57). The therapy offered without any drama whatsoever, by the young detective who is investigating the weird happenings, is pictured simply as a mode to receive and even complete her words by treating them as unremarkable, ordinary, simply what she saw. In Cavell's words:

> The young detective, in giving her an explanation, in a sense of what she saw, bringing her back from strangulation, reintroducing her to language, demonstrating that her words are not shameful, but ordinary and perfectly credible, that the act of speech is hers to define, returns her to her voice—becoming, one can say, her voice teacher. (58)

So, one important aspect of voice (as distinct from, say, speech acts) is that the voice must belong to me, be mine, not in the sense in which I own a piece of property but in the sense that it acquires life within my history. As Sandra Laugier puts it admirably, "In what way is the language that I speak, inherited from others, mine?" (Laugier 2015, 64). Referring to the persistence of this theme for his philosophy, Cavell (1996) recalls that he had, in *The Claim of Reason* (1979), spoken of "something like" having a voice in your own history and compared the ways in which one may be so denied (deny oneself) in philosophy and in politics. "The denial of voice," he writes, "is not the loss of speech, a form of aphasia, and a loss of reason, of mind, as say the capacity to count, to make a difference" (Cavell 1996, 58).

Breathing life into signs that were not so much dead, in Paula's case, as having become ghostly, takes the task of restoring of trust in one's experience and the confidence that one's words are meaningful because there is someone who receives them as meaningful. Trust in oneself, avowal in the first person, requires a sense of the presence of another as a second person—a theme that comes up in several of the chapters that follow. Thus, one description under which this book could be read is that it traces the moods, modalities, and labor that goes into making the everyday inhabitable, to make it count, even as the dangers that stalk the everyday cannot be overcome once and for all. Some of the vulnerabilities of which I speak in the following chapters arise from our forms of life as *human* forms of life. Others are specific to milieus within which I worked, their susceptibilities to the travails of poverty, violence, betrayals, illness, or early deaths that could have been prevented in another milieu. Yet, it is not as if one could treat the human as the given or regard different cultural forms as examples of variations within the human, as if the human voice or the human body were given, knowable in advance. I try to show that a form of life may be described under the sign of cultural particularity as it might be simultaneously seen as a human form of life—one might be exiled from one's culture but still see oneself as belonging to the human form of life, or one may be exiled from both.

   It is helpful here to conceive of the human not as a universal within which different cultures are contained—one could recall Marilyn Strathern's mereological thinking on part–whole relations, that the whole (as in medieval theology or in imaginations of time travel) might be seen as a dimension of the part rather than containing it.[7] Further, the experience of fieldwork also creates an uncanny sense that multiple durations are folded in the "now"—the experience of living one's personal life as well as the life of an anthropologist results in ethnography touching on elements that are autobiographical much as autobiography becomes suffused with one's ethnographic experience. I am not saying that this rendering offers a standard protocol that all anthropologists follow, or should follow, nor that my description captures the normative dimension of ethnography—but if one does allow oneself to be molded by one's ethnography, some such transfiguration of the self, as yet indeterminate and perhaps just a rumbling of what is to come, becomes palpable in the field or retrospectively when one thinks back.

Later in the book (Chapter 11), I elaborate on this insight through the discussion of a recent book by Renato Rosaldo, a book of anthropoetry, born out of a compulsion to recreate the event of his wife's tragic death on a field trip to a remote mountainous region in northern Philippines, not far from where they had conducted fieldwork earlier. The book is striking for its provocation to think anew the relation between ethnography and autobiography. Rosaldo does not so much intend to write on this theme—it is wrenched out of him through the lens of this traumatic event. Still, his weaving of the extraordinary and the ordinary brings up an overarching issue for me that I address throughout this book.[8] In some ways, the weaving of the trauma of his wife's accidental death with ordinary acts like feeding or bathing his two young children alerts us to events that run adjacent to the swirl of emotions of grief and feelings of numbness that are themselves part of the trauma but are also an intimation of a future to come. The sense that the everyday will be returned but in a deformed way draws us into a wider discussion of the relation between what is ordinary and what is extraordinary in thinking of everyday life.

## THE ORDINARY AND THE EVERYDAY: KINDRED CONCEPTS STRAINING AT THEIR LIMITS

In an essay on perfectionist returns to the ordinary, the philosopher Piergiorgio Donatelli (2015) thinks of two different routes that a return takes in the perfectionist register that Cavell introduces in the discussion of the everyday. The first route is that in which an extraordinary event of traumatic loss functions as both an event and a figure of thought to bring forward the uneventful ordinary lives within which loss is diffused. He discusses this possibility through the television series *The Leftovers*, in which a very large part of the human population of the world has inexplicably disappeared. He shows how the protagonist, Lisa, who has lost her whole family—in fact, her whole world—tries to rebuild her life but discovers herself to be beyond repair. In contrast, another television series, *Six Feet Under*, explores the vulnerabilities of life, of loss, death, aging, and illness without reference to an initial Great Loss. From here Donatelli takes us to the philosophical literature and shows how in both Nietzsche and Wittgenstein the return to the ordinary happens after they have overcome the philosophical necessity or the attraction of the large dramatic view of life against which the uneventful, the humble, and the diminutive might be brought forward on the philosophical stage. In Nietzsche's case, says Donatelli, the tragic view (*The Birth of Tragedy*) seems crucial to bring into view, and subsequently to overcome, in order to allow a return to the ordinary as in *Human, All Too Human*. The expression Donatelli uses for a return to the ordinary for Nietzsche is "intimacy with the earth"; interestingly, one of my own interlocutors, a minor leader living in one of the slums also used the expression "friendship with the earth" to allude to the ordinary.[9]

In contrast with (or parallel to) this view of forms of life as vulnerable to catastrophic events, Cavell draws attention to the kind of destruction that consists of small, recurring, repetitive crises almost woven into everyday life itself. What is catastrophic is not a spectacular event but that which is happening repeatedly, undramatically, uneventfully. Yet, Wittgenstein too was once tempted by the picture of getting to the purified essence of language in *Tractatus*, although, as Cora Diamond (1988b) argues, he throws away the ladder (a metaphor for the longing for finding the essence of language) as he finds that if the conditions are too ideal, we cannot walk—"Back to the rough ground" (Wittgenstein [1953] 1968, §107). We might, then, consider these examples—Nietzsche and Wittgenstein, on the one hand, and Cavell, on the other—as different sorts of returns to the ordinary. In the first case, the large catastrophic event leaves its marks on relations even as the ordinary acts are resumed; in the second case, the threats and omens are secreted in the most ordinary expressions and effects, as in Edgar Allan Poe's (1843) claim that, in his chilling stories, all he is doing is relating household events.

In his foreword to my book *Life and Words: Violence and the Descent into the Ordinary* (Das 2007) that exemplified the first impulse of showing what it was to go on in the aftermath of extreme violence, Cavell writes:

> I was prompted to ask myself whether her cases of extreme manifestation of a society's internal, one could say, intimate and absolute violence are comprehensible as extreme states, or suddenly invited enactments,

of a pervasive fact of the social fabric that may hide itself, or one might also say, may express itself, in everyday encounters. (Cavell 2007, xiii)

This putting together of the ordinary and the extraordinary as an essential feature of the texture of everyday life comes out with great force in Cavell's (2010) remarkable autobiography, *Little Did I Know*, which has been the subject of important philosophical commentary.[10] Here is a citation from the text that Donatelli is struck by:

> Put still otherwise, so much of what has formed me has been not events but precisely the uneventful, the nothing, the unnoted, that is happening, the coloration or camouflage of the everyday. The extraordinariness of what we accept as ordinary does not manifest its power over us until we are conscious at the same time of the ordinariness of the extraordinary. A stone on which this coupling breaks we might call a miracle or a holocaust, a departure from and within the ordinary that is not merely extraordinary, but irreversibly traumatic. (Cavell 2010, 61)

By now you might wonder why I have avoided giving definitions of terms that appear in Wittgenstein and are often regarded as constituting a conceptual repertoire of sorts—terms such as *forms of life, hinge, nonsense, agreement, criterion, description, internal relation, private language, aspect-dawning, bedrock.* Surely these are specialized concepts—are they not? Rupert Read (2005) engages the question of the place of technical terms in Wittgenstein and compares them to "magic" words that often make their appearance in texts to conjure something that does not really exist. While I sidestep any detailed discussion of this issue here, I have little doubt that terms that appear in Wittgenstein are not in the nature of concepts that come to us already defined through which we parse out different regions of the real; as part of our lives, concepts are not applied to reality that stands outside and confronts us frontally. Instead, I am interested in the way concepts become or are vulnerable to experience.

In chapters 11 and 12, I take up these issues in greater detail, arguing that one way to think of the open texture of concepts is to think of them not through modes of abstraction through which the different concrete cases are brought under the umbrella of a concept, procedures of inclusion and exclusion, but through projection and the internal limits determined through a feeling of "rightness" of a particular projection from one example to another. As Laugier (2017) writes: "The question of realism is deeply transformed by attention to the particular and by the sensitivity of our concepts to experience (the reverse of what we might call a Kantian conception of the application of concepts to experience). The radical transformation of concepts is what I call our life with concepts: The fact that they are in this world and even often (for ordinary concepts) in or of *the ordinary world*. As Cavell says of the ordinary world, that may not be all there is but it is important enough!"

> But wouldn't those words too be only a *germ*? They must surely belong to a language and to a context, in order really to be the expression of the thought of that man. (Wittgenstein [1953] 1968, 217<sup>e</sup>)

But now think of other scenes depicted in *Philosophical Investigations*—the builders' language (*PI*, §2, 8) that consists only of commands bringing to mind the game of language in the Asylum as Foucault (2003, 149–51) describes it in *Psychiatric Power*: the trancelike state in which I might try to buy a red apple by first assembling everything that is red and then separating out the red apple from the pile in which pencils, toy cars, radishes, lamb, socks, all red in color, are heaped together (*PI*, §1). Or imagine yourself in a society in which one has no attachment to one's words and so people will readily substitute one word for another, or think of the amazement of the child that when the tailor said he sewed a dress, the child imagined there was no fabric that came between the tailor and the dress (*PI*, §195). Or think of the animals that leave their tracks—cows, beetles, dogs, lions, flies—in the different scenes, such as trying to repair a spider's web, or the fly in the bottle,[11] or the dog expecting his master when he hears footsteps, but our inability to say he hopes that it is his master at the doorstep. It becomes clear that if we are to take the pitch and tone of *Philosophical Investigations* as essential to its composition, then we would need to grasp it by means other than the procedures of argumentation that take concepts as neutral intellectual tools standing outside a reality to which they are applied. For some purposes we might assume that the conventional picture of reality that comes knocking at the door and dismantles our concepts might be useful—as the work concepts such as force or velocity might do in physics, at least I imagine it is important for physicists to believe so as a condition of possibility for doing so—for other purposes, we might want to think what the purchase might be to think how our concepts might crisscross each other and shape what appears as the force of the real—to be attentive not just to the "shock" of reality but also to the way the uncanny appears within the scene of the real. As Jocelyn Benoist writes:

> One should overcome the picture of concepts as constituting some kind of "screen" between us and reality—as if we stayed, ourselves, in somewhere outside of reality. Of course we are *in*, and concepts are a very important part of our ways to be within reality—they are as many ways to give importance to things. That is not to say that the image of the *screen* is absolutely worthless. Concepts can indeed become such a screen, when we deal with them abstractly and withdraw, so to speak, from our own life and our belonging to reality. Such abstraction is however only one possible use and *misuse* of concepts. It supposes that we who use concepts forget ourselves as the ones who use concepts and as such cannot see them anymore as something used. They become thus a universe per se and in that way, something like a screen, if not blinds. All the violence of reality is then required in order to break through the screen. (Benoist 2018)

The procedures I have taken in this book are to take the scenes in Wittgenstein and Cavell's attunement to them as integral to their method, as I try to put together a picture of the everyday as lined with skepticism in which the grounds can slip not only because of catastrophic events but also because of the inability to accept the violence internal to human relationships—the desire to escape the limits of the everyday. I am interested in the everyday as the site on which the life of the other is engaged but this other is not the radical Other of either philosophy or anthropology. As an anthropologist I am attuned to concrete others, even daring to suggest that it is in following concrete relations, quotidian turns of events, the waxing and waning of intensities, that we learn to be in the world. I have taken inspiration from Wittgenstein's idea that the task is to lead words back from the metaphysical to the ordinary and to make do with what words we have in hand. While I will deal at greater length with the question of what it means to strive for concepts that are humble, born of the everyday, and the stakes in eschewing explanation in favor of description, or the simple acts of taking away the excitement born of grammatical illusions, here I satisfy myself with evoking a couple of citations from Wittgenstein as guidelines to the philosophy of Cavell and its intimacy with the anthropological closeness to the concrete. This particular relation to concrete others has left an imprint on everything I have written in the following chapters. I treat the philosophical impulses, the anthropological mode of being in a world, literary references that come into the text sometimes unbidden, as well as autobiographical moments, as lying on the same plane in their ability to bring thought into closer harmony with modes of living; it is important for me to see how each of these impulses is able (or not) to receive figures of thought that generate a picture of everyday life and its forebodings, its ill omens, as well as its ability to stand up to these threats. The particular color lent to the experience of the everyday within these scenes of destruction and reinhabitation will vary—its very heterogeneity accounting for the fact the lines between the good and the evil, security and skepticism, striving and endurance are thin and blurred. This is not because the everyday is hard to find but because it is easy to deflect the difficulty of not being able to see what is before our eyes. Consider Wittgenstein ([1953] 1968) saying:

> When philosophers use a word—"knowledge," "being," "object," "I," "proposition," "name"—and try to grasp the *essence* of the thing, one must always ask oneself: is the word ever actually used in this way in the language which is its original home?—What *we* do is to bring words back from their metaphysical to their everyday use (§116). When I talk about language (word, sentence, etc.), I must speak the language of everyday. So is this language too coarse, too material, for what we want to say? Well then, how is another one to be constructed? (§120)

> The aspects of things that are most important for us are hidden because of their simplicity and familiarity. (One is unable to notice something— because it is always before one's eyes.) The real foundations of his inquiry do not strike a man at all. Unless *that* fact has at some time struck him.— And this means: we fail to be struck by what, once seen, is most striking and most powerful. (§129)

## POLITICS IN AND THROUGH THE ORDINARY

When Wittgenstein speaks of our everyday language being too coarse, too material for what we want to say, but asks how another one is to be constructed, he speaks of the temptation to somehow escape the frailties of everyday—this escape will sometimes take the form of imagining a purified language stripped of all ambiguities, expressing a longing for things to be transparent. Wittgenstein's words also express the ordinary fact of our disappointment with our language. For some scholars, this and other similar remarks in *Philosophical Investigations* have been taken to indicate Wittgenstein's conservatism: a host of scholars have opined that Wittgenstein's philosophy is essentially conservative and leaves no room for criticism of our forms of life (Gellner 1959; Kapferer 2016). Other philosophers have argued the opposite: that there is a radical politics and form of critique embedded in Wittgenstein's philosophy that is premised on the idea that any form of criticism generated from within a form of life is bound to remain constrained by existing categories and limits to imagination of the possible, and thus what Wittgenstein is offering is a way of generating critique that can go beyond present possibilities. Alice Crary (2000) makes a cogent case that both sides of the argument are misled by their (mis)understanding of either language as outside of forms of life that it then seeks to represent or by their understanding of language games as confining meaning to affixed and conventional use. This is not the place for a more detailed engagement with issues in this register, but I will make two observations. First, as Crary (2000) says, it is a mistake to assume that Wittgenstein's suspicion of metaphysical arguments leads to a regrettable reticence, if not a disavowal, of the possibility of transformation in political arrangements, but it is equally misleading to assume that Wittgenstein's philosophy leads to an antirealist position in which not only is the kind of realism that rests on copy theories of truth rejected but the very idea of words being world-bound is rejected. An attention to context in thinking of registers of the real as in various theories of reference, or on the ways concepts parse out regions of the real, is not the same as a commitment to a radically relativist position (Benoist 2018; Michael Williams 2007). So the question is: What is the place for political community in this lineage of thought? And what is it to speak of politics as that which encompasses the domestic—or one might say that encompasses the work that women do to repair the everyday, to open routes for return to the everyday?

In Cavell, the relation between the everyday conceived as the domestic and politics conceived as a larger community of consent where consent is not given once and for all but must be earned by allowing expression to the individual to find her voice engages classic questions of political representation. After all, as Cavell says, we must be prepared to represent others and to be represented by others for political community to be formed at all. What is it to earn this consent and what it is to withdraw one's consent from the political community as in civil disobedience (Thoreau 1849) or in satyagraha (M. K. Gandhi 1920)? There is a subtle but significant difference in thinking about *agreement* in forms of life and *consent* in the making of political community—a theme I take up in Chapters 3 and 7 on themes of cruelty and noncruelty. An argument I regard as diagonal to this argument is Laugier's work on care that sees the neglect of care as a political principle, the neglect of female forms of political activity. For Laugier, the issue is not care versus justice but the struggle to reimagine politics by stitching the domestic and the public domains, the imperatives of need and those of freedom, together. In Laugier's words:

> Care is at once a practical response to specific needs and a sensitivity to the ordinary details of human life that *matter*. Hence, care is a concrete matter that ensures maintenance (e.g. as conversation and conservation) and continuity of the human world and form of life. This is nothing less than a paradigm shift in ethics, with a reorientation towards vulnerability and a shift from the "just" to the "important," exactly as Wittgenstein proposed shifting the meaning of importance by destroying what seemed to be important. Assessing the importance of care for human life means acknowledging the vulnerability of forms of life. (Laugier 2016, 208)

The issues may be succinctly stated by asking how the "we" of political community and the "we" of forms of life are constituted.

Are these discussions of consent and care too abstract? Let me give two examples from the ethnographic work of Bhrigupati Singh and Clara Han. Singh's work has been singled out by many for its rigorous reading of Deleuze through the lens of ethnography, but he has also given us some unforgettable figures, such as those of Bansi Maharaj and Kalli. Kalli, a former bonded laborer and a fierce political worker for the rights of the Sahariyas (a lower caste/tribe in a district in Rajasthan), seems caught in the grip of relations she can neither fully accept nor indeed just walk away from. In Singh's Kalli we may find shadows of Cavell's reading of Ibsen's Nora—the woman who refuses the sexual settlement part of the social contract (Cavell 1984). We might say that while Nora decisively declares her autonomy from the community—rescinding her consent to an unjust arrangement in marriage—Kalli makes consent, both domestic and political, a different kind of binding in which justice and care are neither in competition nor smoothly tied to each other but are much more erratic. Since childhood, Kalli was befriended by a Jind (jinn, djin) who provided companionship of the sort that jinns sometimes provide to children (Khan 2006). Once Kalli was married, the Jind became envious of her husband. Sometimes the Jind caused Kalli to disappear; at other times, he caused headaches, made her shun her domestic responsibilities, and in general contributed to a quarrelsome and quickly angered disposition. Sometimes, though, he seemed to recede into the background. Once after being challenged by Kalli's husband either to show his power by curing a sickly, nearly dying grandchild or to accept that he was merely a pretender with no real power, the Jind did show his capacity for care by curing the sick child but exacting the price of moving from the house where he had resided into Kalli's body. This shift from cohabitation to possession created more turbulence but then settled into more predictable rhythms. Smaller shifts are shown in the disposition of the husband and Kalli herself and their relation seems for a while to reach greater equanimity.

The story, however, does not find any easy resolution. Through his accrual of detail, Singh detects conflicts within Kalli herself. In one episode, she found herself pushed deeper into the husband's lineage, seeking the mediation of an ancestral deity of her husband by running madly to the fort where the waning ancestral deity resided. At other times this running away from the domestic ends in intermittent or unpredictable forays into the political sphere. For instance, once she joined a local NGO, confronting police officers and senior state officials over a land dispute and staging political protests as she moved in and out of the local NGO that was fighting for the rights of the Sahariyas. There are all kinds of contingencies in play here. Singh surmises that "she could have traveled with the Jind into a life of seclusion and madness, throwing stones at anyone who dared come near" (Singh 2015, 212). But instead, her aging trajectory reveals to her the vulnerabilities of a failing body. She then discovers the strength not only to fight but also to be caring and kind—able to provide consent and care even though of a varying quality.

Singh speculates whether the peace the Jind made with her husband, and her husband made with her, was because Kalli allowed herself to receive succor from the dense kinship networks in the small town in which she lived. But then he concludes, "Living in Kalli's house for extended periods of time, I began to sense that as with the Jind, the same element, say 'home' may be as much a source of vulnerability as it is a ground for strength and growth. One is no safer for never having left home" (Singh 2012, 213). If the Jind, Kalli, and her husband were socialized, they were not exactly socialized into the following of predetermined rules: the Jind perhaps blocked the path of Kalli becoming a dutiful and docile wife, but his presence in her life also released some potential for fighting injustice through engagement with political action. Her forays into politics that her husband was to come to accept later and her frequent returns to him were indicative of the compulsions she felt to respond to injustice but also to return to the care she craved for herself.

A similar delicacy of description is to be found in the second example I take: Clara Han's work on how a single death contained within a milieu of countless instances of police violence in a poor neighborhood in Santiago creates reverberations in the neighborhood she has studied. Using the delicate expression "echoes of death," Han (2015, 2018) tracks how the smallest of gestures (kissing a photograph of the dead person, blowing a kiss, wishing him a good night), and the recurrence of dreams in which what the dead said to the person who dreamed, allow difficult relations to be spoken out, showing how state violence and violence in the domestic come to be seen as aspects of the same milieu.

A running thread in my discussion of the everyday is that its very ordinariness makes it difficult for us to see what is before our eyes. Hence, we need to imagine the shape that the ordinary takes in order to find it: this could be the shape of the ordinary as the domestic, or as the neighborly, or as having the rhythms of the diurnal in the form of repetition. Depending on how we conjure the everyday, the threats to the everyday will also be seen in relation to this picture of the ordinary. If, for instance, we take marriage and domesticity as providing us with the image of the ordinary, then the threats might be seen through doubts about the fidelity of the partner (e.g., in Othello, as Cavell teaches us); if we see the ordinary as habitation within a world in which we dwell in a taken-for-granted way as an animal lives in its habitat, then the threat might be seen as our existence becoming ghostly (Hamlet), losing that natural sense of belonging (Cavell 1987); if the everyday is seen in terms of a precarious order secured through contract between warring men (Hobbes), then the threat will appear as the sexualization of the social contract (the figure of the abducted woman as analyzed in Das 2007).[12] Framing all these pictures of the everyday is the idea that everyday is a site on which the life of the other is engaged, that it is the space not only of habit but of reinhabitation. In a paragraph that I continue to find compelling for my understanding of everyday life, Cavell (1994) dwells on the abstract conceptual moment in Wittgenstein where he talks about his philosophy having destroyed what was, anyway, a house of cards. Cavell writes, "Could its (i.e. the conceptual moment's) color have been evoked as the destruction of a forest by logging equipment, or of a field of flowers by the gathering of a summer concert, or by the march of an army? Not, I think if the idea is that we are going to have to pick up the pieces and find out how, and whether, to go on, that is go on living in this very place of devastation, as of something over" (Cavell 1994, 74).

The pictures of destruction that are first evoked here (the march of the army) suggest that that those whose actions have (willfully or carelessly) destroyed a place of habitation (a forest, a field of flowers) have simply moved on with little regard to what was destroyed, whereas if we are to live in this place of devastation by picking up the pieces, the rubble, and remaking that place, we would need a different picture of what is destroyed in our lives and what it is to pick up the pieces again. Each of the following chapters is an engagement with this theme in one way or another. But talk of destruction cannot but make us think how remaking a place itself has become the scene of utter neglect of what was destroyed as in the rush of developers who try to buy land on the cheap after a natural disaster in order to build luxury hotels (Pugh forthcoming) while people affected by these disasters await relief within the mass of regulations and bureaucratic processes that govern rehabilitation (Lovell 2013; Adams 2013). In contrast, the miracle of small acts of care, whose incommensurability with the horror is not in question, nevertheless, as Cavell says, "allow life to knit itself back pair by pair" (Cavell 2007, xiv). Note that the acts of care *allow* life to knit itself back; there is a fine balance between agency and patiency in the register of the everyday. In *Life and Words*, I conclude that the ability to allow oneself to be marked by the pain of the other, to allow the knowledge of the other to happen to me, was my kind of anthropological devotion to the world. More than a decade separates that book from this one, but my love for anthropology as a devotion to the world remains the same.

One of Cavell's great achievements is to have shown that subjectivity is expressed in the discovery and loss of one's voice in one's history. Wittgenstein and Foucault have the shared concern of overcoming the picture of the subject as psychological subject. While Foucault's work on the subject is pathbreaking not only because of the manner in which he historicizes the subject but also in his showing, in precise detail, how normalizing power works on the individual body to generate the subject—hence the close connection in his work between subjection and subjectivation. However, as Rechtman (2017) argues, this has created a division in which subjectivation falls to the lot of social sciences and subjectivity is left to the psychologist. In Cavell's profound rendering of the problem of skepticism, everyday life is lined with skepticism, but he does not think of skepticism as simply a problem of epistemology—not "How do we know if the world outside exists?" but "Can I bear to make myself known?" If skepticism about the world was defined as a matter of belief and the difficulty of knowledge—something of a scandal for philosophy—Cavell's skepticism is both dated and gendered. Thus, the skeptic's question on the male side of the problem arises in such worries as how do I know that this child is mine or that it is I who am the cause of this woman's pleasure; on the female side it presents itself as the problem of making oneself intelligible, finding someone who is of the same flesh, to whom I might trust my words. Skepticism is thus taken in the realm of the social and is one site where we can see the culturally specific transfigurations that provide the context for living with such issues. Cavell famously argues that the answer to the skeptic's doubts lies not in providing more information, or more evidence, but simply in acknowledging the flesh and blood character of the other who is before me. The theme of skepticism and the uncanny—accepting one's separateness from the other and yet being able to articulate how one's life might be staked in this other—reappears in many of the chapters that follow.

Philosophers sometimes turn to literature to correct the moralism of moral philosophy (Diamond 1996) or to introduce the human voice that philosophy has lost, they say, in its flight from the ordinary (Cavell 1979). The issue for such philosophers is not that of embracing a counterphilosophy and turning to literature but asking if philosophy can receive from the hands of literature what it has lost in its turn to overdetermined analytical reasoning and its banishing of poetry from its kingdom. In the concluding lines of *Claim of Reason*, after he has discussed how we might read Iago and Othello as figures of thought in philosophy—one as the slanderer of human nature (his diabolism), the other as the enactor of the slander—"the one thinking to escape human nature from below, the other from above," Cavell offers this provocation:

> So, we are here, knowing they are "gone to burning hell," she with a lie on her lips, protecting him, he with her blood on him. Perhaps Blake has what he calls songs to win them back with, to make room for hell in a juster city. But can philosophy accept them back at the hands of poetry? Certainly, not as long as philosophy continues, as it has from the first, to demand the banishment of poetry from its republic. Perhaps it could if it could itself become literature. But can philosophy become literature and still know itself? (Cavell 1979, 496)

The "So, we are here"—the first four words of this last paragraph—echoes the "So they are there . . ." of the previous paragraph in which Cavell attests to how the two bodies lying together in their bridal sheets and their death sheets are emblems of the fact that human beings are not open to ocular proof—how do we who are here relate to the they who are there? I think this is the provocation that the question of the human as separate, as overcome with inordinate knowledge, will pose to the anthropologist with regard to the "they" who are there—the challenge of working out who is the "we" and who the "they," where is the "here" and where the "there."

Making a case for this "texture of being" as mattering for moral thought, and hence for philosophy, Diamond (1983, 163) says, "But we cannot see the interest of literature unless we recognize gestures, manners, turns of speech, turns of thought, styles of face as morally expressive of an individual or of a people." Could one make a similar claim on behalf of anthropology? Let us see.

Each chapter of this book brings into view one aspect of the everyday, picking up strands from earlier chapters that were allusive. In the present introduction, as we saw, I set out my mode of reading Wittgenstein and Cavell in the context of what I think of as a lineage of thought—a *parampara*, the Sanskrit term referring not only to adherence to modes of thinking but also to style and aesthetics as in the works of Cora Diamond, Sandra Laugier, Jocelyn Benoist, Piergiorgio Donatelli, Paola Marrati, and Alice Crary. The signature notion in these authors seems to me the idea that philosophical problems arise in the weave of life, and thus the anthropological tonality of their writing is an invitation for creating particular kinds of connections between philosophy, anthropology, and literature. This introduction argues that the relation between anthropology and philosophy is not grounded in a search for better foundations for anthropology, achieved by launching an inquiry into the human as a general category or the human condition, but rather by finding the human in engaging with the concrete in specific milieus. It is from within this perspective that ideas about the everyday, the ordinary, and the threats to the ordinary, whether in the form of large catastrophic events or in the form of recurring and repeated crises, are tracked in the neighborhoods in Delhi where most of my ethnographic work has been located.

Chapter 1, "Wittgenstein and Anthropology: Anticipations," is like a seed in which my first reflections on the promise of engaging Wittgenstein's anthropology was laid out in 1998 for a series on different philosophers in *The Annual Review of Anthropology* (see Das 1998b). The main theme that I identified was an understanding of culture not as a text to be interpreted through root symbols falling on the axes of nature and culture, nor simply as shared values (a vague metaphor at best), but instead as providing the ability to both forge a belonging and find resources within one's culture to contest it and thus to find one's voice in its singularity within it. The chapter explores the concept of counterculture and finds its alignments with skepticism that takes us in a direction that asks not "How do we know that the external world exists?" but "How do I know that I exist, that I can trust myself in relation to others?" Skepticism is engaged in this chapter as lining the everyday: I use the idea of lining not to suggest a border but to allude to the way a coat and its lining, the exterior and the interior, are joined to each other. Hence, skepticism is not the kind of doubt that can be extinguished once and for all. The idea of forms of life is introduced in its horizontal dimension as "form" and its vertical dimension as "life" showing how forms of life are both, particular to a milieu and as drawing from our common background as humans. How does this double aspect find expression in anthropological accounts?

Chapter 2, "A Politics of the Ordinary: Action, Expression, and Everyday Life," takes us to quotidian scenes through which the state is engaged over infrastructural projects, such as ensuring access to electricity and water in a locality in Delhi that has its origins in unauthorized occupations over land. In many debates over policy and paternalism with regard to the poor, I often have the feeling that for many policymakers and academic experts getting access to water is as easy as opening the tap for water to flow. One of the tasks in this chapter is to simply show the intensity and the kind of labor that goes into the task of getting electricity meters installed in a locality that falls outside the administrative category of a recognized colony, often characterized as an informal settlement. This labor might involve, for instance, getting a map of the residential area prepared and authenticated by several ministries of the government, writing endless letters of appeal, making rounds of administrative offices, and waiting in queues, mobilizing enough support from residents for the project, and preparing affidavits promising regular payments for consumption of electricity. It will also entail warding off violence from the mafia-like interests that develop around illegal supply of electricity and extortion of money. I ask if this work performed by the local leaders and their supporters counts as politics.

The chapter engages the work of the philosopher J. L. Austin on performative utterances. Whereas many scholars have taken the aspect of illocutionary force as the emblematic aspect of such utterances, concentrating on felicity conditions, I take up the more problematic concept of perlocutionary effect where Austin is more concerned with risk and failure of utterances and the instability of context. Asking how the kinds of utterances that Cavell names as "passionate utterances" bring into view the lacing of desire into language, the chapter shows the vulnerability of human expression and action and the different routes through which the world comes to have a say in the successes and failures of performative utterances. Although canonical performances such as "I declare . . ." and "I promise . . ." are by their very nature public and assume a sovereign agent, I look at the kinds of work that go into shoring up such utterances in quotidian action in the everyday before or after the moment of dramatic declaration is over. The aspect of the everyday that is highlighted in this chapter is that of the eventual everyday—a possibility that is entailed in the actual everyday but that requires work that I characterize as a form of the political in the ordinary.

Chapter 3, "Ordinary Ethics: Take One," develops an argument for considering ethics as ordinary. Rather than assigning a separate domain for ethics with its own specialized vocabulary for moral life deployed by experts, this chapter argues that we could think of ethics as a spirit that suffuses everyday life, somewhat like logic, as it permeates everyday activities. Much discussion on ethics accords a centrality to moments of breakdown and to principles for making choices in hard cases. While there is a place in social life for occasions that demand a muscular definition of the good, the bad, the righteous, an exclusive emphasis on such moments eclipses those other moments when moral sensibilities are displayed in quotidian acts of care and sustenance. While recognizing the importance of habit as the flywheel of society, the chapter argues that sedimentation of experience is only one aspect of habit, the other being the innovations and improvisations through which the particularity of the concrete other is recognized.

Carrying the theme of texture and the ordinary further, Chapter 4, "Ethics, Self-Knowledge, and Words Not at Home: The Ephemeral and the Durable," takes up a particular problematic in the depiction of the everyday—that its very closeness makes it impossible to see it. I ask what kinds of emissaries, then, does the everyday send in order for it to be recognized. The chapter pays particular attention to words not at home, by which I mean that the fieldwork experience does not consist simply of collecting stories or coherent narratives with a clear plot and a delineation of characters. Rather, words and gestures swell up suddenly, often, out of context, and provide a glimpse into the turbulent waters that often flow behind the seemingly peaceful and uneventful everyday. Tracking moments such as deathbed statements or moments in a ritual performance when something discordant happens, I ask how such moments signal the risks to which our actions and expressions are prone. Instead of the psychological subject, does the *grammatical person* give us clues with which to think of the self and its opacity? Acknowledging the asymmetry in the first- and third-person stances, the chapter argues for the salience of the second person as the addressee of a speech event and the relevance of the other for giving life to words. The signature theme of finding one's voice in one's history finds ethnographic and literary affirmation in attentiveness to fleeting moments that, from another perspective, might last forever.

Chapter 5, "Disorders of Desire or Moral Striving? Engaging the Life of the Other," takes one case of the dangers posed by desire across religious divides—in this instance, the small event of a Muslim girl and a Hindu boy in one of the low-income neighborhood in Delhi having fallen in love with each other. The scene of desire that transcends religious differences and transgresses a given moral code is a significant motif in the poetic imaginary in South Asia, but it rarely asks how such desire is sustained within the social. Instead, usually such love affairs are presented either in the form of cautionary tales or as allegories of the closeness of love and death. In the case examined in this chapter, the motif shifts to that of inhabiting a life in this difference. While the ambiguity of desire is fully explored in this chapter so that the classic question of whether erotic desire is for an earthly beloved or the divine beloved hovers over the event in all its unfolding, the chapter shows that it is not only the couple but everyone in the family who is given an opportunity to make shifts, to learn how to inhabit a newness. I offer the notion of an adjacent self, parallel to the idea of the neighborhood of actual everyday and eventual everyday, to show a moral sensibility that is not about escape from the everyday but an inhabitation of the everyday through a realization of new possibilities within it.

Chapter 6, "Psychiatric Power, Mental Illness, and the Claim to the Real: Foucault in the Slums of Delhi," brings out the dark potentials of the everyday by focusing on the madness of a young boy and by showing how his illness reverberates in the family and the neighborhood. For his family, the madness leads to an exhaustion of the abilities to care. I place this case within a conversation over norms and normativity within the milieu of neighborhoods steeped in chronic violence. Parallel to the unfolding of events as the madness of this young boy moves between the family and the clinic, I show the slow development of the concepts of psychiatric power over the course of Foucault's lectures at the Collège de France and argue that what gets effaced in much discussion of Foucault's concepts of disciplinary power is the specificity of different kinds of power subsumed under this concept. Thus, for instance, when the scene of madness in Foucault's work *Psychiatric Power* is the asylum, the concern is with the way the psychiatrist imposes a different version of reality on the incarcerated patients not through authoritative knowledge but through tokens of power. In contrast, when the psychiatrist stands in the court of law as the expert witness in the subsequent lectures in *Abnormal*, his power becomes less of imposing a new reality than of providing criteria for distinguishing the criminal and the mad person. As Foucault says, the psychiatrist is no longer present in a therapeutic role; he has simply become the guardian of the social body. Is this conceptualization of the productive power of psychiatry relevant for understanding the scene of madness in poor localities in Delhi? What happens before the psychiatrist or the mental health expert comes on the scene and what happens after he leaves?

It is here that I find that the concepts from Canguilhem that Foucault overwrites—those of *normatively normal* in which norms may be transgressed and those of *pathologically normal* in which the death of normativity itself is encoded—capture an aspect of the darkest side of everyday life in these neighborhoods, and Swapan's case (the protagonist of this story in the chapter) shows how families come to become the scene of trance, illusion, and an exhaustion of caregiving abilities. Yet as Foucault was well aware, the residues that are left in the games of power and resistance after their exhaustion at one threshold of life can come alive at another threshold. One way to read this chapter is to bring forth the concept of aspect dawning from Wittgenstein through which we see how residues become re-animated. As one aspect of power, say its normalizing function as discipline, fades out, another aspect, such as its alignment with sovereign forms of punishment, might find new objects. For Foucault, the archive was the place where individuals who are caught in the grip of the law become available as subjects to the historian, but for the anthropologist, the life of law flows through different kinds of hinges and junctions that, though not unmediated, are not exhausted by the archive.

In Chapter 7, "The Boundaries of the 'We': Cruelty, Responsibility, and Forms of Life," I ask if the state of pathological normativity that is evident in the threats to the everyday in the slums in Delhi and that makes the securing of the everyday an achievement is also something that characterizes the disorders of contemporary democracies. In particular, I ask, What does it mean to belong to a political community in which torture is routinely practiced? What responsibilities devolve on us as members of these communities even if we have never given consent to the practice of torture? Through a triangular reading of J. M. Coetzee's two novels *Waiting for the Barbarians* and *Diary of a Bad Year* in conversation with the philosopher/psychoanalyst Jonathan Lear, I ask what is the nature of violence under Empire? Might we speak of the erosion not only of this or that society under Empire but also of the human form of life in the sense in which the magistrate, a man completely unaware of his own complicity in projects of Empire and the torture practiced in it, becomes a figure of horror to himself? How does one read the creation of a sense of vulnerability by making the time of not-happening as quintessentially the time of happening? A time when violence from the barbarians (a figure that functions as floating signifier ready to be filled by any historically marginalized group) may not have happened yet but is waiting at the door of reality. I show that the figure of the barbarian woman creates the possibility of a future together by a make-believe language that rejects the lure of any standing languages. In these novels, Coetzee destabilizes the notions of author and reader, blocking any attempt at ersatz ethical posturing by narrative devices of a disfigured author function and the dispersal of the reader into different modes of reading. The novels, I argue, resonate with the idea of everyday as *recovered* from the debris of the political community constantly created by stoking the fear of the other in this case but from equally other scenes of destruction within the family, or in scenes of intimacy.

Chapter 8, "A Child Disappears: Law in the Courts, Law in the Interstices of Everyday Life," takes us to a grievous event—that of the disappearance of a child in one of the neighborhoods—to unravel the experience of quotidian violence that lines the everyday in the slums and low-income areas in Delhi. The disappearance of a child is not a rare event in such areas as other works on runaway children or children kidnapped and put in the service of beggars' mafias have also demonstrated (see Steinberg 2019). In many cases, failing to get help from the police, parents resign themselves to such events. In this case, however, a series of contingent events propelled the case into publicity and finally to the court where the persons who had abducted the child were tried and sentenced to imprisonment of varying durations.

In the chapter, I first analyze the judgment of the sessions court to discover that the court produces a sense of facticity but only through the help of certain fictions that are not so much added to the facts as produced by the legal process itself. Paying close attention to the grammatical structure of both written and oral statements—particularly the way tense, mood, and voice are used—I argue that there are different kinds of splits that happen. The judge's pronouncements show a doubling of voice—one voice through which she converts the narrated events into objects recognizable to the law and a second voice in which the law speaks through the voice of the judge. Similarly, the child witness is shown to be split into the witness who *saw* the various acts of horrifying violence done to her as well as the victim who *experienced* these events on her body. Finally, even as a just outcome ensues as a result of court procedures, I show how the minor contradictions that were papered over take us to the life of the law outside the court into the neighborhood where the everyday harassment by police officers, the bribes, and the scandals are the stuff of everyday experiences. The notion of ordinary realism helps me anchor the contradictory affects in which the law embodies both threat and promise.

The next three chapters directly engage the question of anthropological knowledge and its relation to philosophy and literature. Chapter 9, "Of Mistakes, Errors, and Superstition: Reading Wittgenstein's Remarks on Frazer," takes a pivotal moment in philosophy's direct address to anthropology and argues that instead of reading Wittgenstein's remarks as pertaining to a theory of religious belief and ritual as these are commonly interpreted, it is more fruitful to see them in relation to his major preoccupation with pictures of the world produced through what he calls "grammatical illusions." I argue that what Wittgenstein is arguing is not simply that Frazer made a mistake in interpreting rituals as expressions of an erroneous understanding of cause and effect but rather that he was in the grip of a superstition creating false excitement about primitive practices where none were warranted. Wittgenstein draws on our common background as humans: the natural history we might invent to show that, had Frazer paid attention to our primitive reactions as humans—for instance, in turning to respond to a cry of pain or to kiss the picture of a beloved—he might have found other routes to connect the practices of the so-called primitives to those commonly found in his own society. I do a sustained reading of some of the most intriguing comments of Wittgenstein—comments on which very few philosophers (to my knowledge) have responded to ask such questions as what it is to take the facts of my existence upon myself and what it is to imagine that my life could have been otherwise than it is. I hold that such points of connection, rather than a grand foundational gesture, create a more meaningful interface between philosophy and anthropology as also between anthropology and literature. Perhaps we should fear not only the failures of knowledge but also the success of knowledge in arriving at a settlement among these disciplines too soon.

Chapter 10, "Concepts Crisscrossing: Anthropology and Knowledge-Making," takes up a reading of certain classic texts of British anthropology to ask how anthropological concepts are generated. Despite the widespread repudiation of Frazer in social and cultural anthropology, it is interesting to observe how the "common sense" of European societies seeps into anthropological concepts that are held to be general and thus applicable across different societies. This chapter delineates the different ways in which signs and concepts function in the process of translating vernacular terms into anthropological concepts. Looking closely at the terms and practices around which religious beliefs and practices are organized among the Dinka and the Nuer, the chapter shows that the idea of God is transported from the Old Testament notions to generate standards for rendering answers to which terms can qualify to be translated as "God" depending on what is taken to be real and what an illusion; for instance, the reality of God is never doubted by either Evans-Pritchard or Lienhardt, but neither expresses any doubt in their conviction that witches do not exist. A hidden question that animates these discussions turns out to be a version of the older questions: which societies have the concepts and the intuitions that would deem them as ready for receiving the Christian message? As a thought experiment, I draw on different notions of god(s) and of ritual practices (such as sacrifice) from Vedic texts in the Sanskritic tradition and ask what if gods were seen as entities produced through grammar, brought into existence only for the duration of a ritual—ontologically seen to be lying between existence and inexistence as some *mīmāmsā* texts on ritual hermeneutics argue. Would we have thought of the Dinka and Nuer concepts of god or witches or spirits differently? The boundaries that prevent thoughts from other traditions (Indian, Chinese, Arabic, African) to cross over into anthropological concepts or to overlap with them also unfortunately prevent a richer picture of thought from emerging through a genuine openness to thoughts from elsewhere. The chapter also offers a way to think of what Cora Diamond (2004) calls a "crisscross" philosophy as a tapestry of overlapping threads put together patiently and with many hands.

The final chapter, "The Life of Concepts: In the Vicinity of Dying," is written in an autobiographical voice, although there are not many stories I tell about myself. What I mean by the autobiographical voice here is that it is written from an impersonal region of the self that cannot but help watch. There is a famous Sanskrit verse about the parable of the two birds—friends and inhabitants of the same tree, but one who looks on while the other is absorbed in enjoying the pleasures of the world.[13] There are many learned expositions of this verse in terms of the relation of the atman and the Brahman—the empirical self and the supreme self—but for me the verse is less about immersion and transcendent overcoming of experience and more about being an anthropologist. This chapter is my reflection on how thinking and living an anthropological life are joined together like these two birds, but I undertake this discussion through an exegesis of two books on loss—one, a book of poems written by Renato Rosaldo years after the death of his wife, Michelle Rosaldo, and the second, on the women raped and rehabilitated as *bironganas* (war heroines) in the national imagery in post-war Bangladesh. Rosaldo allows the searing grief at the death of his wife to find expression in different voices imagined as those of actual people from his earlier fieldwork. The refraction of his grief into these different voices reveals the omens and premonitions that convey the menace and dangers that lurk in everyday life that dawn on Rosaldo only years after his wife's death. Nayanika Mookherjee finds a way of conveying the fine grains of experience in the extreme history (*charam itihas*) that the women said, they were offering to her, and in which they lived as *khota*—damaged, stained women.

Why is this book also an autobiography? I do not possess the stories and the fragments I arrive at. Instead, in finding my voice through words that I have had to beg, borrow, and steal, I hope it shows what being an anthropologist, or at least one version of being an anthropologist, is. From yet another perspective, if asked to sum up what the book is about, I might say, after Edgar Allen Poe: it is a mere recounting of household events. Such is my understanding of the everyday and of self-knowledge.

# 1

# WITTGENSTEIN AND ANTHROPOLOGY

*Anticipations*

This chapter was written for a series in which different anthropologists were invited to consider the relation they saw between fundamental anthropological questions and the philosophy that provided the grounds (however unacknowledged) in the work of one major philosopher. The series was a visionary project conceived by Valentine Daniel and it was the first time I had found the courage to express my longtime engagement with Wittgenstein's later philosophy on which I had run reading courses at the Delhi School of Economics. I was fortunate that soon after the publication of this essay in 1998, I could teach a formal course on Wittgenstein and anthropology at the New School for Social Research in 1999. It took courage to make this strand of my thinking knowable, public, as if it was the most natural thing in the world for an anthropology department to have a course on Wittgenstein. Then and now, I do not claim the credentials for being a Wittgenstein scholar, but I do claim that his philosophy might appeal to those who recognize the uncanniness of everyday life. In some ways this chapter functions like *bija sutra*—a seed that contained the problems that will become fleshed out through ethnography later. Placed right at the beginning of the book, it will allow the reader to see the distance or closeness among the issues that go on to define the trajectories of my work.

The opening sentence of the paper as it was then said, "I wish to invite reflection in this paper on a certain kinship in the questions that Wittgenstein asks of his philosophy and the puzzles of anthropology." That sentence could well be regarded as defining the domain of this inquiry into everyday life. Consider Wittgenstein's formulation "A philosophical problem has the form: 'I don't know my way about'" (Wittgenstein [1953] 1968, §123). For

Wittgenstein, then, philosophical problems have their beginnings in the feeling of being lost and in an unfamiliar place, and philosophical answers are in the nature of finding one's way back. This image of turning back, of finding not as moving forward as toward a goal but as being led back or turning back, is pervasive in the later writings of Wittgenstein. How can anthropology receive this way of philosophizing? Is there something familiar in the feeling of being lost in anthropological experience? Wittgenstein's fear—"the seed I am likely to sow is a certain jargon" (Diamond 1976, 293)— is to be respected so that the translation of his ideas into anthropology should not be taken as the opportunity for merely a new set of terms. Instead of rendering a systematic account of any one aspect of his philosophy, I shall try to follow a few lines of thought that might interest anthropologists, hoping to convey the tones and sounds of Wittgenstein's words. My thought is not that this will help us reach new goals but that it might help us stop for a moment—to introduce a hesitancy in the way in which we habitually dwell among our concepts of culture, of everyday life, or of the inner. In this effort, the work of Stanley Cavell's thoughts on several of these questions have been crucial for me, acting like signposts in my own efforts to move within *Philosophical Investigations*.

## THE PICTURE OF CULTURE

*Definitions*

Writing in 1997, traumatized by what he had experienced in the unravelling of Sri Lankan society in what was to become a civil war that lasted for twenty-five years, Daniel (1996) coined the term the *anthropography* of violence. He was moved to say, "Anthropology has had an answer to the question, What is a human being? An answer that has, on the whole, served us well, with or without borrowings from philosophers. The answer keeps returning to one form or another of the concept of culture: humans have it; other living beings do not" (194). He went on to discuss how Tylor's ([1878] 1974) founding definition of culture helped to move it away from the "clutches of literature, philosophy, classical music, and the fine arts—in other words, from the conceit of the Humanities" (Daniel 1996, 194). Let us consider for a moment the actual definition proposed by Tylor: "Culture or civilization taken in its widest ethnographic sense, is that complex whole which includes knowledge, belief, art, morals, law, custom, and any other capabilities and habits acquired by man as a member of society" (Tylor [1878] 1974, 1). What is interesting in this definition is not only the all-inclusive nature of culture but also the reference to it as capability and habit acquired through one's membership of society. As Asad (1990) notes, this notion of culture with its enumeration of capabilities and habits, as well as the focus on learning, gave way in time to the idea of culture as *text* "that is as something resembling an inscribed text" (171). Within this dominant notion of culture as text, the process of learning came to be seen as shaping the individual body as a picture of this text, inscribing memory often through painful rituals so that the society and culture of which the individual is a member is made present, so to say, on the surface of the body (Clasteres 1974; Das 1995a; Durkheim [1912] 1995). The scene of instruction in Wittgenstein ([1953] 1968) in the double sense of showing how one—say, a child or a builder—is instructed into a life in language, and also how we as readers are to be instructed through that scene, is quite different.

*Scenes of Instruction*

*Philosophical Investigations* begins with an evocation of the words of Augustine in *Confessions*. This opening scene has been the object of varying interpretations. The passage reads as follows:

> When they (my elders) named some object, and accordingly moved towards something, I saw this and grasped that the thing they called was the sound they uttered when they meant to point it out. Their intention was shewn by their bodily movements, as it were the natural language of all peoples: the expression of the face, the play of the eyes, the movement of other parts of the body, and the tone of voice which expresses our state of mind in seeking, having, or avoiding something. Thus as I heard words repeatedly used in their proper places in various sentences, I gradually learnt to understand what objects they signified; and after I had trained my mouth to form these signs, I used them to express my own desires. (Wittgenstein [1953] 1968, §1)

Cavell (1979, 1990a), who has given the most sustained reading of this passage, senses here the presence of the child who moves invisible among his or her elders and who must divine speech for himself or herself, training the mouth to form signs so that he or she may use these signs to express his or her own desires. Now contrast this scene of instruction with the famous builders' scene, which follows soon after in Wittgenstein ([1953] 1968, §2):

> Let us imagine a language for which the description given by Augustine is right. The language is meant to serve for communication between a builder A and an assistant B. A is building with building stones: there are blocks, pillars, slabs, and beams. B has to pass the stones, and that in order in which A needs them. For this purpose they use a language consisting of the words "block," "pillar," "slab," "beam." A calls them out;—B brings the stone which he has learnt to bring at such-and-such a call.— Conceive this as a complete primitive language.

Why are these two scenes juxtaposed with each other? Does it make sense to treat the builders' language as a distorted version of what it is to teach language? If we transpose the scene of instruction in which the child moves among the adults with that of the builders (treating it as a scene of instruction for ourselves), we might see that even if the child were to use only four words, these may be uttered with charm, curiosity, a sense of achievement. One may say, the child has a future in language. The builders' language, in contrast, is closed. Wittgenstein wills us to conceive of this as a "complete primitive language." Yet as Cavell (1995) points out, there is no standing language game for imagining what Wittgenstein asks us to imagine here.

It has been noted often enough that Wittgenstein does not call upon any of the natural languages from which he could have taken his examples; thus, his game in this section—whether with reference to the child or the builder— is in the nature of a fiction through which his thoughts may be maintained in the region of the primitive. But the "primitive" here is conceived as the builders' tribe, which seems bereft of the possession of its culture or of an undoubted shared language—the language the tribe uses is invented language, not to be confused either with the natural languages found among people who maintain full forms of sociality or with the language of the child.

Wittgenstein's sense of the child who moves about in his or her culture unseen by the elders and who has to inherit his or her culture as if by theft appears to find resonance in the anthropological literature in the register of the mythological (for instance, in the bird nester myths analyzed by Levi-Strauss [(1964) 1969]). Despite the studies on socialization, rarely has the question of how one comes to a sense of a shared culture as well as one's own voice in that culture in the context of everyday life been addressed anthropologically. If asked at all, this question has been formulated as a question of socialization as obedience to a set of normative rules and procedures. But juxtaposing the child with the builders seems to suggest that whatever else it may be, the inheritance of culture is not about inheriting a certain set of rules or a certain capacity to obey orders. As Wittgenstein ([1953] 1968, §3) says, "Augustine does describe a system of communication: only not everything we call language is this system." And then, as if the surest route to understand this concept is to understand it through the eyes of the child, he points out that the words in a game like ring-a-ring-a-roses are to be understood as *both the words and the actions in which they are woven* (§7). The child learns that "we all fall down" is both a chanting of words in unison with others and the enacting of falling down to go in harmony with the words. Unlike the builder whose language, in Wittgenstein's description of the scene, is capable of only machinelike actions, the child's language is not simply about obeying orders but learning what it is to be with others, to "fall down" in a funny, giggly, fun way.

Concern with childhood surfaces in classical anthropological literature but only as incidental to the intricacies of age ranking, rites of passage, and sometimes with reference to attitudes toward what can only be a fictional category of the "average child." Both Nieuwenhuys (1996) and Reynolds (1995) show how sparse the ethnographic descriptions of children and their agency have been in this literature. Reynolds's (1995) work on political activism of children and youth in the volatile and traumatic context of South Africa is special because she shows how tales of folk heroes might have provided a perspective to young people with which to view their defiance of the regime of apartheid even as they had to negotiate questions of obedience, authority, and kinship solidarity within the domains of family and kinship. I would also draw attention to the remarkable account by Gilsenan (1996) and to Das (1990b, 1990c) and Chatterji and Mehta (1995) on the complicated question of what it is for children to inherit the obligation to exact vengeance, to settle for peace, or to bear witness in a feud or in the aftermath of a riot. Claims over inheritance are not straightforward in these contexts, but even in relatively stable societies, anthropological descriptions of culture as either shared or contested have excluded the voice of the child. As in Augustine's passage, the child seems to move about unseen by his or her elders.

Let me go on to the question that the figure of the child raises here: What is it to say that the child has a future in language? There are several scenes of instruction in *Philosophical Investigations*: those pertaining to completing a mathematical series, those pertaining to reading, those pertaining to obeying an order. All raise the issue of what it is to be able to project a concept or a word or a procedure into new situations. "A" writes down a series of numbers; "B" watches him and tries to find a law for the sequence of numbers. If he succeeds, he exclaims, "Now I can go on." What has happened here?

One powerful way of understanding what gives a child the confidence to say "I can go on" is provided by Kripke (1982) with the example of what it is to follow a mathematical procedure or a rule. He points out that Wittgenstein shows convincingly that we cannot speak of an inner understanding having occurred; nor can we say that there are some basic rules that can tell us how to interpret the other rules. Here is how the problem appears to Kripke (1982, 17):

> Here of course I am expounding Wittgenstein's well-known remarks about a "rule for interpreting a rule." It is tempting to answer the skeptic from appealing from one rule to another more "basic" rule. But the skeptical move can be repeated at the more basic level also. Eventually the process must stop—"justifications come to an end somewhere"—and I am left with a rule which is completely unreduced to any other. How can I justify my present application of such a rule, when a skeptic could easily interpret it so as to yield any of an indefinite number of other results? It seems my application of it is an unjustified stab in the dark. I apply the rule *blindly*.

Without going into this argument in any detail, I want to comment on one formulation that is proposed by Kripke (1982): that our justification for saying that a child has learned how to follow a rule comes from the confidence that being a member of a community allows the individual person to act "unhesitatingly but blindly." Kripke gives the example of a small child learning addition and says that it is obvious that his teacher will not accept just any response from the child. So, what does one mean when one says that the teacher judges that, for certain cases, the pupil must give the "right" answer? "I mean that the teacher judges that the child has given the same answer that he himself would have given. . . . I mean that he judges that the child is applying the same procedure he himself would have applied" (90).

For Kripke (1982) this appeal to community and to criteria of agreement is presented in Wittgenstein as a solution to the "skeptical paradox"—that if everything can be made out to be in accord with a rule, then it can also be made to conflict with it. But this skepticism with regard to justification, says Kripke, applies to the isolated individual: it does not hold for one who can apply unhesitatingly but blindly a rule that the community *licenses* him or her to apply. As with application of a word in future contexts, there is no "inner state" called "understanding" that has occurred. Instead, as he says, there are language games in our lives that license under certain conditions assertions that someone means such and such and that his present application accords with what was said in the past.

My discomfort with this description arises from the centrality that Kripke (1982) places on the notion of rule as well as from the processes he privileges for bringing the child in agreement with a particular form of life that would license such blind and unhesitating obedience to the rule.

If we take the teacher in Kripke (1982) to be the representative of the community within which the child is being initiated, then I am compelled to ask whether the "agreement" in a form of life is purely a matter of making the child arrive at the same conclusion or the same procedure that the adult would have applied. Rather, it appears to me that, as Cavell (1990a) suggests, this agreement is a much more complicated affair in which there is an entanglement of rules, customs, habits, examples, and practices and that we cannot attach salvational importance to the learning of rules as the best route to the inheritance of culture.[1] Wittgenstein ([1953] 1968) speaks about orders or commands in several ways: there is the gulf between the order and its execution or the translation of an order one time into a proposition and another time into a demonstration and still another time into action. I do not have the sense that the agreement in forms of life requires the child to produce the same response that the teacher does. To have a future in language, the child should have been enabled to say, "And after I had trained my mouth to form these signs, I used them to express my own desires." There is of course the reference in Wittgenstein to following a rule blindly.

"All the steps are already taken" means: I no longer have any choice. The rule, once stamped with a particular meaning, traces the line along which it is to be followed through the whole of space.—But if something of this sort really were the case, how would it help?

No; my description only made sense of it was to be understood symbolically.—I should have said: *This is how it strikes me.*

When I obey a rule, I do not choose.

I obey the rule *blindly.* ([1953] 1968, §219, emphasis in original)

And then in §221 he explains, "My symbolical expression was really a mythological description of the rule." I cannot take up fully the question here of what it is to speak mythologically or symbolically, but from the aura that surrounds the discussion of these issues, speaking of obeying a rule blindly seems to be similar to the way one speaks of wishes, plans, suspicions, or expectations as, by definition, unsatisfied, or the way one speaks of propositions as necessarily true or false—that is, that they are grammatical statements. When Wittgenstein ([1953] 1968) talks about rules and agreement being cousins, the kinship between them seems more complicated than Kripke's (1982) rendering of either of these two concepts allows.[2]

I want to take an ethnographic vignette now to show the entanglement of the ideas of rule, custom, habit, practice, and example in what might be seen as constituting agreement within a particular form of life. Gilsenan (1996) gives us a stunning ethnography of violence and narrative in Akkar, a northern province of Lebanon, in the 1970s. From the several narratives in this text, one can infer the rules by which issues of vengeance and honor are articulated in the exchange of violence. Indeed, if one reads Evans-Pritchard (1940) on the feud among the Nuer, it all seems like a matter of kinship obligations that can be stated in terms of clear genealogical principles through which feuds are organized. One could imagine that a male child being socialized into such a society could be taught his place in the community in terms of *rules* that he learns, much as Kripke's child learns to follow the same procedures as the adults who are initiating him if he is to learn how to add. But here are sketches from a story from Gilsenan (1996, 165–66) of how a boy becomes a man even as he is being initiated into the rules of vengeance:

> The chosen young man walked, alone and in broad daylight, up the steep hill separating the quarters of the fellahins and the aghast. . . . Everyone could see him, a fact much insisted upon in accounts. At the top of the hill, he approached the small ill provisioned shop owned by Ali Bashir who was standing at the entrance looking on to the saha (public space)

before him. . . . The boy simply said to him: "Do you want it here in the shop or outside?" Ali ran back inside, grabbed the gun, and was shot in the wrist, his weapon falling to the ground. The killer then emptied his revolver into Ali's chest. He died instantly.

Turning his back on those fellahin who had witnessed his deed, the killer—and now hero—walked back down the hill. . . . All agreed that he presented his back to the enemies in a grand disregard for his own safety. No one dared retaliate.

This archetypal *geste* of agnostic indifference filled every requirement of the heroic act. He was superb in exit as he had been on entry. The aesthetics of violence were in all respects harmoniously achieved. My informants all remembered that the senior of their number, a renowned hunter, companion of the lords, and also a paternal half-brother of the wounded man, hailed the young hero when he came down to the lower mosque at the entrance of the village exclaiming: "Ya 'aish! Reja'it shabb!" (Long may you live! You have returned a man!). He saluted one who had gone up the hill a boy and come down a true, arms bearing young man.

Some may argue that the scene of the instruction in Kripke (1982) bears little resemblance to the scene in which this young man is chosen by the elders as the appropriate instrument of revenge. (But then is the example of learning a procedure for solving a mathematical problem a good analogy for what it is to obey rules—a particularly clarifying one, as Kripke claims?) As for the young boy, it is his display of the aesthetics of violence that makes him a man. No one can say that he acted exactly as the elder would have acted in his place, for such scenes are also marked by contingencies of all kinds in which one might end up not a hero but a buffoon. Yet it is through the entanglement of rule, custom, habit, and example that the child has not only been initiated in the community of men but also found his own style of being a man. In fact, the aftermath of the story of this young hero converts him into a source of danger, always looking for some replication of the originating moment of his public biography, and who finally dies in a quarrel as if he were predestined to have such a death. A consideration of that event would take us into a different region of Wittgenstein's thought: the region of the dangers that the otherness of this hero posed for the rest of the community.

Anthropological accounts have suggested that attention to Wittgenstein's discussion on rules and especially the distinction between regulative rules and constitutive rules, as Searle (1969) suggests, may give new direction to questions of how to distinguish the nature of prescriptions in ritual actions and other kind of actions. Humphrey and Laidlaw (1994) not only give a fascinating account of the Jain ritual of *puja* (worship), they also argue that what is distinctive about ritual prescriptions in general is the constitutive nature of rules that go to define rituals.

> Constitutive rituals create a form of activity, by defining the actions of which it is composed. We pointed out that ritualized action is composed of discrete acts which are disconnected from agents' intentions and we said that this feature of ritualization depends upon stipulation. It is this stipulation, as distinct from mere regulation which is constitutive of ritual. Only ritual acts (like valid moves in chess) count as having happened, so the celebrant moves from act to act, completing each in turn and then moving on to the next. This is unaffected by delays, false moves, extraneous happenings, or mishaps. (Humphrey and Laidlaw 1994, 117)

They use this distinction, then, to show the wide variation in the ways of performing the ritual act of puja, which are nevertheless considered right by the participants because they may be said to accord with the constitutive rules. The importance of this formulation is not only that it breaks away from the distinctions between instrumental action and expressive action, or from the overdetermined view of ritual as a form of communication, but also that it addresses some puzzling features of ritual observations that are often ironed out of final ethnographic texts. I refer to the kinds of mundane activities that may be carried on during a ritual but are nevertheless not seen as constitutive of the ritual and hence can be ignored in judgments about "rightness" of a ritual act.

There is an explicit analogy in Humphrey and Laidlaw's (1994) discussion of the constitutive rules of ritual and of chess. Wittgenstein's ([1953] 1968) observations on chess may be pertinent here. He has talked about not only the rules that constitute the game but also the customs—for example, the use of the king to decide by lots which player gets white in drawing lots (§563) or not stamping and yelling while making the moves (§200). But Wittgenstein leads us to a different direction, one in which the entanglement of rules with customs, practices, and examples comes to the fore: "Where is the connection effected between the sense of the expression 'Lets play a game of chess' and all the rules of the game? Well, in the list of rules of the game, in the teaching of it, in the day-to-day practice of playing" (§197). Wittgenstein used the analogy of a chess game to illuminate what it means for language to be governed by rules. In both language and chess there are rules that have no foundation—that is, the rules cannot be justified by reference to reality: they are autonomous, and they could be different. But there are limits to this analogy. The most important difference, as Baker and Hacker (1980) point out, is that the rules of chess are devised to cover every possible situation whereas our language cannot lay down the rules that will cover every conceivable circumstance. Hence there is always a gap between the rule and its execution. Could we say that the constitutive rules of ritual can cover every conceivable circumstance? I suggest that while this is sometimes the ambition of the theoreticians of ritual, as the mīmāmsā school of Indian philosophy claimed (see Das 1983), the embedding of ritual in the forms of life do not allow for this. In fact, a situation of completeness would make ritual like the invented languages of Wittgenstein rather than the natural languages, which are never complete (Wittgenstein [1953] 1968, §18).

Baker and Hacker (1980) suggest that natural language games may be distinguished from invented ones by the fact that the former are mastered only in fragments while the latter are presented as complete languages. The feeling in reading about the builders' language is that they seemed particularly bereft of culture. I suggest it comes precisely from thinking of their language as if it were complete.

An anthropological text, we know, is marked by a certain kind of excess or a certain surplus. Call it thick ethnography, call it fascination with detail. Most ethnographies provide more than the theoretical scaffolding requires. Some argue that this excess is embedded in the emplotment of ethnography as a performance (Clifford 1990). Others speak of the difficulty of portraying ways of life that are "experience distant" to their readers (Scheper-Hughes 1992). I suggest that this excess or this surplus expresses equally the distrust of formal rules and obligations as sources of social order or moral judgment. If culture is a matter of shared ways of life as well as of bequeathing and inheriting capabilities and habits as members of society, then clearly it is participation in forms of sociality (Wittgenstein's forms of life) that defines simultaneously the inner and the outer, that allows a person to speak both within language and outside it. Agreement in forms of life, in Wittgenstein, is never a matter of shared opinions. It thus requires an excess of description to capture the entanglements of customs, habits, rules, and examples. It provides the context in which we could see how we are to trace words back to their original homes when we do not know our way about: the anthropological quest takes us to the point at which Wittgenstein takes up his grammatical investigation. It seems a natural point to break here and inquire into what are "forms of life," "criteria," and "grammatical investigation" in Wittgenstein.

## LANGUAGE AND SOCIALITY

### Forms of Life

The idea of forms of life is what has often been taken to signal the availability of Wittgenstein's thought for sociology and anthropology. Wittgenstein takes language to be the mark of human sociality; hence human forms of life are defined by the fact that they are forms created by and for those who are in possession of language. As it is commonly understood, Wittgenstein's notion of language is to see it in the context of a lived life, its use within human institutions rather than its systematic aspects. But is this enough? Cavell (1989) expresses a serious concern at the conventional views of this text, which in his understanding eclipse its spiritual struggle.

> The idea [of forms of life] is, I believe, typically taken to emphasize the social nature of human language and conduct, as if Wittgenstein's mission is to rebuke philosophy for concentrating too much on isolated individuals, or for emphasizing the inner at the expense of the outer, in accounting for such matters as meaning, or states of consciousness, or following a rule etc. . . . A conventionalized sense of form of life will support a conventionalized, or contractual sense of agreement. But there is another sense of form of life that will contest this. (Cavell 1989, 41)

What Cavell finds wanting in this conventional view of forms of life is that it is not able to convey the mutual absorption of the natural and the social—it emphasizes *form* but not *life*. A hasty reading of Cavell on this point may lead readers (especially anthropologists) to the conclusion that the idea of natural is taken as unproblematic in this interpretation. Let me dwell for a moment on this point. Cavell suggests a distinction between what he calls the ethnological or horizontal sense of form of life and its vertical or "biological" sense. The first captures the notion of human diversity—the fact that social institutions, such as marriage and property, vary across societies. The second refers to the distinctions captured in language itself between "so-called 'lower' or 'higher' forms of life, between say poking at your food, perhaps with a fork, and pawing at it or pecking at it" (Cavell 1989, 42). It is the vertical sense of the form of life that he suggests marks the limit of what is considered human in a society and provides the conditions of the use of criteria as applied to others. Thus, the criteria of pain does not apply to that which does not exhibit signs of being a form of life: we do not ask whether a tape recorder that can be turned on to play a shriek is feeling the pain. Cavell suggests that the forms of life have to be accepted but that it is in the sensibility of *Investigations* to call not so much for change as for transfiguration. A brief political detour into what the figure of transfiguration does as political critique is called for here.

In his luminous paper "Fred Astaire Asserts the Right to Praise," Cavell (2005a) offers a way of thinking of political critique in the context of the terrible record of racial discrimination in the United States by showing how the figure of transfiguration (rather than, say, of political revolution) finds a different route to contesting the legitimacy of existing arrangements. But the claim is both about the political and the philosophical: "I wish to urge the pertinence of philosophical interpretation in such a case as the work of Fred Astaire, a Hollywood song-and-dance man. That this man is accepted as one of the greatest American dancers of the twentieth century . . . perhaps takes some of the sting out of the proposal, but only somewhat" (62). Yet the perplexity of why philosophers routinely dismiss such figures as figures of thought goes deeper for Cavell.

> But I am bound to yet deeper perplexity—surely to myself—by finding that I have to place a further pressure on such an instance as that of Astaire, not merely staking a certain aesthetic claim to his art's promise of shared pleasure, but a certain political claim that his mode of art—one which, we can say appropriates the achievement of black dancing—is not only acceptable to me, but represents a striking adornment of American culture, one which makes my praise of his work an expression of my consent to America's partial democracy happier or more heartened thank it might otherwise be. (62)

In the exquisite reading that Cavell provides of the opening number of a song and dance routine in which Astaire partners with Cyd Charisse from the 1953 Hollywood musical entitled *The Bandwagon*, the figure of transfiguration occurs in the demonstration of how speech may turn into song and walking into skipping, or leaping, or dancing, allowing a song-and-dance man who has been denied dancing—dancing denied to a man whose life is dance—to reclaim his right, even as a white man to an inheritance of dance from black culture. In the unsparing criticism of Michael Rogin's readymade interpretation of the dance routing as an appropriation of black culture, Cavell says, "Rogin's perception of systematic . . . and prolonged injustice," understandable as it may be, "does not allow him to recognize that Astaire's dance of praise is itself to be understood specifically as this painful and deadly irony of the white praise of a black culture whose very terms of praise it has appropriated, even climatically about being brushed with madness in one's participation in it" (Cavell 2005a, 69).[3] The figure of transfiguration— the metamorphosis that Astaire's dance routine shows in reclaiming his dancer's body is described not as "finding a new body but finding the body anew"—the camera's focusing on his feet and his shoes and polishing and waxing by the shoeshine man is to show that "what the black man is doing with his wands and cloth are not labor alone, the object is not to transform shoes but to transfigure the creature on earth who wears shoes" (74). What could be a more politically worthy critique?

I want to turn to a different question now and ask: How does the distinction between the horizontal and the vertical help in showing us what happens at the limit of each? What is it that human societies can represent as the limit? Here I draw from some of my own work to show how such an idea may strike a chord on the keys of anthropological imagination.

For some years now I have been engaged in trying to understand the relation between violence (especially sexual violence) in everyday domestic contexts and violence in the extraordinary context of riots during political events, such as the Partition of India or the violence against Sikhs following the assassination of then prime minister Indira Gandhi. In one of my earlier papers (Das 1996b), I conceptualize the violence that occurs within the weave of life as lived in the kinship universe, as having the sense of a *past continuous*, while the sudden and traumatic violence that was part of the Partition experience seems to have a quality of frozen time to it.[4] In discussing the life of a woman, Manjit, who had been abducted and raped during the Partition and subsequently married to an elderly relative, I argued that while the violence she was submitted to by her husband was something sayable in her life, the other violence was not (could not be?) articulated. The horizontal and vertical limits seemed to me to be particularly important in formulating this difference.

> It is this notion of form of life, i.e. its vertical sense of testing the criteria of what it is to be human, that I think is implicated in the understanding of Manjit's relation to the non-narrative of her experience of abduction and rape. Men beat up their wives, commit sexual aggression, shame them in their own self creations of masculinity—but such aggression is still "sayable" in Punjabi life through various kinds of performative gestures and through story telling (I do not mean to say that it is therefore passively accepted—indeed the whole story of Manjit shows that it is deeply resented). Contrast this with the fantastic violence in which women were stripped and marched naked in the streets; or the magnitudes involved; or the fantasy of writing political slogans on the private parts of women. This production of bodies through a violence that was seen to tear apart the very fabric of life, was such that claims over culture through disputation became impossible. If words now appear, they are like broken shadows of the motion of everyday words. . . . Such words were indeed uttered and have been recorded by other researchers, but it was as if one's touch with these words and hence with life itself had been burnt or numbed. The hyperbolic in Manjit's narration of the Partition recalls Wittgenstein's sense of the conjunction of the hyperbolic with the groundless. (Das 1996b, 23)

I have taken this example in some detail because it suggests, through means of an ethnography, that while the range and scale of the human is tested and defined and extended in the disputations proper to everyday life, it may move through the unimaginable violence of the Partition (but similar examples are to be found in many contemporary ethnographies of violence) into forms of life that are seen as not belonging to life proper. Was it a man or a machine that plunged a knife into the private parts of a woman after raping her? Were those men or animals who went around killing and collecting penises as signs of their prowess? There is a deep moral energy in the refusal to represent some violations of the human body, for these violations are seen as being against our natural history as humans, as defining the limits of life itself. The precise range and scale of the human form of life is not knowable in advance, any more than the precise range of the meaning of a word is knowable in advance. But the intuition that some violations cannot be verbalized in everyday life is to recognize that work cannot be performed on these within the burned and numbed everyday. We reach through a different route the question of what it is to have a future in language. I believe that the limits of the forms of life—the limits at which the differences cease to be criterial differences—are encountered in the context of life as it is lived and not only in the philosopher's reflections on it. These are the times in which one may be so engulfed by doubts of the other's humanity that the whole world may appear to be lost.

In his work on violence, Daniel (1996) calls this point the counterpoint of culture: "The counterpoint I speak of is something that resists incorporation into the harmony of a still higher order of sound, sense, or society" (202). Other accounts of violence similarly suggest that certain kinds of violence cannot be incorporated into the everyday (Langer 1991, 1997; Lawrence 1995). But then how is everyday life to be recovered?

*Everyday Life and the Problem of Skepticism*

In describing what he calls the counterpoint to culture, Daniel (1996) interviewed several young men in Sri Lanka who were members of various militant movements and who had killed with ropes, knives, pistols, automatic fire, and grenades. But it is clear from his powerful descriptions that what was traumatic for Daniel in hearing these accounts of killings was the manner in which the styles of killing and the wielding of words was interwoven. Here are some extracts.

> He was hiding in the temple when we got there. . . . This boy was hiding behind some god. We caught him. Pulled him out. . . . The boy was in the middle of the road. We were all going round and round him. For a long time. No one said anything. Then someone flung at him with a sword. Blood started gushing out. . . . We thought he was finished. So they piled him on the tyre and then set it aflame. (Daniel 1996, 209)

Daniel finds the shifting between the "we" and the "they" to be noteworthy, but what stuns him is the next thing that happened.

This was the early days of my horror story collecting and I did not know what to say. So I asked him a question of absolute irrelevance to the issue at hand. Heaven knows why I asked it; I must have desperately wanted to change the subject or pretend that we had been talking about something else all along. "What is your goal in life?" I asked. The reply shot right back: "I want a video (VCR)." (Daniel 1996, 209)

Wittgenstein's sense of exile of words is what comes to mind here. It is not that one cannot understand the utterance but that in this context when these words are spoken, they seem not to belong—they seem not to have a home. Daniel's (1996) turning away from this event is a desperate one. He lurches toward a hope (211)—the rustle of a hope—wherever it may be found and whenever it may be found. And it is found in a scene of almost quiet domesticity. He recounts an event in the 1977 anti-Tamil riots in which a Sinhala woman is journeying on a train; she is in one part of the compartment and on another seat is a retired Tamil schoolteacher. A mob began to drag out Tamils and to beat them. The Sinhala woman, recognizable easily as a Kandyan Sinhalese because of the way she wore her sari, moved over to his side and quietly held his hand. Some members of the mob entered the compartment, but the gesture of conjugal familiarity persuaded them that the gentleman was a Sinhala, so they proceeded elsewhere. Daniel (1996) thinks of the gesture of the woman as a sign, gravid with possibilities. But what are these possibilities? From a Wittgensteinian perspective, these seem to be only possibilities of recovery through a descent into the ordinariness of everyday life, of domesticity, through which alone the words that have been exiled may be brought back. This everydayness is then in the nature of a return—one that has been recovered (never fully restored though) in the face of madness.

The intuition of everydayness in Wittgenstein appears therefore quite different from, say, that of Schutz (1970), who emphasizes the attention to the "paramount reality" of the everyday and conceptualizes transcendence as momentary escapes from these attentions. It is also different from the many attempts made in recent years to capture the idea of the everyday as a site of resistance (Jeffery and Jeffery 1996; J. C. Scott 1985, 1990). My sense of these approaches is that there is a search in these attempts for what Hans Joas (1996) calls the creativity of social action. Rather than searching for agency in great and transgressive moments of history, it is in the everyday scripts of resistance that it is thought to be located. There is nothing wrong with this way of conceptualizing the everyday, for it has the advantage of showing society to be constantly made rather than given once and for all. The problem is that the notion of the everyday is too easily secured in these ethnographies because they hardly ever consider the temptations and threats of skepticism as part of the lived reality and hence do not tell us what is the stake in the everyday that they discovered.

In Cavell's (1984, 1988b, 1990a) rendering of Wittgenstein's appeal to the everyday, it is found to be a pervasive scene of illusion and trance and artificiality of need. This, to my understanding and experience, is because both the temptations and threats of skepticism are taken out from the study of the philosopher and reformulated as questions about what it is to live in the face of the unknowability of the world (for my purposes especially the social world). Let me depart for the moment from the kinds of scenes of violence that have been described by Das (1990b, 1995a, 1995b, 1997), Daniel (1996), Langer (1991, 1997), Lawrence (1995), and many others. These scenes may appear exceptional to many. Instead, I ask, is the sense of the unknowability of the social world also encountered in other contexts, in the context of normal suffering, so to speak? Some scholars suggest that this unknowability of the social world has been made more acute by the processes of modernity or globalization (see Appadurai 1996, 158–78), whereas my sense is that uncertainty of relations is part of human sociality as it is embedded within certain weaves of social life (Das and Bajwa 1994). But let me take my example from an anthropological classic.

Evans-Pritchard's ([1937] 1976) account of witchcraft among the Azande has often been seen as that society's way of dealing with misfortune rather than with the essential unknowability of other minds. For instance, Taussig (1992) writes:

> To cite the common phraseology, science like medical science, can explain the "how" and not the "why" of disease; it can point to chains of physical cause and effect, but as to why I am struck down now rather than at some other time, or as to why it is me rather than someone else, medical science can only respond with some variety of probability theory which is unsatisfactory to the mind which is searching for certainty and for significance. In Azande practice, the issue of "how" and "why" are folded into one another; etiology is simultaneously physical, social, and

moral. . . . My disease is a social relation, and therapy has to address that synthesis of moral, social, and physical presentation. (85)

It is true that Evans-Pritchard ([1937] 1976) veers in several directions in accounting for the Azande beliefs in witchcraft, including questions about the rationality of the Azande. If we pay some attention to the descriptions that he provides, however, we find not so much a search for certainty and significance but rather a shadow of skepticism regarding other minds (Chaturvedi 1998). Moreover, this skepticism seems to have something to do with the manner in which language is deployed. Evans-Pritchard ([1937] 1976) reports that those who speak in a roundabout manner and are not straightforward in their conversation are suspected of witchcraft: "Azande are very sensitive and usually in the lookout for unpleasant allusions to themselves in apparently harmless conversation" (111). Very often they find double meaning in a conversation (116) and assume that harm would be done to them, as the following instance recounted by Evans-Pritchard shows:

An old friend of mine, Badobo of the Akowe clan, remarked to his companions who were cleaning up the government road around the settlement that he had a found a stump of wood over which Tupoi had stumbled and cut himself a few days previously when he had been returning late at night from a beer feast. Badobo added to his friends that they must clear the road well, as it would never do for so important a man as Tupoi to stumble and fall if they could help it. One of Tupoi's friends heard this remark and repeated it to his father who professed to see a double meaning in it and to find a sarcastic nuance in Badobo's whole behaviour. (115–16)

A pervasive uncertainty of relations is indicated by many factors: the Azande aphorism "One cannot see into a man as into an open woven basket"; the Azande belief that one cannot be certain that anyone is free from witchcraft; and the care that a Zande man takes not to anger his wives gratuitously because one of them may be a witch and by offending her he may bring misfortune on his head. And although a Zande would not state that he is a witch, Evans-Pritchard ([1937] 1976) reports that one may know nothing about the fact of one's own witchcraft (123). Uncertainty about other minds here is linked to a certain alienation from the language that one speaks, as if the language always revealed either more or less than the words spoken. Indeed, it is the intimate knowledge of how Azande converse and interpret one another's meanings that Evans-Pritchard considers important to an understanding of how attributions of witchcraft are made: "Once a person has been dubbed a witch anything he says may be twisted to yield a secret meaning. Even when there is no question of witchcraft Azande are always on the look-out for double meaning in their conversations" (131). Here we have the intuition of the humans as if one of the aspects under which they could be seen is as victims of language that could reveal things about them of which they were themselves unaware.

This idea touches upon the Wittgensteinian theme of language as experience (and not simply as message). He takes examples of punning, or of a feel for spelling: If you did not experience the meaning of words (as distinct from only using them), then how could you laugh at a pun? The sense is of being controlled by the words one speaks or hears or sees rather than of controlling them. There is some similarity to Austin's (1962) concerns with performatives, especially with perlocutionary effect.

A context that I consider decisive for understanding these themes is that of panic rumor. I shall take the example of anthropological studies of rumor to show how the theme of the unknowability of the social world and the theme of humans becoming victims to words come to be connected. Although rumor is not an example that figures in Wittgenstein, I propose that one may find connections in the way in which there is a withdrawal of trust from words and a special vulnerability to the signifier in the working of rumor and the exile of words under skepticism.

Several historians and anthropologists emphasize the role of rumor in mobilizing crowds (Rudé 1959, 1964; Thompson 1971). Historians of the subaltern school see it as a special form of subaltern communication, "a necessary instrument of rebel transmission" (Guha 1983, 256). Other characteristics of rumor Guha (1983) identifies are the anonymity of the source of rumor, its capacity to build solidarity, and the overwhelming urge it prompts in listeners to pass it on to others. The excessive emphasis on communication, however, obscures the particular feature of language that is often brought to the fore when we consider the susceptibility to rumor during times of collective violence (Das 1990a, 1990b, 1998a; Tambiah 1996). Bhabha (1995) poses the question in an incisive manner: What is special to rumor as distinct from other forms of communication? He goes on to isolate two of its aspects: the first is rumor's enunciative aspect, and the second its performative aspect. "The indeterminacy of rumour," he says, "constitutes its importance as a social discourse. Its intersubjective, communal adhesiveness lies in its enunciative aspect. Its performative power of circulation results in its contiguous spreading, an almost uncontrollable impulse to pass it on to another person" (201). He concludes that psychic affect and social fantasy are potent forms of potential identification and agency for guerrilla warfare and hence rumors play a major role in mobilization for such warfare.

Other views of rumor, especially those derived from mass psychology, emphasize the emotional, capricious, temperamental, and flighty nature of crowds (Le Bon [1895] 1960). Something common in these situations is an essential grammatical feature (in Wittgenstein's sense) of what we call rumor: that it is conceived to spread. Thus, while images of contagion and infection are used to represent rumor in elite discourse, the use of these images is not simply a matter of the elite's noncomprehension of subaltern forms of communication. It also speaks to the transformation of language—namely, that instead of being a medium of communication, language becomes communicable, infectious, causing things to happen almost as if they had occurred by nature. In my own work on rumor in a situation of mounting panic of communal riots, I identify the presence of an incomplete or interrupted social story that comes back in the form of rumor and an altered modality of communication (Das 1998a). The most striking feature of what I identify as panic rumors (in which it is difficult to locate any innocent bystanders) is that suddenly the access to context seems to disappear. In addition, there is an absence of signature in panic rumors so that rumor works to destroy both the source of speech and the trustworthiness of convention. This characteristic seems to distinguish perlocutionary effect from illocutionary force. In the latter, trust in convention and law allows promises to be made and marriages to be contracted. But as Cavell's (1979) marvelous discussion of the skeptical problematic in *Othello* shows, it is not enough to say "I do" on the altar to make a marriage in which one can trust not only the other but trust oneself as worthy of love. The mounting panic in which the medium of rumor leads to the dismantling of relations of trust at times of communal riots seems to share the tempo of skepticism. Once a thought of a certain vulnerability takes hold, as Cavell shows (1979, 1994), the world is engulfed without limit.

Unlike Cavell, Michael Williams (1996) considers skeptical doubts to be unnatural doubts. He holds that the experience that we know nothing about the real world has to arise from a particularly striking experience of error. Yet no experience of error, he argues, can give us a feel of a total loss of the world. The threat of skepticism for Cavell lies in our feeling that our sensations may not be of this world. But for Williams this threat arises in the philosophizing of Cavell because he has internalized a contentious theoretical view. Cavell, however, suggests in all his work that skeptical doubt arises in the experience of living. Skepticism is for him a site on which we abdicate our responsibility toward words—unleashing them from our criteria. Hence his theme of disappointment with language as a human institution (Cavell 1994).[5] The site of panic rumor suggests similarly a subjection to voice (comparable to Schreber's subjection to the voices he heard). There seems a transformation from social exchange to communal trance, and if this trance is to be resisted, one has to lead works back to the everyday, much as one might lead a horse gone suddenly wild to its stables.

## COMPLEXITY OF THE INNER

It might be tempting to suppose that the unknowability of the social world essentially relates to the unknowability of the other. But the question of skepticism in Wittgenstein does not posit an essential asymmetry between what I know about myself and what I know about the other. His famous argument against the possibility of a private language is not that we need shared experience of language to be communicable to one another but that without such a sharing I will become incommunicable to myself. The inner for Wittgenstein is thus not an externalized outer—there is no such thing as a private inner object to which a private language may be found to give expression. This view is not to be construed as Wittgenstein's denial of the inner but rather that inner states are, as he says, in need of outward criteria (Johnston 1993; Schulte 1993). Thus, what appear often in our language as intrinsic differences between different kinds of inner states are basically grammatical differences in disguise. Part II of *Philosophical Investigations* begins with the following:

> One can imagine an animal angry, frightened, unhappy, happy, startled, but hopeful? And why not? A dog believes his master is at the door. But can he also believe his master will come day after tomorrow? And *what* can he not do here?—How do I do it?—How am I supposed to answer

this? Can only those hope who can talk? Only those who have mastered the use of a language? That is to say, the phenomena of hope are modes of this complicated form of life. (Wittgenstein [1953] 1968, 174)

The reference to language here is obviously not to suggest that those who have mastered the use of a language have acquired the logical skills necessary to express hope but rather that grammar tells us what kinds of objects hope and grief are. Thus, the inner states are not distinguished by some reference to content but by the way we imagine something like an inner state for creatures complicated enough to possess language (and hence culture). I would like to illustrate this idea with reference to the discussion of belief and then follow the illustration with a discussion on pain.

*Belief*

The question of belief in *Philosophical Investigations* appears as the asymmetry between the use of first-person indicative and third-person indicative. Two observations in the second part of this text are crucial. The first is "If there were a verb meaning to believe falsely it would not have a first-person indicative" (Wittgenstein [1953] 1968, 190). The second, closely related to that observation, is "I say of someone else 'He seems to believe...' And other people say it of me. Now, why do I never say it of myself, not even when others *rightly* say it of me? Do I not myself see or hear myself, then?" (Wittgenstein [1953] 1968, 191).

Wittgenstein is asking, What does a belief look like from the inside? When he says that it is possible to misinterpret one's own sense impressions but not one's beliefs, he is not referring to the content of an inner experience but rather to the grammatical impossibility of inferring one's belief (or one's pain) introspectively. That is why he says that if there were a verb that meant "to believe falsely" it would lack a first-person present indicative. Wittgenstein is not stating a metaphysical truth about belief here but a grammatical one. Even when it is possible to make such statements as "It is raining and I do not believe it," the grammar of the term *belief* does not allow us to make these statements, for we cannot imagine a context for such statements— they violate the picture of the inner in the grammar of the word *belief.*

Anthropologists have wrestled with the problem of belief in the context of translation of cultures. The problem has been persistent: When anthropologists attribute belief statements to members of other cultures (i.e., non-Western cultures), are they making a presumption that a common psychological category of most Western languages and cultures is to be treated as a common human capacity that can be ascribed to all men and women? Such questions have been asked of several categories of emotion (see Lutz and Abu-Lughod 1990; Lutz and White 1986), but the case of belief is special because it has been anchored to questions of universal human rationality, on the one hand (Gellner 1970; Lukes 1977), and the common human condition of corporeality, on the other (Needham 1972).

As far as the side of universal rationality is concerned, the puzzle for many scholars seems to be to account for the apparent irrationality of beliefs like that of witchcraft or of other scandalous statements: for example, that the Nuer believe that twins are birds (Evans-Pritchard [1956] 1970). In his polemic against the anthropological tendency to find coherence in such statements, Gellner (1970) states that only through an excessive charity of translation can such beliefs be rendered intelligible. He seems to suggest that they are either to be taken as evidence of prelogical thought or as ideological devices to hide the power exercised by privileged classes in society (the latter point is made with regard to the category of *barak* among Moroccan Berbers). Gellner warns that "to make sense of the concept is to make nonsense of the society" (1970, 42). Asad (1990) has given a devastating critique of Gellner's method, especially of the manner in which in his haste to pronounce on the irrationality of such concepts he actually manages to evade all questions on their use in everyday life of the society under consideration. Wittgenstein's general view seems to be that there are many empirical assertions that we affirm without specially testing them and that their role is to establish the frame within which genuine empirical questions can be raised and answered (Cavell 1969b; Michael Williams 1996). If this scaffolding is questioned, then we are not in the realm of mere differences of opinion. Thus, to someone who is offering an explanation of the French Revolution I will probably not ask whether she has any proof that the world is not an illusion. If such a question is asked, we shall have to say that our differences are noncriterial differences that cannot be resolved by adducing more evidence.

Thus, for the Azande there are genuine empirical questions about how one is to know whether one's illness is to be attributed to the witchcraft of a neighbor or a wife. The final empirical proof of the cause is provided by the postmortem of a body to show whether witchcraft substance is found in the body. Obviously if one shifts this kind of question to another kind of question in which we ask a Zande if he or she believes witches to exist, one is shifting the frame completely. In this revised frame (in which we are certain that witches do not exist), one can ask questions only about witchcraft beliefs, or witchcraft craze, but not about superiority of one kind of witchcraft medicine over another or whether unknowing to oneself one may be a witch—a source of danger to one's neighbors and friends. What does this mean for the practice of ethnography? One strategy is that adopted by Favret-Saada (1977), who felt that to open her mouth on issues of witchcraft in Bocage was to become implicated in utterances that constitute the practices of witchcraft. Thus, her ethnography becomes an account of the complicated relation that the ethnographer comes to have with the "bewitched" and the "unwitchers." It does not raise questions about the rationality or truth of witchcraft beliefs because there is no way in which such questions may be asked from within the language games of the Bocage. The other strategy is to think of ethnography as a persuasive fiction (Strathern 1988). I shall return to the question of translation. For the moment let me say only that the disappointment in the indeterminate place of anthropological knowledge is perhaps like the disappointment with language itself, as somehow natural to the human. This disappointment is a great Wittgensteinian theme and should perhaps lead us to think that the reason why so-called contradictions in belief do not paralyze one in any society is that one's relation to the world is not on the whole that which would be based on knowing (Cavell 1969b, 1979, 1994, 1995).

## Belief and Corporeality

Needham's (1972, 5) inquiry on the status of belief statements and the problem of translation is on entirely different lines. He states:

> If they [beliefs] are assertions about the inner states of individuals, as by common usage they would normally be taken to be, then, so far as my acquaintance with the literature goes, no evidence of such states, as distinct from the collective representations that are thus recorded, is ever presented. In this case we have no empirical occasion to accept such belief-statements as exact and substantiated reports about other people.

Needham goes on to address this problem through Wittgenstein's idea of grammatical investigation and particularly that an inner process stands in need of outward criteria. However, his notion of "grammatical" does not appear to be that of Wittgenstein's—it is hasty and confuses philosophical grammar with the notion of grammar in linguistics (perhaps it is comparable to a case of surface grammar in Wittgenstein, but I am not on sure ground here).[6] The burden of Needham's argument is that even when we are convinced that a person genuinely believes what he says he believes, our conviction is not based on objective evidence of a distinct inner state: "We can thus be masters, as we are, of the practical grammar of belief statements yet remain wholly unconvinced that these rest on an objective foundation of psychic experience" (Needham 1972, 126).

Now if I am correct that the inner is not like a distinct state that can be projected to the outer world through language in Wittgenstein but rather like something that lines the outer, then language and the world (including the inner world) are learned simultaneously. Needham is right in suspecting that a grammar of belief in the English language and in forms of life in which beliefs are held, confessed, defended, solicited, guarded, and watched over may be different from the way in which similar concepts through which the world and the word are connected in the warp and weft of some other society's life. However, the solution Needham (1972) offers to the problem of translation—that some inner states are accompanied by bodily expressions (such as body resemblance, natural posture, gesture, facial expression) whereas other inner states (such as belief) have no specific behavioral physiognomy—is to misread grammatical differences as intrinsic differences in the content of experience. Wittgenstein's way of describing this idea was to say that the body is a picture of the soul, not that the soul stands next to the body or that meaning simply stands next to the word.

We are thus not going to get out of the problem of translation by an appeal to certain human capacities that are real and universal, as contrasted with others that are artificial constructs of various cultural traditions, as Needham (1972) proposes. That is not to say that we do not *read* the body, or that there are no primitive reactions such as crying out in pain, but rather that we depend on grammar to tell us what kind of an object something is. Inserting the centrality of the body in human society is important not in inferring internal states of mind but in the intuition of language as a bodying forth, as in Wittgenstein saying, "Sometimes a cry is wrenched out of me." Let us now consider this question with regard to pain.

*Pain and Private Objects*

Wittgenstein on pain is a major philosophical and anthropological issue, yet there is no highway of thought available to traverse. It would have to be from the side roads and the meandering in uncharted territories that one would find the relation between Wittgenstein's thoughts on pain and the anthropological task of studying forms of sociality. Consider Cavell (1997), who says:

> *Philosophical Investigations* is the great work of philosophy of this century whose central topic may be said to be pain, and one of its principal discoveries is that we will never become clear about the relation of attributions of the concept of pain, nor about any of the concepts of consciousness, nor of any unconsciousness—neither of my attribution of pain to myself nor of my attribution of pain to others—without bringing into question the endless pictures we have in store that prejudicially distinguish what is internal or private to creatures (especially ones with language, humans) from what is external or public to them. (95)

In some of the most creative anthropological writing on this issue, we find the disappointment with language to somehow be integral to the experience of pain (Good et al. 1992). Wittgenstein emphatically denies the possibility of a private language in this case, as in other cases, that refers to what is internal or private to creatures. But what this means is that for Wittgenstein the statement "I am in pain" is not (or not only) a statement of fact but is also an expression of that fact (Cavell 1997). The internal, as I have stated, is not an internalized picture of the outer—nor is the external only a projection of the internal. In this context, what is unique about pain is the absence of any standing languages either in society or in the social sciences that could communicate pain, yet it would be a mistake to think of pain as essentially incommunicable (Das 1997). At stake here is not the asymmetry between the first-person ("I am never in doubt about my pain") and the third-person ("You can never be certain about another person's pain") but rather that to locate pain I have to take the absence of standing languages as part of the grammar of pain. To say "I am in pain" is to ask for acknowledgment from the other, just as denial of another's pain is not an intellectual failure but a spiritual failure, one that puts our future at stake: "One might even say that my acknowledgement is my presentation, or handling of pain. You are accordingly not at liberty to believe or disbelieve what it says—that is the one who says it—our future is at stake" (Cavell 1997, 94). Some passages from *The Blue and Brown Books* (Wittgenstein 1958) are remarkable in the notion of language as embodied or bodying forth.

> In order to see that it is conceivable that one person should have pain in another person's body, one must examine what sorts of facts we call criterial for a pain being in a certain place. . . . Suppose I feel that a pain which on the evidence of the pain alone, e.g. with closed eyes, I should call a pain in my left hand. Someone asks me to touch the painful spot with my right hand. I do so and looking around perceive that I am touching my neighbour's hand. . . . This would be pain felt in another's body. (49)

I interpret this passage (see Das 1995a, 1995b, 1997) to propose that Wittgenstein's fantasy of *my pain* being located in *your body* suggests either the intuition that the representation of shared pain exists in imagination but is not experienced, in which case I would say that language is hooked rather inadequately to the world of pain or that the experience of pain cries out for this response to the possibility that my pain could reside in your body and that the philosophical grammar of pain is about allowing this to happen. As in the case of belief, I cannot locate your pain in the same way as I locate mine. The best I can do is to let it happen to me. Now it seems to me that anthropological knowledge is precisely about letting the knowledge of the other happen to me. This is how we see Evans-Pritchard finding out about himself that he was "thinking black" or "feeling black" though he resisted the tendency to slip into idioms of witchcraft. In the introduction to this chapter, I talk of Wittgenstein's idea of a philosophical problem as having the form "I do not know my way about." In his remarks on pain, to find my way is similar to letting the pain of the other happen to me. My own fantasy of anthropology as a body of writing is that which is able to receive this pain. Thus, while I may never claim the pain of the other, nor appropriate it for some other purpose (nation building, revolution, scientific experiment), that I can lend my body (of writing) to this pain is what a grammatical investigation reveals.

## THE DARKNESS OF HIS TIME

In the preface to *Philosophical Investigations*, Wittgenstein ([1953] 1968) writes, "It is not impossible that it should fall to the lot of this work, in its poverty and darkness of this time, to bring light into one brain or another—but, of course, it is not likely" (vi). Bearn (1977) writes that the destructive moment of the *Investigations* threatens the fabric of our daily lives, so it is more destructive than textbook skepticism of the philosopher or the cafe skeptic. If in life, says Wittgenstein, we are surrounded by death, so too in the health of our understanding we are surrounded by madness (Wittgenstein 1980, 44). Rather than forcefully excluding this voice of madness, Wittgenstein ([1953] 1968) returns us to the everyday by a gesture of waiting. "If I have exhausted the justifications, I have reached bedrock, and my spade is turned. Then I am inclined to say: 'This is simply what I do [handle]'" (§217). In this picture of the turned spade, we have the picture of what the act of writing may be in the darkness of this time. The love of anthropology may yet turn out to be an affair in which when I reach bedrock I do not break through the resistance of the other. But in this gesture of waiting, I allow the knowledge of the other to mark me. Wittgenstein is thus a philosopher of both culture and the counterpoint of culture.

# 2

# A POLITICS OF THE ORDINARY

*Action, Expression, and Everyday Life*

An important claim that runs through this book is on the nature of everyday life and its dual character—viz., that it is both a space of routines and habits as well as a space that contains the potential of generating the kind of doubts about one's relations to others and to oneself that can become world annihilating. This feature of everyday life is what gives it an uncanny character. Reading the ethnographies of violence that emerged in the nineties and that were still stumbling with questions of how to comprehend the transformation of places such as Sri Lanka from relatively peaceful social settings into war zones and chronic violence, and reflecting on my own work on the violence of the Partition of India into two countries, I detected a tendency to violence that was contained within the everyday. I argued further that if not a cure then at least an interruption in the execution of such violence was to be found in the everyday itself rather than in an escape from the everyday.[1] In the previous chapter I gave several examples of what it means to think of the everyday as a way of inhabiting the very space of devastation yet again—building life, repairing relationships, I had earlier called this gesture the descent into the ordinary (Das 2007). In this chapter I ask how this conception of the everyday allows us to think of a politics of the ordinary as a stitching together of action and expression in the work of bringing about a different everyday—I call this the birthing of the eventual everyday from the actual everyday.

Recently, there has been an interesting turn to think of politics in relation to vulnerability and resistance in which philosophers and critical thinkers have turned attention to failing infrastructure as a major obstacle to finding the ground from which a politics of collective action could be waged.

For instance, commenting on the importance of the demands for infrastructural goods, Judith Butler (2016) speaks of the way a movement may be galvanized for the very purpose of establishing adequate infrastructure or for keeping infrastructure from being destroyed. However, infrastructure is important for Butler because it provides the ground for political assemblies that depend on it. Thus, while accepting Hannah Arendt's notion of political action as gathering for collective action that brings the space of appearance into light, Butler also critiques Arendt for her assumption that the material conditions of gathering are separate from the space of gathering and argues, instead, that "infrastructure now includes not only public media but all forms of media through which, and within which, the space of appearance is constituted" (Butler 2016, 14). While I appreciate Butler's attention to infrastructure in any consideration of what constitutes politics, I am struck by the fact that the street appears here only in relation to the prospects of collective mobilization. In some ways, this replicates the separation between labor, work, and action that provides the architecture for Arendt's theory of action. Elsewhere I have engaged the question of what a politics of need might look like when politics and governance are folded into each other so that political action is undertaken in the everyday itself (see Das and Walton 2015; Das and Randeria 2015).[2] For now I want to take the picture of descent as a mode of doing politics and the theory of political action that it implies.

In my ethnographic work with low-income urban families in Delhi, I would often come across expressions and practices that suggested some kind of a "descent" into the ordinary through evoking such expressions as a "friendship with the earth." For instance, a local leader in Delhi, where I was working, once asked me in jest, "If you fly high, where will you fall?" I replied, as I was expected to, "On the earth." He laughed, nodded, and said, "So our friendship should be with the earth, no?" This particular leader was explaining to me why he worked on local concerns such as how to get tankers of drinking water in an unauthorized colony in which water refuses to flow or even how to ensure that the addresses haphazardly assigned to houses built on land that the inhabitants recognize as "illegal enclosures" (*gheri hui zameen*) or "occupied land" (*kabze ki zameen*) can acquire validity in official documents. I realize that these issues seem banal and more on the side of fulfilling basic needs rather than fighting for ideals such as justice and freedom—what could ever be of theoretical interest, one might ask, in the trivial details in which the perils of everyday life here are expressed?[3] Yet, as I sat in dark rooms without windows, or in the shadow and smells of heaps of waste collected from the neighborhood hospitals or factories, with discordant sounds pouring in from the street, and listened to stories about what it took to get an official document, or the extent of effort a woman had to make to carry gallons of water perched on the back of a bicycle from a tube well or a water tanker and carry it up hilly terrain—I would hear the protests of a Beckett character: "You're on earth, you're on earth, there's no cure for that." I feel that if a conversation between anthropology and philosophy is to have any meaning at all for me, philosophy must learn to respond to the pressure of questions that I encountered in these settings. It is not a matter of some grand gestures of attraction or repulsion that anthropology could make toward philosophy, but a need to respond to the intensity with which the voices in these streets and houses pervade my very being. What is the nature of their intimacy with the world? How does one work on the self to claim an ethical life within these quotidian concerns? How does one come to lose one's world? Said differently, instead of the sovereign subject whose utterances carry force because they are authoritative (I promise, I declare), I am interested in the fragility of the subject and of the context as mutually constitutive of the work of inhabitation and what that entails for a politics of the ordinary.[4]

## THE FRAGILITY OF ACTION AND THE FRAGILITY OF EXPRESSION

Is human vulnerability to be traced to the fact that all human action is vulnerable to failure, or is vulnerability socially constituted? A way out of this binary of a universal ontology of the human versus the social-historical conditions under which some are made more vulnerable than others is to take a fundamental insight from Austin (1962) that knits action and expression together as a way of thinking of the "natural facts" of human life and of the diversity in social conventions that give shape to it.[5] I make here a brief excursion into framing the question of vulnerability of human action through Austin's work on performative utterances because of its essential insights into the various kinds of failures to which human expression and action are subject. I then come to the ethnography that reveals how the risks of failure of human action (and expression) are tied to the struggle for fulfillment of everyday needs that knot the social and the natural into each other.

Let us begin with the Austin's (1962) important insight that in a certain region of language, which he designates as the region of performative utterances or speech acts, action does not follow or precede speech but rather *is* the (speech) act itself. The examples he gives of such utterances do not rely on iconic collection pieces like those pertaining to the "bald king of France is a wise man" (famously used by Russell to debate truth value functions for null sets) but are made up of humdrum verbs. "I *do* (take this woman to be my lawfully wedded wife)," "I *name* (this ship the *Queen Elizabeth*)," among others. Austin's comment on these utterances is worth citing here:

> In these examples it seems clear that to utter the sentence (in, of-course the appropriate circumstances) is not to *describe* my doing of what I should be said in so uttering to be doing or to state that I am doing it: it is to do it. None of the utterances cited is either true or false: I assert this as obvious and do not argue it. (Austin 1962, 6)

If, however, it is so obvious that the examples given by Austin neither pertain to statements that are nonsense nor can be assigned values of truth or falsity, then how do they actually do what they do? What are the conditions under which such utterances succeed? Austin does not ask, "What are the conditions under which these utterances are true or false?" but rather inquires into the conditions under which they are felicitous (happy) or infelicitous (unhappy.) I refrain from rehearsing all the six conditions he enumerates but rather note that these include such things as specifying conventional procedures with specifications of what words are to be spoken, who might speak them, where, and under what circumstances. These external procedures are complemented by a reference to "thoughts and feelings" that certain participants are expected to have and the subsequent conduct that they are expected to follow (Austin 1962, 14–15).[6] In specifying these conditions Austin is also careful in not only laying the felicity conditions but also specifying what kinds of infelicities will make the performance fail. Remarkably, these failures include not only external conditions but also internal states. For example, to say "I promise" when I have no intention of keeping my promise is to speak insincerely, falsely, and would violate conditions five and six of felicity conditions enumerated by Austin. Yet, the puzzle is that a false promise is still a promise and would be grounds for legal action, for instance, in Indian law if a man were to have had sex with a woman he had promised to marry but used the promise only as a ruse to sleep with her (Indian law would recognize this as culpable action).

Austin's remark that explicit performative utterances are "obviously" neither true nor false has spawned much discussion on whether explicit performatives are, contrary to Austin, bearers of truth value (Tsohatzidis 2018). But as Cavell (2005b) astutely observes, what is at stake for Austin is not to jettison truth and falsity to bring down the lofty discussions of truth down to size.[7]

> What intellectual plausibility can Austin be counting on for the suggestion that what he names felicity and infelicity can be seen to provide as philosophically stringent a mode of the "criticism" of speech as does the ancient assessment of truth or falsity? The philosophical stake seems so disproportionate; the dimension of the felicitous turns merely—does it not?—on human conventions, whereas the dimension of truth invokes our fundamental relation to, our knowledge of, whatever there is human or otherwise. But Austin will eventually claim that truth (truth itself, so to speak) is to be understood precisely as a dimension of what he calls the criticism of speech. His aim in his study of performatives is at once to lift the non-descriptive or non-assertional or non-constative gestures of speech to renewed philosophical interest and respectability and to bring, or prepare the ground on which to bring, the philosophical concern with truth down to size. (179–80)

It is Cavell's remark on bringing truth down to size that makes me want to look at how an Austinian theory of the stitching of action and expression might help me in delineating the contours of political action in the areas I studied where the risks of misfires, abuses, accidents, mistakes, and errors were much more palpable than successes. In his marvelous essays on truth, excuses, and pretending, Austin, to my ears memorably, shows that human action might itself be defined as that which is likely to go wrong— yet when a performative act fails we have recourse to a range of excuses that are symmetrical to the many kinds of failures and misfires of performative acts and utterances that Austin carefully maps. Laugier (2018a) explains that a theory of error is essential not only for understanding the character of performative utterances as social acts but for understanding the character of all actions and expressions. The philosophical stakes here lie not so much in isolating a particular region of language and action (the performative) in which the distinction between truth and falsity can be *replaced* by felicity and infelicity but in the realization that cutting down truth to size also ironically means that truth is freed from its tight muscling down to propositional truths. Instead, it comes to roam around in the whole social field pertaining to such questions as the correct appreciation of a situation, deciphering the context, and asking what happens when conventions to guide us are not in place. An exquisite ethnographic discussion of such deciphering of the situation may be found in Han's (2014) depiction of how neighbors home in on "critical moments" in the life of the neighborhood: Does the child who came in to play look like she has not eaten? Is the next-door house plunged in darkness because there was no money to pay the bills? Are sounds of quarrels coming from the adjoining house because of unpaid bills? Kindly neighbors might then "pretend" that they have cooked too much food and ask the neighbor to come in and share or take to other ruses to help—here the pretending is not so much a lie as a different kind of truth either cut down to size or elevated into a moral action while avoiding moralism. These are not opposed stances.

Austin's theory of performative actions has found a fertile ground in anthropology but has been used primarily to delineate the role and function of utterances with illocutionary force that are often public with conventions and procedures in place. In contrast, discussion of the perlocutionary dimension of utterances that are primarily known by their effects has suffered in comparison. Austin thought it was a fatal criticism of his theory that such utterances as "I warn you," "Run," and "Hands up" are not confined to any specific class of verbs. Given the right circumstances any utterance, whether constative or performative, he realized, can have perlocutionary effects by the very definition that such utterances do something *by* saying something and not *in* saying something. Why is this the end of the story, asks Cavell, and not its beginning? He detects in Austin's giving up on perlocutionary effects a certain timidity of philosophy in the face of emotion and passion.

Let us then take Cavell's proposal that asks us to step back and think of the manner in which action and expression are stitched together when convention is *not* in place. Cavell carves out a place for what he calls "passionate utterances" and asks us to reconsider the entire theory of performatives when the point of such utterances is that they put the speaker and hearer into jeopardy by bringing desire into the domain of language. Although anxious to acknowledge the stupendous achievements of Austin and the ground he has already laid in his essay on excuses for understanding the risks entailed in utterances that do not have the background of a stable context, passionate utterances are not simply a subtype of performative utterances. Thus, passionate statements such as "I love you" cannot rely upon shared convention to be successful or unsuccessful but must stake a claim to be unique to *that* speaker and *that* addressee. While dependent on such conventional words as "I love you," passionate utterances must also signal the uniqueness of *that* moment for *this* person speaking *these* words. Further, such utterances single out the addressee—the second person to whom the words are addressed and not the first person who commits herself to, say, a promise or a marriage as in utterances with illocutionary force.[8] While someone breaking a bottle on the hull of the ship naming it (in the British case where Austin's example is located) *Queen Elizabeth* relies on the authority that he wields to make the public utterance effective or felicitous, the one who utters a passionate statement—declaring his love, for instance—makes himself vulnerable. If we were less focused on the action aspect of speech acts and more on expression, says Cavell, we would see that perlocutionary effects are not external to the speech act, as Austin argues, but constitute the internal possibility of the expression itself. Now performative utterances and passionate utterances appear to Cavell not as two types of utterances but as two possibilities of the speech act—the first opening up the possibility of participation in the order of law (as reflected in the orderliness of speech and its ritual or formal character) and the second as the improvisation stemming from disorders of desire in which the speech act renders the speaker and hearer vulnerable to risks. Cavell is proposing not a balance between orderly ritualized speech and improvisations in speech but rather the realization that the double nature of the everyday finds expression in the double nature of speech acts themselves. "From the roots of speech, in each utterance of revelation and confrontation two paths spring: that to responsibility of implication and that of the rights of desire. The paths will not reliably coincide—but to have them both open is what I want of philosophy" (Cavell 2005b, 185). Indeed, Yves Erard (2019) proposes that in a fundamental way how the world enters in the expressions that carry illocutionary force versus how it enters in passionate statements is very different. On some occasions, conventions might not be in place and so the procedure (of, say, marrying someone or naming a ship) may fail. But this is a different kind of failure than the pervasive risk of things going wrong in the case of passionate statements when the public and shared language gives way to the risks of rejection or betrayal in the intimacy of a face-to-face encounter.[9]

A final point I want to make comes from Cavell's earliest work; it relates to the intuitions about words and their meanings that come not from shared opinions but from sensibilities that have been forged by participation in forms of life. A classic passage from his essay "The Availability of Wittgenstein's Later Philosophy" (1962), repeated again in Cavell (1979), gives us a picture of how we learn to project words in new contexts while retaining the sense of their internal consistency (I will have occasion to visit this particular citation again in later chapters).

> We learn and teach words in certain contexts, and then we are expected, and expect others, to be able to project them into further contexts. Nothing insures that this projection will take place (in particular, not the grasping of universals nor the grasping of book of rules) just as nothing insures that we will make, and understand, the same projections. That on the whole we do is a matter of our sharing routes of interest and feeling, modes of response, senses of humor and of significance of fulfillment, of what is outrageous, of what is similar to what else, what a rebuke, what forgiveness, of what an utterance, of when an utterance is an assertion, when an appeal, when an explanation—all the whirl of organism Wittgenstein calls "forms of life." (1979, 52)

Our ability to project words—Cavell's examples of feeding the lion, feeding the meter, and feeding your pride—are all ways in which our relation to particular objects in the world—how it is inhabited by lions and machines and emotions—is disclosed in our ability to project and our confidence that our words will be received. For example, the fact that I can say "feed your pride" but not "feed your happiness" might tell me that pride is the kind of emotion that might grow with flattery but that happiness cannot be increased by flattery. It also shows that words cannot be projected in a solipsistic way since there is an inner constancy to them. For Cavell, this inner constancy cannot be derived from a book of rules; but I think, in addition, there is an idea of the natural that is at play here.[10] The natural cannot be equated with an invariable and universal "given," since different languages will bring out different ways in which ideas of pride are constructed, but the natural cannot be completely equated with the constructed either. Let us say, for now, that it is almost as if our constructions are necessary to show how a particular history of the natural might be disclosed within a particular form of life in this particular corner of humanity as distinct from another one.

I thought it necessary to lay down the salient issues in the network of concepts in Cavell's writing not because I intend to "apply" them to my ethnography or because I see my ethnography as critiquing them. Rather, I feel that a conversation is invited between the philosophical concepts of action, expression, and the everyday and the perplexities that arise in the lives of the people I describe from my ethnographic sites. Can philosophical concepts grow out of ordinary lives so that we do not escape *to* philosophy but add our effort to nourish such conversations? Clearly, I do feel the need for nourishment rather than for policing the boundaries and weeding out foreign elements from our discourses.

Let me briefly recapitulate three important points from the above discussion that I will mobilize in the following sections. First, I use the notion of the everyday to indicate its dual character—viz., that it is a site of routine, reproduction, repetition, and habit, on the one side, but on the other side it is also the place from which doubts, despair, disorders, and improvisations occur. This dual character of the everyday makes it both a secure place and an insecure one accounting for its uncanny character. Second, the image of the everyday, human intimacy, and forms of action and expression are not evident: they have to be conjured as part of our work. Depending on how we imagine the everyday we will imagine the threats to it through related images. If marriage gives us the image of intimacy, then the threat to it will come from adultery; if consent gives us an image of togetherness, then simulation of consent or forcibly obtained consent will be seen as the threat to our everyday life. The point is that the threat to our worlds have to be discovered for each *case*—it cannot be a general discovery. Finally, in Cavell's understanding, belonging to our culture does not translate into an allegiance to our society or our culture *as it stands*, but the forms that the labor of criticism takes must to some extent grow from the disappointments of the everyday. Later on, I will explicitly take on the question of whether critique is completely enclosed within the criteria that we have learned from participation in our form of life or whether these criteria give us the ability to draw out the potentials that might take critique in unexpected directions. For example, could a recounting of mere household events—as Edgar

Allan Poe's stories and their uncanny character reveal—be almost banal at one level and fatal at another? What does it mean to think of our belonging itself as fraught with the possibility of doubt?[11] What is it to inhabit the everyday within the scene of disappointment is an abiding theme of Cavell's work, and these issues, I contend, are necessary to the picture of the everyday that Cavell's work discloses. They invite the participation of anthropology to the project of making the everyday count. These questions do not dovetail neatly with the ethnographic examples I give, but they are the necessary scaffolding for understanding where the descriptions are going.

## MAKING A WORLD INHABITABLE

I return to the local leader whose observation on our friendship with the earth gave me an opening into this chapter. Sanjeev Gupta (I use his own name since he wants to be identified in any papers I write, to assert authorship of his own actions) lives in a neighborhood in Delhi that in official parlance is known as an "unauthorized colony," a type of settlement that is included under the general rubric of "unplanned settlements." The latter is a catchall category that includes official slums, urban villages, *jhuggi-jhopdi* colonies (shanty settlements), and old traditional bazaars. Inhabitants of such neighborhoods enjoy some rights as citizens. For instance, they are entitled to vote and to receive subsidized food through the public distribution system, as well as having access to government-run institutions such as schools and hospitals, but they are not officially entitled to sanitary services, water, or electricity connections since they live in places that are not recognized by the city as authorized residential areas. This does not mean that they have no access to water, electricity, or sanitation, but a lot of work that I characterize as "political" has to go into getting any of these facilities. In recent years, scholars have begun to seriously reflect on the kinds of ambiguities and indeterminacies that mark the position of such settlements in relation to law and governmental regulations (see Chatterji and Mehta 2007; Das 2011a; Datta 2012; Eckert 2006). I am interested here in a limited question that has to do with the kind of a world that is disclosed in the story of Sanjeev Gupta's engagement with the politics of housing, electricity, and water. How do these forms of politics speak to the questions about the relation between the actual everyday and the eventual everyday that I raised earlier?[12]

I want to start by reiterating that though the law defines the status of the unplanned settlements and the various types of administrative regulations to which they are subject to create the impression of an orderly legal process, the boundaries between the legal and the illegal are not at all clear. First, there are bitter rivalries between different government departments about land use. Second, the courts do not speak with a single voice on this issue. As an example, we can look at the ongoing tensions between the Department of Urban Development, Government of Delhi, the Delhi Development Authority (DDA), and the municipal corporation that have different jurisdictions on different aspects of these spaces. Thus, a report issued by the Department of Urban Development in October 2006 states the following:

> The DDA is responsible for guiding planned development in Delhi through successive Master Plans (1962, 1982, 2001). It is also the sole agency mandated to develop and dispose of land in the city. . . . The DDA, however, has been unable to meet forecasted demands for housing, commercial and industrial space, resulting in large scale unauthorized development. . . . Only an estimated 30% of the city lives in planned areas. The poor have borne the brunt of the shortage. . . . The lack of formal access to appropriate housing has led to the genesis of unauthorized colonies in Delhi. . . . Currently there are about 1432 unauthorized colonies . . . providing shelter to about 30 lakh [i.e., three million] people. . . . Unauthorized colonies have been regularized twice in Delhi: in 1961 when over 100 colonies were regularized and in 1977 when over 600 colonies were recognized. (Department of Urban Development 2006, E1–E2)[13]

Though there are different administrative acts that govern these unplanned settlements on such matters as provisions of public services, restrictions over eviction, and claims for alternative housing, smuggled into these official documents is the uncomfortable realization that the government is dealing with many of these issues after the fact—that different kinds of urban settlements have grown by "illegal" occupation of government-owned land often right under the noses of the authorities and that acts of enumeration and classification are running to catch up with this kind of growth from the ground up. Sanjeev Gupta explained the process as follows: "It is not as if there is an existing map on the basis of which a colony is developed. Rather, a map is forcibly put on spaces that have come into being haphazardly, and which continue to grow and change as new opportunities and needs arise." If the poor learn to dwell in these spaces it is by learning what it is to be "thrown" into a political and legal landscape that cannot be deciphered except through their engagement and action on their environment.[14]

Punjabi Basti, located in West Delhi, where Sanjeev Gupta lives, is an area covering 34 acres with a built-up area of 21.59 acres. In its immediate vicinity lie unauthorized colonies and official slums, but situated at a little distance is the affluent area of West Patel Nagar with its bustling markets and middle- and upper-class housing. Punjabi Basti has 2,318 plots (combined houses and shops), though multiple households may live within the same house. Let us take a deceptively simple question: From where do these figures come? How did a house or a shop acquire something as simple and taken for granted as an address? Note that while figures are available for election constituencies or for census wards, Punjabi Basti did not figure as a separate colony in official records until 1995. Earlier, it was assimilated in the larger area of Baljit Nagar. Even now many documents such as ration cards or voter ID cards record the locality as "Punjabi Basti, Baljit Nagar." Until a few years back, streets did not have numbers or names. Certain landmarks were used to divide different parts of the neighborhood—thus crossroads were named after small temples that had come up through local effort (e.g., Gayatri Chowk named after the goddess Gayatri) and certain sites were marked after important events such as the hosting of the national flag on Independence Day (Jhanda Chowk—lit. Flagstaff-Crossing). Boundaries between neighborhoods were fluid. The geography of the area thus reflects an order that emerged from an evolving collective life rather than from official planning or control.

I will not go into the detailed history of the area except to indicate two features essential for understanding the story that follows. The first is that the families of the earliest settlers that we could locate all indicated that they had moved from different parts of Delhi soon after 1976 when a national emergency was declared and the infamous forced sterilization and beautification drive in Delhi was implemented (Tarlo 2003). However, Punjabi Basti did not come about as a resettlement colony—a term that designates areas to which the poor were forcibly relocated during the beautification drive. Rather, many of these families voluntarily moved here because they saw in this time the opportunity to claim empty land.[15] The local term for this process is *jagah gherna*, which literally means "enclosure of a place" and can be used in a neutral way when people are making a reference to the amount of labor that went to enclose a piece of unoccupied land and convert it into a house. Alternately, the term has the connotation of illegality when one voices the perspective of law, seeing the world through the eyes of government officials (see also Khan 2012 for *kabza* of mosques in Pakistan). People could take both perspectives claiming simultaneously that it was their labor that had made the area inhabitable and at the same time conceding that the land had been taken without going through the legal mechanisms that bestow ownership within the formal regime of property relations. Second, Punjabi Basti is spread over hilly terrain, which makes different streets stretch over different levels. Each small segment of this locality can be said to have a slightly different history—part landfill, part rocky terrain from which large slabs were extracted, part forest—and the process of settling the area has required different kinds of labor such as clearing of the forested part, filling out craters created by extraction of large slabs by builders, and leveling the ground to make roads negotiable. I note in parentheses that the kind of labor that had to be put to make this area inhabitable was very different from that required in other places—e.g., where slums developed right in the middle of affluent colonies as construction laborers who had been given permission for temporary shelters converted these into permanent habitation. There was a strong sense of the legitimacy that residents claimed for their actions. As one woman said to me, "Sister, everyone lives over occupied land—all these rich owners of bungalows (*kothiwale*)—did they come to earth owning land? Did they have to put in the kind of labor that we did to make this uninhabitable place into a dwelling?"

As the locality became more settled, a market in housing developed by which early encroachments were converted into "plots" and sold to new buyers. Though such plots and ownership are not recorded in the revenue registers with a *khasra* (plot) number, the rights to buy and sell are recognized within the local worlds. Those living in recognized slums are protected from eviction by legal acts such as the Slum Areas Act of 1956, but the majority of the people living in unplanned settlements have very limited legal protection. An interesting question is, How have areas such as Punjabi Basti been able to protect their dwellings? The story is complex and needs a much more detailed discussion than I cannot provide here.[16] However, I will relate one segment of this complex story to shed some light on the character of everyday life through Sanjeev Gupta's role in the successful electrification of the colony. I note in parentheses that the attempt to get water connections have failed partly because of the material character of these entities—a topic I address in detail elsewhere (see Das 2012b). I will then reflect on the question of what kind of ethical voice we can locate within these projects of dwelling and building.

## ACTING ON THE WORLD: WHAT MAKES ELECTRICITY FLOW?

I was walking with my research collaborators, Simi and Purshottam, up the steep street on which Sanjeev Gupta lives in December 2011. On the corner of the street there were placards announcing the office of an NGO that Sanjeev Gupta has founded and close to it was another one with some information about the West Delhi Congress Youth Committee on which his name appeared prominently, along with other better-known political leaders. A distinguished-looking Sikh gentleman, perhaps in his late seventies, called Hargovind was buying vegetables from a hawker. We stopped to greet him and fell into pleasant chatter.

"Are you going to Gupta Ji's [an honorific] house?" Hargovind asked. Then he went on to comment that Sanjeev was truly a remarkable man. "Our family is the among the oldest settlers here," he said, "so when he first moved in this place in 1980 we kept our distance. But then we saw what he did to make this street inhabitable [*rehne layak*] and my family and many others became his great supporters." Hargovind went on to rehearse a story we had heard many times. It was the story about how that particular street on which we were standing was once much below the level of other streets. During the monsoon, water used to gush downward and would often enter the houses. Sanjeev Gupta, on his own initiative, brought truckloads of loose soil, plastic, and other material and had it lain on the road to raise its level. Because of the narrow lanes, cars or trucks could not reach that spot—so he hired donkeys to carry the load (a practice still prevalent). For Hargovind, the event that marked a complete shift in their relationship was when he saw that a donkey was not able to climb up the street as it became steeper; so Sanjeev Gupta put his shoulder against its back and, putting his weight behind it, he pushed the donkey to help it move up. "When we saw what he was doing for the whole street, joining his own strength [*zor*] to that of the donkey's, we were ashamed—all the households in this street joined him in this effort. You can see that the street is now at a higher level than other streets. It is paved with bricks, cemented, installed with a cow trap so that animals cannot roam around and make it dirty. It is the cleanest street in the neighborhood." When asked to comment on this story Sanjeev Gupta laughed and said, "But if the government does not do anything, we cannot continue to live in this hell [narak], can we?"

I start with this story to give a sense of Gupta's commitment to action. Yet, the improvisations he makes and the vulnerability of his actions to failure alert us to the fact that outside of conventional ritualized action there is also a different way of stitching action and expression together that should be considered for any theory of performative utterances and the force they carry. The paths through which such saying and doing are connected are not straightforward. While Cavell seems to have placed action on the side of illocutionary force of speech acts and expression on the side of perlocutionary effect, the story that will unfold tells us about improvisation, disorder, and vulnerability on the side of both action and expression.

Walking in Punjabi Basti, one is struck by the presence of seven large transformers with high tension wires installed on bits of land that are at the street corners, in the bits of greenery that pass for parks, and, in one case, on the side of a temple. There are no empty stretches of land on which these transformers could be installed, so the electricity company and the residents have done as best as they could.

The story of the electrification of this neighborhood begins with the privatization of electricity in Delhi in the years between 2000 and 2002. When power reforms began in 2002 in Delhi, in light of the heavy losses incurred by the state-owned Delhi Vidyut Board, the latter was unbundled into three privately owned companies. Sanjeev Gupta and many others told us about the terrible harassment that residents faced when electricity officials lodged complaints with the police about theft of electricity. As in most such neighborhoods, people had earlier drawn electricity illegally from street poles to draw lines to their homes, shops, or karkhanas (workshops) to power domestic or commercial appliances. The networks of private contractors and low-level officials of the municipal corporation who were routinely bribed had assured that the residents did not face criminal charges for theft of electricity. Now with privatization they were finding that the game plans had completely changed. Sanjeev Gupta used his position as the president of the zonal congress committee to arrange a meeting (sometime in 2005) between the representatives of the locality and the officer-in-charge form the zonal division of the company to discuss the issue of electricity theft and harassment. Here is the description of what transpired—I juxtapose fragments of the account given by Sanjeev Gupta (in Hindi) over several informal discussions with an account of the issues involved in electrification as given by one of the officers (Vidyut Sir)[17] of the private company who granted me an interview (mostly in English). The fragments come from different moments. It is also the case that Sanjeev was often relating the story in the presence of objects that materialized the story while Vidyut Sir was sitting in a small conference room of a posh private bank that he had since joined.

> SANJEEV GUPTA: After electricity was privatized, there was this big move to install meters—now as you know in colonies like these there were no regular meters—there were local contractors who used to supply electricity for payment by drawing lines from the high-tension wires—or else, many people drew the lines themselves and there were regular payments extracted by the local linesmen and the policemen. We said to Vidyut Sir,[18] "Sir, we have been demanding regular supply of electricity but you do not sanction meters for us. On top of it you file complaints and the police treats us like criminals. They come and catch hold of the person by the neck as if he has committed a major crime, as if he is a murderer. What kind of justice is this?" Vidyut Sir replied that their records showed how much electricity had been consumed in this locality and what was the recovery of money against it. He said vehemently, "I say on that basis, I say that I have proof, I say, that people are stealing—they are thieves." We said, "Sir ji, how can you call us thieves? If you don't give us electricity on the grounds that we are not an authorized colony—and people naturally need electricity—a man wants to run a fan, his little children are burning in the heat—he will get electricity with whatever means—then why call him a thief?"
>
> VIDYUT: My boss and I were both very struck by Sanjeev Gupta's argument. We thought ethically how could we accuse them of theft when we have not responded to their needs? There was a lot of discussion

within the management—from the business angle, there was a market here but could we manage it? There were huge problems of how to identify houses correctly. The addresses were all haphazard; there were no numbers or names of streets. It was a maze.

SANJEEV: I was truly stung by the accusation of theft [lit. "ye baat mujhe bahut lag gayi"—this utterance struck me]. We said, Sir ji, we will remove this stigma that we are a colony of thieves. Vidyut sir, guided us—so did another officer. The big issue was that houses did not have addresses in sequential order, streets did not have names or numbers—sometimes if a linesman was expected to deliver a bill, the client would simply rip apart his meter and say, my house is not C4— that house is in another street.[19]

VIDYUT: We advised them that they had to get a proper map of the area with house numbers in order—they had to submit a list of names of household with proper addresses. Without such a list, we could not install regular meters.

Sanjeev Gupta and some other leaders then organized meetings in the area and persuaded most households to contribute two hundred rupees per household for a map of the area. After many difficulties because of the topography of the area and because houses were not on one level, a private firm of architects finally made a map. After an exchange of many letters, petitions, and pressure from the chief minister's office, the town planner of the municipal corporation finally approved the map. This enabled the BSES to prepare a list of consumers and to install meters in the houses after augmenting electricity supply by installing seven transformers in the area. In the process each house was given a new number, but Sanjeev Gupta managed to get the electricity company to agree to write both the old numbers and the new numbers on the bills so that now in all official correspondence the address appears to be composite of the two numbers.

I do not want to give the impression that all this—the mapmaking, the assigning of new numbers, the installation of the transformers—was achieved by agreements arrived through rational deliberative discourse. Accusations have been made in the locality that all the money that was collected was not properly accounted for. There were fights over the exact location of the transformers—for instance, the leader of the local Dalits complained that the attempts to place transformers in the park that adjoins the streets, named after Ambedkar, where most Dalits in the area live, amounted to an insult to Ambedkar's memory. The gravest threats to Sanjeev Gupta came not openly but in many covert ways from the network of "entrepreneurs" who were earlier supplying electricity illegally and whose business was adversely affected. One day when Sanjeev Gupta was relating the efforts they had to make to complete the project, he suddenly choked up and I saw that his eyes were tearing up. He said, "I was even attacked one night when I was coming home." "What happened? How? Did you get hurt?" "No but they showed me a revolver and told me to stop these activities." "Who were they?" "Oh, the ones who do this *dukandari* [lit., market transactions but carrying a tone of illicit transactions here]—whose *dhandha* [illicit work] would have stopped." "Did you report to the police?" "No, the local police is always on their side." "So what did you do? How do you know you are safe?" "I told you I was not a die-hard Congress man. I am in the Party because I cannot do without it. So those above were informed and they must have talked to them—after all the ones who were intimidating me are also part of the same set up."

It was characteristic of Sanjeev Gupta's mode of relating a story that he refused to name those who had intimidated or threatened him. Clearly, he lived and worked in a context in which people led lives steeped in what he thought of as corruption, theft, and extortion. For instance, when describing an ongoing case of demolition of shanties in an adjoining neighborhood in which many poor people lost their abodes, he predicted that they would be back and would reoccupy the land but that they would have to pay again to the very people who had first encouraged them to occupy the vacant land. "It is the same people who had first allowed them to occupy this land by giving an extortion fee to them, and then had the demolition squads out, and will now again extract money from them." He would only name the "people" as the local *bhu mafia* (land mafia): "You think that land mafias all come from outside with the big building lobbies but there is a local *bhu* mafia too which operates right from within." Once during a discussion of a house that was being renovated close by with expensive materials, I tentatively suggested the name of a prominent local leader as probably benefitting from the activities of building by extorting some kind of "protection money." "You have named him, not I," said Sanjeev and then went on to add, "Perhaps I would say he is sixty percent good and forty percent bad." The general sense was that relations of proximity required that one saw in everyone some good and some bad.

Sanjeev Gupta's shifting moods, his feelings of being powerful and vulnerable at the same time, were clear in most stories he told. The moment that he recalled with great pride was that of the inauguration of the transformers—the most significant aspect of which was that no ceremony was performed to mark the occasion. There was much discussion among Sanjeev Gupta and his friends. As he recalled, they wondered:

> Should we get a Brahmin to tell us the *muhurat* (auspicious moment) for the inauguration? Who should we invite? Should we invite Lalotia (the local MLA)? But then there are others like Krishna Teerath, the MP; she is also from this area and has done a lot for us. Should it be the electricity officials? They are the ones who guided us to overcome every obstacle. Then I decided—no *muhurat*, no inauguration, no leader. When the transformers started functioning and the whole area was electrified, the politicians, the ones who sit above, were amazed.

Relating an imaginary scene in conversation with a politician who might have expected to be invited to inaugurate the placing of the transformers:

E1. Oh, how did *this* happen?
H1. *Arre, ye kaise hua?*

E2. Transformers were put,
H2. *Transformer lag gaye*

E3. the whole area got electrified,
H4. *pura area electrify ho gaya*

E5. and we were not called to inaugurate?
H5. *aur hamen mahurat pe bulaya bhi nahin gaya?*

E6. Oh Sahib, who are you anyway?
H6. *Aji sahib, aap hote kaun hain?*

E7. You are our representatives—we chose you.
H7. *Aap to hamare numaynde hain—hamne aap ko chuna.*

E8. It is due to us that you sit high above.
H8. *Hamari vajah se aap aaj unchi jagah baithe hain.*

E9. Otherwise who were you?
H9. *Nahin to aap the kaun?*

E10. You should have asked after us when we suffered.
H10. *Aap ko to hamse puchna chaahiye tha jab ham takleef mein the.*

E11. Why should we call you for this occasion?
H11. *ham aap ko kyon bulayen is mauke par?*

E12. Did you spill blood and sweat as we did?
H12. *Aapne hamari tarah khun paseena bahaya hai?*

I will comment on the distribution of voices, the play between the past tense and the present tense, as well as the effective use of the vocative, a bit later. Let me first switch to another moment on another day when Sanjeev was relating the same story as we waited under a makeshift arrangement of chairs in the street where we were to be addressed by a representative of the Civil Defense Department on disaster preparedness. With a sadness in his voice as we looked at the narrow, winding lanes and the new constructions on shaky foundations, making it apparent that no relief could be physically rushed here if an earthquake were to hit Delhi, Sanjeev Gupta said, "That day, when the transformers began to function—only we knew from which personage to which other we had to run, who are the people before whom we had to rub our foreheads on the ground—*kis kis ke peeche bhage, kis kis ke samne matha ragda*?" The reference to a gesture that signifies utter abjection may not have literally taken place, but language conveys here the embodied sense of humiliation.

Yet Sanjeev Gupta is not defeated. He plans to take up the issue of water, since other leaders in the area seem to have failed at this task. He shows me about sixty letters he has already written to the Delhi Water Board and the municipal corporation. He has finally succeeded in getting an official of the water board to admit that the official policies are ridden with contradictions. Now that he has an officially approved map of the area, he is hopeful that other issues of sanitation, water, health, and education will be tackled. As he cites the oft-repeated rhetorical statement that circulates in stories, films, and television serials in India: "*Doston, kissa abhi jaari hai*"—friends, the story still continues.[20]

## COMMENTARY

Sanjeev Gupta is not known in the neighborhood for his rhetorical skills. There are others who can bring together mythical motifs, hand gestures, and movements of eyes with great dramatic effect. Sanjeev, people say, is a man of measured words—*nape tule lafzon ka insaan*. Yet, I am impressed that stories are woven around objects by such men and women in a manner that illuminates the interpenetration of persons and things specific to the lifeworlds from which they emanate. In his reflections on the decline of aura, Benjamin (1969, 2008) states that stories told around objects of use belong to their aura: he traces the decline of storytelling to the fact that commodities become obsolete so quickly that they do not have the time to collect stories around them.[21] In Sanjeev and others, I found that public objects—a transformer here, a tube well there, a tile with the picture of a god placed on a rock at the corner of the two roads—gathered stories around themselves that gave experiences of the place a lively quality. Eli Friedlander (2012) comments on Benjamin's notion of aura to suggest that the significance Benjamin associates with a work of art or with experience more generally is the sense that there is more to the object than meets the eye. "The figure of an aura of light emanating from an object and surrounding it, making it slightly more than it is, suggests that there is a space of meaning that comes with the object and allows us to relate to it significantly. This is possible insofar as the object is embedded in tradition" (Friedlander 2012, 147).

The storytelling around objects that we saw in this case was not about being embedded in tradition, or about the memories we carry around objects that come from our childhood, but rather about how objects are embedded in the future that Sanjeev imagines for his neighborhood and for his own place in it. I want to focus on three specific episodes and their related expressions for a closer reading. These are: the open declaration in a public meeting by the official that the neighborhood in which Sanjeev lives is a colony of "thieves" and the entanglement of expressions and actions that follow from that declaration; the confession by Sanjeev Gupta that there is, indeed, not much difference in the moral standing of those who threaten him and those who protect him; and his remarkable performance of the voicing through which he brings the absent figures of the politicians within his discourse through the mode of irony.

It is tempting to analyze these three episodes that make up the narrative tension in his account by using techniques of linguistic analysis such as the shifts between the personal pronouns, the I and the we, the use of the honorific *aap* in addressing that can make the second person, the addressee, into a third person in both literary and spoken Hindu, Urdu, and Punjabi; or the distribution of tenses so that the politician is caught in the immediate past, surprised that events that were so close in time remained opaque, while the residents/citizens speak in the indicative present (Benveniste 1971b). I will return to these issues in this and subsequent chapters. For now, I return to my earlier discussion on how action and expression are stitched together as utterances move between illocutionary force and perlocutionary effect, the orders of law and normativity and the improvisations introduced by desire, emotion, and passion.

Consider the first episode when the official declares that they cannot supply electricity to a neighborhood of *thieves*. The utterance has an element of performance in it and since the declaration is made by someone whose words carry the imprint of the laws of the State, we might say that though the utterance does not in itself make the residents into thieves, the statement is not hollow or void either.[22] In fact, it is because the residents have already been treated as thieves who are being harassed by the police on complaints of theft of electricity that the statement has illocutionary force. Instead of treating it as an indicative statement to which we could attach values of truth or falsity, Sanjeev Gupta turns it into a language game of challenge and counterchallenge: "Sir, we will wipe out this stigma," he declares. This is one point at which we could stop, as McDowell in his powerful analysis of performative utterances implies we could:

> Speech acts are publications of intentions: the primary aim of a speech act is to produce an object—the speech act itself—that is perceptible publicly and in particular to the audience, embodying an intention whose content is precisely a recognizable performance of that very speech act. Recognition by an audience that such an intention has been made public in this way leaves nothing further needing to happen for the intension to be fulfilled. (1998, 4)

Put differently, we might say that McDowell's analysis would separate the aspect of performance from the aspect of action. Performative utterances would be completely on the side of expression, albeit expression in the public domain. This theoretical move knits the inside and outside, intention and action, primarily through the communicative acts in public between one who has expressed an intention and another who has received it. Although offered as a general theory of speech acts, the action under consideration seems to me to be primarily a description of ritualized action appropriate to such contexts as those of religion and law in which we draw artificial boundaries, separating the action that takes place within these boundaries from its ramifications outside (see also Lee 1997).[23] However, once we see ritual action as contiguous to other actions, we see that the punctuation marks we placed around segments of action do not really work. This is why it is interesting to see how the transformation of a simple commercial transaction—a seller supplying a product to a consumer—becomes an ethical action for both the officer, Vidyut Sir, and for Sanjeev. This brings me to the second point: Sanjeev's confession that there is no difference in the moral standing of those who threatened him and those who protect him.

I think it is important to realize that from the dramatic contesting statements about theft, two paths open up for ethical action. On the part of the electricity official, there is an amazing shift of perspective as he reflects on what it is to be denied of elemental needs in the urban context and whether an ethics of commercial action would require him to create the conditions of possibility in which the residents of the neighborhood could construct themselves as "responsible consumers" and not thieves. It is interesting that he did not concern himself with the question of whether they were entitled to electricity as an "unauthorized colony," telling me that as a private company their job was limited to meeting consumer needs, not pronouncing on what policy the government should or should not follow on the needs of the poor—"that," he said, "we leave to the courts to decide." For Sanjeev Gupta, the ethical action is that of wiping out the stigma of being thieves. The materiality of electricity then enfolds in itself questions of what it is to be doing things in a legitimate way—yet Sanjeev is aware that in order to remain alive he must accept the protection of those he considers corrupt, those who intimidate others, who use threats of violence and yet have good and bad points about them. Ethical paths for him are, then, strewn with the general conditions of life in which no one can claim some kind of moral purity. If the relation between the orders of normativity embodied in illocutionary force of utterances and disorders of life are so woven together, Sanjeev Gupta's and Vidyut Sir's actions make it clear that the securing of everyday life as a space of ethical action is at best a striving toward a different everyday rather than an ascent from it into a place from where the world could be transcendentally viewed or acted upon. I circle back to Sanjeev's opening statement that our friendship should be with the earth.

Finally, let us consider the way in which the moment of the inauguration of the new transformers, or rather the significant gesture of *not* inaugurating them, tells us about the political subjectivities in question. After telling me how he decided to ignore the powerful political leaders who have represented the area, Sanjeev Gupta creates an imaginary dialogue in which he distributes his narration between the voice of an imaginary politician and the "we" that represents the neighborhood. Line E1 to E12, where I give an account of this narration, are the English translations of the dialogue in Hindi that is provided in the corresponding H1 to H12. This dialogue brings the imaginary figure of the politician in our presence—in Goffman's (1974) sense these are figures that have been brought forth by the speaker's acts of narration. Sanjeev Gupta is not a neutral narrator here—rather the effect of irony is achieved by such phrases as "Aji sahib, aap hote kaun hain?" (H6) in which the respectful address of *sahib* (meaning a white man, an officer) and *aap* (honorific second person) is juxtaposed with *aji*, a term of address that can put into suspicion the respectful phrases that follow. Interestingly, Sanjeev Gupta's expressions here draw from the powerful ways in which the vocative is used in Sanskrit grammar and aesthetics—usages that have become completely embedded in the speech acts of everyday life as I found in my fieldwork locations. In a perceptive essay on the logic of the vocative, Chakrabarti (2013) argues that in the vocatively inflected name (e.g., Hari becomes Hare, Shakuntala becomes Shakuntale), the issue is neither that of simply sense or, indeed, of reference, but rather of providing a commentary on what follows in the sentence. There are other aspects to the use of the vocative—for example, as Chakrabarty astutely points out, there is a smudging of the boundary between what Frege calls sense (Sinn) and what he calls "tone or coloring" in the context of addressing someone. It is frequently the case that in invoking a god or goddess, for instance, multiple names are used (108 or 1,008 being the ritually appropriate numbers). As Chakrabarti says, to translate a sequence of words made up of synonyms with the same English expression, for instance, would rob the invocation of its power. Take the example of the invocation of the Sun that appear in a famous verse of the Iśāvāsya Upanishad with the series "Pusan, Ekarje, Yama, Surya, Prajapati" and simply translate it as Sun, Sun, Sun, Sun, Sun, and you would have effectively murdered the verse.[24] These two aspects of the vocative— its power to stand outside the sentence as it provides a commentary on the sentence and its ability to use multiple expressions for what in referential terms is the same deity, person, or object intensifying different aspects of the relationship of the person addressed to various episodes or qualities in their biographies—are important to comprehend precisely what is accomplished in the performance with the imaginary politician that Sanjeev Gupta enacts. Since Hindi is not an inflectional language, the word is not modified to indicate the vocative but the addition of prefixes—meaningless sounds in themselves such as *aji*, *arre*, and *re re* perform the function of the vocative in providing a commentary to modify the sentence meaning. By adding a different affective register in the imaginary conversations recalled above, through the grammatical device of vocatives—such as *aji*, *arre*, and *sahib*—we have an enactment where the politician is put in his or her place. The flight into imagination here and the expression of power with which the voter in a democratic society is endowed is, however, fleeting as Sanjeev Gupta later recalls the humiliating nameless events of supplication that only he/they know.

It is thus that Sanjeev Gupta and some of his neighbors gave me the necessary clues for interpreting Cavell's statement that I cited earlier: "From the roots of speech, in each utterance of revelation and confrontation two paths spring: that to responsibility of implication and that of the rights of desire. The paths will not reliably coincide—but to have them both open is what I want of philosophy" (Cavell 2005b, 185).

## WHEN WORDS ARE LIKE WILD HORSES

Speech, however, is a slippery companion. In the next case, written as a short interlude, before I go to the question of inexpressibility, I describe the case of Prem Singh who lives in Bhagwanpur Kheda, a similar low-income neighborhood. Officially this is a recognized colony, but it has no sewage system, though houses have electricity and running water for a few hours every day. The majority of people who live in this neighborhood are Jatavs and Valmikis belonging to the scheduled castes. Although the word *Dalit* is acquiring greater currency now, most people prefer to be known as scheduled castes or simply SCs—terms that act almost as vernacular terms in these areas.

Walking in the street in Bhagwanpur Kheda one cold day in 2003, snuggled among various posters and graffiti on the walls of houses, I found a computer-generated poster in Hindi that read:

*Insaan ke roop mein kutte*
Dogs in the form of Humans
*Unke bhaunkne ka*
Of their Barking
*Na koi samay hota hai*
Neither is there any specific time
*Na koi Seema*
Nor any limit

Led by a vague curiosity, I asked some young boys who had gathered around seeing me read that notice, "Who has put it up?" There were sniggering comments—"Some madman, we don't know, ask the others." As I walked farther, I could see the same poster on crumbling paper in different places. I circled back to the original place where I had first found the notice and as I stood staring at it, Prem Singh opened the door of his house just enough to peep out. He then signaled for my research collaborator, Purshottam, and me to come inside, making a gesture to shoo away the curious boys who had gathered there.

The story of this poster emerged in one burst—it seemed that Prem Singh had been waiting for an opportunity to pour out his version of events. But just to give a brief indication of the setting: Delhi, those days, was in the grip of dengue fever. Public health messages about cleanliness were everywhere. In the better-off localities, the municipal workers were routinely checking on flowerpots and coolers to see that water was not collecting. In the poorer localities where sanitation or cleaning of drains was completely absent, these messages were treated as just words.

Prem Singh related how he felt that something needed to be done about the garbage and the dirt that collected around. The rains had made the stink from open drains overwhelming. So he began to pour buckets of water treated with phenyl, an antibacterial cleaning agent, into the street. However, since there was no proper drainage in the street it ended up as puddles of dirty water. His immediate neighbor, a bus conductor with some standing among the neighbors, objected because his six-year-old son slipped and fell in these puddles once or twice. The verbal exchange of insults and bickering threatened to become a bigger dispute as neighbors started taking sides and people joined in to watch what was going on for sheer entertainment.[25] Prem Singh described this moment:

The fights began to accelerate—at one time I thought this would become a *danga* [riot]. So, I withdrew. Then I thought that man has only the right over his *karma* [action]—if my good action does not bear fruit that is not my fault—look at where I live—how can good acts prosper here?

Yet, Prem Singh was still seething with rage. "I am not a sage," he said.

I wanted people to know that my neighbor was just a useless man [*bekar admi*]. That is when I thought of these words. He is like a dog and just when a dog barks in the middle of the night, other dogs just join in, the neighbors had joined in this chorus of dogs. As I said, there is no time or limit to their barks. The people here, they are just *chuda chamars* [pejorative reference to scavenging]—the government does not care—it is a hell made of garbage, dirt, and disgusting, filthy insects. I thought at least some people who read it, even if they do not want to come out in the open against my neighbor, will understand and the feelings will gather and he will be shamed.

Despite his hopes, though, Prem Singh did not get any encouraging response from his neighbors. He even made a trip to the High Court in Delhi to put up this poster on the walls of the High Court hoping that some spirited lawyer would take notice and file a petition on his behalf. The courts have been known to entertain public interest litigation cases on similar matters, but his actions elicited no response.

But then, Prem Singh says, as his cause was a righteous one, God opened a path. He had been listening to various accounts in Hindi of "Liberation Iraq" led by the American and European coalition of the willing. He then realized that George W. Bush was not only the president of America (Amrica in Hindi) but was also the leader of the whole world. These different fragments of news made him feel that he had been shown a path—when God closes one way, he opens another, he said.[26]

So Prem Singh drafted a letter in Hindi to President Bush, got it translated and printed on a nice paper, and posted it to "White House, Washington, USA." The letter, written in the style in which government applications are made, said:

Respected Sri Bush, Respectfully, I wish to submit[27] that I have heard that you have vowed to clean the world of terrorists and to bring democracy to the whole world. I want to report that my neighbors are spreading dirt in our streets and objecting to my efforts to keep the streets clean. As you are the great leader of the world I hope you will take action in this matter. Your humble servant, Prem Singh (Address)

As it happened, Prem Singh received a reply from the White House that expressed appreciation for his support of President Bush. He showed the letter around as a sign of the rightness of his cause—for many of his neighbors it was a sign of his craziness. "He expects the American president to come here and have our streets cleaned?"—to which Prem Singh replies, "I have always done my duty—as Lord Krishna said, one should do one's karma without any hope that it will bear fruit." For his neighbors, this "karma" is turning into a constant irritation as he floods various government departments with letters and petitions that sometimes go unnoticed and at other times seem to lead to troubling consequences. In one case, he complained to the DDA (Delhi Development Authority) about an unauthorized extension of the house that a neighbor was undertaking, resulting in the neighbor having to pay a huge bribe to the housing inspector who showed up. One can detect a shift in the way the neighborhood has come to regard him from somewhat laughable crank to one who could harm them because of his stubborn character and his seeming lack of care for the consequences his actions generate.

## COMMENTARY

There are three different segments of this story that I want to select for further comment: the reference to his neighbors as *chudas* and *chamars* (pejorative terms for previously untouchable castes), the animal metaphor, and the letter to President Bush and the circulation of the petition form. Each of these segments leads us to think of the allegorical import of this story and the dangers of words that come not from grand events but from within the nooks and crannies of the everyday.

Prem Singh's reference to his neighbors as "chudas" and "chamars," as scavengers, is less a use of a caste slur to insult another as it is a commentary on the neighborhood itself. After all, Prem Singh belongs to the Jatav/Chamar caste as do many others in the neighborhood; these derogatory terms simply would not carry the same force as they would if deployed by an upper caste man. Yet, given the political sensitivities around caste terms such as Chamar in the political culture, such words cannot be allowed to pass from the private realm to the public one. The use of the animal meta-phor then allows the expression of a public insult and challenge—while si-multaneously expressing the squalor and dirt of the neighborhood of which Prem Singh is himself a part.

It is useful for me at this point to take up a suggestive moment in Cavell's (2005b) discussion of passionate utterances where he writes that passionate utterances might be thought of as one among other modes of discourse char-acterized by different perlocutionary objectives. Let us say in declaring my love for you I deny that I need to consider the question of my standing with you and instead claim authority to speak for a particular institution (say, of assuming that you must marry me because I stand in the right institutional relation to you)—"then my passionate declaration becomes something else . . ." Cavell suggests that this something else might be an instance of moralism. Similarly, instead of demanding a response, I speak to stifle your speech, then it might approach hate speech and I might use my words to brand you (Cavell 2005b, 182). Prem Singh's statements do not quite amount to hate speech in the propaganda material way in which slogans against lower castes during caste riots or against another religious group in sectar-ian riots brand the other group (see Mehta 2010). Yet they have the making of something that could spin out of control.

Prem Singh's letter to Bush might seem at first sight like a harmless ab-surdity produced by the global circulation of news—yet the letter was not conjured out of nothing. In fact, Prem Singh, like some others in the neigh-borhood, were used to writing "petitions" to particular gods such as Hanu-man Ji in one of the temples that receives them. The form of the petition (*arji*) is usually in the nature of a request followed by a pledge—if I succeed in such and such task I will give you such and such offering with the name and address of the person seeking the god's intervention and the name of a witness appended to the petition (see also Lutgendorf 1997; Taneja 2013; Ma-lik 2015). Elsewhere I describe the way in which the ritual vocabulary deal-ing with spirits and the legal vocabulary dealing with trials are mutually inflected (Das 2010b). Thus, it seems to me that there is an act of projection through which President Bush is brought within the local world. Yet the ac-tion does not count as similar to the petitions sent to gods within the form of life inhabited in this neighborhood. As Wittgenstein's philosophy makes clear, agreement regarding criteria is not an agreement in opinions but in forms of life. As Cavell explains, when we project words from one context to another, the criteria for determining what is similar to what, what is outrageous, what is funny, what serious, grow out of our forms of life and not from any universal givens or from any book of rules. In the case of Prem Singh there is a sequence of actions with continuous shifts in the way in which these actions are tied to different perlocutionary objectives. One might say that unlike the classic case of illocutionary force in which "I do" might be seen to accomplish the act (if the conditions of felicity are present), in the case of actions with perlocutionary effect, there is a continuing possibility that acts might morph from one to another that could lead to a stitching of different contexts in unpredictable ways or could lead to the erosion of the fragile threads that allow social life by keeping contexts apart. This is one way I understand how the dangers that Cavell gathers under the sign of skepticism grow within the everyday.

### INEXPRESSIBILITY, OR THE WITHDRAWING OF ONE'S WORDS

In the two cases previously discussed, we found speech acts that were pronounced publicly and hence had an element of performance. The third case I want to discuss speaks to the theme of confession and the unbearable character of painful knowledge that women sometimes carry and from which they protect others. I want to loop back to my discussion of Cavell's "traumatic" discovery that philosophy is inflected by the question of gender. One may summarize Cavell's discovery of the gender difference in relation to skepticism as follows: what on the male side of the gender divide presents itself as an issue about the knowing subject becomes, on the side of the female, the issue of her knowability or that of making herself known. In his analysis of the film *Letter from an Unknown Woman*, Cavell shows that the woman was able to speak, as in having a voice, only from the side of death. The case of the woman, Sheela, I present here complicates the issues by asking to whom one can make oneself known.

Sheela's family is among the small number of upper caste families in Punjabi Basti. There are other families in her own kinship network who are scattered over Punjabi Basti and its neighbor Prem Nagar, though some others within the network have been more upwardly mobile and are settled in better-off neighborhoods in Delhi and elsewhere. Upper caste histories in these neighborhoods often reveal that following some kind of adversity—business failure, disinheritance by the parents, elopement, or, as in this case, displacement after the Partition of India—leads to one branch of the family finding a dwelling in a low-income neighborhood. In Sheela's case, her natal family had escaped from the riots in Pakistan, but her father died soon after. So she grew up in her maternal uncle's house along with her mother, two sisters, and five older cousins. She was married at an early age to a much older man, who in other circumstances would have been considered below the status of her natal family. In the course of researching other issues in Punjabi Basti, I got to know her well. And although she never narrated in one long story the facts of her sexual abuse as a child, a little bit of it would come out on different occasions when we were together. For instance, once when she was helping her eight-year-old granddaughter to change into a new dress, she became tearful and putting her hand on her mouth as if to block speech from bursting out said, "Oh god, this is how small I was when . . ." She did not elaborate, but something in her past had rotated and confronted her at this moment (see Bergson 1990 and Das 2007 for the notion of rotation). As a child, Sheela was often slapped, sometimes beaten—*dande padte the*, sticks were rained—not by her other relatives but by her mother. This aspect, though, she recalled with a kind of cheerfulness, commenting that her mother had to perform these actions to signal her (the mother's) dependent status vis-à-vis her own relatives, who, though not well off, had taken the additional burden of dependent relatives. "What could she do—there was a compulsion—*mazboori thi*." Elsewhere I describe this as the aesthetics of kinship (Das 2007, 2012a).

What was wounding for her was that someone in the joint family was forcing Sheela to perform different sexual acts—so though she was not technically raped,[28] she was overwhelmed by when and in which corner of the house she would have to lift her frock or when she would be pinned against a wall and made to kiss. Sometimes there would be a bite mark for all to see—yet she had to constantly make up stories of why her dress was torn or how she got that mark on her face and was constantly scolded for these apparent signs of her carelessness.[29] What compounded the profound hurt was that her mother had apparently failed to notice: when she exclaimed, "Oh god, this is how small I was when . . . ," she was as if coming to the realization that there must have been a willful ignoring, the offer of a daughter as sacrifice, in return for the shelter provided to the destitute sister's family.

Though she let some expressions of her hurt escape in my presence, I never asked and was never told if she had ever told the story to anyone, including her husband. As I have described elsewhere (Das 2007), in matters of sexual violation, there is an agreement in families displaced by the Partition that one does not ask any explicit questions—one allows oneself to be marked by the knowledge that comes one's way. Here the anthropologist's mode of being converges into that of the others in the community. There were two occasions, though, when Sheela did tell me something. Once when I was telling her that there was a discipline called psychoanalysis in which therapeutic interventions consisted of the "patient" talking every week for an hour with the therapist and saying whatever came to their mind in the session, she said that she wished she would find a guru who could understand her without her having to say anything.[30] Then she went on to say that she could imagine "talking" about those things but she could not imagine ever saying out loud the name of the person who had violated her. "I cannot even say it aloud to myself. It is like I am holding something in me, tight as a fist, a coiled snake, and if that came out, the world would be thrown into chaos—*duniya utthal putthal ho jayegi*."

The second occasion arose when we were talking about a death in a household in the neighborhood. Sheela remarked that people give too much credence to the words of a dying person; but who knows what comes to possess them, she said. Her eyes seemed to wander as she said, "My mother said to me on her deathbed—you have to forgive me for a lot, no?" And then Sheela looked at me directly and said, "That was cruel [*ye zulm tha*]—I don't know why my heart was pulverized. Now I feel I understand a little—she asked me such a question—if, I say yes, it confirms that *I* knew that *she* knew—and now with one word, all that will be wiped off? If I say no, then what kind of human being [*banda*] is this who cannot forgive this dying woman?"[31]

## COMMENTARY

I have often puzzled over the fact that Sheela allowed something of her experience to be expressed to a stranger such as myself with no expectations that we would become intimate. I have notes on Sheela's family and their various activities in the neighborhood, but except for jottings I have turned away from any extensive note-taking on these moments that came upon us. Sometimes I think reluctance on my part mirrors the revulsion I saw in Sheela in naming these abuses. I found Cavell's reflections on Walden to provide a way of thinking about this kind of knowledge that we, as ethnographers, sometimes find. (I hope my discussion of the two earlier cases shows that it is not only in such extraordinary moments woven into the ordinary that anthropology finds its fate. But I am puzzled by recent accounts of a "suffering slot" as akin to the "savage slot" to which, it is said, anthropologists gravitate because it is available as a template. No such consolation was available to me. I postpone for now a more systematic uncovering of this move.) Here is the citation from Cavell:

> The writer has secrets to tell which can only be told to strangers. The secrets are not his, and they are not the confidences of others. They are secrets because few are anxious to know them; all but one or two wish to remain foreign. Only those who recognize themselves to be strangers can be told them, because those who think themselves familiars will think they have already heard what the writer is saying. They will not understand his speaking in confidence. (Cavell 1992, 92–93)

Sheela is not a writer or a philosopher as these terms are usually understood, nor is she dealing with impersonal secrets; yet there is that writerly quality in her dialogues when she has allowed me to join her in her puzzles about her own experiences. So I ask what it is about a name that holds in itself such powers of destruction. At the first level of reflection we could link this inability to name to other taboos on the name in this form of life. Thus, for instance, there is general avoidance of proper names in forms of talk, as people will take kinship terms to address even relative strangers. For married women, there is a strong taboo on taking the name of the husband, and it is said that such a practice would shorten the life span of the man. Women usually refer to their husbands by pointing to their relation to the child— "*Munni ke Bapu*" (Munni's father)—or use the simple third-person plural. This taboo is of a piece with other practices in which any expression of intimacy created through sexuality is actively suppressed. Yet this man did not stand in any normative relation to this woman. And in any case, the refusal to name a husband comes from the desire to protect and honor him, while Sheela says she feels nauseous, physically ill, and in the throes of panic if she were to pronounce her abuser's name even silently to herself.

There is another register of proper names that might have a greater resonance with the dread that Sheela feels in uttering the name of her abuser. While it is meritorious to recite the name of any god or goddess, it is only the ritual adepts such as diviners who can safely get a demon to reveal its name. But I believe that there are serious limits to evoking this cultural resonance for the reason that Sheela is not talking about someone else, a third person whether human or demon, but about herself, the first person, and one's relation to oneself is not based on observational knowledge. As Anscombe (1975, 1981), in her classic essay on the first person, argues, one does not use the word "I" to refer to oneself as one would use other pronouns to refer to a second or third person. Although there might be room for debate on Anscombe's claim that the "I" is nonreferential under all conditions, there would be little doubt that I do not have to search around to find whom I mean when I use the first person to indicate myself—the self is not one object among others, I do not infer how I am feeling by observing myself (Wittgenstein [1953] 1968). Yet in Sheela's experience, there is a name embedded in her body that destroys the intimacy she has with herself. She cannot let go of this name without making the universe go topsy-turvy. She cannot bear to make that part of herself known in which this name resides as a hostile alien.

Once acknowledgment of what happened to her as a child comes, it comes as a question. Sheela experiences this dying statement by her mother as lethal because it too is not offered to elicit a response but rather to stifle her voice. One cannot speculate as to what had made her mother so oblivious to the violence her daughter was facing as a child. It is possible that as a dependent relative, her mother was not able to confront her own brother (whether it was he or one of his sons who was the culprit—the *gunahgar*) without jeopardizing the position of her immediate, fatherless family. For Sheela, the labor of letting go is too much to bear. For her, the question asked was like a snare to put her in a terrible double bind and she responded to it by not responding to it at all. What kind of an end is this?

In the case of perlocutionary effects, Cavell is most interested in the fact that "in the case of classic performative utterances, failures to identify the correct traditions are characteristically reparable: the purser should not have undertaken to marry us, but here is the captain . . . you may fly in tears from the altar, but suppose it is only into an adjacent room. . . . Our future is at issue, but the way back, or forward, is not lost" (Cavell 2005b, 184). In the case of passionate utterances, Cavell writes that the risks are of a different order. He gives the example of Carmen's "No, you do not love me," sung in response to Don Jose's protestations of love in his "Flower Song" as a definitive case of perlocutionary sequel or "consequence" in which the end is not conventional or predictable. Also, much more is at stake than a misfire; for what is at stake is that something ends for Carmen, leaves that part of her identity dead of which this man was a part.

In the fateful utterance said from a hospital bed that Sheela heard, she too refused the response, but something of her own identity as the daughter of this mother seemed to have ended. Notice that she referred to herself as a human being (*banda*) and not as a daughter. I cannot say if in going about in her daily life—cooking, sewing, fetching water—she finds the space where the broken arteries of her childhood can be repaired or if her sense of living in a world that cannot see what is before its eyes, such as the abuse of a child, runs parallel to the performance of these activities. I am not the one who is entitled to offer the last word on this subject (cf. Heckel 2010).

## CONCLUDING COMMENTS

What does the understanding of the everyday culled out of a philosophy that Cavell sees as intimately joined to literature and cinema and an ethnography that is decisively placed among the poor have to say to dominant theories of the everyday currently practiced in the humanities and social sciences? For some purposes, I might say that in the end all I have reported are mere household events. But these unfoldings of events (or quasi events as in Das [2015a]) created the texture of the ordinary that might have been easily missed in a lofty aerial view of these lives. In each of the three commentaries I offered one could see that in securing the everyday, the propensity to exile oneself from life and language was ever-present, as was the effort made by each of the three protagonists to bring about an everyday that could be better, more attuned to their desires for neighborhoods and families in which lives could be lived better—however different the tracks in which their actions and expressions slipped. This may be one way in which we may define the politics of the ordinary. In putting my relation to my interlocutors in my ethnographic work along with my relation to Cavell on the same plane intellectually and emotionally, I am not forgoing criticism but advancing a way in which criticism might engage a work positively. The modern concept of criticism if often equated with the sensibility of being either in a court of judgment or in the expression of indignation—but what I found when I tried to interpret Cavell through the lives of my interlocutors, who are also in some ways my teachers, was that his works blossomed, increased in worth as if I had been able to divine the *idea* of his work as distinct from its content or argument. Perhaps that is reflected in a different orientation that I take to the everyday.

Everyday life, after all, has re-emerged in recent years as an independent area of inquiry, as evidenced by several influential books that survey the whole field (Gardiner 2000; Highmore 2002; Sheringham 2008). Other scholars have offered new experimental writing so as to depict the indeterminacy and elusiveness of everyday life that representational theory fails to capture (Berlant 2007; Stewart 2007; Povinelli 2011; see also Thrift 2007). Without making any presumption about recounting all the important issues at hand, I take three strands in the theories I mentioned above for further comment. First, while all major theorists of the ordinary acknowledge the elusive character of everyday life, the methods for making it visible are very different, as are the questions of what is at stake in the everyday. For instance, many artists, explorers of the everyday, experiment with making the everyday visible by traveling through banlieue outside Paris, living in modest bedsitters, and stopping and talking to local people, or, in other cases, riding in the metro and attentively noting the trivial details of the passengers and their interactions (see Sheringham 2008 for a discussion of these artistic experiments). In India artists such as Vivan Sundaram have been experimenting with trash and urban debris to make installations (see Sundaram 2008 and 2012) that express the uncanniness of the everyday urban life. Fascinating as these experiments are, they are much more about reclaiming the quotidian when it is felt to be disappearing under the mass of bureaucratic regulations of life and the circulations of mass media. These are works that make us look at life anew, but I feel that the ordinary appears in these works for the other sensibilities to be enriched—the concrete others actually disappear as the artist produces ordinariness as a work of art.

Second, there are the major French theorists—Henri Lefebvre's three-volume *Critique of Everyday Life* (2002) and Michel de Certeau's *Practice of Everyday Life* (1984) provide the most important theoretical paradigms for thinking of everyday life in social theory today. These authors made it possible to make everyday, unremarkable acts such as walking on the street or decorating the room or smacking one's lips as one savors the meal (Bourdieu 1984) into objects worthy of theoretical interest. For Lefebvre and de Certeau, despite some obvious differences, the interest in the everyday lies in its potential for resistance. Both authors are deeply concerned with the colonization of lifeworlds by commodities, by the State, and with the mass production of sentiment—both think of tactics and strategy as a way in which another production is made possible in the "poaching," retracing, or other ways of consuming that resist the dominant mode of production. Lefebvre is perhaps more concerned with the decline of the political reflected into a retreat into the trivial details of everyday, but a significant concern for both authors is to find in the everyday the possibility for a critique of modernity.

The third strand of argument is best illustrated in the work of Berlant (2007) and Povinelli (2011), who think of the everyday in contrast with the radical or spectacular event and are most concerned by the conditions of the subject under conditions of late liberalism. For Berlant, this condition is captured under the notion of "slow death," while for Povinelli it is the notion of "abandonment" and the low intensity violence, sickness, and death that characterizes her indigenous subjects. Povinelli calls these quasi-events that are elevated into radical events through the apparatus of the State or the mediation of technology, including media technology. These are provocative ways of rethinking what we mean by social suffering under contemporary conditions.

My differences from these three strands of theorizing lie in the fact that my experiences do not allow me to make such sharp contrasts between the authentic everyday life of the ordinary people and the categorizing, colonizing practices of the State, as Sanjeev Gupta's engagement with the political might make clear. On the one hand, I can see the relevance of Berlant's description of the attrition of the subject. On the other hand, I cannot disregard the sheer capacity for pleasure, for performance, and for constant engagement with life that I encountered. Berlant writes: "I am focusing here on the way the attrition of the subject of capital articulates survival as slow death. Impassivity and other relations of alienation, coolness, detachment or distraction, especially in subordinated populations are affective forms of engagement with the environment of slow death, much as the violence of battered women has had to be re-understood as a kind of destruction toward survival" (Berlant 2007, 779). I too have come across the combination of emotions Berlant mentions, but I have also found a measured engagement with the law that is more than tactic, as in the case of Sanjeev Gupta, and rage, as in the case of Prem Singh, and the capacity to argue, engage, gossip, malign, and protect others. The material conditions of these neighbor-hoods, the violence of past events, as well as their striving for a different form of the everyday, are embedded in my descriptions of the three cases I chose for close attention. But these cases have led me to ask further: To what kinds of puzzles do their lives give expression?

I think one important difference in the kind of account Povinelli and I provide from that of the others mentioned here lies in the long intimacy on which ethnography is based. This does not make people transparent to the ethnographer, but it allows one to participate in ongoing projects when emo-tions wax and wane and no one speaks in a single voice. The affects I cap-ture are not simply those of alienation, detachment, and coolness; nor does time have the quality that Berlant describes as "making a life involves get-ting through the day, the week, the month . . ."[32] Instead of generalizations, I have simply followed the routes opened by the puzzles and perplexities, the improvisations, and the knitting of expressions and actions, as my best guide to understanding the philosophical puzzles to which Austin and Cavell give expression. The labor of making the ordinary appear is one way to think of the kinds of political projects that can bring about the infrastruc-ture that gives people the grounds on which to stand—or make them slip into the kind of absurdities into which Prem Singh's neighbors recognized him as having slipped. Or else there is the struggle of blocking expres-sion as a means of protecting one's words for which we do not always have a standing language of politics we can deploy. I take attention to these differ-ent pathways of action and expression as one way in which anthropology finds its footing in the world. Perhaps it might also offer the lure of the concrete to philosophy, as Lévi-Strauss (1963) would have had it.

# 3

# ORDINARY ETHICS

*Take One*

In the previous chapter, we saw the knitting together of action and expression in the conduct of politics in the everyday. In thinking of the everyday and the ordinary I privileged the works of Austin and Cavell for their aspirations to think of philosophical problems as *human* problems that arise in the lives of actual people and not only in the thought experiments in the hallowed halls of philosophy. Cavell, for instance, repeatedly draws examples from what he calls the humble use of philosophically famous words whether in fiction or in Hollywood movies to think of the philosophical problems of inhabiting the everyday that is shadowed by skepticism (see Das 2011b). Austin draws on such regions of everyday life as the offering of excuses and pretending as crucial to his argument about the vulnerability of human action and human expression (Austin 1979a, 1979b). At the same time, Austin's sense that what philosophers can turn into insurmountable problems can be brought down to earth by attending to how we ordinarily use words is salutary for bringing words home. As he says, "For instance, if we are going to talk about 'real' we should not dismiss as beneath contempt such humble and familiar expressions as 'not real cream'" (Austin 1962, 63–64). Austin's notion of adequation expressed as "enough is enough" is not meant to jettison concerns about truth or reality but rather to extend the scope of these notions.[1] Following the sensibilities of this tone in philosophy, I want to lay out a case for thinking of ethics as "ordinary"—grafting it to the theme of vulnerability that I examined with reference to infrastructure in the last chapter. (I call it "Take One" as the themes here will be elaborated from different angles in subsequent chapters.)

Let us first listen to Michael Lambek, whose edited book *Ordinary Ethics* came to be regarded by many as performing a kind of baptism for a new way of doing an anthropology of ethics in that unlike many others, he did not assign a separate domain to "ethics" or a specialized vocabulary with weighty words such as "good," "right," or "obligation" as constitutive of the ethical.

Lambek says:

Human beings cannot avoid being subject to ethics, speaking and acting with ethical consequences, evaluating our actions and those of others, acknowledging and refusing acknowledgement, caring and taking care, but also being aware of our failure to do so consistently. As a species, given our consciousness, our socialization and sociality, and our use of language, we are fundamentally ethical. (2010, 1)

Lambek's discussion here is quite subtle in that he does not take any sides on such questions as to whether human beings are naturally good or whether evil is a necessary and integral part of human existence. He is simply claiming that human beings cannot help engaging with questions about how to live one's life with others and sometimes to engage in evaluative judgments about their own or others' behavior. Diagonal to this view is Arthur Kleinman's (2006) distinction between the moral and the ethical where he designates the moral as emerging out of what he calls "local moral worlds" whereas "ethical" refers to norms that impinge from the outside—the former, he suggests, are more particularistic and context bound, whereas the latter are in the nature of abstract formulations, universally agreed-upon norms for which the criteria are not elicited from any particular local worlds. There is a rich discussion on these issues. Many scholars argue that the distinction between morality and ethics is of little use on the ground as these tend to overlap in the actual flux of life; others argue what is considered universal is a disguised form of the elevation of Eurocentric ideas into neutral ethical concepts; and still others that the processes through which appeals to human rights are made are important to discern—in some contexts human rights are embedded in discourses of power whereas in other contexts activists or human rights lawyers might use them in legal strategies to challenge the powers of the State (Asad 2000; Taylor 1996; Lambek 2010; Faubion 2011; Selby 2014, 2018). Cora Diamond adds a different dimension to these discussions, arguing that describing events, real or imagined, is itself a moral activity. She cautions that when moral life is tied too closely to notions of choice and of freedom exercised in the capacity to choose, other forms of moral activity such as how to describe an event become invisible (Diamond 1996, 102).

Much discussion on ethics accords a centrality to judgments based on an exercise of reason. Proponents of this view argue that objective, universal measures are needed to overcome the subjective dispositions that might otherwise obscure a clear view of the moral landscape (for a critique of this view, see Crary 2007). I argue here, instead, for a shift in perspective—from thinking of ethics as made up of judgments we arrive at when we stand away from our ordinary practices to that of thinking of the ethical as a dimension of everyday life or, even better, as a spirit that infuses everyday life, in which we are not aspiring to escape the ordinary but rather seeking to descend into it as a way of becoming moral subjects. Such a descent into the ordinary focuses our attention to ways in which we are reading the other in everyday interactions. It is necessary for these purposes to overcome the metaphysical picture of the inner as a mechanism engaged in a mental activity of processing what our perceptions are, bringing a judgment to bear on them, and then acting upon these judgments. John Canfield (2004) offers an everyday example from Wittgenstein's *Last Writings on the Philosophy of Psychology* on the classic theme of pretending to argue that what is involved when we seek to decipher if the expressions of pain, fear, or gladness are genuine or not, or if the smile I see on the face of my friend when I greet her is sincere or a mere pretense, is not the application of some universal rule I have learned that enables me to interpret the slight distortion of the face that a smile or scowl produces. Rather, the issue is to relate this smile or scowl to events in our life together—its importance for me. I might ask, for instance, what kind of mutual space I am in with this person and bring a series of interactions in the past or stories I have recently heard that have made a doubt about sincerity raise its head. The question is neither of learning a set of rules nor of evoking transcendental, objectively agreed-upon values but rather of the cultivation of sensibilities *within* the everyday. As Canfield (2004) puts it, in considering the importance that the expressions of the other's fear or gladness have for me, it is important that we do not immediately accept the objective presupposition that what we are dealing with is exclusively the matter of judgment. That would be to assume ratiocination, he argues, in situations where it is absent. In many of these kinds of contexts one is dealing not with judgments about someone being glad to see me but with reactions that his smile produces because it is immediately visible. One reads the other's body (only, not as a text) and gestures but not in the mode of making judgments.[2]

In order to give flesh to this argument, I will offer examples from ethnographies (my own and that of others) to show how we might think of what moral striving is in the everyday from this perspective. I would like to think of these ethnographic descriptions as scenes, somewhat like Wittgenstein's ([1953] 1968) scenes of instruction (see Chapter 1). With the help of these ethnographic examples, I want to reflect on the following three issues: how rule-following is different from the notion of a moral life in the everyday; what it takes to allow life to be renewed, to achieve the everyday, under conditions of grinding poverty or catastrophic violence that erode the very possibility of the ordinary; and what form moral strivings take in the work performed to give birth to the eventual everyday from within the actual everyday. The following sections are not organized to correspond to each of these questions—rather, the questions reverberate throughout the following chapters. I hope that they will help to show that the notions of ethics and morality on the register of the ordinary are more like threads woven into the weave of life rather than notions that stand out and call attention to themselves through dramatic enactments and heroic struggles of good versus evil.[3]

## MORAL LIFE, RULES, CUSTOMS, AND HABITS

In discussing certain virtues in Theravada Buddhism, through which one learns to be attentive to how one inhabits the world with others, Charles Hallisey (2010) offers a discussion of two conceptions of the ethical from the modern West in the light of which we might consider how to think of ordinary ethics. In response to the ancient question of how one ought to live one's life, Hallisey says that one view associated with theorists such as Paul Ricoeur (1994) postulates that ethics are primarily about how one lives well *with* others or *for* others. The second view, articulated in Foucault's work on the care of the self, offers the thought that this same question involves practices that involve the self's relation to the self—concrete practices of self-fashioning that he calls "technologies of the self" (Foucault 1997, 2005). However, before we think that these are opposed practices, we must heed Hallisey's advice that we not set aside one of these conceptions too quickly in favor of the other:

If only because the desire to live well with others frequently provides motive and guidance to those undertaking a wide range of practices of self-fashioning in any particular moral culture or ethical tradition. This is especially the case whenever the practices of self-fashioning entail a critique of the self and a desire to become other than what one discovers oneself to be. (Hallisey 2010, 143)

For Foucault (1997, 2005) too, the self's relation to the self is no simple matter—the mode of subjectivation involves an inquiry into how the subject is invited or incited to become a moral subject. Simply stated, one might say that the mode of subjectivation necessarily involves the work one must do on oneself to bring oneself into accord with or in alignment with a moral tradition that lies outside of oneself (Mahmood 2005), but this mode of subjectivation is not the same as simply learning to obey explicitly formulated rules. Sylvain Perdigon (2011), in his work on Palestinian refugees, finds an analogue to the idea of ethics as inhering in the everyday in the Islamic notion of *al-iman* as the state of veridiction. He describes this state as one in which there is an accord between what one knows in one's heart, what one says with one's tongue, and what one does with one's limbs in everyday practices of kinship (see especially Murata and Chittick 1994). Let us also recall my earlier discussion of Austin and Cavell that such notions of work on the self and with others has to be undertaken in the context of the recognition of the vulnerability and fragility of everyday life particularly noticeable in the contexts of the fragile conditions in which vulnerable populations such as refugees or poor migrants are compelled to make their everyday life (Das 2011a).

In the low-income neighborhoods in Delhi in which much of my later work is situated, I came to recognize the delicacy of maintaining regard for others through the minutest of gestures (Das 2010a, 2010c). Thus, for instance, women would refrain from sweeping the floor right after a guest had left because that might suggest that "we think that guest is just trash." In the two decades of the 1970s and 1980s, when I was conducting fieldwork among Punjabi families in the crowded localities of Old Delhi (Das 1976, 2007), I would watch with some amusement the verbal barbs women directed at each other over quotidian fights: Who threw that bucket of dirty water after doing laundry from the rooftop into the street? Which child had hit one's child? How dare a neighbor engage in crooked speech (*ulti seedhi batein*) and spread rumors about another? Nevertheless, the quarrels would stop when it was time for the men to return home in the evening, though sometimes a woman might place an upturned *mooda* (a bamboo stool) on the threshold as a sign that she intended to resume the arguments the next day.[4] It did not seem right to many women for a tired man who had braved the heat and dust of the streets to be confronted with an atmosphere of discord. One might read this as the patriarchal ideology of a serene home that women were expected to create for men—such gestures surely expressed this idea and sometimes, by the same token, the inability to maintain a serene home could lead to acts of domestic violence (Kelly 2003; Price 2002). Thus, the possibility of speaking of ordinary ethics allows us also to think of the unethical as growing within the forms of life that people inhabit—it is, thus, not a matter of eliciting opinions about what behavior is considered ethical and what unethical or of cataloging cultural practices on which we can bring judgment from an objective, distant position but rather of seeing how forms of life grow particular dispositions. Such an argument has some important methodological implications.

Some authors, such as Leela Prasad, echoing Cora Diamond, argue that modes of narration, especially of painful events, may themselves be regarded as ethical or unethical. For instance, doing something enjoyable when recounting a tragedy in the past would constitute an ethical breach for some of her respondents (Prasad 2010). For me it was not simply a matter of how one narrates an event but rather how the everyday words and gestures that crept into the modes of narration were also folded into ways of acknowledging or withholding acknowledgment to the concrete others within a web of other practices. This raises the delicate question of why and under what conditions one is led to articulate something like a general statement in the form of a norm or when it is that an explicit formulation of a rule or a justification is called for—a point that I will attend to in the later part of this chapter.

For many of the women and men I came to know in my ethnographic work, the way words and gestures were used was not simply as messages but as expressions of the texture of how one is with others. Along with an etiquette and aesthetic of narration, language might be seen, then, to uncover the nature of the world and the self. Hence language becomes much more than a system of communication: it expresses ethical commitments that have become completely embedded in everyday life. For many of my respondents, what was important was not simply the content of communication but also the manner—so that the self-respect, dignity, and honor of the participants in a communication were not harmed. An even more subtle issue was to protect what people said is the "heart" of the other person, *dil rakhna*. The modality of ordinary ethics traverses the lines of public and private in important ways as one moves from considerations pertaining to maintaining the "face" of the other in public situations to "keeping his or her heart" in private, intimate contexts.

It was well recognized by everyone in the neighborhoods I studied that any hint of an insult offered within the public domain could be read, and was sometimes meant, to be an assault on the honor and respectability (*maan, izzat*) of the person who was thus insulted. Such insults were dealt with according to the resources that a family could command. Bourdieu (1990) and Gilsenan (1996) give fine ethnographic analyses of the timeliness or otherwise of a response in both exchange of gifts and exchange of insults so that the calibration of time was of utmost importance. Return a gift too soon and it could become an insult—wait too long to strike back after an insult and it loses all force. Steven Caton's (1986, 2006) exemplary work shows how much the maintenance of face is a matter of being able to wield the right kind of language in interpersonal exchanges and in the way different tribes in Yemen were able to hold their own in the competitive staging of poetry. In short, it seems that an agreement is maintained between various social actors in a given situation by which the fragile balance between enhancing one's own honor and prestige and being mindful of the honor that has to be shown to others is not disturbed. This delicacy of communication is preserved not only in publicly performed actions of greetings and gift exchanges but also in the minutest shifts in words and tones. The agreements that I speak of here are, however, neither contractual agreements nor agreements in opinions; they grow out of the forms of life. Hence, they are also subject to things going wrong from one moment to the next, letting loose a whole series of events that I try to capture elsewhere by the notion of the social as the domain of unfinished stories that can lie undisturbed for many years and then suddenly come alive in moments of tremendous violence (Das 2007). I will give one last example and then proceed to examine why one might invest the notion of the moral in the quotidian efforts that go to maintain these forms of life and regard them as more than mere fulfillment of social obligations demanded by rules and regulations.

My final example for this set of issues is drawn from Khare's (1976) fine ethnography of classification of food and the remarkable way in which the materiality of food provides the ground for expression of closeness and difference in social life in India and elsewhere (see also Prasad 2007). Khare, for example, shows that in a wedding feast kin who are relatively less endowed with material wealth can be given offense by such invitations as *"aaiye aap bhi bhojan kar lijiye"* ("please come—you too partake of the feast") rather than *"aaiye bhojan kar lijiye"* ("please come and partake of the feast"). Notice that in both cases the honorific form has been used but the addition of a single word ("too") manages to offer a subtle insult that will be remembered and perhaps repaid at an appropriate time, or it might simply be swallowed if the addressee is a dependent relative of the host.

If it is easy to use language to insult by these subtle means, it is also possible to use forms of greeting or affirmation to cover up situations that might be fraught with the risk of loss of face for a vulnerable relative or a neighbor. The best examples of this form of behavior arise when the distinctions between gift, charity, and debt have to be signaled without being put into words. I recall going with Manjit, a quite well-off woman I describe at some length in my earlier work (Das 2007), to visit her cousin Manpreet, who lived in very strained circumstances in a one-room quarter with her adult son and his wife. Manjit knew that her cousin did not have access to much cash and also that her position within her joint family was somewhat precarious as her son's wife was not looking after her well. It was winter and Manjit would have loved to gift Manpreet a warm shawl. This was, however, a situation she could not negotiate very easily. She could have bought shawls for her sister and the daughter-in-law, but since there was no ritual occasion to warrant such a gift and since Manjit is the younger of the two, that would have been seen as flaunting her wealth. A gift only for the sister would be seen as if the sister had been complaining to her relatives about the treatment she received. So, instead Manjit thought she might just find a way of leaving some money with her cousin. When we went to her house, her cousin insisted on sending a grandchild to get some *pakoras* (a savory) from the market. We prevailed on her not to get bottles of Coca-Cola (at an astronomical price) on the grounds that I suffered from diabetes but there was no avoiding the money spent on the pakoras, as Manpreet said to me, *"Manjit de ghar tusi roz khande ho—aaj garib bahen de ghar vich wi kuch kha lao"* (You eat everyday in Manjit's house—today have something in the house of this poor sister too). I responded, *"Dil amir hona chahida hai—paisa te haath di mail hai"* (The heart should be flowing with wealth—money is just the dirt of the hand). The reference to money being the dirt of the hand does not imply any opprobrium attaching to money but rather to its ephemeral character—money disappears as easily as the dirt of the hand.[5] I also suggest that such forms of speech, noted for the absence of the specific signature of a speaker or hearer but rather addressed to one and all, do not take the imperative form. Thus, they are distinguished from rules but offer opportunities to express bits of moral wisdom that can be deployed in particular circumstances to do a variety of actions—admonish, console, or help to cover up an embarrassing situation.

As we were leaving, Manjit found a moment to tuck a wad of currency notes in her cousin's blouse (a common place where women tuck a pouch for small amounts of cash), away from the daughter-in-law's eyes. I do not say that this form of interaction is the only one available between more well-off relatives and poorer ones: sometimes the richer relative will accept responsibility for specific tasks—for example, fostering a child for a specific period, fixing a monthly allowance for a specific item of need such as medicine, taking responsibility for meeting the expenses of a daughter's wedding, or agreeing to pay back a high-interest debt through the fiction that the poor relative is only borrowing money for a short period of time though it is known that despite the best of intentions the loan will not be paid back. There are different fictions maintained to save face; in some cases, for example, the child stands in a special relation to an aunt or an uncle, in other cases the facts of dependency are openly acknowledged. A common expression for such ruses is to say *"Dil rakkhan vaste udhaar keh ditta"* (In order to keep the heart I said it was a debt).

As can be imagined, maintaining these kinship obligations is not always easy, especially when the economic difference between the two sides is not all that pronounced. I describe elsewhere the case of a man called Billu who was haunted by his failure to save his brother's life because he did not have enough resources for his treatment (Das 2010b). Often such events lead to lasting bitterness between parents and children, two brothers, or even neighbors, and become the subject of moral reflections on the declining moral quality of "our times." Yet, despite the fact that families in need are often left wanting more help than they can get, ethnographic and economic evidence shows that interest-free loans and gifts from kin play an important part in helping poor families to meet expenditures for catastrophic events such as a medical emergency or for fulfilling other social obligations such as the marriage of a daughter (Collins et al. 2009).

In what way might one think of the performance of these quotidian acts as constituting an "ordinary ethics"? Are the sorts of descriptions of everyday life I offer not *too* quotidian to qualify as forms of ethical behavior? I offer some reflections on the imagination of human action and on the moral as a dimension of everyday life rather than as a separate domain to defend my metaphor of a descent into the ordinary. I attempt to do so by recasting habit as a kind of moral action and by showing how dramatic enactments of ethical value, as in publicly performed rituals or in legal pronouncements on rules, are grounded within the normative practices of everyday life.

Many philosophers and social theorists think of ethical commitment in terms of a leap away from everyday life even when they are sympathetic to the notion of the ethical as a mode of living rather than simply evaluating their own or others' actions. Thus, for instance, Pierre Hadot (1995, 2009) offers the concept of "spiritual exercises" to distinguish practices embedded in ancient Greek philosophy in order to distinguish them from religious practices. All ancient philosophy, he says, has its aim not just to inform but to form. For the ancients (whether masters or disciples), to engage in philosophy is a spiritual exercise "because it is a mode of life, a form of life, a choice of life" (Hadot 2009, 94). Hadot gives moving descriptions of what it is to cultivate a philosophical vision in the practice of one's life—yet there is also a sense of the banality of ordinary existence. Thus, for instance, in speaking of what he learned from Heidegger, Hadot says:

> It remains that de Waelhen's book allowed me to understand what I consider the essential of Heidegger—at least what is very important in what Heidegger brought me, especially the distinction between what we call the everyday, . . . and authentic existence. . . . In Heidegger this becomes the opposition between the everyday, the banal, and a state in which one is conscious of being doomed to death . . . thus conscious of one's finitude. At this moment, existence takes on an entirely different aspect, which moreover generates anxiety—perhaps because of death, but also because of the enigma represented by the fact of existing. (2009, 128–29)

It was in an implicit contrast with this and similar views that I conclude my book *Life and Words*, somewhat scandalously, with the following words:

My sense of indebtedness to the work of Cavell in these matters comes from a confidence that perhaps Manjit did not utter anything that we would recognize as philosophical in the kind of environments in which philosophy is done . . . but Cavell's work shows us that there is no real distance between the spiritual exercises she undertakes in her world and the spiritual exercises we can see in every word he has ever written. To hold these types of words together and to sense the connection of these lives has been my anthropological kind of devotion to the world. (Das 2007, 221)

I say "scandalously" because the kind of philosophical formation that Hadot is thinking of is about scaling heights, whereas I am trying to wrest the very expression of spiritual exercises away from the profundity of philosophy to the small disciplines that ordinary people perform in their everyday lives to hold life as the natural expression of ethics. While I must reserve my reflections on the impulse in philosophy to violence against the everyday for another occasion, my notion of both ethics and subjectivity takes me far away from the sensibilities of philosophers such as Alain Badiou (1994, 2001) who emphasize the importance of the exceptional event that forces a break from the everyday course of knowledge and brings into being a "subject" who was formerly "just a human animal, a mere inhabitant of a given situation" (Hughes 2007).[6] As we shall see in the last section of this chapter, I too take up events that shatter the ordinary modes of living, but I locate the ethical there in precisely the small acts that allow life to be knitted together "pair by pair" (Cavell 2007).

So how should we think of habits and customs that form the texture of everyday life? Because of the strong emphasis on intentionality and agency in our contemplation of ethics, habitual actions are often reduced to "mere behavior." Even philosophers and social theorists who are sympathetic to the role of habit see its value primarily as the enormous flywheel of society. At best, then, habits are considered important at the acquisition stage as means of cultivating good practices in children (Erasmus 1560), while at a later stage they are said to become a ground for securing everyday life as a site of routine (Dewey 1922).

While I do not dispute such characterizations of habitual action, I claim that we can give a different slant to this discussion if we shift from considerations of individual agency and intentionality to the place where we see the individual within the flux of collective life. Here I offer two different considerations. First, I contend that even though we might feel that the values that a society holds dear become most visible at the moment of dramatic enactments—those that Austin (1962) was fond of thinking as having illocutionary force—a moment's reflection would tell us that we get the feel of the rightness of certain actions or pronouncements only when we can take these dramatic moments back and integrate them into the flux of everyday life.

The philosopher John McDowell (1996) expresses this region of thought extremely well. I use his formulation to take the discussion of rules in Chapter 1 further. McDowell argues that our sense of what is right cannot be determined by something else that stands above that action, such as a rule or a reason for doing it this way, since our inquiry is precisely to ask what makes it right to do it *this* way. We are misled into thinking that within any practice we can discern rules, pictured as rails on which any correct activity within the practice must run. Wittgenstein's sharp critique of the mental picture of rules as rails, states: "Whence comes the idea that the beginning of a series is a visible section of rails invisibly laid to infinity? Well we might imagine rails instead of a rule. And infinitely long rails correspond to the unlimited application of a rule" (Wittgenstein [1953] 1968, §218). This is a particularly salient example of the criticism that even in an ideal case—as, say, being given the first few numbers of a series (two, four, six . . .) and being told you must add two to extend the series—one has not been given any firm reason to believe that the application of this rule extends to the invisible rail beyond what has been given as the "visible section" of the series. In other words, when I reach, say, one thousand, I might imagine that a different rule begins to apply—after all, no one has told me that the rule asking me to add two will extend beyond one thousand—so I will then need another rule to extend this rule. McDowell (2000) gives a nice formulation of the difficulties behind the picture of thinking that learning how to obey a rule is to bring an inner mental activity akin to a psychological mechanism that works like clockwork—aligning some kind of mental wheels that can be aligned to objectively given rails on which one's actions will run. We shall revisit this set of issues in Chapters 10 and 11, when we ask in what sense concepts are experiential—for now, I will simply evoke Cavell's marvelous formulation that on the whole we are able to project words in new situations with some degree of confidence that these projections will be understood not because we have access to universal rules but because of the "whirl of organism" Wittgenstein calls "forms of life" (see Cavell 1969a, 52). Following a rule, for Wittgenstein, then, is a custom by which he meant that it is the entanglement of habits and customs that makes following a rule one way rather than another seem right to us. Thus, unlike both Kant and Frege, whose intellectual Platonist conceptions of norms leads us to think that to assess the correctness of an action we must always be able to make at least an implicit reference to a rule or a principle that must be evoked and made explicit, for Wittgenstein it is the quality of practice that makes it evident that performance of explicit rules does not form an autonomous stratum that could exist without the support of other expressions of norms that he called customs and habits. As Brandom states this, "Norms that are *explicit* in the form of rules presuppose norms that are *implicit* in practice" (2008, 20).

Does this critique of rules as embodying norms reduce the phenomena of habit to mere mechanical actions, which would not be subject to considerations of correctness at all? While no one would deny that habituation involves the dulling of the senses to some extent (I do not have to think every step of the process when I cook our daily meals), it also involves heightened awareness and attentiveness to other aspects. For instance, during my fieldwork I came to appreciate the fact that a woman would remember in such a small gesture as serving tea to the family that I did not take sugar in my tea, that one of her sons liked lots of sugar, another liked to have *malai* (clotted cream on top of the milk) to float on his tea rather than mixed in it, and that her husband preferred to drink tea in a glass rather than a cup (see also Prasad 2007 for some nice examples of the expressions of care through the materiality of food).

## DETECTING THE HUMAN

The rightness or otherwise of certain habitual actions, I claim, is judged by the cultivation of a moral sensibility that is able to detect the "human" within actions that might otherwise be termed as the work of automation. Our uneasy relationship with the possibility of the mechanical (as distinct from the animal) was signaled for Henri Bergson through our attention to the comic. Thus, in his book on laughter, Bergson comments on how laughter is drawn out of us, for instance, when we see a runner stumble on a stone and fall or by the victim of a practical joke. The laughable element in both cases, he says, consists of a certain inelasticity, just where one would expect to find a wide, waking adaptability and living pliability of a human being (Bergson 1911, 10). While the comic is, indeed, an important register for expressing the thought that the human can sometimes be seen as a machine—and I can think of numerous occasions when the involuntary bursting of the mechanical or the animal interrupted the solemn performance of a ritual and elicited uncontrolled laughter—the attempts to defeat the mechanical aspect of being human that I was most impressed by was in the region of concealment, as if whatever else a machine can do it cannot possess a body that can learn the language of pretending, of concealing the intentions behind its actions. Here we find the ethical within the habitual or the routine where we least expect it to be—namely, in acts of concealment and pretending through which one's knowledge of the constrained circumstances of the other is hidden when offering a larger than usual gift or in the use of words to recast a debt as a gift. Thus, while gift-giving can be explained as the "normal" or "routine" gesture one performs when visiting a relative or a friend, as well as on ritual occasions, its mode of performance draws on a register of normativity other than simply fulfilling a social obligation.[7]

I argued earlier that gift-giving as a form of reciprocity is fraught with dangers that one might undermine another but also with possibilities of offering help and demonstrating care that is oriented to the specific needs of another. This double nature of reciprocity is recognized by Michael Jackson (2005), who points out:

> When Marcel Mauss invoked the Maori spirit (*hau*) of the gift to elucidate the threefold character of reciprocity . . . he glossed over the fact that the Maori word for reciprocity—appropriately a palindrome, *utu*—refers *both* to the gift-giving that sustains social solidarity and the violent act of seizure, revenge and repossession that are provoked when one party denies or diminishes the integrity (*mana*) of another. (2005, 42)

It is interesting to observe that the families I have worked with in Delhi who engage in endless discussions on the modalities of giving and receiving, what is often at stake is the reading of the body language of the giver and the receiver. In his classic essay on pretending, Austin (1979b) points out that at the heart of pretending is a certain kind of concealment—but that I conceal sometimes to deceive the other and sometimes to conceal my knowledge that, if expressed, will turn out to have grievous consequences for the other. In Cavell's masterful description of the act of concealing, he writes:

> Whatever in me I have to conceal I may betray exactly by the way in which I conceal it. Just *that* is what is concealed: the concealment of what it is up to me to express is a perfect expression of it—the slight edge of my denials, the over casualness of my manner, the hint of autonomanity in my smile or gait or position, each of which I may succeed in concealing . . . there are those who know how to read such concealments. The concealment of what there is to express is an exacting art, like camouflage. You might call it a language: the language of the body. About human beings there are only open secrets or open questions. (1979, 459)

These open secrets or questions, though, are the stuff of both tragedy and comedy, leading one to acknowledge that our human form of life has elements of other lives—of stones, of machines, of animals, of gods, and that habits performed in the dark of reason (Pollard 2008, 2010) do much more than act as flywheels of society; they remind us that in the face of the precariousness of life the mundane rituals we evolve, the way we conceal knowledge that might hurt, the way we continue to secure routine, is what allows our lives with others to be regarded as ethical or unethical.

Finally, I want to make the point that the sensibility by which we recognize the ethical in the small acts of everyday life also alerts us to the lethal ways in which our capacity to hurt others might also be expressed in completely quotidian ways. Pooja Satyogi (2016), in her exceptional work on cases of domestic cruelty in Delhi, recounts how she was surprised to find that many women reporting cases of domestic cruelty would provide narrations that in themselves might appear to be rather trivial but that took on the force of cruelty for them because of the circumstances in which they were embedded (see Satyogi 2019). For instance, one woman who felt completely suffocated in her conjugal family gave the example that, just as she would be getting ready to leave for work, her mother-in-law might ask her to perform a task that would make it impossible for her to reach her office in time. The task—let us say, of peeling a bunch of pea shells with the injunction that the smaller pods be separated and kept in a separate container from the larger ones—performed on a lazy winter afternoon with a group of women working in companionable rhythms might not seem cruel at all, but to a harassed young daughter-in-law who has barely managed to serve everyone breakfast and then get dressed to catch a bus to go to the office, it is an act through which her very existence as a responsible working woman might be put into complete jeopardy. It is thus that the hurts and insults of everyday life sometimes corrode the possibility of building a life together. Whether such hurts and everyday insults are the grounds on which larger spectacular forms of violence that we witness in publicly enacted riots or during warfare are built is a question that has no straight answers but is worth keeping alive. However, the opposite move of sensing how the quotidian asserts itself within scenes of violence of a more massive scale is an issue I do take up. It offers a picture of healing that is also located in unremarkable everyday acts.

## THEN, WHAT ABOUT GOOD AND EVIL?

I have emphasized the importance of habit as the site on which the working of ordinary ethics can be traced. A critic is entitled to ask, though, that in the light of the atrocities that assail our normal sensibilities and of which we are made increasingly aware by a variety of media—news reports, testimonial literature, images on print and electronic media—is it enough to speak of ethics on the register of the ordinary?

There is a vast literature on Abu Ghraib that has grown as the issue of how violence, torture, and illegal intimidation of certain populations is tolerated or even seen as necessary as the security apparatus grows within democracies has become an urgent question. I do not take up this literature in any detail here except to make two remarks. First, that much of the discussion in the literature has been on the circulation of the photographs of torture—with some scholars making genealogical connections with the circulation of photographs of lynching (Apel 2005; Puar 2004) while others argue that the form sovereign power takes now is anchored on the mass circulation of images of pornographic violence and their consumption (Caton 2006). Despite the important contributions this literature makes, the fascination with the figure of *homo sacer* developed in Agamben (1998) has obscured from view the historical depth and contemporary variations in the way judicial reasoning is actually applied to the adjudication of torture cases. A deeper understanding of the forms power takes through the combination of techniques of surveillance and plethora of laws through which terror trials are actually made cognizable in courts needs much more rigorous analysis of not only police practices, court trials, and mining of archives but also work on the adjacent events taking place in police stations and in informal exchanges in the courts in which the terror-accused are held and tried (see Hakyemez 2016 and Suresh 2016 for exemplary work in these directions).

In relation to my present theme of ordinary ethics, let me take up one strand of the argument developed by Caton (2010) that arises and gains in intensity with every war, every genocide, every revelation of the widespread use of torture—viz., that such ordinary people were capable of committing what Caton names as "evil." Caton is not comfortable with naming the kinds of acts committed at Abu Ghraib as simply "unethical" and proposes instead the category of "situational evil" to get out of the universalism versus relativism quandary. Nor does he find Kant's transcendental view of evil satisfactory. As he says, "What is missing in these transcendental views of good and evil is the possibility that ethical conduct is not simply assured by following an ethical code, but that such conduct *emerges* in a given situation" (Caton 2010, 174). Caton then turns to the question of responsibility. He finds Hannah Arendt's (1963) thesis on the banality of evil particularly helpful, in that it takes account of both the bureaucratic machine within which such evil takes place and the individual responsibility of those who claim immunity on the grounds that they were simply cogs in the machine. Arendt, as we know, did recognize that Eichmann was no Macbeth or Iago— Caton, too, recognizes that the evil committed by the perpetrators of Abu Ghraib stuns us by its banality rather than the larger-than-life character of the persons involved. Yet, in the final analysis, Caton would place responsibility on the individual: "Finally, there is no way to determine in advance which individuals will act ethically or even evilly in given situations; in the sense that this is 'spontaneous' the individual, as Kant insisted, is free to choose" (182). I will reserve comment on Caton's conclusion, though I recognize how difficult and tortuous it is to come on one side or another, either that of individual responsibility or that of institutional evil. I propose in my own work (Das 2007) that shifting the question elsewhere to the work of time gives us a different kind of insight into the moral issues at stake, for then the focus shifts from the commitment of dramatic acts of evil to that of how such acts are lived in the course of daily life.

If the problem of evil makes us stutter, so does the problem of extraordinary courage. In recent years, a number of extremely courageous accounts by women who survived terrifying violence have emerged in the public domain (Amy 2010; Talebi 2011; see also Rechtman 2006 and, for the widespread use of torture in democracies, Rejali 2007). These accounts constitute the most remarkable testimonies of both the utter cruelty and evil their authors confronted and their ability to survive in defiance of the powers of annihilation that were let loose upon them. There is clearly no standard template that one can deduce from these accounts—each is remarkable for its singularity. Out of this compelling literature I want to take one classic, stunning account by Shahla Talebi (2011) of her life as a political prisoner in Iran, first under the regime of the shah when she was just eighteen years old and later under the Islamic republic. In prison for nearly a decade, where she was repeatedly tortured, along with her husband who was later executed, Talebi draws a picture of life in prison that Stefania Pandolfo, in her blurb on the book, describes as a creation at the limits of life. But what I want to do here is to ask what the questions are that puzzle Talebi both in prison and out of it. To follow her puzzlement, I feel, is the best way to follow what moral issues might be at stake when we are silenced by the enormity of the violence and the determination to combat this evil, on the one hand, and the irruptions of everyday life in her account, on the other.

I will not attempt to give a depiction of the cruelty and torture, but Talebi's descriptions are the clearest indication that many prisoners did not let themselves be reduced to "bare life." As one example, here is her description of how they "celebrated" the Iranian New Year:

> Prior to every Iranian New Year, we took days to clean up our cells as if they were our homes—we embraced the risk of stealing soil and seeds on our way to the clinic, for interrogation, to our family meetings, so that we could plant our New Year *sabzeh*, the green plants we grow for the New Year as a symbol of growth. (Talebi 2011, 69)

Yet the "we" here is somewhat deceptive, for it hides deep moral divisions that arose in the prison as a result of the terrible circumstances in which the accused were placed. I take one example. As in most prisons and camps, the administrators relied on collaborators, men and women who either could not bear the torture anymore or sought some advantage for themselves or their families through collaboration. It is not difficult to understand how prisoners who had been able to themselves withstand torture and who refused to recant became the harshest critics of such collaborators. When one stands with such prisoners, seeing the prisons and the routine infliction of torture on their bodies and souls, one understands that they must have attributed some responsibility for the unbearable pain they bore to the actions of the collaborators. Yet one can also stand with the collaborators and see that it is only our exaggerated ideas of agency (see Améry 1980 on the impossibility of being able to imagine what the experience of torture might be, however well prepared you think you might be to endure it) that make us feel that we can say with Kant (as does Caton) that in the final analysis the individual is free to choose, since some people were able to hold up against the torturers even while others succumbed. When we read such accounts, our moral sensibilities intuitively cry out for the need to distinguish the perpetrators from the victims, and it is necessary to do so for juridical purposes, but our moral intuitions can fail us sometimes when we are unable to take into account the biography of a "perpetrator"—one made into an instrument of another's will by repeated use of torture, as was the case of child soldiers in the wars in Africa or with the well-documented cases of recruits trained and condemned to perform systematic torture in prisons and camps run by a brutal regime (see Hinton 2013).

I felt I reached bedrock as I read the following paragraph in Talebi on a woman who had collaborated with the prison officials and the disquiet she caused among the women prisoners as she spied and reported on them.

> Fozi's collaboration with the interrogators reached such an ugly and disgusting level that her infamy spread to all the wards and even to the outside world. Her husband, who was able to flee the country and was exiled in Europe, sent her a message of repudiation and abrogated his marriage to her. Her parents stopped coming to visit her for months until she became mentally ill. (2011, 83)

Then, after describing the madness into which Fozi fell, Talebi puzzles:

> Fozi went to sleep [having been forcibly administered an injection by the guards to keep her quiet] while many of us restlessly contemplated the incredible capacity human beings have of becoming so different from one another. Why is it that there are people who risk their lives to ease others' pain, although their own suffering may be even greater, while there are others willing to rescue themselves by walking on the injured shoulders of others? (86–87)

Surely, in face of this puzzle we must see that matters here touch on things far beyond agency, choice, exhortations to duty, and so on through which moral philosophy moves on its accustomed paths. Surely, we must see that while women in the prison might have the standing to pass judgment on collaborators with whom they were forced to dwell. And even as we acknowledge the extraordinary courage of some prisoners such as Talebi, who withstood the torture without giving in to demands for information on their fellow prisoners, we must surely despair that Fozi's husband and her parents, who themselves managed to evade prison and thus could have had little idea of the everyday brutality she faced from prison guards, found it fit to pass judgment on her.

And finally, there is the puzzlement of Talebi upon finding herself falling in love years later when she is in the United States:

> It was 1999, and I was extremely heartbroken following a failed romantic relationship for which my inexperienced heart had no preparation. My only previous experience of romantic love was with Hamid, whom I had lost so violently. And here I was with no regime to take away my love, yet I had lost him without knowing how to make sense of this loss. (2011, 129)

The scandal of the survivor is not that she cannot go on but that she does go on, and this is what appears to shock Talebi, that she can still fall in love, that everyday life can be recovered. In my earlier work, I have shown that for one of my respondents, Asha, it was that life could be re-engaged again and that her own body would betray her by feeling such desire that made her voice deeply divided—re-engaging life and yet turning her own voice against herself (Das 2007).

I suggest that moral philosophy here is taken on paths to which it is not accustomed. Let me go further and state that, just as in the ordinary course of life we might find the presence of moral and ethical formations within everyday habitual acts, so in the cases of the kind of violence described by the testimonial literature the ethical may be found in the impersonal rhythms of the social that allow life to be knitted together again. One of the best descriptions of the kind of process I have in mind is the description given by Heonik Kwon (2008, 2010) of how, in the region of Quang Nam in Vietnam that he studied, villagers began to revive ancestral shrines in the mid-1990s, after a long period of suspicion of religious activities by the Communist regime. Kwon also discovered that, along with rehabilitating ancestors, villagers began to build parallel shrines for the unknown dead in the Vietnam War and the thousands of displaced people who had died in strange places. What does such a gesture of recognition of one's former enemies mean? Kwon places these acts within an ethics of memory and makes the delicate point that such attempts meant that the law of hospitality and the law of kinship—one addressing the stranger and the second one's kinsmen—ran on parallel courses in the life of the community. However, while on the surface one might attribute different meanings to the ways of honoring kinsmen versus finding a place for strangers in the ritual life of the community, in a deeper sense the villagers were also trying to find a way to bring back one's errant ancestors—those who fell on the wrong side of the Vietnam War—to inhabit again the space of the domestic. These errant ancestors, who were expelled from the domestic community, were invited back just as the strangers—American soldiers whose ghosts pressed on the consciousness of the villagers since they too had died away from home—were accommodated in the ritual life. Kwon's work reminds us that deep political divides also fray the sphere of the family. Other anthropologists show how such impersonal forces as a god or jinn might become the bridge by which those divided within one threshold of life by conflicts that cannot be resolved might find a shared symbolic space within another threshold of life (Singh 2009). It seems that the "ordinary ethics" evident in such gestures have the potential to generate an eventual everyday from the ruins of the actual everyday by putting together the rubble and ruins and learning to live in that very space of devastation yet once again.

In my own work on the Partition of India in 1947 and the horrendous violence to which women were submitted, I try to portray precisely what it meant to inhabit that very space of devastation once again (Das 2007). Women not only used such powerful metaphors as "drinking the pain" and "digesting the pain" but also, in their everyday acts of endurance, they protected the children against knowledge they thought would be too hard for them to bear; they allowed life to be lived as best as they knew. Similarly, in Didier Fassin's (2010) work on the lives of terminally ill patients suffering from AIDS in South Africa, the ethical is encountered in the way in which survival itself becomes ethical as life is redefined to include the traces that one strives to leave for the living. I argue that it is in the flux of everyday life that we can recognize and pay attention to the scaffolding of everyday life, as well as the turns it takes within habits, excuses, pretenses, concealments, endurance, and acknowledgment (M. D. Jackson 2005; Reader 2007, 2010)—all these are critical for understanding how everyday life might provide the therapy for the very violation that has grown from within it. In laying this theory of ordinary ethics, I have privileged the voices of women. I hope this gesture will appeal to those who are willing to think from the feminine regions of the self as a way of inhabiting the world with others.

## A CONCLUDING THOUGHT

I have puzzled a lot since an earlier version of this chapter was first published as to why it produced anxiety among some anthropologists that such reasoning posed a threat to the search for the good in society or even to the project of moral reasoning itself. I found a very good clue for understanding some of this anxiety in Cora Diamond's (1997) take on difference and distance in thinking of the moral. Diamond is intrigued by a case reported in the *Washington Post* that produced considerable controversy on the ethics of reporting. The case related to Hobart Wilson, a twenty-six-year-old man who was driving at one hundred mph in the wrong lane and crashed into another car, killing its driver and himself in the process.

The case ignited the interest of a journalist, Chip Brown, because of Wilson's whole attitude to life. He was a man who had fallen off a tractor when he was very young and was disabled as a result of this fall. However, he was defiant toward life, refusing to accept himself as disabled, and spurned anyone who tried to offer him sympathy. He had run afoul of the law many times—convicted of owning unlawful weapons, drunk driving, resisting arrest, breaking into stores, committing burglaries, and several other charges. Fiercely autonomous, he had constructed a contraption on wheels on which he would often buzz around with reckless speed. On the fateful day, he had borrowed his sister's car and was driving with headlong speed in the wrong lane when he crashed into another car leading instantly to his own death and the death of the driver, Gilbert Layton, first described in the *Washington Post* as a "luckless stranger." Testimonies of him by members of his family and his friends showed him to be a lovable, law-abiding, gentle man with a devoted wife and adult children. His death was obviously a grievous loss to his family and friends.

The article in the *Washington Post* produced understandable anger. Many readers wrote letters to the effect that Wilson was an "unworthy subject"—that there was nothing in his life that could redeem him and that if something had to be written about this incident it should have been about Gilbert Layton, the driver of the other vehicle who died in such an untimely manner, for no fault of his own. The letter written by Layton's widow is a searing indictment of the *Post*—"Because Mr. Wilson hated the world, a good man had to die a tragic death, leaving a loving wife, two children and two grandchildren he loved very dearly. . . . To send out a reporter to cover the story of this man is in very bad taste" (cited in Diamond 1997, 206). Other readers wrote from a more impersonal angle expressing righteous indignation that such a worthless person was given space in the newspaper.

In her comment on the write-up and the letters, Diamond says:

The letter-writers treat the story as if it had only one character; but the reporter has given us two characters—and the best lines are Vickie Wilson's [his sister]. She says, of Hobart Wilson, "I think he should have one decent thing said about him," that is what should now be said, now he is dead; and Chip Brown lets us hear her say it. . . . And then there is the wonderful final sentence: Vickie Wilson's words, but Brown's choice as *final* sentence: with its triple negatives: "He's by his father, where won't no one push him no more." (Diamond 1997, 208–9)

In her wonderful way with words, Diamond brings us face-to-face with what she is a master of—viz., making us face the "difficulty of reality"—that even as we fully understand Barbara Layton's rage at the tragic and completely unnecessary death of her husband, we might reserve some compassion for the man who was given such a raw deal by life but who never lost his taste for it. The ability to judge and discern what is right and what is wrong is important, but Diamond is reminding us that we do not have to be judges at every moment of our life. Diamond's reflections connect to my own sense of Fozi's predicament and my own despair at the moralism shown by her husband and her parents (very different from the puzzles Talebi expresses) who could have had no understanding of what being tortured entailed for her in terms of keeping a moral compass intact. Diamond is connecting the theme of the ethics of narration with such issues as the conflict between love and morality—for instance, she takes on the debate between Richards (1971) and Bernard Williams (1981). Richards says that we should accept the moral principle that love and affection should not be based on physical characteristics alone but on those traits of character that relate to acting on moral principles. Bernard Williams (1981) characterizes such a position as "righteous absurdity."

In her own intervention, what Diamond brings out forcefully is the limitation of theories of ethics that isolate individual acts in order to make them objects of judgments and evaluations rather than thinking the fine-grained textures of life in which what might count is not an exclusive emphasis on *action* and *choice* but on the *texture of being* (Murdoch 1956). Diamond thinks of this register of the moral as a responsiveness to life. What matters is not one dramatic moment of decision but the attention to detail that thinking of life entails.

I understand the attraction that dramatizing moral choice holds for many in discussions of ethics. For example, expressing what moved him in the account of moral life in a discussion with Arthur Kleinman, Jackson writes, "Life is a gamble. There are no guarantees, no binding moral codes, no center that always holds. For Arthur, this did not mean that one gave up the idea of the good; rather one conceived the moral life as something that had to be struggled for. And it was the most dangerous and difficult moments of our lives that this struggle is momentarily won or lost—when we become monsters or saints" (M. D. Jackson 2009, 81–82). This is, of course, a possible way of living an ethical life, but for me it is not that one becomes a monster or a saint in one dramatic moment but rather that *how* one engages with one's ordinariness within the everyday scenes of good and bad defines who one is or who one becomes—as did Sanjeev Gupta, the protagonist of the previous chapter.

It occurs to me that perhaps growing up in relative poverty in the crowded conditions of a *basti*, where living conditions were slightly (but only slightly) better than those of the slums in which I work now, has given me a perspective that is somehow in tune with the Jain/Hindu idea that the pursuit of ethics as defined in *general terms* is impossible: For the Jains the frequent expression that "Jainism is impossible" is indicative of this stance to reality (Laidlaw 2013). For Hindus, the idea of Kali Yuga, or the fourth age that is symptomatic of the corruption of existence that time itself brings (Das 1977, 2014), shows the impossibility of following dharma—however, ethics *in the particular* is what human beings can strive for though never fully succeed in. It is because others come forward to help, correct, sustain, forgive, even in the midst of such corruption of time, that ethics become possible. Such are the inclinations I pursue as (and if) we move forward together.[8]

# 4

## ETHICS, SELF-KNOWLEDGE, AND WORDS NOT AT HOME

*The Ephemeral and the Durable*

A running thread in the arguments of the previous chapters was that we do not need to separate any particular domain of life as the domain of the ethical with a specialized vocabulary or named specific virtues—such as the pursuit of the good, or of freedom, or of justice—in order to understand what an ethical life entails. I asked what if, instead of imagining ethics as composed of actions corresponding to the pursuit of these named virtues, we thought of ethics as embedded in the most ordinary of actions? These actions might retrospectively be named as virtues, but they are not undertaken in pursuit of that virtue. Further, the same actions pursued differently might easily be transfigured into a negation of ethics (see also Das 2015c, as well as Chapter 3). For example, it seems odd to imagine that if a person saved someone who was under attack from a dangerous criminal and even risked his or her life in doing so, the aim was the pursuit of "courage" rather than that of saving the person who was in danger. Others may well say of this action that this person showed great courage but the imperative to act came from another source than that of demonstrating one's courage. Further, the very same actions that may be described or evaluated as "courageous" or "good" under some contexts could morph into something else with a slight shift of context. An example I offer in Chapter 1 is that of a much-admired young man in Gilsenan's (1996) ethnography of everyday masculine violence and narrative in Lebanon who was at one time celebrated for his courage in confronting an enemy right in his territory and then having killed him, turning back to go down the hill, fully exposed to the others who had witnessed this shooting and showing no signs of fear. Yet the same kinds of actions began to be regarded as a nuisance when the young hero became inclined to convert every occasion as a scene for the display of his own courage rather than paying any heed to the delicate task of maintaining enough peace for ordinary life to be sustained. This ambiguity is often discussed in terms of a conflict of values, but we might ask instead if there are other ways of thinking that rest less on notions of judgments and evaluations from the third-person perspective and more on thinking of individual actions as embedded in the flow of life. What might such a description entail?[1]

As I stated earlier, there is a healthy and vigorous debate in anthropology as to whether ethics is best seen at the moments when the ordinary routines of life break down, thus making ethical dilemmas visible, or whether ethics are woven into forms of life and anthropology's task is to make this weave of life visible—to disclose what it looks like (see Lambek et al. 2015). There is a palpable anxiety among many anthropologists that if we cannot produce external, agreed-upon criteria through which we might be able to distinguish and judge what is ethical and what is unethical, moral life and anthropological thought itself might fall into a limbo. There is a particular picture of the anthropologist as akin to the judge in a court of law that makes many anthropologists privilege the moments when their informants can stand outside the flux of life and pronounce judgments on the conduct of their fellow beings. However, as Sainsbury (1996) argues persuasively, the assumption that concepts, like sets, have sharp boundaries fails us precisely at the moment when moral issues are at stake. For instance, in some debates on abortion, he says, one can feel a real sense of shock at the realization that there is no set of persons with close boundaries: the concept "person" is vague at just that relevant point. Let us take a different way of thinking of ethics, as an expression of our "being-with"—a way of living our lives with others.[2]

Take Cora Diamond's idea of ethics, which I discuss in the last chapter in relation to the problem of moralism. She writes:

> We may then think that there is thought and talk that has as its subject matter what the good life is for human beings, or what principles or actions we should accept; so then philosophical ethics will be philosophy of that area of thought and talk. But you do not have to think that; and

Wittgenstein rejects that conception of ethics. Just as logic is not, for Wittgenstein, a particular subject with its own body of truths, but penetrates all thought, so ethics has no particular subject matter; rather, an ethical sprit, an attitude to the world and life, can penetrate any world and thought. So the contrast I want is between ethics conceived as a sphere of discourse among others in contrast with ethics tied to everything there is or can be, *the world as a whole, life*. (Diamond 2000, 153, emphasis added)

What does thinking of "the world as a whole, life," entail for ethnography?[3] Juliet Floyd (2018) asks a compelling question as to whether Wittgenstein's notion of forms of life is a Weltanschauung. Interestingly, her answer is "no" and "yes." No, because Wittgenstein, she says, does not offer an intuition or description of the world as a whole grasped in the traditional philosophical (and one might add) anthropological way; yes, because he is asking for a revision in how we see the world as a warping and weaving of life-forms. "It is internal to such weaving of procedures," she says, "that our uses of words are not reflective of one sort of thing that a culture is or has to be" (Floyd 2018, 87).

Would the modification of life with the adjectival everyday—i.e., "everyday life"—provide a different lens with which to take forward our notions of ethics or, rather, ethical life in anthropology? There has been considerable debate on the feasibility of such a concept as "ordinary ethics" and I engage some of this debate in the previous chapter—here my task is to ask what kind of imagination is needed to make everyday life visible against the default position that the everyday is purely the site of routine and repetition. It is not that I think that routine and repetition are unimportant, but I argue that everyday life cannot be seen simply as the residue of these routines.

### IMAGINING THE ORDINARY

In his essay "Being Odd, Getting Even," where he tries to work out Descartes's inheritance by the literary, as in Emerson and Poe's rendering of the question of self-knowledge (hence of skepticism), Stanley Cavell (1988a) makes explicit the task of *imagining* what picture of intimacy, closeness, ordinariness we might conjure as a method to think of the everyday or the diurnal.

If some image of human intimacy, call it marriage, or domestication, is [or has become available as] the fictional equivalent of what the philosophers of ordinary language understand as the ordinary, call this the image of the everyday as the domestic, then it stands to reason that the threat to the ordinary that philosophy names skepticism should show up in fiction's favorite threats to forms of marriage, namely in forms of melodrama and of tragedy. (176)

Cavell goes on to explain that in his book *Pursuits of Happiness* (Cavell 1981) he is posing a question with regard to this picture of human intimacy. The question is whether a pair in romantic marriage who outside the idyllic world of Eden are likely to accumulate hurts, pains, disappointments, can nevertheless remain friends. In the case of *Pursuits of Happiness*, Cavell's answer was a "yes," expressed in their willingness to be remarried—that is, to turn the disappointments into a commitment to a future together through mutual education in which the course of this togetherness or the end is not given in advance. In the case of his second book on film, *Contesting Tears*, the answer was a "no" since the women in these melodramas prefer a life of solitude and sometimes even touch madness in the attempt to overcome the arrogation of their voices by a dominant male figure (Cavell 1996).

The problem of what cannot show itself or shows itself through forms other than that of revelation is a complex one and is relevant for the particular feature of everyday life—viz., that its very ordinariness is what hides it from view and hence it cannot be *unearthed* to reveal something hidden. Heidegger's ([1927] 1967) notion of appearance pairs showing with announcing—thus disease cannot be seen but it announces itself through symptoms, or time can never show itself except through its positive emissaries through which one can track its work on bodies or landscapes. While appearance seems a very important concept for tracking how a particular modality—say, that of living as refugees—might be rendered anthropologically (see especially Perdigon 2015), the idea that everyday life as modality has to be imagined (rather than logically inferred) and that different images of the everyday will render different ways in which being-together might be described is central to the idea that everyday life is both closest to us and the most distant from us.

If everyday life is a modality of living, as I claim, then Cavell's formulation provides a very good guide to think what image of everyday we might conjure in order to make explicit what the labor of the achievement of everyday involves and what it is to fail in this achievement. I take two ways of imagining the everyday—one as a willing acceptance of repetition, everyday as *habituation*, and the second as a mode of *reinhabitation*.[4] As the reader can readily detect, these themes were already present in the previous chapters. Now I want to deepen the account by dwelling on the way that the significance of certain moments, or events, or gestures, or expressions initially escapes one in both one's ethnography and one's life, dawning on one only after a long period. Thus, the announcing that Heidegger pairs with showing is not something one can decipher immediately:[5] sometimes a method of critical patience is required for deciphering how small details matter in the weave of everyday life and at other times this dawning comes in a flash like the sudden recognition of the resemblance between the face of a granddaughter and her grandmother.[6] Thus the movement is not necessarily from immersion to reflection or from first-person to third-person perspective, as we shall see later, but is anchored in the being-together as a mode of living to which I made reference earlier.

## HABITUATION, REPETITION, AND ITS UNDERCURRENTS

As I discuss in the previous chapter, traditional views of habit saw it as a flywheel of society—its most precious conservative agent, as William James (1890) puts it. While one aspect of habit is certainly that it is seen to fix our tastes and aptitudes, narrowing the range of the possible (Ricouer 1966, 283), the emphasis on this aspect is not unrelated to the value we place on durability. But durability implies some flexibility and capacity for evolution—thus Ghassan Hage (2014) argues that habit has a double aspect—that of the sedimentation of experience, on the one hand, and a generative capacity for responsiveness to a particular milieu, on the other. In the previous chapters I drew attention to the importance of ordinary ethics in terms of the ability to counter the automation or mechanization of action by attentiveness to small details within what looks like the sedimentation of habit. I showed how this attentiveness was expressed in what looked like unremarkable acts such as noticing the specificity of someone's need, or taste, or disposition and modifying a habitual action just a little or cultivating the small disciplines through which care is dispersed within habitual actions. Important as these points are to contest the notion that habit is a sediment of repeated actions, as if humans were machines performing the same actions without thought or will, I realize that I did not go far enough in thinking that the creativity of everyday life might lie not only in the small changes and forms of attentiveness but also in the volatility that might lie just below the surface of habits. Cavell calls the combination of familiarity and strangeness of the domestic the uncanny of everyday life (Cavell 1988a). In Poe's inheritance of Descartes, Cavell states, a sense of dread can overcome us in the mere recounting of household events. Habit then might be the form of human action in which we might experience life as deeply familiar and at the same time find it deeply strange, distant, and impersonal. Though I have argued for many years now that everyday life is shadowed by skepticism and that belief and doubt are aspects of each other (Das 1998a, 1998b, 2007, 2012a), this aspect of the everyday is often completely elided in anthropological renderings of the everyday. The challenge, as I see it, is not to find a solution to this problem of skepticism but to learn to maintain it as part of everyday life, of habituation—what Laugier (2015) calls "ordinary realism" and places within the ethics and politics of care (see also Aucouturier 2015).

While I take the notion embedded in the expression "forms of life" that "form" and "life" are two related dimensions—corresponding to the idea that the social and the natural constantly absorb each other—much of classical anthropology considered life to be the mysterious force that could be tamed by rendering it under the rubric of the social (Das 2007). A classic discussion might be found in Durkheim:

> I do indeed take it to be obvious that social life depends on and bears the mark of its material base, just as the mental life of the individual depends on the brain and indeed on the whole body. But collective consciousness is something other than a mere epiphenomenon of its morphological base, just as individual consciousness is something other than a mere product of the nervous system. If collective consciousness is to appear, a *sui generis* synthesis of individual consciousnesses must occur. The product of this synthesis is a whole world of feelings, ideas, and images that follow their own laws once they are born. They mutually attract one another, repel one another, fuse together, subdivide, and proliferate; and none of these combinations is directly commanded and necessitated by the state of the underlying reality. Indeed, the life thus unleashed enjoys such great independence that it sometimes plays about

in forms that have no aim or utility of any kind, but only for the plea-sure of affirming itself. I have shown that precisely this is often true of ritual activity and mythological thought. (Durkheim [1912] 1995, 426)

However, notice that the "life unleashed" announces its independence from an "underlying reality" and has no other aim than affirming itself. These are important moments in the text but are tamed through an overbearing sense that ultimately the social is itself the ground of all being.

## A ROTATING FAN, A HOT SUMMER AFTERNOON, AND A SISTER'S COMPLAINT

An episode that makes a very brief appearance in my book *Life and Words: Violence and the Descent into the Ordinary* (Das 2007) is of a woman who on her deathbed had said to no one in particular, "Do not cover me in a shroud sent from my brother's house." I describe how at such moments when an in-junction from a dying person comes unbidden and unanticipated, the relatives are thrown in a terrible bind. Should they respect the last wishes of the person? But then dying people are known to be vulnerable to the mischief of spirits and ghosts—was it the woman's own voice that spoke? In this case it would have been a terrible insult to the natal family of a woman to refuse this last gift that proclaims the conclusion of a long gift-giving relationship between the natal family of a woman and her conjugal family and the inheritance of this gift-giving relation by the next generation. Indeed, the mourning rituals assign a central place to the brother, or the mother's brother, of someone who has died. According to Hindu notions of marriage, a girl is gifted by her father to her husband and the gift-giving relation continues even beyond her death in the special obligations a mother's brother inherits toward his sister's children (Das 1976; Trautman 1981, 2000). The contamination of this "pure" relation between brother and sister either through greed or through the corrosion of all relations with the passage of time is a cultural theme that finds expression in everyday talk, in soap operas, and, at least until the last decade, in many Hindi films (see, for instance, Das 1976; Trawick 1990; Bennett 1983). Yet a dying wish to deny the brother the right to provide a shroud was so dramatic that it stunned everyone, but no one was inclined to talk about it.

I cannot construct this story through an archive of lengthy narrative in-terviews, but because I had interacted with Sita's (the woman's) family for many years, I remember many instances of small talk in which an underlying current of grudges she bore against her brother and his family would surface and then disappear. One day on a hot summer afternoon, in 1972, as we sat in a small room in her brother's house fanning ourselves despite the slow rotating ceiling fan that was dispersing the hot air all over the room, she said, "Your uncle ji [referring to her brother] has never ever acknowledged that we [her husband and she] had gifted that fan when your uncle ji first moved to Delhi."[7] I had heard similar complaints often about various relatives since this topic was a staple of conversations among women. In this case, after a few years of her brother moving to Delhi from a small town, her own husband (an army officer) had died of a heart attack. So my sense was that she had lost the sheen of a privileged relative and resented the fact that she was always on the verge of an economic breakdown. It was only after years of hardship that her two sons were finally able to complete their education and get well-paying jobs; even then she never got the respect that she thought was her due from her sons' respective wives.

Sita did not ever let herself get into open fights with her brother or, later, her sons. She maintained a stance of self-sufficiency, slowly spending more and more time as she grew older in an ashram in Vrindavan—the holy town of Krishna and Radha. There were many stories of resentments that were woven into the texture of these relations that were on the surface marked by civility, adherence to the rhythms and routines of everyday life. Only inert objects—the fan, an elaborately embroidered phulkari (a heavy, colorful, scarf) she had crafted "with her own hands," a set of cushion covers—were allowed to be brought into conversations with a sense of something wrong or, rather, something not being quite right within Sita's relationships. Thus, for instance, she would say, "Do you think this cushion cover is too bright for the Delhi heat? Do you feel these days children do not like to eat homemade biscuits?"[8] It was in these general third-person utterances that one was invited to identify which second person was being addressed. Maybe my brother's wife tucks away the cushion behind other cushions because it is too bright (said with a tinge of irony), but the message to be inferred was that no one in her brother's house wanted to acknowledge her gifts properly—hence acknowledge *her*. I have called these kinds of exchanges "the aesthetics of kinship": they maintain the equanimity of a willing acceptance of everyday life while also gnawing away at the hinges on which it moves.

In fact, there is a name in Punjabi for such emotions, expressing a combination of hurt and feelings of neglect and the genre of complaint that I describe—it is known as *gila* and could be translated in the first instance as "reproach." Often coupled with two other Urdu terms—*shikwa* (reproach) and *shikayat* (complaint)—these terms mark different circles of intimacy. Thus, one might express *gila* and *shikwa* against one's close relatives, one's lover, and, on occasion, against one's own heart—*shikayat* has a more formal connotation. Thus, I might say that the child complained to the teacher ("shikayat ki"), one would not say "gila kiya" unless close intimacy had developed between the two.

There are many literary uses of the word gila that capture the rhythms of intimacy in which to express a reproach is also to express love; rather, the reproach *is* a particular moment in the give and take of love. In one of the families I know, in which a close relative had complained to another relative that when she was sick, her sister-in-law had not come to visit her in the hospital, a fight developed when the sister-in-law refused to come out of her room to greet the relative on a subsequent occasion. Matters escalated until the two women stopped speaking to each other (*bol chaal band ho gayi*). Explaining her action of having complained about her sister-in-law, which set the turbulence in their relation and in time came to implicate a whole segment of the kinship group, the woman said, "*Apne samajh ke hi tu gila kitta si na*" (Regarding her as my own did I express the reproach, no?). In her eyes, the sister-in-law had betrayed the intimacy twice over—first by not visiting her in hospital and second by not even recognizing that her reproach was an expression of disappointment in love, not an impersonal complaint or a complaint born of enmity.

Sita was not as close to me as some other women, so I was only allowed to register these small signs of close relations being corroded though there were no large villains—only the sadness of a fate that had made a once proud sister and mother into the relative who came close to receiving charity from her close kin. I had thought that kinship moved here on the established grids of mutual visits, gifts on the appropriate occasions, gossip, a gathering of news about all the dispersed kin—in other words, life as usual. If I had sensed the undercurrent of disappointment in the substance of the relationships in Sita's life, I did not fathom the extent of her anger against her brother until the words denying him his right to offer her a shroud were uttered. I too felt a disappointment with myself. I had thought that I was almost a family member, but the apparent routines and habits of this family had hidden from me the sadness and the slow growing apart that was going to shred the delicate weave of their relations. In retrospect, Sita had died when I was in my thirties and perhaps it was only with the passage of time that I would become someone to whom women would trust their stories much more. At least I learned that familiarity could dull you toward the strangeness that is happening right before your eyes.

Many years later, my mother-in-law was dying in the ICU of a hospital in Kolkata. I became panic-stricken when she suddenly began to demand cigarettes and a bottle of wine—putting a closed fist on her mouth as she said, "*phoo phoo korbo*," blowing imaginary smoke and taking an imaginary bottle to her mouth. Theoretically I knew about the ICU-produced psychosis, but I did not want any relative to be in the vicinity of my mother-in-law in case, I told myself, they infer all kinds of wrong notions about how she had lived her life. My mother-in-law was a very pious person; rules about purity and pollution were second nature to her. We were never allowed to touch eggs and then touch milk without first washing our hands to prevent the transmission of pollution. Deeply perturbed, I consulted a priest who advised me to take a small piece of fruit, have her touch it, and then feed it to a cow. I smuggled a small apple in the folds of my sari, I touched her hand to the fruit and then in our street in Kolkata I approached a neighbor who kept a milch cow in the backyard. The cow ate the fruit; we offered prayers to the nearby Kali temple; my mother-in-law lost her cravings and died as much of a peaceful death as is possible in an ICU.[9]

I talked to the priest later and asked him why had she expressed such strange desires—she who had not stepped out of the house since my father-in-law died, she who had said that with his death all color had gone out of her life when urged by us to wear, not the stark white of a widow's sari, but one with a slight dark border. The priest was very hesitant to say much but he indicated that one must be very careful that at the time of death a dark or dirty force might enter the body and thus one becomes the bearer of that entity's desires—bound to it rather than to one's own karmas and one's one own *samsakāras* (dispositions).[10] It is the ritual work performed by the mourners that assures a safe passage to the dying (Das 1977; Parry 1994). Throughout the liminal period when the dead person takes on the form of a *preta* (ghost), we were enjoined to observe many taboos to protect her and to protect ourselves. Even then, until the mourning period was over, the rituals in which she was named referred to her by adding the modifier preta (ghost) to her name, and I felt crushed by the sound of the word preta added to her name during the performance of these rituals. A kindly relative tried to reassure me that the preta was like the holy ghost—not a bad spirit but a messenger—for he saw me shrink every time the word was pronounced. I have seen many deaths, but unlike the sanitized versions in the reformed rituals of the Arya Samaj, which are the favored rituals of my side of the family, the rituals conducted according to orthodox Hindu custom were brutal. Not all one's studies of texts on the rituals of death—the *Garuḍa Purāṇa* or the *Antyeṣṭi Saṃskāra*—can protect one from the feeling of the brutality and the cruelty with which one is made to face death when it comes to the singularity of the life that has been extinguished. But worse perhaps is the idea that a single sentence on your deathbed or a single gesture could negate what your life was about, and it is only the subtle understandings with others—the work of a lifetime—that could protect you from these kinds of unforeseen, unbidden expressions that might come out of your mouth but, you would want to believe, were not yours. This was the first meaning of the volatility of routines and habits that, far from making you into mechanized automatons, can lay bare the fragility of the accord you might have had with the sense of your life as a whole.

In her insightful commentary on Cavell's (2010) philosophical autobiography *Little Did I Know*, Paola Marrati (2011) makes the following observation:

> What I would like to call attention to is [the] idea that our need for prophecy does not come from the hidden nature of the future, but from our natural, others would say existential, incapacity to know what is plainly in front of us: that we live in time, that we live in the world, that we live with others—in peace and in blood. What is truly mysterious, then, is not the content of such truths, but why they are and remain surprising to us; the problem of knowledge they raise, therefore, is not how knowledge can successfully explore, conceptualize, or categorize the world and its objects (humans included), but how knowledge eludes us, how we manage not to know what in a sense we cannot fail to know. (Marrati 2011, 954)

One aspect of this denial of what is before our eyes is a failure of acknowledgment (to use Cavell's vocabulary)—the simple acceptance of the flesh and blood character of the concrete other with whom everyday life is lived. My reflections on terms such as gila and shikwa and the way they are used in kinship relations points to the acknowledgment of the pains and hurts (outside of Eden or in the purer times than that of the present degenerate age of Kali Yuga in Hindu notions of time) that engaging with the concrete other entails. Our sense of life as a whole as ethical involves us in finding ways of containing these disappointments and not allowing them to be converted into a curse on the world. A life with the other, as Michael D. Jackson (1998) notes, consists of a myriad of minor moments of shared happiness and sympathetic sorrow, of affection and disaffection, of coming together and moving apart, so that what emerges is far from a synthesis to which one can assign a name or pin down as something one can know. There is no single key that will open the secret of what inhibiting a life together has meant in terms of habits, routines, repetitions, and their undercurrents that are continuously addressed and contained through such work as that of minor repairs—the way women darn tears in garments with the delicate placing of one thread on another.

The other aspect of opaqueness, as revealed by the dying statements of the two women, is that what one learns about oneself surprises one. Is the placement of habit and routines at the heart of everyday life also a way of concealment of the way in which we cannot bring ourselves to actually experience that which is unfolding in our own story? How is this opacity of experience tied to the opacity of the self?

## THE OPACITY OF THE SELF: WHAT DOES THE FIRST-PERSON PERSPECTIVE ENTAIL?

In a justly famous paragraph on his inability to mourn the death of his son, Waldo, Emerson wrote:

> There are moods in which we court suffering, in the hope that here, at least, we shall find reality, sharp peaks and edges of truth. But it turns out to be scene-painting and counterfeit. The only thing grief has taught me, is to know how shallow it is. That, like all the rest, it plays about the surface, and never, introduces me into the reality, for contact with which, we would even pay the costly price of sons and lovers. . . . In the death of my son, now more than two years old, I seem to have lost a

beautiful estate, no more. It cannot get it nearer to me. (Emerson [1844] 1969, 472–73)

It appears astonishing that what Emerson is mourning here is the loss of his ability to experience reality and not so much the loss of his son. If, however, the first half of the essay is about the vertigo the author feels as if grief is to be suffered without feeling it, the rest of the essay is about the various losses he enumerates—most of all our inability to be certain that we stand on sure ground, that we touch experience (Cameron 2007). Cameron argues in her insightful essay on this topic that grief occasioned by the death of the author's first child begets the other losses enumerated in the essay. Mourning seems to do its work here, according to Cameron, in the manner in which grief initially attached to a single experience comes to pervade all experience in an impersonal manner. She also reads Emerson's references to the body as macerating, as wasting away, as signifying the inability to speak of the death of the child, as the experience of the death of the self.

In a different reading of the same essay, Cavell argues that accompanying the sense of alienation from his own experience, there is also the pervasive sense of the essay as steeped in the imagery of birth. Cavell then detects an even darker shade of grief when he wonders if the analogies to sacrifice—say, in Isaac's promised death to Abraham's mission—might raise for Emerson the question "Must I take Waldo's death as a sacrifice (a 'martyrdom,' he says, thinking of Osiris) to my transformation?" When Emerson says that grief has nothing to teach me, he is overcoming an illusion that any publicly available institutions such as religion could offer consolation. "Nothing is left now but death"—the issue is not that he does not know how to go on but to make sense of the fact that he does go on. In this re-engagement or, rather, reinhabitation of life, experience slips away from hands that cannot clutch at it "as if language has difficulty reaching phenomena, leave aside clutching it" (Cavell 2003, 118). I will not take up the philosophical register of this essay—especially Cavell's argument that out of this inability to touch experience is born the philosopher father's birth into philosophy—but instead ask, What does it mean that we might be fenced off from our own experience of loss? To *suffer* grief without being able to feel it. Is there a difference between first-person and third-person perspectives on this loss? How should we read the dominance of first-person pronouns in Emerson's essay—I, we, my, me—as the problem seems to be not that of the opacity of other minds but one's own inability to relate to what is going on within one-self? What pictures of the inner and the outer do these scenes evoke?

The theme of the asymmetry between first-person and third-person per-spectives is a classic one and might be summarized by saying that in typical first-person statements one does not first search for evidence of, say, what is one's belief regarding any particular state of affairs and then come to know that this is one's belief. Nor does one *infer* one's inner states—one's state of hunger, one's pain, or one's sense of desolation—by *first* examining the evi-dence and then coming to a conclusion, whereas for any other person one might need to do precisely that. For instance, I might infer that the baby is hungry from her wails or, in the case of a child, by her question "Is there some-thing to eat?" In Wittgenstein's famous formulation on the asymmetry be-tween the first person and third person in the particular case of belief, "If there were a verb meaning 'to believe falsely' it would not have any significant first-person present indicative" (Wittgenstein [1953] 1968, 190). While it might be perfectly possible to say for another person that he or she believes something falsely or holds beliefs that are false, it is not possible to say that of one's own present self. One could, of course, say that of one's past self. As we saw in the discussion on belief in the first chapter, the question is not that of establishing if a statement in which I attributed a false belief to myself in the present in-dicative tense was *empirically* correct or false but rather that it would consti-tute a grammatical (or criterial) error in Wittgenstein's sense of grammar.

There is a complex and rich literature on these issues, and it is not my intention to engage the fascinating questions about first-person access or the question of first-person authority, except insofar as these help me find ways to understand the utterances I described. Thus Sita's wish that she not be wrapped in a shroud coming from her brother's house, which seemed to come as a surprise to everyone, or my sense of panic that I was unable to grant first-person authority to an expression of a wish in an ICU, what from all external experiences looked like an expression of a dying wish. Although a distant view of these matters might ascribe such reluctance on the part of Sita's relatives and my husband and myself in terms of the fear of breaking social norms, I think much more was at stake than social standing. (I do not deny that in some cases it would be a matter of preserving social norms but that would carry very different affects.) As the argument proceeds, I hope to be able to establish the centrality of the second person to find a dif-ferent way to get to the issues of first-person access and authority. For now,

I ask that even as it is crystal clear that first-person statements about belief cannot grammatically accommodate "falsely believing," could one simply extend this argument to all sensations, expressions of wishes, or desires? Without disputing Anscombe's (1981) wonderful insight that the first-person pronoun does not primarily "refer" to me and thus cannot be seen as a simple substitute for the noun that my name indicates,[11] I believe that the relegation of the second person to the margins of discussion on grammatical personhood obscures the kinds of issues that come to the fore when we consider experiences of the kind I describe or the issue that Emerson so eloquently touches on about the opacity of one's own reactions to powerful experiences of grief or even love.[12]

Let us take three short lines Wittgenstein adds in expanding the thoughts on the authority of first-person statements. These come from the same section of *Philosophical Investigations* from where I gave the earlier citation on the impossibility of "believing falsely" in the case of a subject in the first-person present indicative tense.

> At bottom, when I say "I believe . . ." I am describing my own state of mind—but this description is indirectly an assertion of the fact believed.
>
> One can mistrust one's senses, but not one's own belief.
>
> The language game of reporting can be given such a turn that a report is not meant to inform the hearer about its subject matter but about the person making the report. (Wittgenstein [1953] 1968, 190$^e$)

I want to take two thoughts from these citations that have relevance for my argument that Wittgenstein is suggesting that a first-person statement about belief has two aspects: one is that it is a description of my state of mind and the second is that it is also asserting something about the state of affairs that might be judged as "true" or "false" depending on the evidence. It might turn out that my belief about the earth being flat can be shown to be wrong or I might have been mistaken in believing that the person I happened to have seen in the rally in support of the then president elect was my friend Michael. I can learn to correct such beliefs and, depending on the nature and intensity of what I stated as my belief, such corrections may or may not have any consequences for my feelings on the matter. Instead, the weight comes to be placed on application of reasons to processes of decision-making regarding which beliefs to hold and which to correct.

As an example of this reflective stance, consider Korsgaard (1996, 113), who says: "The reflective structure of human consciousness sets us a problem. Reflective distance from our impulses makes it both possible and necessary to decide which one we will act on; it forces us to act on reasons." Richard Moran (2001) makes the perceptive point that the picture of the reflective self here is of one who halts ongoing acts to step away and observe her beliefs from an impersonal third-person stance. What is important here, Moran observes, is that the beliefs I am reflecting on are *my* beliefs, I can choose to change them or choose to hold on to them, for I am *responsible* for what stance I take toward my own beliefs or desires. However, what I find fascinating is that the individual is imagined here as engaged in reflection *all alone* and that the question of whether all cases of revision or correction involve issues of judgment or if something else is at stake is not really engaged. For instance, as I said, I might have believed that the earth is flat and now, given the evidence that it is a sphere (maybe I was shown a photograph taken from the moon), I have changed my beliefs (or could these be opinions? views?). But unless this belief of the flatness of the earth involved a revision of my whole cosmology, this distant fact of it being a sphere might have little emotional impact on me. Now consider my second example: I discover that it was not Michael but someone resembling Michael who I saw at that rally. The immediate relief I feel is of a different order because of the particularity of my relation to Michael and our shared past and my assumptions about what kind of relation with the world I share with him. Because the discussion of truth and falsity of beliefs in thought experiments basically tries to express first-person statements in the form of propositions, the weight is on the side of reportage.[13] It falls short on the side of asking what kind of testimony to the self is being offered here. In this sense, statements about belief might not be very good models to think about first-person statements on sensations or emotions. When Emerson says, "In the death of my son . . . I seem to have lost a beautiful estate, no more," there is nothing in the realm of facts that is at issue—rather the question is "How is it with you?"

Now one of the important dimensions in Wittgenstein's discussion on first-person authority is that he introduces a hearer: the first-person statement is not a private soliloquy—there is someone to whom my statement is addressed. For instance, "a report is not meant to inform *the hearer* about its subject matter but about the *person making the report*" (Wittgenstein [1953] 1968, 190ᵉ). Without going into much greater detail, my argument is that presence of the second person here wards off the possibility that first-person statements are about experience that might be rendered as completely private. Or that talking to myself means that I have invented words and expressions that carry meaning only for me.

> Why can't my right hand give my left hand money?—My right hand can put it in my left hand. My right hand can write a deed of gift and my left hand a receipt.—But the further practical consequences would not be those of a gift. When the left hand has taken the money from the right, etc., we shall ask: "Well, and what of it?" And the same could be asked if a person had given himself a private definition of a word; I mean, if he has said the word to himself and at the same time has directed his attention to a sensation. (Wittgenstein [1953] 1968, §268)

As we can see from this and several other paragraphs in *Philosophical Investigations*, the philosophical therapy Wittgenstein offers is to enable the reader to loosen the grip of a picture of the inner as hidden or private in the sense of being completely cordoned off from the public and shared character of language. Then, to ask how first-person statements are both about facts in the world and about the person making the statement is not to claim that these two aspects can be completely separated—one directed outward and the second inward—but to acknowledge that the inner and the outer are not entities separated by boundaries but each lines the other. The world counts—it has a say. However, how the world counts is somewhat different when we think of the first person as taking a third-person stance and a second-person stance. In the first case, the facts that are to be taken account of are "impersonal" facts: I am a person among other persons or I am dependent on the public nature of the words that are the only ones I have at hand. In the second case, I seek someone who can receive the words that give testimony to myself. Cavell argues that Wittgenstein's comments on the private language argument are attempts to uncover a fantasy or a profound fear—that not only am I completely unknown but also I am either powerless to make myself known or what I express is beyond my control. This fantasy of a private language, using Cavell's words, "relieve[s] me of the responsibility for making myself known to others. . . . It would suggest that my responsibility for self-knowledge takes care of itself—as though the fact that others do not know my (inner) life means that *I cannot but know it*" (Cavell 1979, 351, emphasis added).

There are others who have linked the issue of first-person voice with the issue of responsibility. For instance, Moran (2001) too argues that while I might take a third-person perspective on myself—considering myself impersonally as someone with a certain character and history, with certain beliefs and desires—just as I consider others, this equivalence between first-person and third-person stance would leave out of consideration the fact that I am responsible for my character and my desires. The subtle shades of difference between Moran's and Cavell's renderings of "responsibility" seems to lie in the fact that while Moran shows great insight in stating that my self is not just one person among others who happens to be me, his notion of responsibility is embedded in a judicial model of responsibility as in a court of law in which responsibility is directly linked to culpability and must be borne alone.[14] For Cavell, however, my self-knowledge cannot be formed independently of my relation to others and responsibility takes the form of the work I must do to in order to make myself known or at least intelligible—in other words, to be responsible for my expressions. And although Cavell does not make it explicit as to who the addressee of my expressions is, his examples, especially from Shakespeare or from the Hollywood couple in *Pursuits of Happiness,* seem to me to privilege the small community formed in the conversation between the subject and an intimate, concrete other.[15] Might one suggest that the addressee—the one in relation to whom I perform the labor of making myself known—is the second person and not the impersonal third person, although there will be contexts in which I might find myself in a position where I must assume a third-person addressee?

The story of inhabiting life with others is of course not a straightforward one. It is possible that the voice of Sita from the deathbed was meant for her close circle of kin—one from whom she was asking for her hurts to be acknowledged—that in their collective wisdom they recognized that she was not seeking to make a public statement. She might have even counted on them to restrict the circulation of the words drawn out of her in anger or hurt. There are other women I know whose lives had been much more disrupted by the Partition of India and its violence and who saw the necessity of containing the poisonous knowledge that had seeped into their relations with the grievous events of mass murders and rapes. Their care for the world was expressed in their modes of reinhabiting, making the very space of devastation flourish again through the small acts of care they offered—attending to children, to repair of relationships through the ordinary acts of bringing gifts to which, indeed, Sita had devoted her life. I do not know and cannot know how to go further, but I do know the difference in the aesthetics of kinship in this kind of world between trusting your words to the care of the concrete others with whom you have shared *this* kind of past, *this* kind of laughter, *these* kinds of tears, and releasing it to a public that might mutilate your words by treating them as if they were just like other objects in the world. We are now in the scene of kinship relations, and anthropology should have something to say on that.

## KINSHIP AS BEING-WITH AND THE SPACE OF THE SUBJUNCTIVE

In his recent influential essays on what kinship is and what it is not, Marshall Sahlins (2013) speaks of kinship relations in terms of mutuality of being. At first instance, I was surprised at what seemed like flogging dead horses: Is not the point that kinship is not about biology except as it is constructed in different societies something we drill into our undergraduate students? Were we reviving the contentious debates on substantivist versus nominalist theories of kinship that raged in the sixties?[16] As Maurice Bloch (2013) asks in his comment on a *HAU* symposium on Sahlins's book, What does the "is," a verb denoting being, tell us about kinship? And how does mutuality of being as a definition of kinship help us to distinguish kinship from other forms of relatedness? Unlike Bloch, I do not think the issue is that of giving a precise definition of kinship without which a scientific inquiry would be doomed.[17] Concepts, I argue (Das 2015c, chapter 11), do not have to be sharply bound in order to be useful. What concerns me more, however, is that Sahlins makes only peripheral references to the relation between intimacy and violence that I see as integral to kinship. Sahlins does call witchcraft the negative aspect of kinship, but it is not only in witchcraft accusations that we can see the dangers of kinship. Instead, I argue that intimacy—whether imagined as kinship, or the domestic, or even as the character of life itself—has, by definition, a double character. Because human beings not only care for each other but are also dangerous for each other, kinship or any other form of relatedness poses a major challenge to such projects as to how one is to live one's life (Das 2007). In Cavell's signature theme, the problem of skepticism in philosophy is not primarily about doubts about the existence of the external world but about the psychic existence of the other in one's life. One might say that a grammatical expression of this mutuality is found in the dialogical scene of the first person and the second person as the speaking subject and the hearing subject.

Sahlins's argument that kin participate *intrinsically* in each other's lives is important. They share a "mutuality of being" and are "members of one another" as Janet Carsten (2013) describes it, augmenting her comments with a stunning example of this mutuality of being and of almost living each other's lives. Here is how she describes a childhood memory:

> One of many family stories that made a vivid impression on me as a child was told by my mother, Ruth, who related how, as a young woman in her mid-twenties, she had once been on a journey, about to catch a train from one European city to another. Standing on the platform, she suddenly had the feeling that something was wrong at home. For no obvious or explicable reason, instead of taking her intended train, she took a different one—travelling in the opposite direction—and went directly home. On arrival, she discovered that her brother, to whom she was extremely close, had just received a diagnosis of leukemia. He died just a few weeks later and, as the manner in which Ruth told of these events made clear, her life from then on was irrevocably changed. (245)

Carsten goes on to draw attention to the fact that such remarkable examples of mutuality do not exclude the opposite characterization of kinship as dangerous, or as imbued with negative affects, or as "ambiguous" (see Peletz 2001). The issue, though, more than that of kinship being "ambiguous," is that when shadowed by skeptical doubt or the simple corrosion of time, our relations (and not of kinship alone) can actually devastate us. In an account of my own childhood (Das 2009), I too describe just such a relation imbued with just the same intensity and intimacy once upon a time between my eldest brother and me. As a caption of a photograph in which a little girl stands in the security of her big brother's enveloping body read, "I do not know how such love grew between us." A little ahead, the concluding sentence in the last paragraph of the essay was: "But when years later he was to go and kill himself, I felt like a house from which every light had been switched off, one by one" (Das 2009, 208–9). The significance of an event of this kind lies not in showing us that kinship is "ambivalent," for that is too mild a term for the kind of failures of kinship I describe there. The ties of kinship and intimacy should have surely attuned me to my brother in the way Carsten's mother was attuned to her brother. You should have known, I said to myself, that such dark feelings were playing havoc with another life to which your life was so irrevocably joined. For years afterward (and even now), I had to work hard to keep at bay the dangers that I felt were coming from me, to protect my family or those who became close to me from myself. Perhaps this is why when Cavell (2010) speaks in his philosophical autobiography of the little things he did for his children such as putting on the heating and preparing their breakfast as "healing the wounded arteries of his childhood," I understand just how such small acts might be the only way to claim your existence once again. Sahlins, though, gives little attention to how this mutuality of being is constantly endangered and repaired.

There are, of course, other ways in which one can depict how societies or individuals might stand up to the conditions of injustice, violence, untimely deaths, and other violations inflicted on them. For instance, Michael Puett (2014, 2015) gives a remarkable reading of ritual theory in ancient Chinese texts that speak of rituals as creating a subjunctive space in which by enacting an "as-if" reality the individual is educated in self-formation through which he or she can break his or her normal patterns of response to contingencies of life in a world marked by strife among kin, battles over succession, and warfare. Puett contests the dominant explanations of these rituals as enacting a worldview through which norms or rules for action might be instilled in the individual. Instead, he maintains that there is an explicit recognition of the "as-if" character of the rituals in these texts for they know that the harmonious world of kinship created in rituals is at odds with the real strife between fathers and sons in bitter battles of succession. Yet it seems as if by the ritual techniques of naming, role playing, and offering gifts to spirits an attempt is made to fortify the person to act as a pious son and to keep spirits at bay, but there is perfect awareness in the ritual texts that this is an enactment of wishes, that rituals inevitably fail to produce this kind of person or to keep strife in the real world at bay. Are rituals then an enactment of ideal worlds as opposed to the realm of the actual? Matters, as we shall see, turn out to be more complex in Puett's own writings when put in conversation with others.

A similar dark view of kinship is present in Favret-Saada's (2015) remarkable book on the order of witchcraft and the therapeutic process of dewitching in the Bocage. One strand of her argument is that forms of bewitching and dewitching in the Bocage were rooted in the property relations of farm families and the lines of fissure these created. However, it seems to me that the processes that bring the darker side of kinship to light are found in other contexts too. So, we might take this text as going beyond the context of farm families to provide insights into the nature of kinship and relatedness in everyday life itself.

In the Bocage, bewitching is a diagnosis arrived at by an expert (a dewitcher) through careful consideration of a client's description of a set of diffused anxieties that result from a series of misfortunes affecting the productive and reproductive capacities of the head of a farm family. The witch, then, is someone who wants to take away the vital force necessary for survival from the owner as head of the farm family. With masterly precision, Favret-Saada shows how the dewitcher uses a combination of strategies ranging from reading tarot cards to the rapid deployment of her (the dewitcher's) voice that rises to a crescendo, bringing images before the mind that flash with the speed of advertisements. Traversing from this kind of work performed in the presence of the dewitcher to other kinds of work performed in the house but under her instructions, the dewitcher attempts to effect a shift such that the head of the farm will be able to overcome the resistances he might have built toward the psychic work necessary to make him a proper head of the farm—not only legally but in terms of his own psychic reality. What is it that is required of the head to truly embody his legal position? To come to terms with the psychic realization that this is the kind of person he must now become? The legal regime of property in the Bocage requires that one becomes an individual producer, autonomous and with full rights of ownership, by "despoiling, eliminating, and expropriating one's immediate forebears, collateral kin, and even one's wife"—for claims of other men over the farm must be extinguished and women must be placed within a position of dependence within the farm economy (Favret-Saada 2015, 91). This form of everyday violence, says Favret-Saada, is legal and culturally acceptable. Yet, not everyone has the psychological wherewithal to accomplish this task. Dewitching then becomes a form of therapy in which the dewitcher and the wife in the bewitched couple come to establish a subtle cooperation in altering the psychic reality of the reluctant farm head. There is a whole complex of techniques, manipulation of material objects, the tenor of the voice, etc., that are brought together in the dewitching process that produce real effects. In the shifting of the psychic reality the person becomes more than himself, as Mme. Flora—the tarot card reader with whom Favret-Saada worked—brings about a distinction between the client as the person he is and what he must become as he begins to embody the great principles of "law, justice, and truth" (61). Dewitching, as she puts it, is not just another technique of self-assertiveness; a certain legal, but very real, violence is necessary to produce a happy farmer.

Favret-Saada's analysis resonates deeply with my own understanding of a common "family drama" I encountered in my fieldwork wherein, upon the death of a father, the ascension of the brother to the position of the head of a household incites a melancholic sense of the inevitable unfolding of a lethal conflict between brothers over property, succession, and even the right to propitiate ancestral deities. The two great epics of the Hindus, the Ramayana and the Mahabharata, attest to the power of this *originary* conflict as a story enshrined in kinship that is tragic but inevitable. Favret-Saada forcefully reveals our common vulnerability—not only to an external world of powerful institutions that can and do inflict violence but also to the terrifying realization that therapy itself might be a means for making us the instruments of that violence. This is perhaps why the people she worked with insisted on a distinction between dewitching and cure from both physical and psychic ailments.

In Favret-Saada and Puett, then, we have two remarkable but contrasting views of how rituals work. Although located in very different milieus and studied with very different methods, both authors seem to argue that rituals enact a pedagogy of sorts. For Favret-Saada, the dewitcher opens up a channel to evil—less dramatically put, he enables a transformation of dispositions that allow the farm head to overcome his hesitation with regard to the necessary and legal violence he must commit in order to be a successful farm head. In the case of ritual theory from ancient China, the pedagogic project is aimed at interrupting our normal patterns of behavior, but ritual theory knows in advance that the ritual space offers, at best, a temporary refuge—as Puett says, it is not the space in which one could live or, more forcefully, even if we could, we might not *want* to live in this "as-if" world. Both views of ritual embody a melancholic view of what it is to inhabit the "real" world, but while in the case of the Bocage dewitching, rituals create durable dispositions, in the second case, the subjunctive world is too beautiful, too harmonious for one to inhabit it, except temporarily. Puett seems to imply that we must not put our faith in the idea that such dispositions can last for we would be disappointed or even destroyed if we allowed such hopes to flower. I think Puett is right to be alert to these dangers of the "as-if" worlds, but the subtlety of Puett's reading is that he does not portray the ritual world as a world of hallucinations or that of a catharsis provided in a world in which social relations have become otherwise blocked. His conclusion, instead, speaks of how this ritual space and other "as-if" spaces we create are to be seen as helping to cultivate sensibilities that are developed over time through the tension between rituals and our lived reality. "We are constantly creating pockets of 'as if' realities, and the disjunction between these pockets and the patterns that we fall into in our lived reality is the basis for us to transform ourselves. But what we are seeking is not to become more like the person we are in these as-if spaces. The goal is rather to learn to respond to situations well—an ability we gain through the endless work of training ourselves through ritual activity" (Puett 2014, 550). Yet it is not entirely clear to me as to why the "as-if spaces" are seen as temporary, while the real world of strife is seen as durable. Could it be, I ask, that these "as-if spaces" also last forever, even though the modality in which they last is different from that in which the durability of official doctrines or of machinelike repetitions we might perform as dutiful subjects to norms might last?

Let me turn to a somewhat different (if not unrelated) place given to the ephemeral, the fleeting, by looking at Andreï Makine's novel *Brief Loves That Live Forever*. Set in the Soviet Union, the protagonist, an orphan now entering middle age, recalls the fleeting moments, the brief loves, that taught him what it is to be free of the weight of symbols that represent the most durable, authoritarian structures of Soviet society. The titles of the different stories that make up the tapestry of his memories are themselves eloquent: "She Set Me Free from Symbols" (the first story), "An Eternally Living Doctrine" (fourth story). The therapy that is offered from these enduring symbols of officialdom and the hollow promises of the revolution are not backed by any authority of, say, tradition or a resistance movement, yet they free the protagonist from the hallucinatory effects of the grandstands and the ever-present weight of propaganda. As he muses: "This obsession with what lasts causes us to overlook many a fleeting paradise, the only kind we can aspire to in the course of our lightning journey through this vale of tears"; "We prefer to fashion our dreams from the granite blocks of whole decades. We believe we are destined to live as long as statues"; "The paradise that taught me not to take myself for a statue"; "What remains is a fleeting paradise that lives on for all time, having no need of doctrines" (Makine 2013, 53, 67). At no place in the book is the oppressive brutality of the regime denied—indeed, many of the characters bear bodies broken by torture or by the hard labor of the camps—yet, the ability for love, however brief, whether frenzied or chaste, bears evidence that the protagonist is not psychically annihilated. Ironically, the statues that, it appeared, would last forever are now in cemeteries, whereas the brief loves imbue the narrator with a taste for life and, in their own modality, last forever.

At the end of this section, then, we have come to different pictures of what it is to think of textures of life and the disorders of kinship and intimacy. In Cavell's rendering of these matters, there is one picture of human intimacy that we might describe as a cautiously aspirational one. His question, which appeared right at the start of this section, bears repetition: Could a pair in romantic marriage who are likely to accumulate hurts, pains, disappointments, as time goes by, nevertheless remain friends? The ability for such friendship lies in a deep understanding of what fidelity might mean when it cannot be proclaimed once for all but must be won through a discovery repeatedly, diurnally, of what counts as important for *this* pair, for *this* relationship in all its particularity.

With Favret-Saada, the darker vision of everyday life is shown in the power held by the social to mold the individual in some picture of what it is to come to adulthood through vanquishing one's dispositions that make one hesitate in relation to societal demands for violence—urging the annihilation of others who come in the way of achievements sanctified by social norms. Favret-Saada's picture of everyday life is one in which the normality of such processes as succession to the position of a head of family or inheritance of property hides the undercurrents of violence that circulate as rumor, accusations of witchcraft, and other potentially destructive affects that make language itself lethal. In Puett, this darkness of a world at war with itself is mitigated only in ritual that creates a harmonious subjunctive space but one that cannot be inhabited for long.

Finally, for Makine, the real lies in the fleeting moments, in the brief loves that manage to breathe life into the frozen statues that the weight of official symbols and injunctions turn us into. The opposite of this vision of how to think of the ephemeral might be the violence of the fleeting moments, as in Sita's dying injunction that risked bringing the shadows that fell on her kinship relations out in the domain of publicity. These varying ways in which kinship and ritual, or the actual and the subjunctive, or the actual and the eventual, are aligned open the path to thinking that the ethical is much more diffused into one's life lived as a whole (in fragments, in fleeting moments) rather than in individual acts that can be separated and judged. Perhaps the brief loves that rescued the protagonist of Makine's novel from stonelike existence are saturated with the Soviet context—or perhaps they are indicative of the fact that we have to work out what fidelity to relations outside the recognized codifications (or within them) means for our moral and affective lives.

## CONCLUDING THOUGHTS: A PLACE TO REST

In his remarks on certainty, Wittgenstein says:

> You must bear in mind that the language-game is so to say something unpredictable. I mean it is not based on grounds. It is not reasonable (or unreasonable). It is there—like our life. (Wittgenstein 1969, §559)

But if everyday life has the texture of this uncertainty, which inflects our relation not only to the world but to self-knowledge, how does anthropology create its concepts and how do our modes of living with others affect the way we render our experiences in our fieldwork knowable? There is a very interesting passage in Cavell's early work on Beckett (Cavell 1969b) when he is reflecting on what he has called a characteristic of Beckett's language in *Endgame* that pertains not only to its use in dialogue but its grammar—its quality of unnoticed or unexpressed "*hidden literality*"—by which he means that the words strewn about seem to lack comprehensibility until we realize that their meaning was completely bare, open to view. The terse quality of the dialogue invites comparison to the posing of riddles, but there is another technique that Cavell identifies for which he says there is no literary form or figure with which one could compare it. Here is his description of this technique:

> It is a phenomenon I have often encountered in conversation and in the experience of psychotherapy—the way an utterance that has entered naturally into the dialogue and continues it with obvious sense suddenly sends out an intense meaning, and one which seems to summarize or reveal the entire drift of mood or state of mind until then unnoticed or

unexpressed. I am remembering a conversation in which a beautiful and somewhat cold young lady had entered a long monologue about her brother, describing what it was like to live for the summer with him in their step-mother's New York apartment, telling of her fears that he was becoming more and more unhappy, more than once mentioning suicide; a beautiful young man like that. And then she said: "When I was in the shower, I was afraid of what my brother might do." The line came at us: I seemed to know that she had not been talking about her fears for her brother, but of fears of him. "What would your brother do?" But she had become perplexed, we were both rather anxious, the subject got lost; The line, however, stayed said. It would not be quite right to say that something was revealed but there was as it were an air of revelation among us. (Cavell 1969b, 128–29)

Through various stunning examples in the play of how, within an utterance, a word suddenly swells up in intensity to convey a completely different meaning from what the conversation seemed to have been about, Cavell makes the claim that Beckett's characters have a tale to tell but that they are not going to find anyone who will trust that tale or, let us say, be mad enough to trust that tale. Thus, one of the characters in the play, Hamm, says Cavell, wants death and his entire project is to achieve this death but suicide is not an answer for him—"for he cannot imagine his death apart from imagining the death of the world." But in contrast to other imaginations of the death of the world as in Lear or Hamlet, or Christ, there is no language of redemption. For Cavell, the aesthetic of terror of the kind produced within the calm everyday flow in some kind of scene of the "shelter" that Hamm expresses, resonates with the kind of terror that living with the nuclear bombs produced, for the disaster is not yet to come—it has already happened.

I could go through years of field diaries and take out words and statements of precisely this kind—and many of these appear in my ethnographic accounts. A woman saying within a focus group discussion on reproductive rights, the suggestion of a dark meaning, "I cannot call my husband as Father of so and so—I call him by his name," and my realization that the woman wishes a little bit of death to be visited on her husband on every such occasion and how that was tied to years of neglect as she lost six or seven pregnancies (Das 2015b) or a woman saying about the deathbed statement of her mother about her need for forgiveness, "This was cruel" (Chapter 2). The ethnographic moments I have described in this chapter are precisely about words and gestures of this kind: they are not about the plot line of the story or the examination of kinship and ritual as *beliefs* by putting them in a structure of typified experiences. At one point in *Endgame*, Clove says, "The end is terrific," to which Hamm responds: "I prefer the middle." And Cavell has much of importance to say on being an eschatologist versus being just in the middle in this scene when finding a cure for being on earth is not the issue, perhaps enduring this condition is. I stop at this point.

# 5

# DISORDERS OF DESIRE OR MORAL STRIVING?

*Engaging the Life of the Other*

The last chapter showed the dark side of kinship in which the sudden appearance of utterances, such as deathbed injunctions to kin, put a tremendous pressure on what I called the second persons, the presumed addressees of these injunctions, to decipher how to follow them. In this chapter I try to show a still different side of kinship in which modalities of being-together are revealed in an ethics of hospitality in the process of making a stranger into kin.[1] If everyday life is the site on which the life of the other is engaged, how are unexpected events such as falling in love with the "wrong" kind of person absorbed within kinship relations for love to flower in the space of the domestic? What implications does a case such as the one I discuss in this chapter have for the moral striving I observe in the low-income neighborhoods I studied? If desires have the power to disrupt commonly agreed-upon notions of morality, what happens to those who do not put these desires under the constraints of a received moral perspective right from the start, to which Diamond's discussion in Chapter 3 alerted us? One aspect of the everyday I have emphasized is the hard work it takes within the everyday to contain the potentials for violence. This chapter, I hope, will show the complex ways in which desire is seen as simultaneously disruptive for the normative order and creative for allowing expression to what goes beyond the expectations of social roles and responsibilities.

This view of moral life is deeply influenced by a notion of the everyday in which how I respond to the claims of the other, as well as how I allow myself to be claimed by the other, defines the work of self-formation. The realization of these moral ideas, in what Cavell calls the picture of Emersonian perfectionism, is not premised on a pregiven, objectively agreed-upon idea of the common good; nor does it rely on virtues that are named within a vocabulary of their own. Rather, Cavell envisions a moral striving that in its uncertainty and its attention to the concrete specificity of the other is simply a dimension of everyday life (Cavell 1990b). In this picture of spiritual becoming, what one seeks is not to ascend to some higher ideal but to give birth to what sometimes Cavell is moved to call an adjacent self—a striving in which the eventual everyday emerges in a relation of nextness to the actual everyday (Critchley 2005). Against the dominant understanding of morality as the capacity to form *moral judgments* in which the crucial requirement is that we should be able to take an abstract, nonsubjective vantage position from which we can orient ourselves to the world (the third-person impersonal perspective), I argue that recourse to such an ideal position could equally provide a cover for evading the imperative to be attentive to the suffering of the other. I am not suggesting that there is no room for moral judgments in our lives or that people do not apply abstract standards derived from, say, a rule of conduct found in what they consider to be authoritative traditions but rather that whole areas of moral life remain obscure if our picture of morality remains tied to some version of following rules and judging others on impersonal standards alone.

In order to give conceptual and empirical depth to the notion of nextness or an adjacent self as one way to think of moral striving, I wish to develop what used to be called an extended case study of the marriage of a Hindu man and a Muslim woman in one of the low-income neighborhoods in Delhi. I offer this case study not as an example of larger social processes of, say, social change or social conflict in the spirit of illustrating a general argument, but rather as a mode of engaging a singularity through which I can show how a range of complex forces brought into being by the simple fact of a boy and girl having fallen in love fold themselves into intimate relations and come to define what Henrietta Moore calls "intimate aspirations" (personal correspondence). In the later Wittgenstein, I remind the reader, there is a stringent critique of the notion that the correct projection of a concept is already laid before us—thus, he says, when we assume that we know what following a rule means, we have a picture of a rigid line or grid on which our actions will move. Yet this picture produces only the buried mythology of our language (Wittgenstein [1953] 1968).[2]

What would be the opposite of this notion of "projection" along the imagery of an ideally rigid rail line? We could draw upon Foucault's notion of eventalization, which he argues is a way of lightening the weight of causal thinking in our intellectual projects, of interrupting given constants and instead thinking of gestures, acts, and discourses through which the imagery of the rigid line on which action will unfold can be made to stop (Foucault 1996).[3] One ethnographic mode of writing that we could draw from Wittgenstein is to think of the scenic as capturing a particular way in which a mode of conversation or a course of action is dramatized so that various voices (that of the child, of the skeptic, of common sense, of the philosopher) are allowed expression (Wittgenstein [1953] 1968). In the last chapter, I took words that seemed to have escaped from any plotline of the story and yet carried an intensity of the sort that, having been said, these remained said even if not acted upon.[4] Here I use another ethnographic insight derived from Wittgenstein—viz., the idea of a scene. I hope to show how something as simple as a Hindu boy having fallen in love with a Muslim girl becomes a seed scattered in the soil of the everyday. It carries within it the potential to unleash great violence but also carries an opportunity for intimate aspirations to be realized by all who have to re-create their relations around the couple. While I will try to frame this kind of nascent happening with an account of political affects to show how such an act can morph into Hindu-Muslim violence, how it can become the subject of police investigations, court cases, and parliamentary inquiries, I will also carry it into the life of this couple, whom I call Kuldip and Saba, and their relationships. My descriptions of the mode of engaging this event in the everyday will, however, take the form of scenic descriptions that evoke Wittgenstein's scenes of instruction (as in a child learning to read) or dramatizations of skeptical doubt (as in the parable of the boiling pot). I hope that, by presenting the singularity of this case in this mode, I will be able to show how the notion of nextness or the adjacent self allows for some calming of the turbulent potential of this event. It is a picture of moral perfectionism as a striving—the play of uncertainty, doubt, and the deepening of intimate relations within a whole weave of life.

## THE EXPLOSIVE POTENTIAL OF HINDU-MUSLIM MARRIAGES

The potential for violence in Hindu-Muslim relations involving the sexuality of women is a long-standing theme of political rhetoric in India and has been addressed in administrative and judicial practices through the concern for "public order." Deepak Mehta (2010) analyzes how exchanges of insults between Hindus and Muslims in the public sphere were articulated around the themes of the sexualized body of the Prophet, the emasculation of the men of the other group, and slights concerning the sexuality and purity of women. He analyzes the genres of insult and shows how they were written not so much to evade the British censor as to be recognized in the eyes of the colonial state as literatures of insult. However, heaping insults and humiliation on the other is only part of the story; the other part is the theme of desire that crosses the normative boundaries of religion, which has fascinated poets, writers, and filmmakers. Within this field of desire, fraught with the possibilities of tremendous violence, how are loving couples enabled to negotiate the treacherous waters of Hindu-Muslim sensibilities, the difficult realm of law, and the dense kinship universe of each person?

In her pathbreaking work on love marriages in Delhi, Perveez Mody (2008) offers the notion of "not-community" to depict the complex interaction between law, publicity, and intimacy. She argues that ideas of liberal citizenship are both enabled and punctured by new forms of intimacy, as demonstrated in the legal trajectories through which such issues are addressed in India. In a fascinating account of how the law negotiates the sensitivities around Hindu-Muslim relations, Mody's work brings out the contradictions embodied in legislative acts, such as the Special Marriage Act of 1872 in the colonial period, that, on the one hand, provided legal protection for individuals who chose to marry without parental consent and yet, on the other, constrained these choices by various other qualifications—specifically, by restricting the law's application to those who explicitly renounced membership in any religious community. Not only at the legislative level but also at the levels of police procedure, adjudication, and public-interest litigation, the ambivalence regarding Hindu-Muslim marriages often bursts into publicity of one sort or another, as is evident both in the literature of the nineteenth century and in the newspaper and other reportage in our own times.[5] For such couples, negotiating the terrain of parental consent, community approval, or even a complete break with previous kinship relations might bring into play a whole range of effects that are the stuff of cinema and literature. Most anthropologists have been reluctant to explore the profound implications of such a situation. Even Mody, because she was constrained to follow cases that had already burst into national publicity, is not able to show us how questions of ethics, morality, and intimate aspirations are negotiated outside the realm of publicity, though she does show that when couples are successful in getting parental consent, they are careful to maintain a fiction of "arranged marriage."

Outside the realm of publicity, conjugal and sexual relations are not always placed under the constraints of the kinds of norms of purity and respectability with which Mody was concerned. During his fieldwork in villages in Madhya Pradesh that were in the vicinity of the Bhilai Steel plant established as a public sector undertaking in collaboration with the USSR in 1955, Jonathan Parry (2001) was surprised to find the variety of conjugal and sexual arrangements among lower caste Satnamis. As Parry points out in his acute analysis, the institution of secondary marriages—a term that could cover customary conjugal arrangements that are permitted but do not have the sanctity of first or primary marriage to concubinage—allowed considerable relaxation of norms of endogamy, sexual purity, and monogamy.[6] While arguing that there is a move now in these communities toward marriages that on the surface look like "companionate marriages," Parry demonstrates that these new norms do not instantiate a move toward "purer relations," as Giddens (1992) seems to hypothesize, nor can these transformations be understood independently of the interventions of the local police and the new kinds of norms of monogamy instilled among workers by the management of the steel plant.

What interests me in Parry's description, for the purposes of this chapter, is not so much his ironic depiction of the middle-class Indian who holds forth on the sanctity of marriage among Indians (the man with the briefcase who is the generic figure who will engage every foreigner he happens to meet on the superiority of arranged marriages in India over the "love marriages" in the West) but Parry's own privileging of the male point of view. I understand that it is not easy for male anthropologists to enter into close relations with women, but I am struck by the total absence of any of the voices of women whose own perspectives on what is going on is always refracted through one or the other male voice. Here are two compelling scenes depicting the main protagonist Ankalu's "errant wife" and then Ankalu's own unsuccessful attempt to find a woman to replace her immediately to avoid loss of face.

> On the night in question Ankalu and Kedarnath were sleeping out in the street. Around 2.00 A.M. Kedarnath got up and climbed over Ankalu's compound wall to join the latter's wife. Coming back, his silhouette was spotted by Dakshin, who went to investigate. Kedarnath pleaded his discretion, to which Dakshin was disinclined by the circumstance that his own brother's wife had previously run off with Kedarnath. An enormous hullabaloo ensued. The whole *para* (quarter) was woken; Ankalu's sons manhandled the wife, confiscated her jewellery and turned her out of the house; and the *kotval* was summoned—the village watchman whose duties include reporting misdemeanours to the police. (Parry 2001, 790)

What follows is some attempt to have the matter adjudicated in the local panchayat with no decision emerging, and in the end Ankalu expels his wife from the conjugal home, partly on the insistence of his adult sons. Parry then gives this vivid description of Ankalu's search for a new wife:

> By the second panchayat, his sons had stiffened Ankalu's resolve. His wife was sent away. Mounted on powerful motorbikes, next morning Ankalu roared off with five friends around the peripheral villages in search of a new one. In each a fortifying drink and the party would call on the *bhandari* to ask if *koi rarhi-chharve baithi hai, kya* ("Is there any widow or abandoned woman sitting here?"). But as Somvaru had warned, it was not that easy and these sorties continued for several weeks. Sometimes the search was combined with one for a bride for his son and nephew, enquiries about which were hopefully concluded with: *Aur mere laik koi hai?* ("And is there anyone suitable for me?"). Several times the posse was directed to a temporarily husbandless woman "sitting" in her *maike* (her natal home) only for her to declare she would consider the proposition if Ankalu would register some land in her name, for where would she be if he died or divorced her? Once he sought out his second wife to ask if she would return, but was angrily sent packing. (791)

Parry offers these descriptions in support of his argument that, unlike in some other parts of India (for instance, in the case of the *khap* panchayats in Haryana, which are local level panchayats particularly concerned with sexual propriety), any outrage or violent repercussions are muted in these cases. Yet, he fails to go any deeper into the texture of relations—behind the performance of male honor what are the affects? I was reminded of Amritlal Nagar's (2011) description of male talk in his novel *Seth Bankemal* when the protagonist is heartbroken at the death of his wife and his friend admonishes him for stooping so low as to grieve for a woman. Especially when he could get hundreds of other women for the asking! What Nagar manages to convey is not contempt for women or indifference to the event of this loss but the *concealment* of the emotions that are running through the bereaved husband and his friend's male talk.

For a better understanding of the texture of erotic relations and the waxing and waning of erotic intensities, we might turn to the stunning ethnography of Shahbad, Rajasthan, penned by Bhrigupati Singh (2015). In the chapter entitled "Erotics and Agonistics: Intensities Deeper than Deep Play," Singh too describes a milieu in which extramarital liaisons—"settlements" as the people in the area describe them—are common but involve a delicate interlacing of aesthetics and ethics. For instance, there is the temporal unfolding of relations beginning with the gambits used by men to test out if a relation will go further; the visual pleasures and dangers of eroticized bodies on display watched from near or afar; genres of speech and song rife with resonances, suggestive gestures, and a whole physiognomy of words through which legitimate or clandestine futures are forged and sexual desire finds expression. A performance of bravado similar to the scenes in Parry are frequent in Shahbad too in which insults and sexual innuendos might be exchanged, but Singh captures the uncertainties, the courting of risks that might enhance the pleasures of agonistic intimacies or turn into feuds among neighboring villages or caste groups. There is much showing off but also much heartbreak, as when a wife discovers a "settlement" that a husband has kept secret from her. Actions do not have the mechanical quality they do in Parry's descriptions of the public performances of Ankalu.

In the low-income neighborhoods I have studied, extramarital alliances, love affairs, and elopements are also the stuff of rumor and games of honor and shame. The strategies by parents or estranged spouses usually consist of some cases becoming volatile, while in other cases parents opt for a style of "management" (*manage kar liya*) through kin pressure, payment of money, or, in cases that threaten to become volatile, by the intervention of the local leaders or the police. However, it is acknowledged that an elopement across the Hindu-Muslim divide could lead to an explosive situation since such local events immediately get grafted into national sentiments of forcible conversions or bring the militant Hindu organizations (less frequently Muslim organizations) into the politics of the local.

That Hindu-Muslim marriages carry a potential for violence is obvious to everyone in these neighborhoods. I give an example of a political pamphlet that was circulating at about the time that the case that I describe occurred. The pamphlet was produced and distributed by Akhil Bharatiya Vidyarthi Parishad, the student wing of the Bharatiya Janata Party (BJP), known for its militant defense of a Hindu nationalism that has consistently put into question Muslim belonging to the nation.[7] The pamphlet shows how the anxieties around terrorism and Islamic jihad that have gained fresh ground because both global and national discourses on terrorism and security are folded into the older rhetoric of the Muslim tendency to "seduce" young and gullible Hindu girls.

The pamphlet, written in English, which was distributed to students at the prestigious Jawaharlal Nehru University in 2009 and found its way in one of the localities through a student who was taking classes in a tutorial college in the vicinity of the university, carried the following warning:

Few days back a Malayalam Daily; Kerala Kaumudi exposed shocking revelations about a jihadi organization named "Love jihad" which has been conveniently ignored by rest of the media. The allegation that Muslim men entice Hindu and Christian women into marriage for reasons other than love, as part of an Islamist conspiracy, has recently been investigated by Kerala Police and has brought out some ugly details. The August 31 issue of Kerala's foremost newspaper, Malayalam Manorama, carried an extensive report on how a Pakistan-based terrorist organization is planning, abetting and financing the enticement of college students from different communities in the State to become cannon fodder for its jihad in India. The report terms such young women as "Love Bombs."

The exposé continues:

Trapping naive Hindu girls in the web of love in order to convert to Islam is the modus operandi of the said organization. Already more than 4000 girls have been converted to Islam by these Jihadi Romeos. Special branch of Police started investigation when marriages of such large scales were reported within last 6 months. As per the instructions of this organization, the recruits need to trap a Hindu girl each within the time frame of 2 weeks and brainwash her to get converted and then get married with her within 6 months. Special instructions to breed at least 4 kids have also been issued. If the target doesn't get trapped within first 2 weeks, they are instructed to leave her and move on to another girl. College students and working girls should be the prime target. Having completed their mission the organization will give 1 lakh Rupees and Financial help for the youth to start a business. Free mobile phone bikes and fashionable dresses are offered to them as tools for the mission. Money for this "Love Jihad" comes from the Middle East. Each district has its own zonal chairman to oversee the mission. Prior to College admission they make a list of Hindu girls with their details, and target those who they feel are vulnerable and easy to be brainwashed.

This pamphlet was based upon newspaper reports in both regional and national dailies. The issue came up when the Kerala High Court was hearing the anticipatory bail petitions of two young Muslim men, Sirajjudin and Shahan Sha, on the charges that they had abducted two girls from a local college and had forcibly converted them to Islam. The parents of the girls had brought a habeas corpus petition before the court. In the course of hearing the anticipatory bail petition, the court had observed that every citizen is entitled to "freedom of conscience and the right to freely profess and propagate religion as enshrined in Article 25 of the Constitution." "This right," the court further observed, "did not extend to the right to compel people professing a religion to convert to another religion."[8] As this event unfolded, it spread to a hearing in the Karnataka High Court and a police inquiry into the activities of the alleged Love Jihad organization, as well as the People's Front of India, a Muslim group alleged to be involved in funding these activities. The police did not find any organization by the name of Love Jihad; nevertheless, the deputy general of police reported in court that a spurt in conversions of Hindu and Christian girls was suspected and would be investigated in greater detail. A militant Hindu rights group, Sri Ram Sene, announced that it would send 150 party activists to keep an eye on suspicious activities of couples and immediately stop any "Love Jihad" activity they might identify. Members of Catholic organizations in Kerala also took notice of these events. K. S. Samson, the head of the Kochi-based organization Christian Association of Social Action, announced that the organization would cooperate with the Vishwa Hindu Parishad (a right-wing Hindu group) to identify girls who were being forcibly converted from Hinduism and would expect reciprocal cooperation for saving Christian girls. An unnamed police officer is reported to have stated that certain fundamentalist groups that had been carrying out vigilante attacks against couples who marry outside their respective communities had now started using the label "love jihad" to justify their attacks.[9]

I point to such pamphlets and forms of publicity to show the aura of suspicion that surrounds marriages that cut across communities, especially the Hindu-Muslim divide.[10] While there might be intensification of rumors and a heightened sense of danger at some moments and at others the intensity might wane, people in the neighborhoods in Delhi and other places are very aware of the potential for violence that such marriages might unleash. In two of the neighborhoods in Delhi in which I conducted fieldwork, local peace committees composed of Hindus, Muslims, and Sikhs have been created at the initiative of the local police, in association with the neighborhood branch of the Congress Party. They work to track down rumors and to mobilize support to defuse any violence that might escalate in response to local or even national events. I do not want to suggest that members of the police force always play a peace-maintaining role or that some political parties are more tolerant or, as the local parlance would have it, "secular" in accepting such marriages than others, but there are interesting local histories that account for different sensibilities even at the level of the neighborhood.[11]

In the context of tracking some of the publicity materials that these committees have generated, I learned about nine cases of Hindu-Muslim marriage, as well as other intercaste marriages that created considerable tension in the two neighborhoods over eight years (2003–2011). As I describe the manner in which social relations were continuously reconfigured in this one case, I make only occasional reference to the other cases. However, my discussion is informed by the wider field of forces that operate in them all. My technique of description is to place myself within an imminent and emerging story, depicting scenes of conversation, evasion, fear, and elation, rather than taking a transcendental view from a distance after the story has already acquired clarity. I was sometimes accompanied by my research assistant and colleague, Purshottam, and sometimes we would end up talking to

Kuldip's family together while at other times I could catch one or another member of the family in the house or in a tea shop nearby. I also stopped often to have tea with women who were sitting in the street, making small objects to sell, chatting, or simply "taking in the sun" in the winter months. In recreating the scenes of conversation, I use the present tense to convey the fact that what I describe is not a retrospective rendering.

## A STRANGER IN MY HOUSE

Purshottam and I are walking down the street when Leela Devi's sister-in-law, Savita, happens to open the door of their house. She insists that we come in to have a cup of tea. Leela Devi is not home today—normally, being the eldest woman in the house, she is the one to greet us and give us news of what has been happening. It is clear that Savita is bursting to tell us something. (This and other conversations all took place in Hindi and have been translated by me.)

> SAVITA: Did you know that Kuldip [Leela Devi's eldest son] has gotten married?
> VEENA: No, when did that happen? Congratulations. Where are the sweets?
> SAVITA: What congratulations? He has brought a Muslim girl into the house [*muslamani bitha li hai*, lit., "has made a Muslim girl sit in the house"]. No one in the neighborhood knows. They are both constantly running here and there [*idhar udhar bhag rahen hain*], hiding from her parents, who are threatening to kill Kuldip and they [the parents of the girl] have also lodged a police case of abduction. Didn't sister [Leela] tell you?

Over the next few days, we visit Leela Devi several times, because she seems anxious to talk and keeps calling both of us to come and visit her—yet when we meet, she can only skirt around the issue. Thus, what we can gather are broken fragments.

It is afternoon, and Leela Devi, Purshottam, and I are sitting in the open courtyard while she washes some clothes squatting on the floor near the water tap. Suddenly there is a flurry of movement, as sounds of loud knocking erupt. Before we can react, Leela Devi has hurriedly arisen, wiped her hands, rushed us into a little adjoining room, where old TVs and a broken sofa are piled up, and locked the door from outside. We can hear some kind of contentious conversation taking place. Leela Devi sounds placatory, saying he is not here—he was ill—that is why he has not returned your money, but he will. Finally, the men leave, but their threats hang in the air. It turns out that these were two tough men sent by some people from whom Kuldip has taken credit. When Leela Devi finally comes to open the door of our room, I can see that she is trembling.

She tells us the following story:

> You know how good Kuldip was in his studies. He got a scholarship to IIT. [The Indian Institute of Technology is an elite engineering school. As it happens, Kuldip's scholarship was not to IIT but to ITI, one of several Indian Technical Institutes set up by the government as vocational training centers. These are highly valued by families in lower-income neighborhoods, but they train students to be technicians, not engineers. This pattern of slight deception about his accomplishments was typical of Kuldip s stories about himself.] But he did not complete that degree, because he set up a tutorial college in partnership with a friend. He said, "I can make much more money setting up a college on my own." But his partner deceived him. He ran away with the money they made jointly. See how brilliant he is; his photograph is in the papers [she shows me an advertisement in a two-sheet tabloid called *Careers Today* that has Kuldip's photograph]. Now the moneylenders are after him. What between these moneylenders and the RSS guys,[12] we are afraid to leave the house.

I mutter something about how sorry I am and say that if they need any help they should tell me. But she continues to talk, almost to herself:

> For the last two years, things have just not worked out. Earlier my husband got so many TVs and cassette players to repair. [A room had been built as an extension of the house and as a storefront for the repair shop.] But now he does not get much business. For the last two years there has been this *chakkar* between my son and Saba. We did not know, but his grandfather knew. And in truth he encouraged Kuldip.

It is hard to translate the term *chakkar*, but its meaning in this context might best be conveyed as a tangled web, though the word "affair," which is also used, gives a more straightforward translation. What did the encouragement of the grandfather mean? I had learned earlier that the grandfather, who was a retired employee of the postal department, was considered relatively well off by local standards because he had both a regular pension and other sources of income. One of these was from a local shrine in the small urban settlement (*kasba*) where the ancestral home was located. It seems that, after the Partition of India, many Muslims from this town either migrated to Pakistan voluntarily or were forced to leave because of the communal violence. One such family was the shrine keeper of a local pir (saint), about whom not much was known. The shrine remained abandoned for a while, but someone used to go and light a *diya* (earthen lamp) every evening on the raised platform that is often taken to be the grave in which the dead saint resides, since his body is not subject to death or decay. One day a visitor, who did not know that the overgrown, abandoned site was a shrine, had gone to relieve himself there at night, but the diya chased him away. The very same night, Kuldip's grandfather dreamed that the spirit of the pir, named Bhooray Khan, had come into him, and he took upon himself the task of becoming the manager of the shrine. He cleaned up the place and slowly, through the medium of dreams, he began to construct the history of the local pir. He has since filled in details, making his own biography of the pir, on the model of the usual urs[13] stories of a Muslim saint who is handsome and pious. According to this generic rendering, the pir is on his way to his betrothed's house when some village women plead with him to rescue their cattle from a group of raiding bandits. The handsome young man agrees to do so but dies in the ensuing fight with the bandits, though he is able to restore their cattle to the women and is consequently consecrated as a pir (see Amin 2015). According to the grandfather, he also received the boon of being able to cure various ailments. Although he has never studied Arabic, he can dream of Qur'anic *ayats* (verses); he then recites them over a glass of water or another material object, and blows over the water, which he can now use to cure ailments. It is not clear from his description whether he sees the verses or hears them, but in any case, he says he gets knowledge— sometimes he calls this knowledge *gyan* and sometimes *ilm*. Both terms can have generic and specific meanings in the context of healing cults but are differently anchored to Hindu and Islamic ideas of knowledge, respectively. His son, Kuldip's father, has also inherited this ability to dream cures. The family, however, considers itself to be firmly Hindu. Kuldip's mother and father are devout worshippers of the mother goddess, Vaishno Devi, who demands vegetarianism of them. The grandfather and the children are exempt from these requirements placed by the mother goddess. The grand-children, Kuldip and his siblings, have not inherited this ability to dream. The grandfather believes that each grandchild will show his disposition and that nothing can be imposed by way of an impersonal religious belief.

Therefore, I suspect, when Kuldip fell in love with Saba he confided in his grandfather, relating the difficulties they were facing and the fact that they were both hesitant whether they would be able to withstand the pressures that are built into a marriage outside one's community, especially a Hindu-Muslim marriage. I will let Kuldip speak about this. The occasion was a poignant one, since, after hiding from Saba's relatives and running all over north India from one sympathetic relative to another (sometimes Kuldip's, sometimes Saba's) and living in various cheap hotels, they had run out of money. Saba was pregnant and soon to give birth. Meanwhile, negotiations between various relatives had been continuing, so Saba felt reassured that her parents or brother would not risk a communal confrontation by killing Kuldip or her, as they had earlier threatened to do. Kuldip's mother invited them to come back. This was now more than a year after they had first eloped.

KULDIP: When I first saw her, I did not even notice her very much. Actually, one of my friends was going out with a girl. He used to ask me to come with him, and his girlfriend brought Saba along so that they would not be conspicuous—a girl and a boy alone attract the attention of all kinds of bad people. I do not know how it happened, but then I knew that she was the only one in the world for me. But I did not know if she would be able to stand the rigors of a true love [*saccha pyar*].[14]

SABA: First I was offended, but then his sincerity won me over. Still, it was difficult, because everyone in my family knows how I have immersed myself in the verses of the Qur'an. I was the first girl in my family to have learned how to read the whole Qur'an. I know only enough Arabic to recognize the verses and to recite them, but I am not like others, who learn just a few verses. So I knew how hurt and upset my father and brother would be. But once I acknowledged to myself [*khud kubul kar liya*] that I loved him, I thought that this is what I must do—this is what I have to do [*yeh to karna hi karna hai*].[15]

The story that followed is similar to other stories of strategies followed by couples to combine the resources of helpful kin and friends and to somehow get the protection of the law to evade the feared violence that such a marriage can generate (Mody 2008). Thus, for instance, before Kuldip and Saba eloped they took care to leave a written statement with the local police station through a lawyer, with copies in the hands of some friends, to the effect that Saba was voluntarily leaving with Kuldip in order to get married. Saba feared that her father might lodge a complaint of abduction against Kuldip (which he did), and she was advised that such a letter would come in handy against police harassment or criminal charges, were they to be levied against Kuldip. Like many other eloping couples, they had first gone to the Tis Hazari Court in Old Delhi in order to get married under the Special Marriage Act of 1954, but, as Mody describes in her book, it is not a straightforward matter for an eloping couple to get married in the court. The banns of the intention to marry have to be publicly posted for thirty days in advance, in addition to the requirement of several official forms of certification, including one from the local police station testifying to residence of the couple in a neighborhood in Delhi.[16]

Many young men of the RSS or other Hindu fronts monitor these banns in order to prevent such marriages. Recall that the Sri Ram Sene said that they would send 150 activists to stop "love jihad" marriages and the comment of the anonymous policeman I cited earlier that this threat should be seen as a continuation of the usual strategies of threatening and intimidating couples from different religions who wish to marry. However, Mody also points out that there are various kinds of services offered in the courts that are not part of the formal legal system but have nevertheless become a part of the everyday life of the court. One of these services is that of the Arya Samaj, a Hindu reform organization that has historically combined a progressive agenda of Hindu reform with a strong anti-Muslim stance and a program for reconverting Muslims to their "original" Hindu state. Brill's first *Encyclopaedia of Islam* (1913–1936), in its chapter on India, mentions that the Arya Samaj had been active in the work of reconversion and that the Rajput Shuddhi Society (Rajput Purification Society), which was affiliated with it, had brought 1,052 Rajput Muslims into the Hindu fold between 1907 and 1910 (Houtsma et al. 1993).

In any case, with the help of some friends, Kuldip and Saba were able to contact a local Arya Samaj priest, who offered to convert Saba to Hinduism and to perform an Arya Samaj wedding for them, which would be recognized by the court. Thus, they could simply register their marriage rather than have to wait for the court procedures such as putting up the banns that might put them at risk. Both Kuldip and Saba pointed out to me that this was not the only option they tried.

> SABA: I really had no objection to being converted—I thought if one of us has to do it, why not me? They gave me a different name—Seema—not too different from my own name, so that I would not become disoriented. The priest actually told me that it is customary for all Hindu girls to get a new name on marriage. There was not much ritual or anything—just *yag* [in Sanskrit, *yajna*, fire sacrifice] and circumambulation round the fire and putting vermilion in the parting of my hair. Kuldip said to me, "Don't take anything to heart—this is just for legal purposes. No one is going to stop you from reading the Qur'an or saying your *namaz*."[17] But still it was interesting [using the English word] that no temple would agree to marry us—only the Arya Samaj agreed.

> KULDIP: Actually, we also tried the mosque. I wanted to become a Muslim, but there they insisted that we must bring an affidavit signed in a court that I was willing to be converted out of my own free will. The mufti of Fatehpur Sikri told me that I would have to study the Qur'an for at least three months before I could know that I wanted to accept Islam and before they could assure themselves that it was a genuine case of wanting to convert and not simply a ruse for getting married. Actually, all these are excuses—these days no one wants to take a risk [using the word "risk" in English].

> SABA: All these are just excuses for doing nothing—to cover up the fact that they don't want the hassle. They think the RSS guys will come and take *panga* [a colloquial expression meaning to pick a fight]. And then they don't want to deal with irate parents. The fact is that my parents are very conscious of their high caste status—we are Rajputs, and Kuldip comes from a lower caste.

> KULDIP: Oh yes, this is a *kaum* [community] that should welcome those like me who genuinely want to accept Islam, because this community grew by conversions. Only later did they come to realize that someone like me who has received the light of Islam is like a gift from above [*uppar wale ki den*]—like a precious newborn—to be received on one's eyelashes [an expression denoting extreme delicacy]. But they were bothered about caste and parents and RSS.

*Disorders of Desire or Moral Striving?* 163

I wanted to talk more but there were always interruptions. I give some further texture to Kuldip's intriguing references to his attraction to Islam, as well as its relation to the manner in which his father's and grandfather's unstable relations to Islam played in the life of the household, by stitching together several short conversations from different times after Kuldip and Saba had moved back into Kuldip's parents' house and after the birth of a son to Saba.

> LEELA DEVI: I do not know when our days will turn. I pray day and night to Mata Rani [the mother goddess], saying, "Don't turn your face away from us." Earlier my husband used to have visions of her, and she used to guide him—do this do that. But now there is no business—everyone gets new TV sets and no one seems in need of repair.
>
> VEENA: Is she angry because something wrong has been done?
>
> LEELA DEVI: Who is to say? It is the mother's wish. I keep trying to divine what is the matter. Is it because Saba might have become a Hindu? But who can take away the *saṃskāra* she has?[18] So I thought maybe when she is lighting the evening lamp [at the domestic altar] or maybe she does something not quite right in the puja [ritual worship] so I tactfully stopped her from doing that. Maybe He [her husband; a common way of referring to one's husband, since it is taboo for a woman to pronounce her husband's name] has started drinking. He might even be eating meat. He is inclined that way, though the goddess has imposed very strict dietary restrictions on him. People criticize me for bringing Kuldip and Saba home—the RSS boys are after us. I told one of them, "You can get many people to defend your Hindu *dharma*. But as for me, I am a mother. Where will I get my son again if I lose him?" I say, "Mata Rani, forgive me—don't punish me for loving my son."

Here, with a different inflection, Saba:

> Though I told you that, when they did all that *shuddhi* [purification] and conversion, both Kuldip and I knew that this was just for the law, it did have some influence on me. I began seriously to learn how to do puja. It moved me to think that this is what Kuldip grew up watching and doing—and then I thought that, so long as I do not perform *sajda* [the

Islamic term for prostration][19] before another god, I do not offend against Allah's glory. I would fold my hands and bow my head in respect, but I would not touch my head to the altar. That is why I thought I have not rejected Islam. Allah too knows and blesses lovers [*Aasbikon par to Allah bhi fida bai*—lit., "Even Allah is enchanted by lovers"].

On yet another occasion, sitting in the *barsati* (a room on the side of the open terrace) that had been now assigned to Kuldip and Saba as a "Muslim" or "Islamic" space (since the family did not make the subtle distinctions that scholars make between the two) and having tea:

SABA: But then Mummy Ji [referring to Kuldip's mother] began to be somehow uneasy with my performing puja and all. She said, "You have learned to read the Qur'an and to say the *namaz* since you were such a little girl—how can we take away from you all your saṃskāra? Maybe the goddess herself does not want us to take you away from what is dear to your heart and from your Allah."

KULDIP: Here in the barsati we keep the Qur'an and everyone supports Saba—they know she has to perform the rite at the right time. Anyway, women are not allowed to go to the mosque, so all that has to be done at home.

VEENA: And you, how do you relate to all this?

KULDIP: Well, I have also started reading the *namaz*.

SABA (interrupting): Actually, that was really quite amazing. Papa Ji [Kuldip's father] says he can dream the right *ayat* to be read when he makes a cure. But he is under some kind of order from Mata Rani not to say *Bismillah*. I have watched him perform all this, and I cannot understand how Allah *mian* does his work.[20] But He [referring to Kuldip] is like he's intoxicated with this [*is cheez ka nasha chad gaya hai*]. The other night he woke me up at three in the morning and said, "Teach me how to read the namaz." I said, "Now?" And he said, "Yes." I can tell you I know how long it takes even for a person born a Muslim to learn the proper way of reading the namaz—but he seems to pick up so fast. It is hard to know what Allah wants.

VEENA (to Kuldip): So do you think of yourself as Muslim now or as Hindu? Or does it not matter?

KULDIP: I am a Muslim now. Of course, I stand with my mother when she performs *arti* [waving of lamps and chanting] in the evening before the image of the goddess. I too used to be a complete devotee of the goddess. And of course I will take part in the annual rituals to honor the ancestors. But sitting in temples or making offerings—all that is over. Now I think that something compels me to learn more about Islam. I go and hang about in the mosque. I have talked to the elders there, and they now see that the light of Islam has come into me. They now agree that a great mistake was made in not admitting me earlier—but now I have recited the *kalma* [profession of faith].

Saba corrects him to say "*kalima*," and he recites for me "*La Illaha Illal-lah Muhammadur Rasullullah*"—"There is no God but God, and Mohammad is his Prophet." Then he says shyly that Arabic does not yet sit on his tongue properly.

It turned out that each person in the family was trying to make slow shifts in his or her orientation to the divine, to prayer, and to ritual performances, as well as adjustments in the question of to which community he or she belonged. Kuldip's mother became closer to the goddess as she tried to see that anything that angered the goddess in relation to the presence of a Muslim girl in the home was somehow neutralized. Her husband, who had earlier been able to dream both in an Islamic and in a Hindu idiom, felt the weight of betrayal toward the goddess. But he was losing his ability to cure, so he shifted his allegiance to a local Sufi *baba* (an honorific for a holy or wise older man) known as *khichdi baba*. Khichdi is a popular dish of rice and lentils, but in popular parlance it also refers to an unruly mix.[21] Once when I was talking to Kuldip's grandfather, he said that since Allah had given them small bounties such as the blessing of the pir, he was now demanding what was due to him (*apna hisab le rahen hain*). Kuldip took on the Islamic name Mohammad as a sign of his commitment to Islam but limited its use to the mosque or among Saba's relatives. His grandfather had a dream in which a new basti (settlement) was being formed, in which he saw a mosque and, like a watermark on a sheet of paper, a temple behind it.[22] Consulting a book on how to interpret dreams from an Islamic perspective, he informed me that the dream was a good omen, since if you see a new basti with a mosque and a market it means Allah has blessed a new endeavor—as for the temple, he could not say. Dreams, he tells me, are the last bit of prophecy Allah has bestowed on humans, provided you know how to interpret them, for Iblis (Satan) also uses dreams to delude men (see Das 2015a for a discussion of dreams in the practice of another, more established Muslim healer in a similar neighborhood).

As I indicated earlier, Kuldip had something of a trickster quality, as in being able to make ITI appear as IIT or in managing his debts with the dexterity of a gambler—taking loans from one type of person (a relative) to pay off another (a moneylender). Perhaps this is why the grandfather was relieved to have a good dream. However, Kuldip's luck did not hold for long—there was added pressure from his uncle and aunt, who shared the house with his parents, because his unsettled debts were creating a scandal in the neighborhood. Kuldip had gone a long way toward "becoming Muslim" but had neither been circumcised nor partaken of beef—the two ultimate tests in local understanding that conversion is complete. After one particularly ugly event, in which one of his creditors threatened to have him beaten up, he left with Saba and their son for Aligarh, where some of her relatives stay in a Muslim neighborhood and where he was able take on a Muslim identity (name, beard, and regular prayers in the mosque, while still avoiding beef and deferring circumcision). Although I could not meet Saba and him after they left, they maintained regular contact with the family, and his mother told me that the creditors had forcibly placed a family on the top floor, who paid regular rent to the creditors and were expected to stay until the debt was paid off. Kuldip's four younger brothers became the major conduits for contact between his conjugal family and his parents. In addition, tentative gift exchanges between the affines were established by each side, sending appropriate gifts of sweets from the market for Diwali and Id-e-Milad the two major festivals of Hindus and Muslims respectively. Kuldip's younger brother laughingly told me that Kuldip was trying to put Saba in purdah, to observe the veil, and that Saba was vigorously resisting on the grounds that even her orthodox father had failed to do that. After a year had passed, I heard rumors that Kuldip had failed to establish himself economically, that a tutorial college he had set up with borrowed money in Aligarh had failed, and that he might be returning to his parents' house. The first indication of this was that he had sent his son to spend the summer in Delhi.[23]

Not all such marriages across religion or caste seem to show the same complexity. While marriages across communities are by no means rare, the reactions range from quiet acceptance to violent fights. Thus, for instance, Namita, a girl from the *baniya* caste, fell in love with a Muslim boy from the same neighborhood, eloped with him, and converted to Islam. Her parents would have nothing to do with her and had cut all connections, but she was hopeful that over time they would forgive her. By contrast, when a Hindu girl, Sonia, ran away with a hawker, a Hindu from a similar lower-caste background, it was not caste or religion that was the issue but the sheer fact of her running away and the question of family honor. Her mother and uncle (her father had abandoned her mother) lodged a case of abduction with the police on the grounds that she was a minor. The couple was produced in court, where Sonia alleged that her mother was trying to engage her in prostitution and that was why she was opposing their marriage. Her mother was reduced to silence and amazement that such coarse language could (as she said) "come out of her daughter's mouth." The court ordered Sonia to be placed in Nari Niketan (a government-run custodial home for girls and women who might have been raped, who have been rescued from brothels, or who are otherwise in danger of being sexually or physically violated) until she attained legal majority. The family then relented and withdrew the case, which legally then ended in a "compromise."[24]

I do not wish to go into the full geography of these cases here, although an understanding of the changing forms of intimacy in urban India would require us to do that. Instead, my aim is to reflect more deeply on the case of Kuldip and Saba to ask what moral projects might be embedded in everyday life in the context of the agonistic belonging of Hindus and Muslims as neighbors in the same local worlds (see Singh 2015)—local worlds that are, however, inflected with national and even transnational imaginaries that shape Hindu and Muslim identities. What idea of everyday life might we propose here? And how might our understanding of the moral depart from the idea of morality as the capacity to make abstract moral judgments or to deploy a vocabulary that marks off the domain of the moral from everyday life?

## EVERYDAY LIFE AS AN ACHIEVEMENT

The term *everyday* covers a wide range of meanings: it tends to perform different kinds of functions in the oeuvre of different writers as we saw in Chapter 2 (see also Das 2015c). Rather than attempt to give an account of these different theoretical positions, here I will show how two specific intuitions about the everyday become important sites for understanding the sense of the moral as the generation of an adjacent self, as we have seen in the case of Kuldip and Saba. In his magisterial work on the everyday, Fernand Braudel (1979) speaks of the coordination of the durability of the long term with the minute fluctuations of low-level occurrences. In the last chapter, I tried to give different unfoldings of the relation between the ephemeral, the fleeting, and the more durable structures of society in the case of ritual and kinship.

For Braudel, behind the visible institutions of state and market lie many kinds of "basic activity which went on everywhere," the volume of which he called "fantastic." What Braudel tries to do for material life, covering the rich zone that he calls "infra-economics," one could do for the moral life. The big events that become visible because of their capacity to break into the public realm have both an antecedent life and an afterlife. These eventologies of the ordinary in the light of what comes after, as Shane Vogel (2009) elegantly puts it, require one to wait patiently to track how something new might be born. In the case of Kuldip and Saba, we see that there is not one single conversion as a turning away from a previous mode of life but rather a slow flowering of the discovery of how Saba might become the daughter by marriage of a home in which the identities Hindu and Muslim are, in any case, in an unstable relation to one another. Moreover, we see that Islam holds an attraction for Kuldip, though the specific dimensions of Islam with which he finds affinity will come only later. Each member of the family is given an opportunity to learn how to inhabit this newness, and I have tried to track closely and respectfully, to the extent that they would allow me, the ordinary moments interwoven with extraordinary events, such as Kuldip's desire in the middle of the night to learn how to say the namaz, or Kuldip's grandfather's dream that a new basti was being formed and his vision of a mosque and an old ruined temple that is never completely erased, a scene that he could interpret as a harbinger of good things to come.

There is another vision of the everyday in both Freud and Austin, which Cavell describes as "not being awake." In his words, "Each harbors, within sensibilities apparently otherwise so opposite, a sense of human beings in their everyday existence as not alive to themselves, or not awake to their lives" (Cavell 2005d, 214). What it is to become awake to one's life might be thought of by analogy with Cavell's reading of Thoreau and his pond—of Thoreau taking the time to relate a hundred details, such as the transformation of water into ice or the significance to be found in bubbles within the ice. This attentiveness to minute shifts in actions and dispositions is one way in which to inhabit the everyday: one sees something like it in the changes Kuldip's mother notices through the mediation of her mother goddess or in what Saba tries to bring about in herself so that she can connect to Kuldip's childhood. There are, of course, pressures from the lack of money, and one could hardly hold Kuldip up as some kind of moral exemplar. But, beyond his attempts to elude his debtors and perhaps some underhanded dealings here and a bit of misrepresentation there, his love for Saba brings a possibility for newness into his life. This is the possibility that, even when the national rhetoric is vitiated by a vision of a strong Hindu state in which the presence of Muslims is barely tolerated, a small community of love can come about and, at least in some lives, break the solidity of oppositional identities. This imagination of a small community of love insulates it from a wider anonymous and impersonal public—giving yet another example of the difference between a second-person perspective and a third-person perspective. As Charles Hallisey suggested to me, for Kuldip and Saba, it seems that each can be an "I" if they are also a "we." We should not read such sentiments as instantiations of global movement or aspirations for "purer" relations, as Parry rightly warns us—but nor should we assume that a love that braids together a striving for the divine and a striving for a particular other to whom one relates as a singular being cannot flourish in these neighborhoods. The improvisations in which Kuldip and Saba engage would not have been possible without the improvisations made by Kuldip's mother and his grandfather much as a musician's improvisations must take place within the improvisations of the whole orchestra. Or to put it another way— the ethical and aesthetic intertwining of "what is important" in Laugier's (2018b) persistent attention to the importance of importance finds a connection here with life in the everyday.

In a provocative essay on evil and love, Leo Bersani (2008) asks whether love can overcome evil. He invites us to think of a different way to conceptualize love and, indeed, relatedness. Developing Freud's great insight that, in love, to find an object is always to re-find it, Bersani argues that love is inseparable from memory. Thus, the loved object is already a bearer of other memories (of the mother, of an infantile, idealized self)—it cannot, despite claims to the contrary, provide an openness to the other. Bersani makes the extraordinary claim that the "beloved becomes the lover as result of being loved" and thus defines the task of love as embracing the reality of the other as one's own. In other words, what one has to overcome in love is, first, the inability to love oneself and hence the inability to love the other. Without going into the full development of his argument, what I take from Bersani's remarkable essay is the idea that love provides us with the opportunity to realize our "virtual being," which is not the idealized infantile self but rather, in my vocabulary, an adjacent self that is allowed to come into being. That course entails losses that we might even mourn—the most important loss being the security of anchorage in a solid, given identity. I find it salutary to understand that, in this urban environment, in this household struggling with everyday wants and needs, this labor of opening oneself to a different vision of what it might be to receive the other should be performed. Even before the marriage, there were indications in this household that Hindus and Muslims are not completely locked inside their identities; perhaps this instability constitutes the condition of possibility for such love to be born and to find a home. It is a picture of the moral in which we might lose the profundity of moral statements through which much of philosophy, theology, and religion (including that of the religious experts in these very neighborhoods) stages the moral. What we gain is the simple capacity to inhabit the everyday and to perform the labor of discovering what it is to engage the life of the other.

What, then, of the scholarship on Hindu-Muslim relations that has long argued that there is a profound history of hostility between Hindus and Muslims, within which the only hope for peace lies in settling for relationships in the "marketplace"? In Louis Dumont's famous formulation:

> We are faced with a reunion of men divided into two groups who devalorize each other's values and who are nevertheless associated. The association, quite inadequately studied, has had a profound effect on Hindu society and has created Muslim society of quite a special type, a hybrid type which we are scarcely in a position to characterize, except by saying that, lying beneath the ultimate or Islamic values are other values presupposed by actual behaviour . . . [there is a] permanence of psychological dispositions to the extent that each Muslim, Christian, or Lingayat has something of the Hindu in him. (Dumont [1969] 1980, 211)

It is interesting that Dumont does not ask himself whether there might be a "Muslim," for instance, within the "Hindu." Nor does he imagine that a traffic in categories might be normal in the social life of nations and persons.

However, one might refer to the long history of the attraction for the Christian or the kafir in Sufi poetry as involving a pedagogy of the soul in which a pious Muslim comes to piety after overcoming the longing for the kafir (or the Christian) beloved. As J. Andrew Bush (forthcoming) observes in his delicate reading of Kurdish Sufi poetry, the non-Muslim kafir is a tendency within the pious Muslim self. Acknowledging this tendency, he says, is both a way of cultivating humility and a reminder that small acts of infidelity proliferate in the lives of ordinary Muslims.[25]

The thesis of "devalorization" of the story of attraction across religious divides has a strong hold on many scholars and is important as a cautionary tale. Thus, though many scholars have provided evidence of "syncretic" practices in folk religion, Peter van der Veer (1994) cautions against reading a history of harmony or mutual respect into these practices. Instead, he argues that Hindus seek out Muslim shrines not as an expression of devotion but because they assume that, like untouchables, Muslim healers are able to master the spirit world and to expel malign spirits. He then goes on to conclude that the Muslim practice of saint worship is thus incorporated into impure practices typical of lower castes in a Hindu worldview. Others argue that relations between Hindu devotees and Muslim pirs are much more nuanced (Saheb 1998; Werbner and Basu 1998; Amin 2015). Terms such as "the Hindu worldview" or "the Islamic worldview" are, unfortunately, so totalizing that they leave little room for an exploration of the moral projects people might pursue because they assume that all the steps are already taken or that following rules that characterize moral pursuits are like following a pregiven grid.

To pay attention to the possibilities for both hurt and care within the contentious memories Hindus and Muslims have of each other, possibilities that increase or decrease in intensity along with the larger political projects within which their identities are implicated, is to assume neither that we can find solace in such binary oppositions as faith and ideology (Nandy 1990) nor that all relationships across the Hindu-Muslim divide are doomed to failure from the start. Instead, we might pay attention to the manner in which moral striving shows up in everyday labors of caring for the other, even in contexts where a mutual antagonism defines the relation—or, as Singh (2015) formulates it, where the relation between neighbors might be defined as one of "agnostic intimacy" in which one locked in conflict with another at one threshold of life might find that there are other thresholds of life in which one becomes, despite all expectations, attracted to that other.

# 6

## PSYCHIATRIC POWER, MENTAL ILLNESS, AND THE CLAIM TO THE REAL

*Foucault in the Slums of Delhi*

In placing Foucault among my interlocutors in the low-income areas that figure in this book and even bringing myself to call these "slums," what do I hope to achieve in this chapter? My aims are not really very lofty. In her inspiring book *Knot of the Soul*, Stefania Pandolfo (2018) hopes to bring about a real conversation between Islam and psychoanalysis through an exploration of how figuration or exemplifications works in these two paths of healing. Though she talks about the agony of culture and of a cultural tradition being reduced to the status of a living ghost, the memorable Imam with whom she converses on theological matters seems to have a very sound grip over and appreciation of the beauty and salience of the Islamic concepts of desire and of disorders of the soul. My entry into questions of madness and healing are of a different order. The protagonist of the story in this chapter is, in one sense, Swapan—a young man whose relation with his family and his neighborhood is ridden with tensions and conflict and who suffers from a psychiatric illness—but in another sense the protagonist is the neighborhood itself.[1] The healers in this neighborhood work with a variety of therapeutic practices regardless of whether they are trained biomedical practitioners or ayurvedic or Islamic healers. The world is full of spirits and ghosts and jinns; medical technologies such as injections and antibiotics and even new technologies such as kidney transplants come to live along with these densely populated figures of spirits and minor gods. It is hard to characterize the therapies as "folk" or "traditional" or "modern."[2] While

Pandolfo documents beautifully the disquieting presence of Islamic healing as the jurisprudence of the soul, which seems to have a haunting presence in her writing, I am struck by Donatelli's (2019) astute description of
my project in these neighborhoods as showing the minute texture of how
the vital "embodies the grand and the sublime, how a whole form of life,
splendid or miserable alike—is to be found in such minute moments" (53).
Let us see what critical potential might be generated from these minute moments. Unlike a conversation between two traditions (say, Islam and psychoanalysis), I am interested in seeing the crisscrossing of concepts and
technologies, asking what are the hinges and junctions (often creaky) that
define the nomadic character of power that flows between different points
such as that of the family, the psychiatric hospital, the police station? What
residue does each kind of power (sovereign, disciplinary, normalizing) secrete in the everyday as one confronts what could be named as the madness of the milieu itself?

In *Affliction* (Das 2015a), I analyze the case I present here through the
texture of Wittgenstein's *Philosophical Investigations* as providing a way to
do ethnography of psychiatric illness differently than in the dominant mode
of locating oneself in the clinic. Wittgenstein's notion of the double nature
of the everyday in which he shows through a series of examples how the everyday contains in itself the urge to deny the everyday, giving it a trancelike character, is particularly salient for understanding how madness or its
threat lines the ordinary (see Das 2007, 2015a). But so is Foucault's magisterial work on psychiatric power and especially his impulse to do philosophy
through the archive of concrete cases of madness in eighteenth- and early
nineteenth-century France in order to trace how one might understand the
working of power on the governance of life. In putting these two different
kinds of formulations in conversation with each other, I hope to show how
a form of life might be unfolded in expected and unexpected ways. Even in
the face of failures and abandonment, it is difficult for me to write as if all
one might learn from this unfolding is the erasure or cancellation of a form
of life. Even if one is sure to lose the game of the struggle with illness and
death, the way the game is played by those inhabiting these milieus is surely
worth describing.

Wittgenstein asks: "Does what is ordinary always make the *impression*
of ordinariness?" (Wittgenstein [1953] 1968, §600). If everyday life is the place
where the ordinary and the extraordinary fade into each other, how are

boundaries drawn and how are they crossed as the question of the real is engaged in relation to madness that moves between the family, the clinic, and the court? How do genealogy and ethnography open different paths to the question of subjectivation and how to be with the other? As we have seen in the earlier chapters, in his various remarks on the concept of a boundary Wittgenstein makes clear that he does not think of concepts as having boundaries with a clear division of the inside and the outside. Instead, he offers such terms as "family resemblances" or "field for force" or actions such as pointing to a region of space where you might stand without drawing a boundary around it (e.g., §71, §76, §79, p. 219ᵉ). In that spirit I want to think of madness in relation to everyday life not as completely outside everyday life but as woven into it as a possibility contained in the everyday. By traversing the concepts of normal and abnormal in a number of theorists, I try to show how concepts stand not in a vertical relation to the flux of life but as produced within and through everyday life, including the everyday life of the anthropologist.[3]

## FOUCAULT ON PSYCHIATRIC POWER AND THE MICROPHYSICS OF DISCIPLINE

In his lectures comprising *Abnormal* (1974–1975), Michel Foucault (2003) proposes the concept of normalizing power as a different modality of power than either sovereign power or disciplinary techniques. In the previous year, in his lectures comprising *Psychiatric Power* (1973–1974) he had placed greater weight on the tactics deployed in the asylum to impose "reality" on the patients (Foucault 2006). Taken together, it seems that Foucault took psychiatric power and the emergence of the figure of the abnormal as crucial for delineating how sovereign power and disciplinary power were redistributed in nineteenth-century French society. The contrast that he made between the repressive power embedded in institutions of law and punishment and the productive power expressed in internalization of norms has been enthusiastically adopted in the social sciences in general terms as providing an overarching frame for understanding the important transformations that took place in contemporary societies. At the same time, much less attention has been paid to the cadence and rhythms of psychiatric power, as Bernard Harcourt put it in the course of a discussion in 2015 at Columbia University. For instance, how is the movement across the strategies deployed by psychiatrists, the resistance offered by patients, and the subject formation of patients actualized at different moments in Foucault's writing and beyond? The rhythms underlying these movements give a more nuanced picture of what is specific to psychiatric power then general sweeping statements about the replacement of sovereign power by disciplinary power in modern societies or fixing these modes into typologies. Although, as I will argue, the reason why the psychiatrist comes to represent the workings of disciplinary power shift between the lectures Foucault gave in 1973–1974 and 1974–1975, it is important to remember that he drew repeated attention in both sets of lectures to the fact that disciplinary techniques are already available as a mode of creating docile subjects in the army or in school. What, then, is specific to psychiatric power? What does it add to these existing regulations?

First of all, let us reiterate that in Foucault's formulation, power is not "possessed" by the psychiatrist. In the first lecture in *Psychiatric Power*, Foucault clearly states what was to become his signature theme: "Power is never something that someone possesses, anymore than it is something that emanates from someone" (Foucault 2003, 4). Rather, power is the name that he gives to certain tactics of management that are released in the asylum that result in the capture of the patient's body, actions, time, history, and biography by the regime of the asylum. These tactics of management—the relays, networks, and dispersions that he puts under the name of power—however, include not only the examination of the life history of the patient through which her whole life is placed under scrutiny (somewhat akin to confessional techniques in the monastery in certain Christian orders, as Foucault points out) but also the use of physical punishment, withdrawal of food, and other body techniques effected by the agency of the "servants" in the asylum. Foucault is clear that control over the patient is not something that can be established once and for all: for every maneuver of the psychiatrist, the patient produces a countermaneuver. He gives examples of how the patient (e.g., the hysteric) may produce symptoms that do not fall into the isotopic classification prevalent, and thus such symptoms challenge the psychiatrist to bring the new symptoms under his control through new techniques. This game of maneuvers and countermaneuvers points to one important characteristic of disciplinary power as embodied in psychiatry—viz., that every new tactic in the exercise of disciplinary power produces a residue, which accounts for the fact that even more areas of the life of the patient have to be brought under the disciplinary regime. Thus, despite the occasional statements about the colonization of whole society by discipline, or power that runs in the smallest capillary branches of the social, the capture by discipline is always incomplete: it produces residues that remain uncolonized or are presented as "yet to be colonized."

Foucault's descriptions make it abundantly clear that the authority of the psychiatrist is established not through any demonstration of the greater prestige of psychiatric knowledge or its demonstrated scientific efficacy at that time (actually the stakes for psychiatry are precisely to find recognition as a branch of medical knowledge) but through tokens that signal the dominance of the psychiatrist in the asylum. Thus, Foucault says, "leaving aside for the moment the problem of why in fact such a practice could be seen as a *medical* practice, and why the people who carried out these operations had to be doctors, it seems that, in its morphology, in its general deployment, the medical operation of *the cure performed by those whom we think of as founders of psychiatry has practically nothing to do with what was then becoming the experience, observation, diagnostic activity, and therapeutic process of medicine*" (Foucault 2003, 12, emphasis added). In fact, Foucault is clear that the techniques of disciplining used in the asylum had been already worked out in other institutions but that with the opening of law to psychiatry as "expert testimony" these techniques come to be redefined as "therapeutic" for the patients, who are also cast in the role of guardians for protection of the social body. So what exactly was it that the doctor added in this game of maneuvers and countermaneuvers?

It is true that sometimes Foucault renders the shifts that occur between the eighteenth and nineteenth centuries as a complete shift from sovereign power to disciplinary power (or from law to norm), but the overall structure of the argument in *Psychiatric Power* assumes that just as there were disciplinary islands in the midst of institutions in which the dominant mode of power took the form of sovereign power (e.g., certain religious orders), so he posits the family within "disciplinary" societies as the island in which the form power takes was that of sovereign power: "Just as the disciplinary form of power existed in medieval societies, in which schemas of sovereignty were nevertheless present, I think forms of the power of sovereignty can still be found in contemporary society" (Foucault 2003, 79).

Foucault continues, "I was going to say that the family is a remnant, but this is not entirely the case. At any rate, it seems to me that the family is a sort of cell within which the power exercised is not, as one usually says, disciplinary, but rather of the same type as power of sovereignty" (Foucault 2003, 79). Later, in the same lecture, he goes on to call the family a switch point, the junction, ensuring the passage from one disciplinary system to another. At this point in his thinking, the family is also the institution that has to absorb the individual who is not educable or who cannot be disciplined by the regulatory regimes.

An important point to which I draw attention at this stage of the argument is Foucault's characterization of madness as error and the transformation of the doctor in the nineteenth century as the agent of what he calls "a surplus power of reality." What kind of power is this? For Foucault, if one had to define this power, the following provisional description could be offered: "Psychiatric power is that supplement of power by which the real is imposed on madness in the name of a truth possessed once and for all by this power on the name of medical science, of psychiatry" (Foucault 2003, 133). In other words, the problem nineteenth-century psychiatry gives itself is to deal with the simulation of reality in madness: its cure consists of creating a regime of discipline within the asylum which, through a series of deprivations, forces the mad to confront their own reality as "simulation" or "madness." The real, then, is imposed on madness not through reasoned argument but through an asylum strategy that magnifies the tokens of knowledge and power in the asylum. While in the earlier book *Madness and Civilization* (Foucault 1988) there was a fascination with madness as the discourse of unreason on reason, now madness has become much more prosaic. The power to impose reality on the mad relies much more on punishment and on simulated falsehoods created by the strategies of the psychiatrist that mirror and reverse the delusions of the mad person—strategies that can be implemented only within the asylum. For example, if someone is delusional in thinking that he belongs to royalty and is panicked that the guillotine awaits him, then a theatrical creation that simulates that reality—through, say, a tribunal that holds a trial and declares him innocent—will effect his cure. Foucault calls this kind of narrative the "classical cure" and cites the paradigmatic cases described in a widely used textbook by Philippe Pinel (famous for removing the chains in which the mad were usually bound in the asylum) that was prevalent in the eighteenth century and was found even in the earlier part of the nineteenth century. Foucault concludes that only by incorporating the language of madness within itself (as in the performances staged in the asylum) could psychiatric language intensify the real and act as the supplement to the power through which the real was established over the delusions of the mad in the space of the asylum.

Let us summarize the major features of the psychiatric "cure" and its implications for our understanding of two aspects of the cadences and rhythms of the play between sovereign power and disciplinary power.

First, the therapeutics that psychiatry releases at this point (until the early nineteenth century) are enacted through ritualized scenes in the asylum that Foucault describes as a "battle scene" in which the confrontation is staged between the will of the psychiatrist as expressed not in any individual consciousness informed by new knowledge into the causes or treatment of madness but in the tactics, punishments, deprivations, etc., enacted in the asylum. The repeated characterizations of these scenes as "theatrical" or "ritualized" spaces is very interesting because, similar to theater and ritual, what madness creates is an "as-if" reality. Might the difference, then, between ritual and theater, on the one hand, and therapy, on the other, be that in the case of theater and ritual, these performances know themselves to be creating a simulated reality, while in madness the simulation is not a knowing simulation but replaces the access to reality itself? A corollary that follows is that the outcome of the battle between psychiatrist and patient is that the patient must forgo his delusions and be stripped of the hold of the "as-if" reality by the kinds of punishments and deprivations that are enacted in the asylum. Thus, the doctor here is recast as someone who is the agent of an intensified real.

Second, one never reaches a conclusion in this battle: each victory on the part of the psychiatrist creates a residue through the patient's ability to produce new symptoms. This is best demonstrated in the case of the hysteric in whose case the very simulation of symptoms that the psychiatric knowledge cannot understand leads to a greater hold over the life of the patient whose whole life comes to be put under the psychiatric gaze. Foucault calls the hysteric the "antihero" and notes that the very resistance the hysteric puts up, in this case, authorizes greater subjection and the creation of subjectivity through such modes of subjection.

Third, while the category of "crisis" disappears from medical knowledge in general because the development of statistical medicine and pathological anatomy create the space for reading symptoms in a new manner, in the case of madness the notion of crisis remains crucial because psychiatry is called in on behalf of sovereign power (either the family or the state) to give a decision: Is this person mad or is she a criminal, as in the case of motiveless crimes adjudicated in courts of law? Or is this child fit to be part of the family or must she be removed to an institution, as in the case of a child experimenting with sex? It is not the patient who calls in the psychiatrist to give her symptoms a status, character, and specification (as in differential diagnosis) but the family or state that wants the disciplinary authority of psychiatry to intervene at the point of decision to draw a line between madness and nonmadness, fiction and reality. It is true that later Foucault argues that with the discovery of instinct as psychological category the more generic category of the abnormal is born, but for our purposes the idea of psychiatric power as manifested not only in the policing of families but also in making the psychiatrist an agent for the imposition and intensification of the real has important implications.

Finally, if the asylum is the place where the psychiatric drama unfolds—combining in itself the power to regulate, to punish, and to redefine the real—the family is the hinge between a form of power that is sovereign (as in the power of the father) and disciplinary institutions, a junction at which the individual comes to be moved between different disciplinary institutions (school, army, asylum).

We shall see how these features, as well as the hinges and junctions between the different forms that power takes, are present in the case study I revisit, but they are present only as echoes through which we see how a dynamic play of forces that produce what, following Povinelli (2011), one might profitably call "quasi-events" (Das 2015a) but with an important qualification. Povinelli defines "quasi-events" in this way: "If events are things that we can say happened such that they have a certain objective being, then quasi-events never take the status of having occurred or taken place. They neither happen nor not happen. I am not interested in these quasi-events in some abstract sense, but in the concrete ways that they are, or are not, aggregated and thus apprehended, evaluated and grasped as ethical and political demands in specific late liberal markets, publics and states, as opposed to crises and catastrophes that seem to necessitate ethical reflection and political and civic engagement" (Povinelli 2011, 13). Thus, Povinelli's interest is in tracking those moments in which either through statistical aggregation or through mediatization these quasi-events that embody suffering that is routine and cruddy are made to gather such weight that they might become the subject of state attention. My interest takes a related but different turn. I hope to see the unfolding of these quasi-events in which sometimes the family opens itself to the state or to medical institutions that appear at one threshold of life (Singh 2015) and at other times they become dormant or absent, corresponding to different rhythms and cadences of both disciplinary power and sovereign power. Before I turn to these issues, though, I need to make a quick foray into the neighboring concept of normalizing power that makes a brief entry into the lectures of the following year but then is swallowed within disciplinary power.

## NORM, NORMALIZATION, AND NORMALIZING POWER

In the following year (1974–1975), Foucault organized his course around the figure of the abnormal. This time we encounter the psychiatrist not in the asylum but in the courtroom and, as he says, "psychiatry no longer seeks to cure, or in its essence no longer seeks to cure. It can offer merely to protect society from being the victim of the definitive dangers represented by people in abnormal condition" (Foucault 2003, 316). I do not propose to go through a full genealogy to demonstrate how this transformation happens, but I will pose some specific issues with regard to normalizing power.

In his lecture of January 15 of that year, Foucault cites Georges Canguilhem's (1991) book *The Normal and the Pathological* for the ideas he considers historically and methodologically fruitful. First, he draws attention to the general process of normalization in the eighteenth century and the multiplication of its effects. Second, he cites the "important idea" that the norm is not defined as a natural law but rather by the exacting and coercive role it can perform in the domains in which it is applied. The point Foucault emphasizes in Canguilhem is the element of the norm on which a certain exercise of power is founded and legitimized. "Canguilhem calls it a polemical concept. Perhaps we could say it is a political concept" (Foucault 2003, 50). It is interesting to see which aspects of Canguilhem's discussion are elided and what consequences these might have in the different trajectories that the discussion of norm takes in these two authors.[4]

Canguilhem famously states with reference to health: "Strictly speaking, a norm does not exist, it plays its role, which is to devalue existence by allowing its correction" (Canguilhem 1991, 77). It is pathology, he says, that renders possible physiology and medicine. Pathology also defines life itself as dynamic, for a life unmarked by any disease would be abnormal. There are two paths for discussion that these observations open up: the first is what makes knowledge possible and the second is how a living body relates to this "absent" norm. In Canguilhem's words, "If health is life lived in the silence of the organs, then, strictly speaking, there is no science of health. Health is organic innocence. It must be lost, like all innocence, so that knowledge may be possible" (Canguilhem 1991, 101). Thus, the historicity of scientific discourse must begin with the infractions; only through error can nature be known. On the epistemic level, I see a rapport between Canguilhem and Foucault, but while Canguilhem is concerned with the way that the individual not only incorporates norms but also generates new norms, Foucault ends up assimilating normalizing power into disciplinary power. For Canguilhem, disease is an experiment with life leading him to think of the polarity in life, the two kinds of original modes of life: the normatively normal in which the normal constants may be transcended and the pathologically normal in which the death of normativity itself is coded. Thus, while Canguilhem expresses the gap between the norm and the multiple actualizations in terms of a series of negatives—failure, monster, negative value, error, mistake—he clearly sees that new norms are generated by disease, as Goldstein's clinical observations on patients with head wounds who settle for a more restricted environment exemplified for him. Thus, while both Foucault and Canguilhem go together some of the way, for Canguilhem disease is a debate with the milieu and in that sense the process of normalization must generate not (only) resistance but a different debate with the milieu (see Han and Das 2015).[5] In contrast, by assimilating normalizing power to a modality of disciplinary power, the subject comes into being not so much by her investment in the norm as by becoming penetrated by it, as discourse passes through the subject almost like a bolt. The psychiatrist as a figure of authority establishes the "truth" of his knowledge by psychiatry's readiness to absorb what becomes insoluble in other domains, such as the impasse created in law: for instance, in his discussion in *Abnormal*, Foucault shows that faced with motiveless crime, law encounters an impasse—the criminal must be punished, but in the absence of motive she cannot be punished.[6] At this point, room is made for the figure of the psychiatrist whose testimony converts the crime into an illness, yet the knowledge wielded by the physiatrist is itself shaky and insecure in relation to medical knowledge based on clinical pathology and statistical knowledge. In several places, Foucault compares the figure of the psychiatrist to that of Ubu—the sovereign as grotesque (cf. Foucault 2003, 28n20). The function of psychiatry becomes that of isolating those who are seen as dangerous: the career of the dangerous individual that will receive elaboration through the security apparatus of the state is launched, but I must leave this story now to turn to the dimension of the subject.

## THE SUBJECT: IN WHOSE CONSCIOUSNESS DOES THE DISEASE/INFRACTION ARISE?

For both Canguilhem and Foucault, the subject is not a phenomenological subject but one created through specific modes of subjectivation that have historical specificity. Yet, for Canguilhem it is the experience of the patient and not simply deviations from the norm measured through laboratory procedures that gives rise to medical knowledge. One might say that the founding moment for medical knowledge is the suffering consciousness of the patient. The creation of new norms lies at the cusp of vital and social norms and it is the living subject that generates new norms—though these are inferior norms effective only in more restrictive environments. Medical knowledge and the normativity of life are generated together: the norms being actualized have a double character in what becomes sayable and in what is normalized. Despite the impression sometimes created in Canguilhem that individual norms are generated through the decisions of a sovereign subject, in fact it is in relation to the milieu (in debate with it) and in variations in the individual life course that new norms are generated. The individual is the site for the play between disease and life. For Foucault, however, the investment in the norm occurs on the model of a force: at times it seems like the norm passes through the individual coming as a bolt or penetrates the individual rather than being internalized through a pedagogical process. At least as far as the discussion in *Abnormal* is concerned, newness is tracked more at the level of public institutions and in the switches between judicial and medical discourse than in the experimentation between the individual and her disease. Unlike Canguilhem's individual, Foucault's individual is standing before the court as the accused, or he or she is in the confessional, or caught in sexual infringements and handed over for psychiatric evaluation by the family or the village. As the case of the accused Jouy, discussed in *Abnormal*, a youth marginal to the village who was caught after the sexual violation of a little girl, the infringement arises in the consciousness of the family, and once it reaches the public prosecutor the accusation becomes one of the disturbance of public order.[7] It is not the suffering individual who demands or seeks psychiatric care, rather the individual is made into the accused in the process of becoming a psychiatric object of action. In Jouy's case, "it seems, moreover, that the village itself had taken responsibility for the affair and had transferred it to a completely different level from that of the slaps expected by the young girl. The mayor was gripped by the case, and it is the mayor who called in the public prosecutor. Furthermore, after the report of the psychiatric experts, the entire population of Loupcourt, the name of the village, keenly desired that the little Sophie Adams (the girl) to be confined in a house of correction until she came of age" (Foucault 2003, 290). We could say that the object on which psychiatric power operates is different from either the individual or the population—this object, as Foucault says, is the social body. After the discovery of instinct, Foucault shows that the crime/psychiatric illness pair fade as characteristics attached to particular types of persons. Instead, the discovery of instinct in psychology universalizes the potential for the abnormal as a potential to be found in every man or woman. Later, another revision will allow the potential of crime to be attached to specific social groups defined by race, as today terrorism has come to be defined as a potential inhering in Muslims as a community.

Let me summarize, for my purposes, three questions that can be posed at the intersection of the two books I have discussed: First, if the psychiatrist in relation to the individual patient is the agent for the intensification of the real but the techniques used are derived more from available regulatory regimes rather than medical knowledge per se, could there be others through whom this function of the real—i.e., dismantling the as-if structure of the real that the mad person has constructed—could be accomplished? If so, then what are the mechanisms through which this might happen?

Second, if the form that power takes in the family is that of sovereign power and if the dominance of regulatory regimes results in the family being forced to absorb individuals who are not "normative" in the new dispensations of power, then what disorders does this create in the family? Does the family end up replicating the structure of crime and punishment that sovereign power uses in the public domain (recall that for Foucault the family can never act as a simple agent of the state or of medical power though it is deeply shaped by these)?

Third, in relation to the real, is madness to be placed on the side of error and pathology exclusively, or does it have possibilities for the creation of new norms by shifting the debate that the individual might have with his or her milieu?[8]

## ETHNOGRAPHY IN COMPANY OF GENEALOGY

In Foucault's description of madness, the psychiatrist is always present in the place of decision whether this be in the therapeutic ritualized scenes in the asylum; the point of impasse in the court when the law is presented with a motiveless crime; or as the one who certifies who can be removed from the family or the village as the "dangerous individual." Although the family is present and is regarded as a crucial institution and the hinge or junction for flows between sovereign power and disciplinary power, we do not see how madness unfolds within the family. I want to make a shift in this scene to ask: what happens before the arrival of the psychiatrist and after his disappearance? In my depiction of Swapan's case that follows, I understand it primarily by thinking of the tempo of skepticism as it engulfs everyday life. Taking a cue from narrative medicine in which patients with psychiatric illness are often characterized as having lost the "self," I argue that what had been lost was not something that resided in the person but a way of *being in the world*. Thus, a description of madness, I contend, would require that we tell the story as if the person was located not inside the body but in the network of relations, affects, and encounters. In effect, to understand madness we would have to ask what forms of life could grow the kinds of words that a person like Swapan, the protagonist of this account, speaks. I take the opportunity now to open up some issues in tandem with Foucault's picture of normalizing power.[9] In order to do this, I will take certain points in the story when the family opens itself to both the intervention by the state and the intervention by a psychiatric institution. I hope to show that what we get are echoes of the powers that Foucault delineated, but these never crystallize into a decisive consolidation of psychiatric power or disciplinary power, leading one to think harder (or more closely) about what constitutes the norm and what its infringement.

The young, twenty-year-old boy Swapan lived in a low-income neighborhood in Delhi in the family composed of his father, mother, older brother, and younger sister. The large, sprawling neighborhood located in West Delhi where Swapan lived started as a cluster of *jhuggis* (temporary shanty houses) built by refugees from Pakistan erected as temporary shelters in 1947 as they fled the massive violence and chaos of that period. There were also clusters of jhuggis constructed in different phases by migrants from nearby villages—primarily members of "untouchable" castes who migrated in search of work. As the refugees and migrants became more affluent, they converted the *kaccha* (mud and brick) houses into *pucca* (cement and brick) houses, adding rooms, terraces, and shops. The neighborhood, however, does not have the legal status of an authorized colony, so the provision of public services such as sanitation or the supply of clean drinking water is in a dismal state. Thus, people live in a state of economic and legal precarity, but this has not reduced them to passivity. Elsewhere (Das 2011a; Das and Walton 2015) I describe the specific forms that political action takes in negotiations of patron-client ties, legal strategies, and use of electoral politics in order to get a measure of security for housing, provisioning of water, electricity, or other services. Aspirations for education, secure jobs, or wealth are expressed in many ways: getting private tutors for children so that they can pass their exams and get admission in college; attempting to find "connections" that might open pathways to a government job; mobilizing social and political connections that the population density of slums might open up. Simone (2004) argues people in such circumstances act as the infrastructure. Despite these efforts, though, the actual routes toward upward mobility are achieved through somewhat clandestine activities, such as participation in party politics that includes the underside of politics, becoming middlemen in the complex web of relations between illegal transactions and provision of services, land grabbing, and many other such activities always on the borderline of the legal and illegal.

It is in this environment that Swapan's madness unfolds. In the following pages, I zoom in on various points of crisis that shifted the fragile agreements within the family and the neighborhood, opening the family to local agents of the state at one time and psychiatric confinement at another. In each case we see that the moves and countermoves between these different actors lead not to consolidation of power but to a secretion of residues that then morph into contests over the real in which neither the patient nor the psychiatrist are able to prevail.

My interactions with Swapan did not begin with a crisis. Rather, in the course of weekly morbidity surveys that a team of researchers at ISERDD was conducting in 2001[10] in the sample households in this neighborhood, Swapan's mother and sister were reporting frequent minor injuries that remained initially unexplained and were later admitted by them to be caused by Swapan's frequent bouts of anger and physical fights. A visiting doctor who was helping during this survey had suggested that Swapan's family should consult a psychiatrist—before this the family had consulted local diviners because it was thought that he might be suffering from the machinations of some mischievous spirit with unsatisfied desires. None of the diviners had been able to identify the spirit that was causing mischief. The main concern in the family was that Swapan had failed in his tenth-grade exam and he was not able to hold any job that could make him economically productive. From these diffused anxieties, the case moved to more crystallized moments of crises.

First, Swapan's mother's complaints against him began to take on an urgency.

"He wanders around." "What can I do?" "He just does not agree" (*manta hi nahin hai*).[11] He saw what that doctor from Amrika (America) had written on a paper (advising the family to see a psychiatrist) and he got very angry. He said, Do they think I am mad? He wanted to tear it and throw it away. As I describe elsewhere (Das 2015a), it was becoming more popular in the neighborhood to believe that psychiatric treatment might be able to help in cases where a diviner could not locate a malevolent spirit in a person suffering from some form of madness. But Swapan's family did not seem to be invested enough in him to find the time to take him to the outpatient department (OPD) of a public hospital, and private providers in the area were not yet treating such cases with anything except by dispensing sleeping pills.

The first crisis that the family identified as indicative of some kind of serious disorder occurred at the end of the year when Swapan consistently refused to bathe or eat. He was smelly and dirty, but above all, the refusal to eat food cooked by the women of the house, especially one's mother, was seen as a complete abrogation of relationships. "He says he will not eat anything touched by my hands," said his mother. "I am *his own mother* and he won't eat things touched by my hands. Now you tell me . . . [*ab aap batao*]."[12] However, there was no effort to involve any other institution. Even within the kinship group Swapan's mother was not on good terms with his uncles and aunts who might have otherwise mediated in the conflict.

Over a few months, the relation between the mother and the son had deteriorated to an extent that Swapan's mother felt completely overwhelmed. Urged by his mother, I asked Swapan, why he did not want to go to the doctor. "Who will take me?" he said in a challenging rather than despondent tone.

Taken by surprise, I said, "I will." The following conversation ensued:

SWAPAN: My problem is not that I am mad. My problem is that no one takes interest in me. [He used the English word "interest"—*mere mein koi interest nahin leta*.]

VEENA: What do you mean, no one takes interest in you?

SWAPAN: See, I failed in my tenth exam. I was always a good student. Math is my only weakness. I could not pass the math exam. Now what my mother wants is that I should work in a factory—*work in a factory* for 1500 rupees a month. Earn money. But I will not work in anyone's factory. I want to pass my exam.

MOTHER (directly addressing me): You know our financial condition. How much money have I spent on him? We say, be ashamed—a big man—sitting and eating at home—look at your sister—are you not ashamed?

VEENA: But what he has is an illness. [Turning to Swapan] What you have is an illness. Like you have blood pressure or something—you take medicine and you will feel better. [I was trying to impress on his mother that his behavior was not a result of a moral defect so that the game of blame might be calmed somewhat.]

SWAPAN: Will I be okay (be cured)? [The Hindi expression "*theek ho jaunga*" encompasses both nuances of *normal* and *cure*.]

I did manage to take Swapan to a psychiatrist accompanied by his mother and an aunt, but after two visits the consultations stopped because, although the psychiatrist was not charging a fee, the family was not able to come up with the money or time to take him there and to buy him medicine. As the psychiatrist explained to me, if Swapan had to depend on his parents for transport and medicine, he would not be able to sustain the treatment.

## SUSTAINING THE REAL

In the cases of madness encountered in Foucault's *Psychiatric Power*, the delusions of the mad were grand delusions and the treatment in the asylum consisted of instilling the reality of the madness in the patient by the use of punitive power—such as dousing with water, deprivation of food, or else by staging an illusion that would free the patient of his illusion (e.g., by staging a mock trial that declares the patient who thinks he is royalty and thus destined for the guillotine to be innocent). But in the case of the slums, the "as-if" reality is both quotidian and pervasive—for example, the hope that getting a degree, learning English, will get the person a "good government job" or, even better, the possibility to become a "film star." Swapan, in some ways, was simply taking the promissory notes of the modern state at face value.[13] The reality the mother was trying to impose on Swapan is the reality of the slums—a factory job, or intermittent positions in courier companies as delivery boys, or other positions that boys accepted as they overcame the dreams of their youth. In such cases, one might describe the normal as in a stage of "pathological normativity" in the sense that Canguilhem uses the term to show how disease leads to the setting of new norms by the individual that allows her to function by restricting the environment. Swapan's madness was indicative of the fact that he refused this form of normativity, and the psychiatrist too recognized the impossibility of imposing the "real" on his condition. Swapan was not so much "resisting" psychiatric power as interrogating what it would mean to be cured if the cure was to accept the demeaning reality of the slum that the future lay in a low-paying factory job rather than a "respectable" job that he felt he was capable of achieving.

## THE SHAPE SOVEREIGN POWER TAKES

In the middle of January 2004, an event occurred that signaled another crisis, as told by Swapan's mother.

> Last night Swapan beat me up so badly that I lost consciousness. Gudiya here, she was crying out loudly, "He is killing my mother." Swapan locked himself in the downstairs room fearing the neighbors would come out and perhaps beat him up, but the neighbors did not want to get involved. His father was not at home, nor was my elder son at home. Gudiya and I snuck out in the street and went to a telephone booth from where we called the police. Now, what could we do? There was danger to life [*ab kya karte—jan ka khatra tha*].

The upshot was that two constables from the neighboring precinct came to the house. At first, they were sympathetic to the account of the episode given by Swapan's mother and sister. They shouted at Swapan. "What kind of son are you? Aren't you ashamed? Your sister is studying for her twelfth grade. She needs peace. Don't you know how much pressure is put on the brain when one studies for a board exam? And look at you—sitting and eating on your parents' charity." A policeman even slapped Swapan. At this point, some neighbors summoned Swapan's father from his shop. His father seemed to have given a different version of events to the constable, who now began to admonish the mother. "Why don't you love him? Why don't you give him food? Is he not the child of your womb? Is your daughter more your child?" The neighbors intervened and said that the fights in the family were disturbing everyone. The constables took Swapan to the police station. In a panic, Swapan's father begged a local leader to do something for his son. They went together to the police station and Swapan wrote a letter of apology and promised to behave in the future. Such mediations by local leaders, who resemble the Big Men (Godelier and Strathern 1991), help to create what I call "brokered selves" (Das 2004).[14] Swapan's mother was crying as she told me: "At that moment in the police station, he [her husband] became his [Swapan's]. He [her husband] gave me *dhoka*—betrayed me. He told me that Gudiya and you can go to your sister's house or wherever you wish— my son is going to stay here." "Now I have become the enemy," she said. "I fear for my life."

An important point Foucault makes with regard to the family is that the form its power takes is that of sovereign power—thus the individual subjected to disciplinary regimes is not the isolated atomized individual directly put under surveillance by the state or the disciplinary power of medicine but one who had been hooked into the disciplinary institutions through the power of the family. While the family of the seventeenth and eighteenth centuries, he argues, was homogenous with other apparatuses of sovereignty, and hence also fuzzy in its boundaries, in the case of disciplinary institutions it is the microphysics of power through which family is not so much dissolved as concentrated, limited, and intensified (Foucault 2003, 82–83). Interestingly, in the case of Swapan, when the police were called in to avert an emergency within the family, they could not decide whether to side with the father or the mother.[15] There is a performance of the regulatory power of the police but the exercise of "discipline" is not sustained: if the family here mimics sovereign power, its anchor in the power of the father is more like a parody because the resources for the intensification of the family as a cell of sovereignty have been dissolved by the conditions prevailing in the slums. The strategies, relays, maneuvers, and countermaneuvers certainly leave some residues, such as a warning to Swapan as well as the more active role that the neighborhood begins to take in the matter of Swapan, but these are not residues on which either form of power could be further consolidated.[16]

## THE PSYCHIATRIST ENTERS THE SCENE

One evening soon after this event, Swapan beat his mother badly by stealthily gaining entry to her side of the house. In desperation, she made a phone call to her sister and said, "My life is in danger." Her sister called Rajan (my colleague) and asked that we all should come to their house urgently. I told her that I did not want a stalemate between the maternal kin and the paternal kin. I said, "When you can assemble together someone who can represent the paternal side and someone the maternal side, then we can meet to find a way out." She promised to do so.

When we reached their house, the mother's sister and the father's sister were there. It seemed the father had been there but had just left for the shop. Seeing me, Swapan's maternal aunt began to tell me how much her sister (Swapan's mother) had suffered. I noticed a very important division of voices along the wife-givers and wife-takers. The mother's sister as the accuser took on the role of those who had given a daughter to the house. The father's sister was representing the "wife takers."

"How long will *our sister* keep getting beaten up by *a son* of your side?" Notice that Swapan was now assimilated into the wife-receivers. He was not the son of the mother anymore but a member of the agnatic lineage to which his father's sister also belonged. The father's sister appeared ashamed and said that she agreed that something needed to be done. "But how can we call the police against our own 'son?'" she asked. I again put it to them that it would be better to treat Swapan like a patient rather than a criminal. We wondered if the various prescriptions he had from the previous visits to the psychiatrist would serve as some kind of certification that Swapan should be in a hospital. I offered to take them to the psychiatrist so they could discuss the difficulties with him.

Swapan's mother, his maternal aunt, Rajan and Simi (my two colleagues from ISERDD), and I went to the polyclinic. In the psychiatrist's office Swapan's mother started to cry, so the aunt asked the psychiatrist what they should do under the circumstances. They wanted Swapan to be admitted to a private hospital, but they had no money. The psychiatrist explained that it would be very expensive to admit him to a private facility and suggested admission in the Institute of Human Behavior and Allied Sciences, which is a public hospital for treatment of psychiatric disorders. "Oh, that is the *pagalkhana*—the mad house," exclaimed Swapan's aunt. "But we have heard that they tie up patients and beat them there."[17] I was nervous that it might be difficult to get admission there, because they have a long waiting list and I did not have any influential friends who could intercede on our behalf. The psychiatrist said, "I don't know if my reference will count at all, but it may help." He wrote a referral requesting that Swapan had been under his care and because he was noncompliant and had shown violent tendencies, it was not possible to care for him at home and so hospitalization was recommended. Armed with this referral we returned to their home. I was still trying to ensure that the family took the responsibility of any decisions they made in this regard.[18]

Swapan's paternal aunt agreed that they should try to get the men of the family and some neighbors to take Swapan to the hospital, if necessary by force. She said that her brother (i.e., Swapan's father) and she had no objection to this course of action. "Be certain," said the mother's sister, "later don't tell me that you took away our son a 'boy' of our house into an asylum." "No, no, do what you wish." Thus, the paternal voice embodied in the father's sister was allowed to serve the paternal function of decision-maker. Both genealogy and carnality had been taken into account and we see again the dispersal of the father function—only not in the way Foucault delineates for the family in "disciplinary societies" in which he sees it as analogous to the multiplication of the king's bodies in the mutual acceptance of heterotopic sovereignties in the game of "societies of sovereignty" (Foucault 2003, 82).

The next day we get a phone call from Swapan's sister, Gudiya. Her paternal uncles had come in the morning. Her uncle (father's brother) had explained to Swapan that no one was abandoning him, that he needed treatment and that as soon as he was better, they would bring him back home. He was taken to hospital and admitted. He did not resist admission or treatment any longer. Swapan was put on medication and was discharged after a month.

In this period, Rajan and Simi (my colleagues) visited him once a week but I had to leave for the United States soon after. When he was discharged from the hospital, Swapan was told that he must attend the outpatient department once in two weeks. He would receive medications at the nominal price of ₹10 (approximately 25 cents in 2004) per visit.

At this moment in the unfolding crisis, the family did act as the sovereign through the agency of the father's elder brother. However, the family is not the diminished cell whose power intensifies by the restriction of the proliferation through which various others are included: the exercise of sovereign power is the moment when the child can be plugged into the disciplinary regime of the asylum though the asylum itself is hardly capable to enacting the kinds of ritualized scenes Foucault describes and Swapan ends up not giving up his own reality but intensifying it as revealed in the following episodes. First, I describe a letter he wrote when he was about to be released from the mental hospital and then a brief scene between us—Swapan and me.

## EXCERPTS FROM A LETTER WRITTEN (IN HINDI) ON THE PATIENT SHEET BY SWAPAN WHILE IN HOSPITAL

Deservedly worshiped Mummy and Papa,[19]

I want to say this to you. Now I have no complaints against Mummy, Gudiya and Nitin. Now I, love you all very much. . . . I pray that mummy and papa, must come here [to visit]. If they come, I will be encouraged. By their not coming I will be broken. To mummy, forgiveness from me—I want to be [stand] defeated by her—I also pray to Gudiya that she should forget my beatings and forgive her brother.

I had commented on this fragment in the narrative in my book thus: "I don't draw attention to this letter to say that finally the tensions were resolved, but to point out the ambiguous way in which Swapan gestures towards the crime of the mother as being both the one from whom he seeks forgiveness and the one he forgives. The juxtaposition of the sentences—forgiveness *from* me as well as I stand defeated—point not to a resolution but to an uncertain future" (Das 2015a, 103). Here too the episode leaves residues that were to make the final leap Swapan took toward the intensification of his own reality become lethal as he gave up on the mental health clinic altogether.

The end of this story for me corresponded to the end of interactions with this family as they suddenly moved away from the neighborhood. It goes as follows: Toward the end of the month after his discharge from the hospital, Swapan had an adverse reaction to the drugs he was given and his tongue started swelling and hanging out. He was taken to a local practitioner (by his father) who administered an injection. Swapan got better but now decided on his own to take only one of the prescribed medicines. When I learned this, I told him that we must talk to the psychiatrist at the OPD. Simi was with him at the OPD the next time and she asked the attending psychiatrist as to why Swapan was not getting psychotherapy—his discharge sheet had said he would be receiving counseling. The attending psychiatrist looked at the file and said that it was the wrong file. Another file was summoned. Swapan was taken to another psychiatrist—another set of medicines was prescribed. I felt dejected as I thought that they do not tie up patients and beat them anymore, but with three minutes per patient in the crowded OPD, mistakes will happen.[20]

On my last visit to his house that winter, Swapan said to me, "Aunty, do you have a PhD?" I replied yes but was intrigued by the question. He said, switching to English, "You must be good in studies." In the entire time I had known him (close to five years), I had never spoken to Swapan in English—never assumed that he could speak English. So I said, "Swapan, you are speaking in English!" He replied proudly, ". . . Yes in the hospital I met a professor like you. He told me my English is good, and in the hospital I was speaking in English and he helped me." Then, after some reflection, he added, "Perhaps now my career will be made."

Foucault says of the residue that the working of disciplinary power in the eighteenth century created residues in the form of abnormalities and irregularities. It was upon these abnormalities and irregularities that the nineteenth-century system drew profit and reinforcement of power that was finally to be turned into the normalizing power of disciplines. The greatest difference between Foucault's account and the cases I have encountered in the field (not only Swapan but also those possessed by malevolent spirits; a Hindu obsessively enacting the drama of having been abducted by Allah, the Islamic God; a ghost who attaches herself to a healer; a young Muslim girl possessed and troubled by one Mr. Tyagi whose identity no one could discern; a girl settling for a psychiatric diagnosis as a means of handling her father's anger) lies in the fact that the residue was not marshaled for a normalizing power to colonize new areas of life. Rather, these residues settled into the interstices between different modalities of power, sometimes producing new ways of engaging life and at other times producing death in the form of a "letting die." I am hesitant to think that this "letting die" is simply the work of the biopolitical state as would be the case if we confined "letting die" to the exceptional cases of birth, reproduction, and technological dying, as suggested by Rabinow and Rose who contend that these are the sites in which residues of the "letting die" aspect of biopower settle.[21]

If Swapan had killed his mother, which he repeatedly threatened to do, the discourse of the moral monster might have been activated in court, but several factors that emerged contingently and intermittently from actions of neighbors, kin, the police, the psychiatric institutions, and even the anthropologist and her colleagues prevented this eventuality. We can see that in inserting his desire (for English and for modernity) in the hospital setting, Swapan created a series of doubles: first, the doubling of his mother as the tormenter and the victim and then in the figure of the professor (doubling the mad professor and the anthropologist professor) representing a world out of reach but that could be still intermittently touched.

## THOUGHTS FOR A CONCLUSION

In revising the case of Swapan along with a rereading of Foucault's lectures on psychiatric power, I set for myself an experiment. As every anthropologist knows, however intimately one comes to know people in one's field sites, there is opacity to events and people that one encounters. My ethnographic impulse was one in which I tried hard to decipher "what is going on." This is more difficult than it seems at first sight, for as I argue elsewhere (see Das 2015c, 71), the characteristic of the ordinary—that we cannot see it directly precisely because it is before our eyes—means that we have to imagine what the labor of making the everyday appear entails. In thinking of Swapan and many other such cases, I was compelled by Wittgenstein's formulation on the trancelike character that everyday life can take and the scepter of madness that lines the everyday.

The delusions I encountered were not grand delusions—they were anchored in the concreteness of everyday reality of the slum. So, I ask myself,

Why does Foucault matter to me? After all, not only are his notions of disciplinary power and the specific form psychiatric power takes closely tied to historical events in France, but also there is no purchase for me in the idea that the form power takes in societies like India will replicate what is happening in the West today at some future time in the inevitable march of biology becoming the motor of history. The attraction of Foucault lies for me in the details—for instance, in his isolation of psychiatric power as speaking on the name of medical authority to impose a version of reality that would replace the delusional reality constructed by the mad person. The exquisite ironies he unearths from the historical record show that medical authority in eighteenth-century France rests on nothing more than the magnification of the symbols of psychiatric power in the asylum. Similarly, it is in the mechanisms of hinges, junctions, switches, and impasses that we see how restless and mobile are the strategies, relays, maneuvers, and counter-maneuvers as they move in the interstices of the given fault lines of a society. Yet, it is not that Foucault gives us the social and Wittgenstein the existential. Rather, we might use Wittgenstein's idea of "aspect dawning" (Wittgenstein [1953] 1968, 194$^e$–195$^e$) to argue that the matter is not of one theoretical formulation being right and another being wrong. Looking closely at mechanisms of power made me realize that cases from urban slums might demonstrate a different life of the residues of each attempt to colonize madness than was available to Foucault from the archives, however fruitful this engagement between philosophy and history has proven to be.

To return to Swapan's case, one commentary on Foucault it offers is that if madness is located primarily in the asylum and the court, it will perhaps reveal the anxieties of psychiatry more than it will reveal the various ways in which the mad person's reality confronts other realities. Even more striking is the fact that at least one of the psychiatrists in Swapan's case recognizes that Swapan has a good understanding of who has a stake in his cure and who in his madness. If our concern is with the expansion of psychiatric knowledge, then the patient's resistance becomes of interest because it opens the path for more areas of the patient's life to be brought under the disciplinary power of the asylum or of medical science itself. However, we could bring a different lens with which to see Swapan's move from one crisis to another: sometimes his symptoms were in the nature of a challenge (his refusal to eat food cooked by his mother, his refusal to bathe) and at other times they were a search for a foothold in which his aspirations could find a place (his learning English). It suggests to me that the patient is not simply offering countermaneuvers as a form of resistance but trying to find ways toward an ordinary realism, even the ability to inhabit what Canguilhem called a pathological normativity. Wittgenstein helps us in thinking what it is to lose your foothold—to fall into a trancelike everyday. Many people in these very localities managed to find succor within the everyday, striving toward an eventual everyday that seemed more modest but demanded formidable work on the environment or on repair of relationships.

The tragedies, small or big—of untimely deaths, or of falling into addiction, madness, or a temptation to simply withdraw from the world as the world withdrew from oneself—were never fully evaded. But in the heterogeneity of life as it was lived, one saw that the subjectivity of a person, though constituted significantly by the forms of subjection to which one was exposed, was not exhausted by the subject positions. In Foucault I find that the potentiality of the residues gives his theories of power a dynamism—as in Wittgenstein I find that the ability to concede that the doubts that line the everyday are doubts against which one is neither allowed to win nor to lose—opening the path for me to imagine an ordinary realism. That some, like Swapan, will not find their way back to the ordinary leaves us with a melancholy that ethnographic work also inevitably entails when one has to say, with Wittgenstein, my spade is turned. Yet, not right at the beginning, for each of us must find her own path to understand what it means to respond and how.

# 7

# THE BOUNDARIES OF THE "WE"

*Cruelty, Responsibility, and Forms of Life*

The kinds of concerns around "pathological normativity" that I delineated in the last chapter made me turn to the literary to ask[1]: If the present conditions of our life are framed by practices of violence perpetrated through the apparatus of the state with the connivance of citizens, then what kind of responsibility devolves on us, members of such political communities, even if we have not given our explicit consent to such projects of spectacular or hidden violence? Do such conditions that make our societies unjust in an overall sense make our thought itself clouded? How might we then recover the ability to think otherwise? In this chapter, I shift registers to follow these questions through a triangulated reading of two novels of J. M. Coetzee—*Waiting for the Barbarians* (1982) and *Diary of a Bad Year* (2007)—along with the interpretations of these novels offered by the philosopher/psychoanalyst, Jonathan Lear (2008, 2015). The issues regarding ethics, responsibility, and the vulnerability of our forms of life are now approached from a different angle, but they continue to be animated by the overall project of the book.

An important feature of Coetzee's novels is that the form of writing seems integral to the task of generating ethical thinking by inviting the reader to form a relation to the novel that is not based on the authority of the author. Thus, the protagonist in his novels is someone who might be seen as a version of Coetzee—even though the most explicit doubling happens only in *Diary of a Bad Year*, in which the aging writer is even named JC and, like Coetzee, is an exile from South Africa, who, sometime in his past, has written a novel called *Waiting for the Barbarians*. If the author figure is thus somewhat deformed in his novels so that his authority is not at all evident in this fictional space, the reader is also addressed in more ways than one, leaving some choices open as to how we as readers will respond to this question of responsibility. This stance to the ethical mirrors my understanding of the nature of ethnographic authority and my sense of the anthropologist's relation to the persons she encounters in the field as somewhat similar to the relation between an author and her characters as Richard Rechtman (2017) provocatively suggests.

The main question I ask in my reading of Coetzee is this: Might we speak of something like a *human form of life* even though we know that the human is neither transparent nor simply given but is encountered within the forms life takes in one corner of humanity versus another? How might we attend to the fragility of life in the sense of a *human* form of life? The themes of fragility and vulnerability have been pervasive in the earlier chapters, but I feel that the time has come to pose this question in explicit terms given that, on the one hand, some writers feel that the relevance of anthropology would be lost if we bypass questions of cultural differences while, on the other, others claim that given the challenge posed to the whole of humanity by pictures of planetary extinction we need to go beyond the human to include all sentient beings into our structures of thought (e.g., Kohn 2013). I am sympathetic to these concerns but also feel that the idea of the human has not been explored in the kind of depth that Wittgenstein and Cavell invite us to do.

## A HUMAN FORM OF LIFE

As is well known, Wittgenstein did not provide a sustained discussion of the notion of form(s) of life: references to this expression occur only five times in *Philosophical Investigations*, though there are other occasions when the phrase resurfaces, such as in Wittgenstein's remarks on certainty (1969).[2] This lack of a sustained discussion is not because the notion of form of life was peripheral in Wittgenstein's philosophy but because he thought of it as an ordinary expression—not one that could serve as a conceptual schema—hence, he elucidated it with examples from ordinary life showing how thought arises from immersion in a form of life. Also, consistent with the form of writing in *Philosophical Investigations* that sets the appropriate tone for reading it, we find several voices in conversation—those of accusation and temptation and a countervoice, the voice of calm that reinstates the ordinary (Cavell 1979).

Rather than rehearse all five occasions in which the term "forms of life" appears in Wittgenstein, let me take the remark that he makes in *On Certainty* to which I made a reference in Chapter 4: "You must bear in mind that the language-game is so to say something unpredictable. I mean it is not based on grounds. It is not reasonable (or unreasonable). It is there—like our life" (1969, §559). A form of life, then, rests on nothing more than that we agree, or find ourselves agreeing, on the way that we size up things or respond to what we encounter. In Stanley Cavell's perceptive remarks, nothing is deeper than the fact or the extent of our agreement (Cavell 1979). But given that Cavell also says that I cannot know in advance as to what I am in accord with, might one say that what it is to have agreement in a form of life is not a matter settled once and for all but has to be secured by the work that is done on the everyday?

There is some debate in the literature as to whether a form of life corresponds completely to the boundaries of a given community—hence Wittgenstein is evoking an ethnological sense of a shared culture of habits and dispositions, rules, and customs or whether the expression refers to a single human form of life. But the issue as I see it is not an either-or kind of issue. As elaborated in Chapter 1, I follow a lead from Cavell's (1989) remarkable analysis of the two separate dimensions of the expressions "form" and "life"—or a horizontal dimension corresponding to "forms" and a vertical dimension corresponding to "life"—to ask how these two dimensions relate to each other. Elsewhere (Das 2007, 2015a) I try to track the difference in expressions within the experience of violence—one that was "sayable" within a form of life and one that could only be shown. My point was not that there is no language to "represent" the latter but that by withdrawing their words (through which violation could be represented) from circulation, women tried to contain the poison that could not be put into the world and would violate the very sense of life as human life.

The crucial point here is that the experience of or encountering of violence reveals one's vulnerability not only to an external world but also to the other with whom one inhabits the world. Even more terrifying is the thought that the fragility of our agreements reveals everyday life *as a whole* to be vulnerable. Cavell argues that it is only by accepting the finitude and fallibility of our existence as human, the flesh and blood character of the concrete other, that we can restore some calm to the tendency of violence against the everyday that our modes of thought make possible.

Let us take this thought forward by asking how forms of life also contain in them forms of death and what this recognition does to the possibility of a different kind of ethics or moral life than theories that take the position that we already have the conceptual repertoire for defining the moral—according to these theorists the only virtue needed is that of courage to embrace it. Coetzee's novels question this "common sense" about moral life precisely by taking us to a point where the fragility of our agreements reveals and puts into question our life as humans. Let us start with *Waiting for the Barbarians* to see exactly how literature responds to this challenge.

## THE BARBARIAN AS THE PERIPHERY OF THE CIVILIZED AND WHAT HAPPENS TO BARBARIAN WOMEN

In some of his recent essays, Jonathan Lear (2008, 2015) emphasizes that if we are inhabitants of an unjust social order it is likely that our own possibilities for thought will be tainted by the very injustice we are trying to understand. Philosophical reflection by itself, he says, is limited here in two ways. First, there is the danger that reflection will itself be an illusion of "stepping back" to an impartial perspective. Thus, the crippled nature of our thought will be enacted in reflection rather than addressed by it. Second, in conditions of injustice, he argues, we suffer deprivation in imagination: we fail to envisage possibilities for life and thought. Thus, if we restrict ourselves to exploring the breadth, depth, and logical structure of our concepts *as we have inherited them*, we may repeat, rather than understand, unjust thought.[3] We need to create new possibilities for thought under these conditions, but how are these to be created? Here, a simple injunction to rational thought does not solve the problem, as I shall show ahead.

Although I appreciate the attention to the distortion of thought that comes from our conditions of life as emphasized by Lear, it seems to me that there are other ways of conceptualizing thought—e.g., as in Wittgenstein's notion that thought is that which is alive in language. My own writing on the work women performed in the context of terrible violence done to them and that, to cite Cavell's (2007) insightful formulation, allowed life to be knitted back in slow rhythms, "pair by pair," evoked the ordinary as a place of reinhabitation through quotidian acts that were incommensurate with the enormity of the horror but were nevertheless an important way of standing up to the horrific. This is neither an optimistic nor a pessimistic picture of the world—the violence was what it was—and the best picture of healing I could offer was the ability to contain the poison that could make future generations vulnerable to the curse of the violence by re-establishing the relation with death.

I want to take this thought further and ask how the notion of care for the world is to be articulated in the conditions of unjust societies, such as in the life of Empire as depicted in *Waiting for the Barbarians* or in political communities that mask the ubiquity of practices such as that of torture under notions of political necessity as depicted in *Diary of a Bad Year*.

The literary critic Matt DelConte (2007) summarizes the main lines of the plot of the first novel as follows:

> *Waiting for the Barbarians* portrays the ethical awakening of a nameless magistrate, who, after witnessing the brutal torture of "barbarians" by the Empire he serves, begins to recognize his own complicity in the Empire's colonizing agenda. Suffering from anxieties of sexual and political impotence, the aging magistrate, also the novel's narrator, initiates a (mainly physical) relationship with a "barbarian" woman, a member of the tribe that the Empire seeks to vanquish and a victim of its torture. After eventually "releasing" the woman back to her people, the magistrate is imprisoned and tortured by the Empire who suspects him of colluding with the barbarians. Ultimately, the Empire's contingency is revealed and most of the outpost's inhabitants flee in fear of a presumed barbarian attack. The novel ends with the magistrate reclaiming, principally by default, his post to a depleted barracks, still unsure of his own relationship to the barbarians and to (literal and figurative) colonization. (DelConte 2007, 436)

DelConte characterizes the tense as a "four wall present tense structure" and argues that this form makes it possible to see the events not as rendered retrospectively but in terms of an unfolding self-awareness in which the course of events is not given in advance to the magistrate in whom the protagonist and the narrator are collapsed. "Simultaneous present tense narration occurs when a narrator tells of events *as* they take place; the narrating-I is the experiencing-I" (DelConte 2007, 428). The shape of this ethical awakening that DelConte alludes to is the realization by the magistrate of his own complicity in the project of Empire even as he is horrified by the torture.

DelConte's main interest is in showing how the four-walled present tense allows the novel to acquire an open-ended texture to engage readers in the visual economy of the difficulty of seeing what is before their eyes. An important feature of the four-walled present tense narrative is that it eliminates the time between experience and narration and is thus seen as an "unnatural" form of narrative, unlike the retrospective narration in which the distinction between story and discourse can be maintained or the historical present tense narration in which the course of the future is known and alluded to even if the tense is the present tense. Further the present tense simultaneous narration does away with a narratee within the ontological space of the fiction—within the story world it is not clear as to who is receiving the narration. Nor is a reader standing outside the space of the fiction directly addressed—such as one might find in such literary devices as "Dear Reader" or implicating in the narrative someone who will find the letter in the bottle. This absentee narratee instigates one as reader to become the direct audience of the author. The magistrate in whose voice the narration takes place is himself unaware of how his life will unfold within the ontological space of the fiction—so if life under Empire is the stuff or the matter on which a world of possibility is created, it is not "life as such" or "life itself as biological life" but life as it unfolds and refolds.[4] This does not mean that the magistrate does not offer any reflective comments or diagnosis of what is unfolding, but such reflections are evolving in new directions as experience reveals to him in which kind of life he has been implicated. Consider the following diagnostic moment, which we might also characterize as the moment of awakening, which comes to the magistrate only after he has directly experienced the scene of torture. I think Coetzee's stake is to enable the reader to listen to such a moment and not to turn away from it—the absent narratee in the space of fiction is what allows the reader (if she finds she can bear it) to insert herself in the place of this absent narratee, to receive the story as if it was hers.

What has made it impossible for us to live in time like fish in the water, like birds in the air, like children? It is the fault of the Empire! Empire has created the time of history. Empire has located its existence not in the smooth recurrent spinning time of the cycle of the seasons, but in the jagged time of rise and fall, of beginning and end, of catastrophe. Empire dooms itself to live in history and plot against history. One thought alone preoccupies the submerged mind of the Empire: how not to end, how not to die, how to prolong its era. By day it pursues its enemies. It is cunning and ruthless, it sends its bloodhounds everywhere. By night it feeds on images of disaster: the sack of cities, the rape of populations, pyramids of bones, acres of desolation. A mad vision, yet a virulent one. (Coetzee 1982, 153)

The centrality of the metaphors of rising and falling, of crisis, becomes evident to the magistrate but the other character of time—viz., of time as waiting—seems obscured to the magistrate though it is evident to Coetzee as he borrows the title of Cavafy's poem "Waiting for the Barbarians" in which the whole issue is that the barbarians do not come but the waiting has already become a way of living. Is a way of living the same as a form of life?

Anthropologists Ghassan Hage (2009) and Vincent Crapanzano (1985) argue that what defines and sustains such a form of life in which there is no route to go forward or backward is waiting. If fearful anticipation is the main affect of this form of waiting—at checkpoints, in crowds, in cafes, on the school bus, if the barbarian or the terrorist is just one moment away only it did not happen this time but it will happen the next time so we better be watchful and suspicious of every object we see lying around that might, after all, contain a bomb, every string of words we overhear that sounds foreign— the world as a whole becomes pregnant with unforeseen dangers. This is simply the other side of the vulnerability and fragility of our world as a whole. Lear, in his analysis of this novel, also makes an important theoretical leap in characterizing waiting itself as a form of life or the life that Empire embodies. It is not a temporary break in the otherwise secure routines of everyday life. Waiting itself is not intrinsically lethal—think of all other microactions and -dispositions waiting produces in a more benign society, such as the building of relationships as in Valeria Procupez's (2015) work on housing cooperatives, or the *rasa* of waiting as in the lover's wait in Sanskrit aesthetics, or as in the Wittgensteinian moment when my spade is turned). It is only when it becomes a form of life that the lethal potential of waiting is revealed.

In waiting as a way of life, we come to imagine that the potential is always standing at the doorstep of reality—so polite conversation might cover up the fact that the time of not-happening is also the time of happening, a time when Empire is in the phase of preparation, waiting for the attacks to happen, oiling the factories in which weapons are being forged, intelligence operations that are scoping out the enemy territory. Our complicity in these acts does not have to be demonstrated to anyone; it is there. Our ordinary talk, polite teatime conversations, and conventions not to discuss politics with guests over dinner—in all this the barbarian (terrorist) is everywhere and nowhere. Those who fall on the side of the barbaric must ask if there will be an end to this mode of warfare on behalf of Empire. As the magistrate can see, though, Empire is not a linear process—it is a circular one. In the end when the magistrate has himself been tortured for assumed complicity with the barbarians, he can only address one interlocutor and his address reveals that what is at stake for him is now not simply what Empire does to the barbarians but what is it does to its "civilized" citizens.

> He deals with my soul: every day he folds the flesh aside and exposes my soul to the light; he has probably seen many souls in the course of his working life; but the care of souls seems to have left no more mark on him than the care of hearts leaves to the surgeon.—"I am trying very hard to understand your feelings towards me," I say. I cannot help mumbling, my voice is unsteady, I am afraid and the sweat is dripping from me. "Much more than an opportunity to address these people, to whom I have nothing to say, would I appreciate a few words from you. So that I can come to understand why you devote yourself to this work. And can hear what you feel towards me whom you have hurt a great deal and now seem to be proposing to kill." (Coetzee 1982, 135–36)

> "No, listen!" I say. "Do not misunderstand me, I am not blaming you or accusing you, I am long past that. Remember, I too have devoted a life to the law, I know its processes, I know that the workings of justice are often obscure. I am only trying to understand. I am trying to understand the zone in which you live." (145–46)

If the notion of waiting as a form of life made sense in relation to the structure of potentiality and the overriding affect of living in anticipation, then the magistrate, at the point at which he reflects the structure of a life lived in accordance with the law, must come to see the opacity of the world in which he has participated.

> I did not mean to get embroiled in this. I am a country magistrate, a responsible official in the service of the Empire, serving out my days on

this lazy frontier, waiting to retire. I collect the tithes and taxes, administer the communal lands, see that the garrison is provided for, supervise the junior officers who are the only officers we have here, keep an eye on trade, preside over the law-court twice a week. For the rest I watch the sun rise and set, eat and sleep and am content.

When I pass away I hope to merit three lines of small print in the Imperial gazette. I have not asked for more than a quiet life in quiet times. (Coetzee 1982, 126)

But a quiet life and a quiet passing away is precisely what will not be granted to the magistrate, for there are no innocent witnesses in the world in which Empire creates and then feeds on images of disaster. Is the population of the civilized world that contributes to its maintenance without directly participating in torture fenced off from the zone of life in which the torturer lives? What is the texture of this fencing off? I am inclined to think that what is being fenced off is not agreements on conventions but the fundamental threats in which we fail to see how life slides into nonlife or the human becomes the monstrous (not simply in a legal sense but in a sense that threatens our very sense of what it is to have a human life). A passage from *The Claim of Reason* is instructive on the horror at the possibility of human identify itself being capable of being dissolved.

> We are more or less accustomed to think of this response [to classical tragedy] as made up of pity and terror, as if what we witness is the subjection of the human being to states of violence, to one's own and to others; for example, terror at the causes and consequences of human rage, jealousy, ambition, pride, self-ignorance. . . . But suppose that there is a mode of tragedy in which what we witness is the subjection of the human being to states of violation, a perception that not merely human law but human nature itself can be abrogated. . . . The particular mysteriousness in Hamlet's motivation may be in persisting in looking through his events for an object of terror. We should try looking at him as a figure of horror to himself. (Cavell 1979, 419–20)

For the magistrate, the problem is that the torturer is not a figure of horror to himself: the horror the torturer evokes does not lie in his taking a monstrous shape but in the human shape of things in which he can still engage.

I am trying to imagine how you breathe and eat and live from day to day. But I cannot! That is what troubles me! If I were he, I say to myself, my hands would feel so dirty that it would choke me. (Coetzee 1982, 126)

I stated in the beginning of this chapter that I was trying to imagine what it means to speak about a common sense of the human or that which is natural to the human. But we might find this common sense precisely at the moment when it is expelled from a form of life—only of that which is the human can we speak of its inhumanity. The brilliance of Coetzee lies in locating that expulsion of the human common sense in the mystery that a torturer can behave like an ordinary human being. In such cases it might be more appropriate to speak not of a form of life but of a form of death that has been produced from the womb of the everyday within a structure of Empire.

Lear argues that the concept of the barbarian lends a false unity to disturbing acts. If one person steals a cow, it becomes an act of the barbarians. The narrator sees that the concept "barbarian" (as the concept of the terrorist today) is what makes it possible to inflict punishment on all for the act of one. But if we stretch the narrative toward the barbarian women, we can either see an intensification of the confusion that such unjust forms of life create, as does Lear, or we can glimpse a structure of eventuality that might suggest a possibility that cannot be articulated yet in the ontological space of the fiction but which we as readers might be able to give form. *This possibility lies in the barbarian women's make-believe speech.* Lear characterizes the relation with the barbarian women as follows:

The barbarian woman captures him, as it were, not simply because she is barbarian, but because she has been tortured. She has been maimed, scarred, virtually blinded, and forced to experience the unimaginably horrible. The narrator needs to understand what difference it has made to be marked by evil; he feels compelled to respond; but mostly he flails about with familiar ambivalent routines. He treats her poorly, as male masters have long done to female slaves; yet he tends to her scars with religious devotion. His confusion is everywhere manifest in his actions. (Lear 2015, 16)

This is an apt enough description, but it does not capture the fleeting moments of aliveness that sometimes spark up in the scenes with her with the rhythms of his devotion in washing every wound and scar on her body or filling her with something called "the truth." For the sake of brevity, just take one scene:

> In the makeshift language we share there are no nuances. She has a fondness for facts, I note, for pragmatic dicta; she dislikes fancy, questions, speculations; we are an ill-matched couple. Perhaps that is how barbarian children are brought up: to live by rote, by the wisdom of the fathers as handed down.
>
> "And you," I say. "Do you do whatever you want?" I have a sense of letting go, of being carried dangerously far by the words. "Are you here in bed with me because it is what you want?"
>
> She lies naked, her oiled skin glowing a vegetal gold in the firelight.
>
> There are moments—I feel the onset of one now—when the desire I feel for her, usually so obscure, flickers into a shape I can recognize. My hand stirs, strokes her, fits itself to the contour of her breast.
>
> She does not answer my words, but I plunge on, embracing her tightly, speaking thick and muffled into her ear: "Come, tell me why you are here."
>
> "Because there is nowhere else to go." (Coetzee 1982, 39)

But does this woman's body, to which she says they did not do as much harm as they did to others—for instance, they did not burn her with the red hot iron fork, only brought it near her eyes, only touched a corner that left a marble-like scar so that she can only see sideways now—contain the possibility of a makeshift language emerging? I remember some of the women who had survived the violence of Partition and the way they sometimes could not help but offer a gesture of care—even to husbands who had become violent and crazed by the imagination of what enemy hands had done to "their women" or the account of two women, raped and abducted and made pregnant by the same man who was to be repatriated back to Pakistan but who snuck out of the temporary shelter in which they were placed to see the father of their unborn children "one last time." In such structures of eventuality do we see the bondage to the idea of female obligation or the chaotic origin of desire in the most unlikely places? What is the place, then, of the erotic in such scenes of brutality? I suggest that we can get a better understanding of the relation between the magistrate and the tortured barbarian woman and see how flickers of the human might be detected in scenes of decay and death if we read such possibilities through the protagonist of *Diary of a Bad Year*—an aging double of Coetzee in whose relation with the luscious Anya Lear too recognizes not simply the compensatory desire to find one's youth again but a response to a metaphysical ache that encompasses in it the fact that we live in a world in which torture has become accepted and seeps into our lives even in the discourses of the liberal and progressive voices, and yet as we face death we want to leave things alright for ourselves even if we are not able to do so for others.

## DIARY OF A BAD YEAR

As readers of Coetzee know, every page in *Diary of a Bad Year* is horizontally divided by a line between two or three sections. The protagonist of the novel is, as I said earlier, JC, who might be a version of Coetzee but is not a substitute of Coetzee's voice as an author. JC is engaged in writing a set of opinions (he calls them strong opinions) for a German press—so these opinions are clearly meant for a public readership, though not in his native English language. The lower part of the page oscillates between the voices of JC and Anya, his young and beautiful (even ravishing) Filipina secretary who he employs to type out his dictated notes since his own eyesight is failing but also because he is, despite himself, fatally attracted to her. JC's musings over what is happening in his life move from the incongruence of his attraction to Anya in the face of his infirmity and old age, his dreams about what he wants from Anya and himself, and how this might relate to the anguish of inhabiting a political community that allows, at its extreme, torture to be justified.

In Lear's (2008) reading, the purpose of the split page is to block, even defeat, ersatz ethical posturing and promote genuine ethical thought in the reader by turning around his whole soul. As he says, "One reason to divide the page is that gives Coetzee a way to address different parts of our soul at more or less the same time—not just put an idea in us but to turn the whole soul around" (Lear 2008, 71). We might ask though, how does the revelation of what is going on in his life at the time that he is pinning down his strong opinions help to address the whole soul? Here is where we need to introduce what else is happening on the lower part of the page. The first change that occurs in this part of the page is when alongside JC's musings we find Anya beginning to relate to what he is saying and also to the way she comes to participate in her own way of acknowledging his fantasies and dreams about her. Finally, toward the middle of the novel we also get a third division where we hear the conversations between Anya and her live-in partner, Alan, and at least one prolonged scene toward the end of the novel when all three are in the same conversational space and during which something is resolved through conjunctions and disjunctions in the way different kinds of desires come together or fall apart. I want to suggest that in the figure of Anya we have the suggestion of a reader who allows her soul to be turned around by the very manner in which she is able to "read" not so much the contents of his text but him, whereas in Alan we have the reader who receives JC's text as the kind of "opinions" we find in the expressions of talking heads in newspapers and television shows.

In order to illustrate my argument, I will take one example of the way that the lower part of the page, when read across, has an impact on the way that we understand the upper part taking us to a point where we (the readers) begin to wonder about our complicity in the injustices of our society. Reading the page across the book, the main problem appears to be not that of torture of the barbarians under Empire but the fact that democratic societies engage in torture. I take two passages to show this connection.

> Every account of the origins of the state starts from the premise that "we"—not the readers but some generic we so wide as to exclude no one—participate in its coming into being. But the fact is that the only "we" we know—ourselves and the people close to us—are born into the state as far back as we can trace. The state is always there before we are. (Coetzee 2007, 3)

And later in the book, in opinions gathered under the title "On National Shame":

> It is plain as day that the US administration, with the lead taken by Richard Cheney, not only sanctions the torture of prisoners taken in the so-called war on terror but is active in every way to subvert law and conventions proscribing torture. We may thus legitimately speak of an administration which, while legal in the sense of being legally elected, is illegal or anti-legal in the sense of operating beyond the bounds of the law, evading the law, resisting the rule of law. . . . Their shamelessness is

quite extraordinary. . . . In the new dispensations we have created, they implicitly say, the old powers of shame have been abolished. (Coetzee 2007, 39)

I think here is the fundamental problem of violence within democracies: if we imagine the uses of a mythic past in instituting the state to which we voluntarily submit ourselves so that instead of the war that in this mythic past is seen as the state of nature we might become a political community ruled by law, then the problem that torture reveals is that this community, which we are now powerless to opt out of, has become one in which talk of allegiance to law reveals the "anti-legal stance" of those who refuse to be shamed by the revelations of how they evade, in fact use, the law to justify lawlessness in the infliction of torture. As Lear says, instead of blood guilt we as citizens now inherit this shame. So then, part of the turning of the soul would be to be to relearn the meaning of shame.

The lower part of the page, the yearning for Anya, is both a yearning for a reader and a desire that JC himself sees as widely inappropriate for a young person—but what do such desires indicate? First, as his reader, Anya is not looking at the finished piece of writing but is part of the enterprise of producing it, deciphering his speech and his writing, "Because it is too much to expect her to read my handwriting, I record each day's output on a Dictaphone tape and give her tape and manuscript to work from"(Coetzee 2007, 31). And then soon after:

So we proceed in this error strewn way. "Acquiring an italic identity. What does she think I am—Aeneas?" "Subject hood" The citizens of the state roaming the streets in their black hoods. Surreal images. Perhaps that is what she thinks it is to be a writer: you rave into a microphone saying the first thing that comes into your head; then you hand over the mishmash to a girl, or to some aleatoric device, and wait to see what they will make of it. (Coetzee 2007, 52)

Above we have the clearest indication that dividing the page into sections is not simply literary virtuosity or a stream of consciousness outpouring to give personal "depth" to what are public opinions or analytic writing—after all, anybody can divide up a page into sections—but why is this story of his infatuation with this young apparition with a "tomato-red shift" that is "startling in its brevity" (Coetzee 2007, 3) so central for turning the soul around? As the story unfolds, we see that Anya is not simply the girl with the beautiful body and the empty mind but the one who as reader deciphers what it means for him to write. So let us turn to what the nature of his desire for her is in his personal musings.

As JC first watches her as he sits waiting in the laundry room, his thoughts are not only about her but also about how he sees her seeing him.

> As I watched her an ache, a metaphysical ache, crept over me that I did nothing to stem. And in an intuitive way she knew about it, knew that in the old man in the plastic chair in the corner there was something personal going on, something to do with age and regret and tear of things. (Coetzee 2007, 7)

In a blinding insight that Lear offers of these moments, he says that JC's erotic attraction to Anya is to be seen as an aspect of his own preoccupation with his decay and dying. JC is looking for a way to die and related to that is his need for being able to birth his writing (compare this discussion with my discussion of Emerson's sense of his birth in philosophy through the death of his son, Waldo, in Chapter 3). Lear states that it is not as if Anya was the natural mother of the miscellany of opinions but that she becomes an occasion when a long-held pregnancy can be brought to fruition. I would add that without the fantasy of an erotic relation that leads one into learning how to die, the opinions could have sunk into "an opportunity to grumble in public, an opportunity to take magic revenge on the world for declining to conform to my fantasies" (Coetzee 2007, 23).

Consider two scenes of a desire and an ability to acknowledge this desire despite its inappropriateness. One in a second diary that JC has written that he does not make public but sends to Anya—she calls it his "soft opinions" and hopes he will publish these some day. The passage I refer to is a dream about his mode of dying.

> A troubling dream last night.
> I had died but not left the world yet. I was in the company of a woman, one of the living, younger than myself, who had been with me when I died and understood what was happening to me. She was doing her best to soften the impact of death while shielding me from other people, who did not care for me as I had become and wanted me to depart at once. (Coetzee 2007, 157)

He has had dreams earlier of dying in a whorehouse—but even when he has this dream, we learn from an earlier private musing that he finds the meaning of *this* young woman, Anya, as the appointed one to lead him to the gateway of death as somehow incongruent. "This young woman who declines to call me by my name, instead calling me Señor or perhaps *Senior*—is the one who has been assigned to conduct me to my death? If that is so, how odd a messenger, and how unsuitable! Yet perhaps it is in the nature of death that everything about it, every last thing, should strike us as unsuitable" (Coetzee 2007, 61).

On the same page in the third section, we hear a conversation that Anya is having with Alan (her partner) who prods her on what kind of fantasies she imagines JC having about her, and it is a perfect illustration of what JC earlier calls "paranoid reading."

> Don't be silly Alan. He is not going to give me his fantasies to type if it is me he is having fantasies about. Why not? May be that is how he gets his kicks; making the woman read his fantasies about her. It is logical in a back-to-front way. It is a means of exercising power over a woman when you can't fuck her any more. (Coetzee 2007, 60)

In contrast to this "paranoid reading" is Anya's own acknowledgment of both how she had stoked his sexual fantasies out of a sheer sense of a certain kind of response that might even have been a form of power over him but that ultimately resolves into an acceptance of this erotic relation as that of helping him to learn how to die. Perhaps the most moving passage in the text is the following concluding one in the lowest section of the last two pages in the voice of Anya:

> I will fly to Sydney. I will do that. I will hold his hand. I can't go with you. I will say to him. It is against the rules. I can't go with you but what I will do is I will hold your hand as far as the gate. At the gate you can go and give me a smile to show you are a brave boy and get on the boat or whatever it is you have to do. As far as the gate I will hold your hand. I would be proud to do that, And I will clean up afterward. I will clean your flat and put everything in order. I will drop *Russian Dolls* and the other private stuff in the trash, so you don't need to have sinking thoughts on the other side about what people on this side are saying about you. I will take your clothes to the charity shop. And I will write to the man in

Germany, Mr. Wittwoch, if that is his name, to let him know that is the end of your Opinions, there won't be any more coming in. (Coetzee 2007, 226)

And parallel to the lower part of the page is the upper part on the last page of the second diary—his soft opinions.

By their example [Tolstoy and Dostoevsky] one becomes a better artist; and by better I do not mean more skillful but ethically better. They annihilate one's impurer pretensions; they clear one's eyesight: they fortify one's arm. (Coetzee 2007, 227)


## CONCLUDING THOUGHTS

If Lear is right that J. M. Coetzee, the author, writes to promote ethical thought and an important component of that journey is to defeat the reader's desire to defer to the moral authority of the novelist, then if one has read Coetzee's novels well, one cannot proffer a firm conclusion but must stop at showing the different signs with which one might find a path to ethical living or ethics as a spirit through which our ordinary lives are lived. For me, the most important moments come in the life of the magistrate when he has to learn to listen to the "make-believe language" in which the barbarian woman and he speak. The four-wall tense structure of the novel and the place created for the reader in the absent narratee allowed me to give a better shape in my thought to the various injustices but, most of all, to the violence that democratic societies tolerate and perpetrate in which my life too is implicated. In JC, one feels addressed by a literary character so that the ontology of the fiction gives way to the life it is addressing: I learned that the structure of defenses we set up—as in JC's critique of liberal intellectuals who are opposed to torture but still can see it is "necessary at times"—replicates the structure of the law. As I write in a long essay on ordinary ethics (Das 2015c), even if I have never participated in anything that would support torture or the violence perpetrated in riots that are a regular feature of Indian life, I can never imagine I have led a blameless life. How then to prepare for the crossing over beyond that gate in a way that might leave things somewhat "okay"? Anya was not the natural mother of the opinions JC produced, but surely in her last reminiscences of how she will hold his hand, and how he will be a brave boy who will give her a smile as he passes over, we can glimpse the possibility of a love that is both motherly and intensely erotic. We might think that J. M. Coetzee, that novelist who hints that he does not probably understand women, might have given birth to Anya or in accepting to clean up the mess after him she might have given birth to Coetzee the novelist. Our responsibility to the present when we live in such unjust societies and feel helplessly compromised by the shame we feel may well lie in an open acceptance of such a life so as to not turn it into the useless grumblings that sometimes pass for criticism.

# 8

## A CHILD DISAPPEARS

*Law in the Courts, Law in the Interstices*
*of Everyday Life*

> The lie might become a saving fiction that held a kind of truth.
>
> —A. S. BYATT, *POSSESSION*

In the month of April 2011, an eight-year-old girl child living in one of my field sites, a shanty settlement in Noida in the national capital region (Delhi), was abducted, forcibly restrained, tortured, and raped until she was rescued four months later under somewhat mysterious circumstances. The case was adjudicated in a district sessions court in which the accused, a neighbor, and his two accomplices (his present wife and his ex-wife) were found to be guilty of wrongful confinement, aggravated rape, and attempted murder. The main accused was sentenced to life imprisonment without possibility of parole. The two women were each sentenced to seven years of rigorous imprisonment with labor. This chapter comes closest to depicting not only the brutality and cruelty that can surface at any time in these circumstances but also the futility of regarding such institutions as those of the law as located exclusively in courts or exemplified in propositions denoting the "ought" versus "is." As Max Weber says, what is distinctive to the legal point of view is to determine what normative meaning ought to be attributed to a verbal pattern having the form of a legal proposition but if we take the sociological point of view we should ask what actually happens (Weber 1978, 311). Yet, matters are not as simple as that, for what happens is not so easy to decipher. What I hope will become clear is that though I am giving a lot of weight to the analysis of the legal judgment, the perspective I bring to it is honed through my intimacy with the neighborhood in which these events took place. Said otherwise, technical knowledge, whether of medicine or of law, takes on a different character when we see it as located in a lattice of relations that stretch from poor neighborhoods to clinics, to laboratories, and to police stations and law courts.

I will strive here to provide a detailed analysis of the legal judgment and the supporting documents produced in court, followed by an analysis of related events outside the court. First, I try to show how legal technology produced "facts" in court. I then take up what seemed like minor contradictions within the documents and oral testimonies and navigate the processes through which these discrepancies were ironed out in court, resulting in a narrative that could lead to successful prosecution of the case and justice for the victim within the limits of legal proceedings. However, the same minor contradictions are later shown to have a different life in the neighborhood from which the case originated. I argue that once we undo the solidity of the narrative that the court is obliged to fix and look at each microevent that makes up the case, we see that truth and falsity, fact and fiction, certainty and skepticism, are mutually implicated. What happens in court is not a straightforward representation of events but rather the result of the work of the little tools of knowledge (Becker and Clark 2001)—such as the police diary, the police memos, or the charge sheet—performing the production of veridical accounts. However, the same documents can be made to tell a story that is diagonal to the story that was made to emerge in court in the sense that while fulfilling one aim—justice for the victim—it also produced another end: the legitimacy of the actions of the investigating officer whose behavior outside the court was regarded as embodying the illegitimate use of power by residents of the slums where he was posted. The stable conceptual furniture that many feminist scholars have come to expect in rape cases then begins to disperse into the finer grains of what makes up the texture of law. In deploying the idea of "fictions" of law, I contend that these do not unmake the law as much as they make it by rendering complex forms of violence as intelligible, parsing them into recognizable categories corresponding to correct procedure that the law in the courtroom might recognize and track.

Because of the tireless work of feminist historians and social scientists, as well as feminist activists, the subject of rape and sexual violence in India has acquired both depth and cogency. Yet treating courts of law as bounded entities for understanding the working of the law, and the assumption that we can draw boundaries around a single case, has yielded a picture of legal subjects and objects in terms of a stable set of concepts through which sexual violence is sought to be depicted.[1] For instance, in her analysis of the working of rape law in colonial India, Kolsky (2010) uses legal judgments to show that cultural assumptions about the unreliability of Indians as witnesses put extra burdens in rape trials on objective and reliable forms of proof. She argues further that medical jurisprudence and forensic investigations were geared toward finding proof of resistance rather than extent of injury, since it was assumed that false accusations of rape were frequent. Thus, it was men who were seen as vulnerable to false accusations rather than women as vulnerable to violence. Kolsky cites the infamous Hull warning, read out to juries as late as in the eighties, proclaiming rape to be an accusation "easily to be made, hard to be proved, and harder yet to be defended by the party accused tho' never so innocent" (Kolsky 2010, 110).

In my own work on rape trials in courts, I demonstrate that judicial logic relied on the assumptions of male sexuality as consisting of unmediated natural impulses for which society provided an education by judicial theatricality through which divisions between "good women" and "bad women" were publicly demonstrated (Das 1996a, 2008). Rape was thus converted into an *intelligible* act for the law, and punishment could be made commensurate with which kind of woman had been raped and *whose* refusal to consent was to be counted as "true" and whose as "mere pretense." Pratiksha Baxi's (2014) landmark study of rape trials in district courts, which looked at processes of adjudication rather than judgments alone, takes these discussions in new directions. She demonstrates that judges not only applied technical legal reasoning to arrive at judgments but also read the "social" as it unfolded during the presentation of evidence within the adversarial process—thus the high rates of "compromises" in rape cases were indicative of the way in which judges gathered many cues from the interactions between the lawyers, the witnesses, the accused, and the defendant that went beyond the weighing of judicial evidence to set aside the criminal nature of the offense and to treat it as if it were a civil dispute. The point is that a decision is only one of the outcomes of a legal case. There is also postponement, delay, harassment, obstruction, compromise—processes that Megha Sehdev (2018) calls the texture of the law, the relation between what goes on inside the courtroom and its entanglements with life outside. This chapter is then not so much a criticism of the feminist literature as an attempt to bring to light the swirling multiple potentialities that a case such as this one reveal.

## THE ABDUCTION OF A CHILD: THE COURT TAKES COGNIZANCE

In the case of *Government of India v. Sudhanshu and Others* (2011), a charge sheet was filed in the Sessions Court of Gautam Buddha Nagar against the accused, his former wife, and his present wife under Sections 365, 326, 344, 307 Indian Penal Code (IPC) for wrongful confinement and restraint. The charges of rape and attempt to murder were added later. As stated earlier, Sudhanshu was found guilty of both charges and sentenced to life imprisonment without possibility of parole; his two wives, Rita and Poonam (one former wife and one to whom he was currently married), were found guilty of wrongful restraint and subjected to imprisonment for seven years with labor (*sashrama*).[2] The proceedings and the judgment are in Hindi whereas the documents produced before the court are in both Hindi and English. Let us look at the structure of the judgment to see what constituted evidence and how the judge was able to discern and separate truth from falsity. The court notes that, according to the instructions issued by appellate courts, the name of the victim will not figure in the judgment—she is referred to as either "the victim" (*pidita*) or by the initials "Kh"—though the accompanying documents produced in court do identify her. In fact, the court depends on proper identification of names, places, sketches, and photographs for establishing the "reality" of the events (as opposed to suggestions of fabrication by the defense) but allows generic terms such as *mukhavir* (police informer) for some others when it deems that identifying such persons by name would jeopardize future investigations. In such cases, the particularity of the person is made to disappear as he appears as a general type. Yet, as we shall see, the assumption of procedure as rule-following, as if actions roll on a grid, constituted the condition of possibility so as to move from the stage of presentation of facts to their evaluation as credible or not. There are other cases in which lapses in procedure come to take center stage and strictures are passed on the sloppiness of police documents, leading to dismissal of the case because of inadequate or inadmissible evidence.[3]

An important argument I pursue here is that the court produces facticity, but certain fictions are implicated in the procedures through which legal facts are produced. I do not mean to say that the court is able to conjure facts out of thin air. As Yan Thomas (2011) shows in the case of Roman law, fictions were not added on to facts but rather were engendered by the law itself. These legal fictions might take the form of negative fictions, positive fictions, and equivalences created between the spoken and the written, between what is said in court and what might be presumed to have happened outside. Taking the false to be true—for instance, taking a pigeon for a predatory bird in a French court in order to take advantage of a particular provision relating to predatory animals in order to compensate a farmer for the loss of his crops as Latour (2010) shows, or taking the deity for a jural person who has rights (Davis 1997; Mehta 2015)—is not an effect of belief but a creation of the legal institution itself. I will show the relevance of these issues as we proceed, but for now let us return to the judgment.

The judgment opens with a brief description of the case in which, after identifying the victim's mother, Babita, and her residential address, it is stated that she (the mother) submitted a written disposition in the police station number 20, Noida, District Gautam Buddha Nagar, that her minor daughter Kh, age eight years had gone to school on April 30, 2011, and had not returned home. This case was registered under Section 365 of the IPC (kidnapping or abducting with intent to forcibly confine a person). A suspicion was expressed in this document against a man called Kalu, but on investigation he was found not to have been in Noida that day. A search for the missing girl was launched in which police notifications around her disappearance were placed in several newspapers and through radio and TV announcements. While the publicity did not produce any actionable information, the investigating officer, Balwan Singh, is supposed to have learned much later from another source, a police informer (mukhavir), about the place where the girl was being forcibly confined. Accompanied by the police informer, two women police officers, and two other witnesses, he went to the house the accused had rented in a nearby village and found the girl there in a room in which all three accused had forcibly confined her—all three were present there at the time of recovery. The girl was found to be in a serious medical condition and was taken for treatment and medical examination to a nearby government hospital and later transferred to a referral hospital. The court states that because of her serious medical condition, her testimony could not be taken immediately but it was recorded after her condition improved. This is why initially the charge sheet had mentioned wrongful confinement and restraint, but later additional charges of rape and attempted murder were added. I noticed the absence of any specific dates in this part of the summary (i.e., when did the police start the investigation? on which date did the police informer give the information and when did the investigating officer begin investigation?).

After the initial recounting of the case, the court lists the names of the witnesses for the prosecution that include the victim, her mother, the investigating officer, a recording clerk, and two doctors who had examined and treated her in the hospital. The documents produced before the court are primarily: (a) *naksha nazri* (spot report) prepared by the investigating officer, Balwan Singh, (b) forensic reports, (c) the police diary maintained by the police officer with supervisor's comments from time to time, and (d) copies of different petitions, police notifications sent to the newspapers, TV stations, with information about the girl and appeals for help.

The court heard the arguments of the defense lawyers that alleged that the defendant was falsely accused because of an old enmity between the victim's mother and the accused who used to be neighbors and had frequently got into quarrels over access to municipal water, which had to be collected from a public municipal pump since there was no regular supply of water in the houses. The court did not find it difficult to dismiss the argument put forward by the defense, since the claim that the grievous and multiple injuries on various parts of her body were a result of a fall was simply not tenable in the light of the medical reports.

The court asked six questions: Was the girl under sixteen years of age? If yes, was she less than twelve years of age? Was the victim abducted from her rightful guardian with intent to perform culpable actions in secrecy? Did the accused perform sexual acts with the victim against her will? Did the (three) accused in their common intention (*samanya aashay*) perform other actions or create any conditions under which, if the girl had died, they would have been guilty of murder?[4] Did the (three) accused use any objects for cutting or piercing or did they use fire or any heated objects that could have led to charges of murder if the victim had died? In parsing out these questions, the court used different components of the documents that had been assembled before it and matched them with the statements of witnesses for corroboration. It also cited precedents to frame how the testimony of the victim should be heard in addition to precedents cited during the sentencing stage (see References for the list of appellate court judgments cited).

The court notes that in the definition of rape given under Section 375 IPC, the victim's age is of utmost importance, and it then goes on to settle that, both on the basis of the documents and medical tests performed, the girl's age is less than twelve years. For the remaining questions, the court analyzes the witnesses' oral accounts, but, as we shall see, the approximately eighty pages of documentation, including the police diary, play an important role in determining the credibility of the oral testimonies offered in court. However, these documents are not taken as constituting evidence with regard to dates, places, etc., on their own.

The judgment starts with an analysis of Prosecution Witness 1 (PW1), who is the victim, and makes the following general observation[5]: "PW1 is the victim. Because she is the accuser, therefore her direct witness is of utmost importance. Because rape or sexual assault is done in states of solitariness [*ekant*], it is often the case that, except for the accused and the victim, there are no other witnesses available. The victim alone is the witness of such actions and the one most capable of telling what happened to her and who did it." A little later, the judge states:

> In a tradition-bound society such as India where the *asmita* [identity, pride] of a girl and a woman is a very sensitive issue with which not only the prestige of the particular girl or woman but also of the family is tied and if one becomes the victim of sexual aggression, keeping in mind the dishonor that would ensue whether the victim is married or unmarried, and the darkness in which her life will be plunged, attempts are made to keep such incidents secret. When even if such an incident happens, a woman wants to avoid acknowledging it, then the possibility of filing a false report of sexual exploitation becomes very weak.

The judge went on to cite nine earlier judgments that had held that testimony of the victim did not require corroborative evidence if the testimony was reliable and free of contradictions. In fact, the judge's statement about women in tradition-bound societies like India echoes the observations made in *Om Prakash v. State of U.P.* (2006) in which an accused had been convicted and sentenced to ten years of imprisonment for trying to rape a woman who was pregnant near the premises of a district court. On appeal, the Supreme Court had reduced the punishment to seven years since it held that the High Court had not been able to establish that the accused knew the victim to be pregnant at that time. In the course of giving its decision, the Supreme Court stated as part of obiter dicta that "it was settled law that the victim of sexual assault is not treated as an accomplice and hence her evidence does not require corroboration from any other evidence including the evidence of a doctor." The observation of the court went as follows:

> In normal course a victim of sexual assault does not like to disclose such offense even before her family member or before the police. The Indian women [sic] has a tendency to conceal such offense because it involves her prestige as well as the prestige of her family. Only in few cases, the victim girl or the family member has courage to go before the police station and lodge a case. In the instant case [sic], the suggestion given on behalf of defense that the victim has falsely implicated the accused does not appeal to reasoning. There was no apparent reason for a married woman to falsely implicate the accused after scathing her own prestige and honor.

The citing of precedents and framing her own observations in identical terms to that of the Supreme Court judge in the obiter dicta performs two functions here: it establishes the importance given to the testimony of the victim and it reiterates a particular picture of modesty, family honor, and prestige.[6] Note that once the child's age was established, the rape would have been a statutory offense and hence not in need of such questions as establishing consent. But the "facts" here are of a different nature—the courts have shifted from the idea that accusation of rape is easy to make and that men are vulnerable to false accusations to the position that women do not make false accusations of rape that would compromise their own prestige. Even though different kinds of cases put different pressures on the courts regarding the reliability of the victim's testimony,[7] where the case is of statutory rape, the observation seems to be superfluous until we realize that placing such resounding faith in the testimony of the victim also validates the police procedures that were followed, as I shall show later.

## EXAMINING THE TESTIMONY OF THE VICTIM: THE LAW SPEAKS THROUGH THE JUDGE

In the style of judicial prose, the judgment first states, "Now what is to be seen is if the victim comes out as authentic on the test of believability" (*viswasniyita ki kasuati par khari utarti hai*). The court then summarizes the main narrative of the abduction, confinement, rape, injury, and rescue and then repeats these very same events now using the words of the victim. In reading these words we should be attentive to the tense structure of the sentences in order to see how the event is recreated in court and also what the relation is between the time of happenings and the time of telling.

The court's own summary of the events is framed by the statement: "*Sankshep mein abhiyojana kathanak is prakar hai*" (In brief, the story of the accusation takes this form). After identifying the name and address of the victim's mother, the court states that she had submitted a registered complaint at the police station at Sector 20 that her minor daughter, aged eight years old, had gone to school on April 30, 2011, and had since not returned home. The complaint was registered under Section 365 of the Indian Penal Code. There was a suspicion expressed against a man Kalu in this report but on investigation he was found not to have been in Noida that day. Meanwhile, a missing person report was sent for publicity to senior police officers, different newspapers, Aakshvani (radio), and Doordarshan (television). In this period, the victim was recovered along with the three accused from Salarpur (a nearby village) on the basis of information provided by a police informer. The condition of the victim was very serious at that time, so she was admitted to hospital and her testimony was obtained later when she had recovered somewhat. Then the fact that this action was done by the three accused—Sudhanshu, Rita, and Poonam—came to light. On the basis of the testimony given by the girl, the events of her abduction, forcible confinement, infliction of injury and grievous injury, and rape by Sudhanshu in the pursuit of their common intention came to be known. Then the charges were enhanced under Sections 326, 344, 307, 376 IPC (i.e., enhanced to include charges of rape and attempted murder).

After giving the summary of the events, the court goes on to summarize what follow-up action was undertaken by the police. This includes the preparation of a spot report duly attested by witnesses, recording of evidence, preparation of a charge sheet, and the filing of charges in court. For the moment, I will skip this account and move to another register in which the events are again recounted using the words of the victim offered in the course of her testimony and cross-examination by defense counsel.

At this juncture of the argument, I make two points: First, the statements are all made in past perfect—so this is an account of action completed and allows for certainty and linearity in the sequence of narrated actions. Second, there is an ample use of the passive voice—e.g., "*Kalu ghatna ke dauran Noida mein nahin hona paya gaya; Sudhanshu dwara uske saath balatkar karne ki jaankari hui; vivechak dwara naksha nazri taiyyar ki gayi*" (Kalu was found not to have been in Noida at the time of the incident; her rape by Sudhanshu came to be known; the spot report was prepared by the investigator). I suggest that the grammatical devices of past perfect and the passive voice reflect the sense that it is not the judge who is pronouncing on the incidents; rather, it is the law that is speaking through the voice of the judge.[8] There is an uncanny resemblance to the use of the passive voice in ritual or sacred injunctions—for instance, the first verse of the *Ishopanishad* says, "tena tyaktena bhunjitha" (by him who has renounced [desire] enjoyment may be had). In the case of ritual (in Vedic texts) the injunction cannot be attributed to any person—the text simply relays the order of the world. Analogically in the case of law, the use of the passive voice in the judge's summary of events indicates that it is not the judge who is speaking; rather, it is the law that speaks through her voice. Note that at this stage the primacy in the passive voice in verb declensions puts the emphasis on the *actions* and not yet on the *persons* accused. The attribution of legal responsibility for these actions will appear at a later stage in the judgment.

In her much-cited paper on cultural techniques and sovereignty, Cornelia Vismann (2013) refers to the importance of grammatical voice in establishing how actions might be jurally recognized as accomplished through the device of the "middle voice" even though they cannot be attributed to a person. Because of her larger interest in the medium as enabling the performance of actions by nonpersonal agents in a syntactical-jural sense, she privileges the Greek grammarians' rendering of the middle voice as standing between the active and the passive voice: certain actions, she says, do not arise from persons who encounter something; rather, the medium suspends the need for clear assignments. Attractive as this formulation is, it is based on a misreading of the middle voice. As Benveniste (1971a) clearly shows in his comparative analysis of the middle voice in the Indo-European languages, the Greek grammarians were misled into thinking that the middle voice arose as a mediation between the original dyad of active and passive voice. Rather, Benveniste argues that the original opposition was between active voice and middle voice and pertained to action performed for the other and action performed for oneself, as in the Panian schema (*parasmaipada* and *atmanepada*), and pertained to the place of the subject as either exterior to the process signified by the diathesis of the verb or interior to it. With the disappearance of the middle voice in vernacular dialects, many of the functions of the middle voice shifted to the passive voice—in the present case, the use of the passive voice signifies more the exteriority of the judge to the process, ceding that place to the law. This is an area of thought that could be developed much more, but I leave it as a marker for further work to come.

### TESTIMONY: THE VICTIM'S WORDS

In the next stage, a summary account is given of the different witnesses produced by the prosecution and the defense. Of these witnesses, the testimony of the victim is considered to be of the utmost importance. There are some contradictions between the oral testimony and the written documents that are noted, but oral testimony is considered more important as the court acknowledges that minor contradictions do not invalidate the account of the witness to whom these events happened.[9] I offer a selection from the detailed testimony to show how facticity and credence are produced so that the words of the victim, a child victim, are made to carry weight.

> It has been stated clearly in her witness by the victim that on the day of the incident she had gone out to play *after* returning from school. The accused Sudhanshu came there and telling her that her aunt Rita was calling her, he took her hand and dragged her toward the tempo (a motorized rickshaw) in which Rita and Poonam were sitting. They took her to Salarpur Bhangel where she was forcibly confined to a room they had rented.
> On her asking to be taken back to her mummy, the three beat her up badly, they severed part of her tongue, wrenched out her tooth with pliers, and threatened that if you repeat "mummy-mummy" we will gouge out your eyes.

The accused Sudhanshu did many "bad, bad, actions" (*gande gande kaam*) on her. In describing the collusion among the three it was related by the victim that when the accused Sudhanshu did the bad things to her, Rita and Poonam would turn their backs toward her and look the other way.

After cataloging further atrocities against her—including insertion of a pestle in the vagina, sprinkling red chilies and pouring Phenyl (a cleaning agent), locking her up whenever they left the room in which she was forcibly confined, and throwing her on the hard floor leading to a serious head injury—the judgment cites her verbatim—*uske swayam apne shabdon mein*—in her own words:

> I said to Sudhanshu, Uncle, please take me to my mummy, then these three hit me grievously [*mil kar bahut pitai ki*] and said—calling mummy-mummy [*bahut mummy-mummy karti hai*]—then they severed my tongue and he said [pointing to the accused]—for now I have just severed your tongue, then I will gouge out your eyes and will play marbles with them.[10]

The importance of the child's own words come out as more detail is added:

> Sudhanshu did wrong acts with me many, many times—he used to have a mobile on which he had videos of many boys and girl doing bad things and he used to see them when he did bad things with me. He used to put his place of urine in my place of urine—it used to hurt me a lot but I could not scream because my mouth was taped. I would also bleed.

As Baxi's (2014) acute analysis of testimony given by a child survivor of rape makes clear, the child witness is put into the double bind of embodying in her own words the adult categories of "rape" and also retaining in the very same words the innocence of childhood so as to escape the charge of having been coached to implicate the accused in a false case.[11] Here a child's words for sex, recognizing the sexual organs only as organs for urination, establish the authenticity of her words. In the summary of the part of judgment that lays out why the child is found to be credible, we see that though the words repeat the earlier summary given by the judge, which had performed an agnostic version of the truth of that summary, now subtle shifts in the tense structure begin to move the account toward its being authorized as a true account. In the words of the judge:

In this manner, the victim has during her examination as prosecution witness given a detailed account of her having been abducted by the accused, having been submitted to tremendous pain, injury, rape, and grievous harm by the accused.

The judgment continues, "This witness has been cross-examined. During the cross-examination, too, she has corroborated the earlier statements made during the main examination." Here the tense structure makes a subtle shift. Instead of past perfect (completed action), the sentence structure first posits her as the witness of her actions and then portrays the same actions as if being observed by another person:

*swayam ko 4.00 baje khelne ke liye akele nikalna, road par sitti ki dukan ke paas se swayam ko abhiyuktagan dwara le jaana, us din khel kar ghar na aana, . . . pair pakad kar sir se patakne par sir se bahut khoon nikalna . . .*

[lit. of herself, at 4:00 P.M., for playing leaving alone; from the road near the sitti shop, of herself, by the accused having been taken; that day, not returning home after playing; having been grabbed by the feet and flung on the floor, a lot of bleeding from the head happening]

Interspersed with this description is the switch to the past perfect when the victim's words are again directly cited. Thus, the judge says in the middle of this string of sentences—"The victim has clearly stated the reason for not having returned home on the day of the incident after playing—'I had not returned home on the day of the incident because these people had taken me'—the witness pointed toward the accused." Notice that in the embedded citation from the victim, the action is portrayed in the active voice (rather than the passive voice) and the action and the intelligibility of the event is accomplished by the pointing function of the hand.

We can see two important functions that the shifts in the tense structure of the verbs as well as the move between active and passive voice accomplishes. It splits the juridical person standing before the court into a victim and a witness, but it is in rereading the child's words and translating them by the judge in a legal language that makes them carry judicial weight. Baxi's (2014) astute point that the child witness is seen to be embodying both the adult categories of rape and the innocence of childhood is indeed borne out here; however, it has to be supplemented by the fact that it is in the repetition of the child's words within a different grammatical structure that accomplishes the law's requirement of her taking the stance of a witness to the very acts that she had experienced.

I will not provide a detailed discussion of the testimony of the other witnesses except to note that the mother's testimony was discussed primarily as collaborative to the testimony of the victim and to refute the claims of the defense that she had an enmity with Rita (the first wife of Sudhanshu and one of the accused) and hence had falsely implicated them in the case. I turn now to the testimony of the police officer, who is described as the "aupcharik sakshi"—the technical or formal witness—as well as the references to the documents as establishing a paper trail from the time that the charge sheet is filed and the case admitted to court.

## TECHNOLOGY OF THE LAW

Many scholars note the importance of paper trails in establishing bureaucratic facts (Gupta 2012; Hull 2012; Mathur 2016; Suresh 2016; Vismann 2008). The weight of paper in the form of legal files, petitions, and written judgments often generates a counterarchive in which, in addition to formal documents, people create their own archives in the form of photographs or letters (Sehdev 2018) or as comments added in the margins to formal documents (Hakyemez 2017). However, let us first look at the nature of the files presented in court trials and the role they play in determining facticity. In their introduction to the edited volume *Little Tools of Knowledge*, Becker and Clark (2001) draw attention to "reports, protocols, dossiers, questionnaires, and tables" as coeval with our era and their role in creating a picture of authority as based on objectivity. Moreover, it is not only the existence of these tools of knowledge but their genre, styles of narration, organization of discourse, and the balance between what are considered to be material objects seen as if they were in nature in a pure unconceptualized state and the testimony of words that are deployed to produce objectivity and facticity in courts of law. In the light of these observations, let us now look at the specific ways that paper files are created as ways of recording and stabilizing microevents that are themselves products of police procedure.

In his work on terror trials in a Delhi court, Mayur Suresh (2016) gives an example of the production of "evidence" by the Special Cell of Delhi Police against an accused he calls Mohammad Hanif. In the course of the investigation of this case, police personnel accompanied Hanif to the city of Mahipal in South India where he was supposed to have received explosives from his handler. Hanif is supposed to have pointed to a public telephone booth from where he called his handler and to document this act, a report to that effect, called "Pointing Out Memo," is prepared by the accompanying police officer, duly witnessed by two others. A particularly absurd scene is played out in court when a public call office owner (pseudonym Anthony) who has been the subject of an "Identification Memo" is produced in court to recount how he identified the accused as having made the phone call. During his cross-examination, Anthony is found to be surreptitiously looking at his hand and the defense counsel shouts out that he is not answering from memory but is reading something inscribed on his hand. Immediately demands are produced that the writing on his hand must be photocopied, with objections from the prosecuting counsel that only originals can be submitted in court, evoking the counterdemand from the defense that in that case his hand should be cut off and presented as a material exhibit. But this court drama aside, the point Suresh makes is that written memos are the mediums through which the world enters the file and the file in turn circulates back to the world. But there are other ways of reading the plethora of written documents produced by the court that point to both how the worldly events that constitute the crime and its investigation are revealed and how other events are concealed. Let us return to the documents before the court in the case of Kh in order to dwell on this point further.

The judgment refers to an objection raised by the defense counsel that the registration of the case is very delayed (*tahreer bahut vilambit hai*). According to the defense counsel's objections, as summarized by the judge, "the incident is said to have happened on 30.4.2011 and the *tahreer* [document showing the case registration] is given on 30.5.11 and there is no clarification offered by the Prosecution." The court does not find any merit in the objection, as the judge explains:

> The witness in oral testimony [i.e., the victim's mother] has clearly stated that on 30.4.2011 on the victim's failure to return home, she [the mother] searched for her in many places but the girl was not found. Then she went to the police post to file a missing person report but the persons at the police station [*thane walon ne*] said that she must first bring a photo of the missing girl, only then will they launch the search and will register

an FIR [First Information Report]. On the date 2.5.2011, she had gone to the police station with a photo—then the police officers said we will launch a search for the girl but did not write a written report. Then on 30.5.2011, she filed a written report in the police station.

The judge then comments that the clarification offered by the oral testimony is completely satisfactory. The judge explains that complaints are often heard that on approaching the police station by a victim, a report is not immediately filed by the police and adds that this was a case of a disappearance and "in such a situation it is quite natural (*svabhavik*) for the police to demand a photo of the disappeared person." The judge concludes that the oral testimony confirms the account given by the victim. In overruling the objection of the defense and treating it as a minor slip in procedure that should not be allowed to derail the main case against the accused, the judge was following the many exhortations contained in judgments of higher courts that the severity of the crime of rape should not be obscured by consideration of minor discrepancies.[12] However, in treating the failure to register an FIR as a minor lapse in procedure, the judge overlooked the possibility that such delays might be indicative of pathologies in the processes by which a crime might be erased from the records altogether. It is of some significance that the delay in registering the case was not allowed to invalidate the story of the victim. Instead the judge turns to the question of what kind of procedure the police followed.

First of all, the judge establishes the importance of the account provided by the investigating officer and the record of the investigation in the daily diary (*roznamcha*) maintained by him. "Although this witness is giving evidence in his formal capacity [*yadyapi yeh sakshi aupcharik sakshi hai*] in the present circumstances his testimony is very important because it is through him that the victim has been recovered and the accused have been arrested red-handed [lit. *mauke par giraftar kiya gaya*, arrested at the site of the crime]."

Using the same linguistic mode as when the evidence given by the victim was being recounted (of oneself having been . . .), the judge notes the following specific procedural actions performed by the investigating official. For the sake of simplicity, I will not use the cumbersome grammatical structure but, instead, render the main points in intelligible English.

This witness has deposed that on May 30, 2011, while he was immersed in his work at Police Station No. 20, he received the information regarding the suspicion of Kalu in connection with case number xxx/2011 and he prepared a spot report on the area from where the victim had disappeared. This has been submitted as Exhibit D.

The details of his interrogation of the suspect Kalu, the information gathered from neighbors, and the report of his phone calls were all recorded in the diary on May 30, 2011. On investigation, the suspect was found not to have been in Noida the day of the disappearance. He was thus removed from the list of suspects.

On June 22, 2011, information was sent to relevant offices for notification under the Missing Persons Act along with descriptions of the missing girl. On subsequent dates, July 13, 2011, and July 21, 2011, information was sent to television stations and to the Child Help Line.

The judge notes that the witness had clearly stated that on information supplied by a police informer, the abducted girl was recovered from the room where she was forcibly held by the three accused and a "memo of recovery" had been prepared on the spot. This memo was signed by the father and mother of the victim and with their consent a copy was given to the three accused. The truth of these events had been testified under oath and it had also been stated in the memo that at that time the girl was in very serious medical condition and hence had to be immediately admitted to hospital.

The judge goes on to describe other investigative acts, such as getting the girl admitted to the hospital, and comments in detail on the various injuries (seventeen as in the forensic report), their seriousness, and especially the evidence of brutal rape by the serious vaginal injuries. The judge notes that the police diary contained detailed descriptions of each interrogation and also described in detail how the girl was recovered. According to this story, when the other leads had gone cold, the investigating officer learned from a mukhavir (police informer) that the victim had been abducted by Sudhanshu and his two wives and was being forcibly restrained in a room that they had rented in a nearby area. Accompanied by the said police informer, two female police officers, and two witnesses from the nearby market, they had gone to the area where the mukhavir pointed out the house and then left. The girl's parents had been brought to the spot. After some resistance from the accused the investigating officer was able to forcibly enter the house where they found the victim crouched in a corner. When she saw her parents, she ran to her mother and cried pitiably while hugging her. The "recovery report" memo had been prepared in the presence of the parents and the original signed by the two female officers, the witnesses, and the parents had been submitted as an exhibit in court.

The judge dismissed the suggestion by the defense that the girl had been coached to give false testimony. The overwhelming forensic evidence, as well as the lingering evidence of the injuries—Kh's missing teeth, her lisping due to the severing of part of her tongue, the burn marks on her face—provided dramatic evidence of the truth of the accusations. Yet these became "facts" primarily through the matching of oral testimony with the written forensic documentation. In the language of the judgment:

> The investigating officer, having taken his fellow female police officers, two independent witnesses from a public call office, and having called the victim's parents and with them coming to Rajeev Colony, from where the mukhavir having taken them to the said place, the mukhavir's leaving that spot after having pointed to the house; asking people in the neighborhood who had gathered there to come forward as witnesses and their having refused to do so, saying that they had nothing to do with the affair; and on knocking at the door, the accused Sudhanshu having opened the door a bit, then seeing the police having forcibly attempted to shut the door; and the police officer on having entered the house with the female police officers hearing the moaning sounds; on seeing the girl lying in a corner and her parents recognizing her; the child having been enclosed in an embrace by her parents; the child having pointed to the three accused and saying that they had kept her forcibly in that room, and beaten her, and severed her tongue, etc., *is recorded.* [emphasis added]

The medical officers who treated her in the emergency ward of the nearby government hospital gave oral testimony, as did the clerk at the police station who entered the complaint on the computer. The oral testimonies confirmed the near-fatal injuries she had suffered, in the case of the former witness, and the timing of the recording of the FIR, in the latter case.

I will consider the defense argument and their fate in the court very briefly. On behalf of the main accused, Sudhanshu, the defense argued that he was being implicated through false charges because of an enmity that had developed between the victim's mother and him when he was living in the same area. He attributed the enmity to the quarrels over shared municipal water for which people had to line up near the municipal pump. The court held that since this motive had been brought up by the defense it was up to the defense to provide legal proof, and they had failed to provide any document or witnesses that would support this claim. As for the two women, the court held them responsible as accessories since the victim's testimony had clearly implicated them and they had been found in the room from where she was recovered. The court paid attention to the defense argument that in her cross-examination the victim had named only Sudhanshu. The court pointed out, for instance, that the victim had deposed in her testimony that when this accused "would do bad things to her . . . forcibly putting his place of urine in her place of urine" (to use her own words) the two women would turn and look away. Their participation in beating her, putting red pepper in her eyes, aiding in inserting a pestle in her vagina, and other acts of torture is of interest to the court for showing their complicity and of establishing common intention, but the question of any specific motives assigned to the women does not emerge.[13]

The judge found all three accused to be guilty under separate charges of abduction, forcible restraint, rape, and attempted murder under different sections of the Code of Criminal Procedure (cited earlier) and commented on the heinous nature of the crimes. As the judge summarized, "This cruelty has not only broken her body but has also psychologically shaken her inner self. It would not be wrong to say that the actions committee by the accused are at the extreme limit of the sexual exploitation of women." The main accused Sudhanshu was awarded life imprisonment without possibility of parole, and the two women were given the sentence of imprisonment with hard labor for seven years each. Requests for leniency were made at the sentencing stage by the defense counsel on the ground that this was the first criminal offense committed by the accused and also that he and his wife had two small children. The court, however, saw no reason to exercise any leniency. Some of the observations that the court made in the main judgment and in the sentencing phase have relevance for its understanding of how what happens in court is aligned to events outside it. It is, however, not the formal pronouncements alone but also the traces left in the documents through gaps, discrepancies, and specific words that give us clues on how the world enters the file, as Suresh (2016) felicitously frames the issue. That question might be complemented by asking how these very gaps and discrepancies are accounted for in the world outside the court. In the next section I attempt to offer observations on both issues by seeing how the neighborhood in which these events happened provided commentary on the legal process by means of conflicting interpretations, rumors, and forms of avowal and of distancing.

## ALIGNMENTS: THE FILE AND THE LOCAL WORLD

Let us take another look at the written words inscribed in the petitions, the police diary, the different memos prepared, the spot reports, media announcements, and medical records not exclusively from the point of view of the work they performed as little tools of knowledge in the court but also so as to see what they reveal through stories that circulate in the neighborhoods such as in the shanty settlements or slums from which Kh came.

In relation to the discrepancies that the court rightly dismisses as being minor as far as the question of the guilt of the accused is concerned—such as whether she was abducted from the jhuggi (shanty) as the spot report submitted to court stated or from the road while she was playing there, or, for that matter, the delay between the date of the incident and the date when the written complaint was filed in the police station—do they convey a different register of information about the life of law in the neighborhood as distinct from its life in court? In his analysis of bureaucratic texts generated in the mid-eighteenth century consisting of the records of a church consistory that acted as a kind of moral court dealing with quotidian matters such as family quarrels, Sabbath desecration, or dereliction of household duties, David Sabean (2001, 67) states that though the disputes brought before the church consistory were banal in themselves, they provided a window into the complex negotiations that ensued among the "disputants, delinquents, neighbours, kin, court members, clerk, and audience." Sabean's emphasis is on emplotment, narrative style, and ways of channeling discourse that these court records reveal. The analytical strategy I follow is somewhat diagonal to the formal analysis: it tries to fill details from the discourses generated in the neighborhood around this and similar cases around abduction that can show the contingencies through which a case might or might not reach the stage of criminal trial in court. How might we read the gaps in the inscriptions when we place them in the hurly-burly of neighborhood life rather than within the plot structure to which court narratives conform? What do they reveal about the role of the police in the everyday life of the neighborhood?[14]

Let us first take a detail that appears quite inconsequential from the point of view of the gravity of the matter under consideration: the FIR produced in court stated that the girl had gone to school and had not returned home on the day of the incident. During the testimony given by the victim, she had stated clearly that she had gone out to play and had been dragged by the accused to his tempo in which his wife and his ex-wife were seated and together they had forcibly overcome her struggle to escape. At various points of the judgment, the presiding judge cited earlier rulings that in a rape case the court must not be swayed by minor contradictions. For example, the judgment cited an earlier judgment of the Andhra Pradesh High Court (*State of A.P. v. Ganguli S. Murthy*, 1977) that "in rape case the court should examine the probabilities and should not be swayed by minor contradiction or minor discrepancies in statement of witness." In view of the gravity of the injuries and the overwhelming forensic evidence of rape, these were indeed minor contradictions from the point of view of the law. But these discrepancies along with the delay of more than one month in filing a written report also point to the kind of intimidation in accessing the legal mechanisms that people living in slums routinely face.

A number of petitions—some handwritten and some typed on a computer—fill out a story that was only briefly touched on in the judge's words when she stated that it was not unusual to find delays in registering an FIR at the police station. In the first handwritten application submitted by Kh's father that is dated May 1, 2011, there is a request to file a missing person's report. The letter states the name of the complainant and gives the information that his daughter is missing since 9 P.M. the previous night and requests that an investigation to find her should be immediately launched. The first application is to the chauki-in-charge, Jhandupura—a police post under the jurisdiction of the Police Station, Sector 20. This application is followed by a complaint launched a few days later to the superintendent of police in which it is stated that when the missing girl's father had gone to inquire about the state of the investigation the police officer had hurled obscene insults at him and accused him of doing "netagiri"—rabble-rousing. A further complaint launched on May 30, 2011, stated that the police were refusing to register an FIR. The complainant expressed great dissatisfaction with the police and expressed a suspicion against a neighbor whose brother-in-law had been visiting and was seen by the missing girl as taking photographs of another girl in the area. The said neighbor had threatened the complainant that he would implicate him in a false murder charge and further challenged that "if you spend Rs. 2000 in this case I will spend Rs. 5000. I will see what you can do." The petition stated that when the complainant had gone to report this intimidation, the police officer had turned on him and said that he was falsely trying to implicate an innocent man—"*your daughter was missing from school*" (emphasis added). In his complaint, the petitioner stated that he suspected the police to be in connivance with the culprits and that they were trying to protect the culprits. Meanwhile, the parents had put up handwritten posters all over the neighborhood describing the missing girl and asking for help and information. Thus the "mistake" in the first FIR that stated that the girl was missing from school seemed not to have been an innocent mistake but a fabrication that directly contradicted what the parents had reported in court in order to lay the grounds for the allegation that they were trying to falsely implicate "innocent" neighbors with charges of abduction whereas the girl had left of her own accord. That this was later modified was because of the intensity of feelings in a "public" that finally gathered around the case—a point I come to later.

Before I come to one final petition that used a more formal format, I wish to draw attention to the fact that the language used in these handwritten petitions was very much the language of intimidations and threats that circulate in everyday interactions in the neighborhood. Thus, "*tere ko murder case mein phasa doonga*" (I will falsely implicate you in a murder case); "*tu 2000 kharch karega to mein panch hazar kharach karronga—dekhta hun tu kya kar lega*" (If you will spend Rs. 2000, I will spend Rs. 5000. Let's see what you can do); "*badi netagiri karne chala hai*" (Trying to be a leader?); "*unhonen file daba di*" (They suppressed the file); "*vakeel doosri taraf walon se mil gaya*" (The lawyer connived with the other side); "*police ke roznamche mein hamesha kuch khali page rehte hein*" (There are always some pages left blank in a police diary). These expressions, some of which find their way into the applications and petitions by the complainant, capture the everyday experience of interactions with the police. Indeed, while formal surveys about the experience with state institutions such as the police would lead one to think that in general the coercive arm of the state fails to penetrate into the slum areas where, ironically, one of the functions of leadership is to provide protection to their followers from the harassment by police (see Das 2011a), one can pick up the omens and traces of the coercion exercised by the police and the sense of insecurity and suspicion with regard to neighbors and even friends and kinsmen or kinswomen it creates. That the police would have asked for a bribe when attempts were made to register an FIR, or that Kh's father would have suspected the police to be in connivance with some neighbors he named in the first complaint (it turned out wrongly), caused no surprise to anyone. On visits to this area (and to other such low-income neighborhoods) I would often find a small group of policemen from the local precinct sitting on a cot outside a jhuggi or in a small one-room clinic of a local doctor who was also a money lender. People harbored great suspicions that a particular neighbor was a mukha-vir or police informer and point to telltale signs of extra income in his or her lifestyle; others pointed to false cases in which they were implicated out of jealousy or rivalry. In other words, police procedures inside the courts were seen to be belonging to a different life of the law than the actual prac-tices that were seen as both routine and clandestine in character. Yet one also finds that law courts were not seen as entirely alien institutions: people also tried to access law courts in order to get stay orders against evictions, to register local NGOs, or to legalize registered societies in the pursuit of particular goals such as to get a court order for supply of regular water, to get maintenance from an estranged husband, or to contest criminal charges of dowry (Das and Walton 2015; Sehdev 2018). In a survey of three neigh-borhoods in 2012, we found little less than 5 percent of people who said they had any involvement with a court of law—yet at the level of discourse of legal terminologies, threats of legal action, and finding ways of warding off police action against oneself there was considerable engagement with the state institutions, including what we may designate as the law (see Das and Poole 2004).[15]

Let us consider a final petition/complaint both for the texture of its lan-guage and the double relation it has to what is happening outside the court and subsequently what happens in court. A petition dated June 30, 2011, by the girl's mother is addressed to the district magistrate of Noida with cop-ies to various high level officials such as the police superintendent, the po-lice commissioner, the chief minister, etc., with the subject line "Requesting legal action in a case of filing of wrong FIR and negligence in investigation of missing person." After repeating the details of the incidents and the threats by the neighbor whose brother-in-law against whom suspicion had been expressed in the earlier written submissions, this petition goes on to say that the neighbors living in the jhuggis were spreading false rumors about the incident and were trying to mislead the police. In the complainant's words:

> All kinds of allegations that are not fit to be repeated are laid against anyone who tries to help me. As a result, far from coming forward to help me, no one is willing to even talk to me. When I go to the police post to inquire about the case, at least two people unknown to me follow me. For the past one month, I have gone and cried and lamented at the police post [*rota bilakhta raha*],[16] but the police there have not even written a report. Acting on the case is miles away. Sir, the main point is that my daughter has been missing from somewhere near my house since 9 P.M. on April 30, 2011, but in connivance with the criminals and in order to save them it has been written in the police report that she was missing from school.

The petition states that the incorrect entry in the FIR that the girl was missing from school is "a living, breathing example (*jeeta jagta udaharan*) of the connivance of the police with the criminals and that a proper investigation should be undertaken on this aspect of the crime." As compared to the handwritten petitions, the Hindi used in this petition is sanskritized formal Hindi and bears the marks of the help given to the mother in drafting the petition by members of a local organization. This is an important indication that the case was coming into the light of publicity before the police decided to act on the complaint.

## POLITICAL INTENSITIES: LOCAL ISSUES
## PROPELLED INTO PUBLICITY

In this section, I turn to some of the contingent events related to a larger political turmoil in Delhi that led to an intensification of political mobilization and attendant affects to which local events such as the issue of missing children and police corruption came to be grafted.

As a leader of the anticorruption movement in 2011, Anna Hazare, a social worker and self-professed Gandhian, started a hunger strike on April 5 of the same year and declared that his fast would continue until anticorruption legislation drafted by activists in the movement was accepted by the government. My intention here is not to give a detailed account of the movement but to see how this movement affected events within the neighborhood from which Kh had been abducted. As momentum gathered in the city in support of Anna Hazare, the local branches of various political parties began to hold rallies and candlelight vigils to support the demands of the movement. New leaders emerged in the locality hoping to get party tickets for the 2012 Assembly Elections in Uttar Pradesh, or at least hoping that they would be noticed by the higher ups in party organizations for the votes they could deliver. Two women living close to Kh's jhuggi joined a newly formed party whose leader hoped that he would garner enough support to be counted as controlling a "vote bank." While I cannot go into any detail here on such political strategies,[17] I simply note that police corruption in the slums came to be joined to the issues of corruption at the national level that the anticorruption movement had brought to the forefront. Thus, demonstrations in front of police stations began to mention the negligence of police in pursuing cases such as that of Kh. This neighborhood also happened to be near the village of Nithari in Noida where the skeletons of more than a dozen bodies of children had been discovered in the drain of a rich businessman's house in 2005–2006, in which case also villagers had alleged that police had repeatedly refused to register FIRs. In 2011, the owner and his servant were still being prosecuted on criminal charges, which made the whole issue of disappearance of children and the police indifference to such episodes politically volatile (both the accused were found guilty and given death sentences in 2017).

At least two groups of local activists—neighborhood level cells of the Centre of Indian Trade Unions and of Janwadi Mahila Samiti (the women's cell of Communist Party of India [Marxist, commonly known as CPI])—had taken up the cause of the disappeared girl. Women from the Janwadi Mahila Samiti had been especially helpful in giving guidance to the family. After her recovery in September of that year, Janwadi Mahila Samiti continued to offer help and to draw attention to the negligence of the police (for instance, see reports in *India Today*, September 3 and 5, 2011, as well as in the vernacular press such as *Amar Ujala*). Members of the National Human Rights Commission had also visited Kh in the hospital and demanded an inquiry into police negligence. The point is that suddenly from being a local event of limited relevance, the case threatened to become an issue of regional if not national importance. There is little doubt that senior police officers came to take notice only after the disappearances of children became a vociferous issue. Thus, in a statement reported by *India Today*, An-

ant Dev, the police superintendent of Noida, stated, "We are investigating if this is a case of child trafficking and if money had changed hands" (*India Today*, September 3, 2011). The report of such an inquiry by the police has never been made public, although in 2018 panic rumors about the disappearance of children and lynching mobs resurfaced in many areas in the country.

As far as the family of Kh is concerned, they were able to ward off the danger of further violence by the accused if he were to be acquitted because the legal process is quite opaque to them. The threat of violence never fully disappeared: Kh's elder sister was married off into a faraway village and rarely visits the family in Noida and her younger brother was sent to the natal village of Kh's mother to be brought up in his grandmother and uncle's home since there were fears of retribution. And although Kh attends school she is not allowed to leave the small house they have now been able to build. There are rumors in the neighborhood about the source of money for the house—whether it is the money given to them as per the court orders or whether this is hush money given so as to block investigations into suspected rings of child traffickers. We cannot know; but we can see the effects of such speculation in the premonitions and omens. As in Kh's case, witnessing an event (e.g., an unknown man taking a picture of a girl in the neighborhood) can release suspicions and rumors. Any idea of childhood innocence repeatedly evoked in abduction cases (Mankekar 1997; Rajan 2003) evaporates in the air; instead, we are left with the picture of a little girl with burn marks, face distorted with pain, fear, and an overwhelming knowledge of the evil humans are capable of—a girl who continues to refer to her abusers as "uncle" and "aunt" in her testimony.

## ADJACENT STORIES: WANING INTENSITIES

The great intensity that had been built around Kh's story dissipated in time. Now if you ask about her, people even a few blocks away will say, "Which girl? What abduction? Here a girl is abducted every day." The sense of crisis, the public anger, the currents of collective energy that seemed to have run through the locality have ebbed as have the reputations of the leaders of the anticorruption movement. And even if it is an exaggeration to say that a girl is abducted every day, it captures the generalized fear in which parent of young girls live. For instance, in 2014, a nephew of a local leader was murdered during an altercation with his friend who impulsively plunged a knife into him. The murderer was absconding. After three nights, the local leader went around the neighborhood announcing that if the boy did not surrender within two days his (the leader's) henchmen would "lift" every girl in that street where he suspected the murderer was hiding. The threat of "ladki utthva lenge" (we will abduct [lit. "lift"] the girl) hung in the air). The neighbors put pressure and the man accused of murder was forced to surrender at the police station within the stipulated time. All this background story was absorbed in official accounts as the instance of police vigilance, but wrapped into that story were other stories of random arrests, bribes, and the battle for ascendancy between two different leaders. People knew that they could not count on the police—yet it is interesting that the mediation of the police and the courts is also now part of the unfolding of such stories.

In 2017, the rumors of men sneaking into people's houses and chopping off the braids of young women as a sign of dishonor and sexual assault were everywhere, as were reports of instances of lynching as the form that "people's vigilance against the consumption of beef" was taking. Within these shanty settlements, vigilant groups of young men were formed echoing reports in national media of vigilante methods against all kinds of "crimes"—sneaking beef across the borders of states, chopping off women's braids under the cover of darkness, thefts, and kidnapping. The groups of young men, it was said, would keep an eye on the neighborhood against all kinds of crimes. Stories began to circulate of fearsome men sighted—men who were naked but dripping with mobile oil on their bodies coming at night and sneaking into people's homes to steal things or to cut off women's braids to dishonor them. One man who was coming home late after a night duty was surrounded by a vigilante group and nearly lynched until someone recognized him. The intertwining of facts, fictions, rumors, and the morphing of local stories into national ones and vice versa needs careful unravelling and critical patience—simply catching conversations in cafes and passing interviews that mimic journalistic methods will not do. Much as such conversations as one catches floating around point to an ominous landscape, they have to be tracked in a resolute way even if what knowledge we anthropologists get remains indeterminate and lends itself to multiple constructions of the real.

## CONCLUSION

I will do nothing more than recount four points that have emerged from a close reading of the judgment and the bureaucratic documents produced before the court, on the one hand, and the manner in which the case became a window through which to view the violence that seeps into everyday life, on the other. I do not wish to sweep away the power of the detail through which I came to appreciate just what it means to embrace a resolute realism in the face of such overwhelming odds as Kh and her parents faced. Yet, it is through the details that my understanding of the entwined relation between language and law and the open texture of legal discourse emerged—this is the understanding I share in these concluding moments of the chapter.

First, consider what it means to say that the production of facts in the course of a court trial entails fictions that are not simply added to facts but are produced by the law itself. While many scholars will recognize that legal definitions of persons or objects can go against our quotidian experience—e.g., discerning if a provision relating to animals can be applied to runaway slaves or deciding if a pigeon is by definition to be treated as predatory—to the extent that such equivalences or attribution of predicates violate an ordinary realism around things and persons, they may be seen as fictions created by the law (even judgments sometimes use this terminology—see note 4). I go further, though, and argue that even when no such definitions are provided, the very fact that written bureaucratic documents must use narrative genres—including specific plot structures and characters such as "police informer" recognizable to the law, as well as melodramatic expressions in order for a "factual" report to be effective in court—shows the limits of the arguments that such reports carry authority because they represent objective facts. Instead, the fictions entailed in the creation of facts is premised on an intertextuality between legal discourse and popular culture such as the visual and aural language of films.

Second, the language of the law, not only at the level of narrative and plot structure but also at the level of grammar, allowed three different durations to be laid upon each other. In particular, I showed how the split between the same action narrated in the past perfect tense and then repeated using an intransitive past continuous as if events that had happened were being seen in the here and now created a split in the testimony of the victim between her *experience* as the victim and her ability to see actions that were done to her as if from a third-person perspective or from the vantage point of a witness. At the same time, the court also brought in the past in the form of citations of precedents to frame how the testimony being presented was to be evaluated—e.g., as in the statements from precedents that the victim of rape is not an accessory to the act or that minor contradictions do not negate the credibility of the child witness. These rhetorical strategies, along with the copious use of the passive voice, framed the judge as simply the medium through which the law spoke. While these grammatical features created the formal conditions for the performance of legitimacy of the law in court, they also signaled the anticipation of future actions, such as the movement toward the judgment within the confines of the case, and also the anticipation of future review by appellate courts.

Third, while the judgment and the punishment accorded to the accused produced a just decision for the victim within the limits of the law, it also established the legitimacy of the procedures followed by the investigating officer by the manner in which it established "facts." The legal decision warded off the immediate dangers that the victim and her family would have faced if the accused had been released, but it also concealed the intimidations at the hands of the police, suspicions of complicity between police and child traffickers, and other pathologies of the law as experienced by the residents of slums and shanty settlements that found expression in the various petitions that were submitted to the police by the parents and were subjects of popular protests at the height of the anticorruption movement in these neighborhoods.

Finally, the patriarchal assumptions of the law are evident in the way in which the torture inflicted on the girl was treated as secondary to the rape. Thus, it was not considered necessary to inquire into the separate criminal acts committed by the women accomplices—it was taken to be sufficient to establish their complicity in the will and desires of the male perpetrator of the crime by evoking common intentions. As many feminist legal theorists have pointed out, it is important to give weight to the variations in the concrete conditions of women's lives constituted by class, race, and caste. A very generalized recourse to "patriarchy" is too blunt an instrument to do justice to the microphysics of power and to the fact that a multitude of consequences follow in which justice may be produced through the entanglements of truths and lies. In taking the law to be about what unfolds not only in courts but also in the experiences of police practices, threats, and intimidations that define its texture in the lives of the poor, I hope to have shown that people in these neighborhoods bear the weight of inordinate knowledge of which we can only get a fragmentary understanding when a case such as that of Kh breaks into publicity. Still, I take it as a necessity to show the resolute spirit of realism with which people seek a plethora of legal remedies, despite their adverse experiences with state institutions, in order to ward off the everyday emergencies they face in such neighborhoods.

What does this account tell us about doing anthropology after Wittgenstein? I return to Donatelli's (2019) discussion of forms of life, splendid or miserable alike, giving us a different perspective on how criticism unfolds than is available through the neoliberal dispositif of statistical aggregation and of mediatization.[18] As Donatelli states the point, a different way to generate a critique from *within* these forms of life would entail the overcoming of an impulse to generate *two* orders of description in which one is the order of everyday life in which embodied obligations, traditional modes of being-with are embedded in thick worlds of communities (even if in corroded forms) and the *second*, the apparatus of law, medicine, social work, police, and bureaucracy that impinge on the first one and against which the former have no resources to resist. Instead, Donatelli argues, if what we had was *one* order of description showing how lives are made and remade with the legal and political tools at hand, then the possibility of a different kind of criticism would not be extinguished right from the start. Sanjeev Gupta, Swapan, and Kh and her parents demonstrate different possibilities for engagement with the state and its apparatus of governance with all the risks of success and failure. A different form of criticism might emerge from the ability to stand with them as they navigate these tools of governance, as I have tried to do, rather than pronouncing their life forms as defunct or erased from the world.

# 9

## OF MISTAKES, ERRORS, AND SUPERSTITION

*Reading Wittgenstein's Remarks on Frazer*

In this and the following two chapters, I move to a different register of writing, taking up ways in which anthropology has responded to philosophy, how theological ideas seep into what look like the neutral and secular apparatus of anthropological concepts, and how literary and autobiographical moments count for me in the making of anthropological knowledge for self and others. In a remarkable afterword to a forthcoming book in which a number of anthropologists provide their comments on Wittgenstein's *Remarks on Frazer*, Sandra Laugier reflects on the relation between anthropology and philosophy: "Given that philosophy has long claimed to take up the task of anthropology, this leads to the question of how anthropology can in a sense claim to be philosophy—not through a kind of upgrading of its status but rather because it illustrates the philosophical method Wittgenstein proposes: attention to ordinary human forms of life in their unity and diversity; that is attention to forms of life and life forms" (Laugier forthcoming, 209).

Yet, Laugier is much more cautious than many anthropologists who find a founding moment for how anthropology might find its foundations in philosophy in Immanuel Kant. In fact, she proposes that one might think of a certain growing apart of philosophy and anthropology at this moment when philosophy came to attend to the human as a separate domain of inquiry, for it inaugurated the human as a *general* concept for moral investigation, reducing the particular to an instantiation or example of the general. At the same time, description as an analytic was subordinated to the task of explanation of the general. The problem Laugier poses for anthropologists is a deep one—

viz., if differences in forms of life and the attention to detail that defines ethnographic work are not simply *instantiations* of something like a human condition that can be taken as a given, known in advance, then in what way might one formulate the idea of the human that Wittgenstein thinks cannot be simply jettisoned?[1] I propose that the answer Laugier is seeking lies in thinking more resolutely about such expressions as "our common background as humans" and what Benoist (2018) posits as the "primitive form" in Wittgenstein. Explaining that Wittgenstein's primitivism is not a reductionism—rather, it is about the kinds of reactions produced out of the human in the background of which forms of life might be said to surface—Benoist cites the following passage from *Philosophical Occasions*: "The game doesn't begin with doubting whether someone has a toothache, because that doesn't—as it were—fit the game's biological function in our life. In its most primitive form it is a reaction to somebody's cries and gestures, a reaction of sympathy or something of that sort. We comfort him, try to help him" (Wittgenstein 1976, 414; 1993, 381).[2] The point Wittgenstein is making is that the reaction elicited from us is to respond to that physical pain; doubt whether the pain was simulated might well come later, but it is not the first reaction. Of course, it is also part of human forms of life that people can be trained to suppress that primitive reaction or even learn to make use of it for perpetrating cruelty, but this does not negate the fact that there is a natural background of human life against which alone we might trace how forms of life surface.

Wittgenstein's *Remarks on Frazer's "Golden Bough"* are of special interest in this context precisely because in his criticisms of Frazer, Wittgenstein elicits the ways in which Frazer falls into error and, more grievously, into superstition (in the philosophical sense) and erases from his thought any reference to the most natural reactions he might have had if he were willing to trust the fact that there was a common background to the human and from that point of view everyday practices of English society he was familiar with carried a resonance with practices he was describing as having a sinister element. In the next chapter, I arrive at the surprising finding that even though later anthropologists explicitly distanced themselves from Frazer, the anthropological concepts they honed to render other societies intelligible to their audiences relied on concepts that once again showed an ignorance of their own assumptions about such entities as ritual, or god, or prophet. It is not my claim that these were deliberate distortions but rather that a close reading of these texts shows how difficult the task of delineating what one might characterize as a human form of life woven into distinct forms of life proves to be.

This chapter was first written as part of a collaborative effort in which different anthropologists commented on different parts of *Remarks on Frazer* (see da Col and Palmié forthcoming). I have retained the structure of the earlier version of this chapter in what follows. I think it provides a very nice entry into the question of what we understand by thinking and how we live with our concepts. But as the famous story of Abhimanyu, the young son of the hero Arjuna in the Mahabharata who is killed in battle, tells us, even when one has found a way to enter into a battle formation, to get out one has to risk one's life.

## PART I: SOME OPENING THOUGHTS

As is well known, Wittgenstein made a departure from the *Tractatus* when he acknowledged that there was no single definition of a proposition that could provide a fit for the diverse forms it takes in the world.[3] Thus, the contact between language and reality is not a singular once-and-for-all achievement, which we either reach or fail to reach by the layering of a system of names against a system of objects. Yet, the question of the kind of contact between language and reality continues to be the single most pressing issue in what are called the second Wittgenstein and the third Wittgenstein (Moyal-Sharrock 2004, 2009). Departing from the *Tractatus*, our experience of how to relate words to worlds in Wittgenstein's later work is one of disappointment, for we may succeed and then flounder repeatedly. This is a stance mirrored in the form of writing especially in *Philosophical Investigations* ([1953] 1968) and *On Certainty* (1969), when paragraphs come to an end abruptly and then begin again later as the same thought reappears with a new example or a different formulation. How, then, are specific (or singular) relations to be found between language and reality or in the way words are found to be world-bound?

My basic idea in this chapter is to depart from the many discussions that take Wittgenstein's *Remarks on Frazer* as giving us a *theory* of religion or ritual, emphasizing its expressive or symbolic dimension as against James Frazer's evolutionary or historical one (Bouveresse 2008) and to think, instead, of *Golden Bough* as providing to Wittgenstein a provocation to reflect on issues relating to the internal (as distinct from an external) relation between language and the world (or worlds). There is, of course, some risk in taking the *Remarks on Frazer* as forming a well-thought-out argument on the part of Wittgenstein. As Peter Hacker (1992) notes, these are a rough set of notes: "In commenting on them, it should be borne in mind that they are incomplete, unpolished, and not intended for publication. If one wants to learn from them, they should not be squeezed too hard" (278). All this is true—and one must be cautious that even the device of treating these remarks as numbered, as in the present translation and my own comments, is nothing more than an editorial convenience: this device should not be equated with the apparatus of the numbered remarks as in *Tractatus* or in *Philosophical Investigations*.

Anthropologists might have something important to offer to this conversation. The trajectory of disavowal and occasional return to Frazer within anthropology (see Stephan Palmié's excellent introduction to his forthcoming translation of *Remarks on Frazer*) attests to a deeper issue here than Frazer having simply confused the instrumental and the expressive dimensions of social action or his having been mistaken in thinking that rituals in primitive societies mistook the nature of the world by attributing efficacy to ritual or magical action. Anthropologists, after all, have been deeply engaged with the issues of how to think of language, gesture, and performance in rituals (and religion) as not simply evidence about how mistaken primitive societies were about the nature of the world but about something else— be that society, cosmology, concept formation, or efficient (as opposed to material) causation as found, respectively, in Émile Durkheim ([1912] 1995), Claude Lévi-Strauss ([1962] 1966), Eduardo Viveiros de Castro (1992), and E. E. Evans-Pritchard ([1937] 1976). More generally, we might ask how does one think of the real in relation to what some call semantic opacity of rituals (Severi [2007] 2015) and others call the braiding of the ordinary and the extraordinary in the form of miracles (de Vries 2001)?

The concepts that I signal in the title of this chapter—mistake, error, and superstition—have some resemblance to each other, but there are also subtle differences between them, of which Wittgenstein gives us a detailed geography. The cases that interest him most, though, are those in which we are misled by our language either because it captures us within a given picture of the real or because it goes idling. How are such cases to be brought to the surface of our thought? What is the harmony between language and the world that is implied here? When is a statement to be seen as a mistake, when an error, when superstition, and what might be the stakes in distinguishing them?[4] I do not discuss here the notion of shadows that are always present as the potential of a word, allowing it to move to new contexts, for they do not play exactly the same role that errors and superstitions do. Instead, they block the notion of a straightforward or obvious way in which words or gestures might be aligned to the world through aspects of reference. In *Philosophical Investigations* (the therapeutic voice?), Wittgenstein says: "My aim is to teach you to pass from a piece of disguised nonsense to something that is patent nonsense" (Wittgenstein [1953] 1968, §464).[5] What is the nature of the disguised nonsense in Frazer as Wittgenstein sees it?

Let us first consider how Wittgenstein makes a distinction between mistake (or error) and superstition (see Travis 2009).[6] As distinct from a mistake, Wittgenstein seems to suggest, superstition is something produced through grammatical illusions (grammar in the sense of philosophical grammar or criteria that are grown within a form of life), leading to the feeling that something that is quite banal or commonplace is really exciting and in need of explanation. One example Charles Travis (2009) gives from *Philosophical Investigations* is of the child amazed that a tailor could sew a dress, imagining that he had nothing else to work with except his hands and pieces of thread. Thus, a casual expression—a tailor made me this dress—becomes the cause of excitement, if (mis)interpreted as the extraordinary event of the dress being produced by sewing, adding one thread on another without the materiality of the cloth (see *Philosophical Investigations*, §195). Wittgenstein then seems to fault Frazer not simply because he read expressive acts as statements of fact but also because he wrongly added excitement to ritual acts without seeing what kind of geography of description could provide the scaffold that supports them. I submit that much is at stake here because it misleads Frazer into a direction that turns out to be fatal for understanding how to render cultural difference and context-saturated meaning into a problem for anthropological thought. One of the paragraphs in *Philosophical Investigations* concludes by saying, "When we do philosophy, we are like savages, primitive people, who hear the expressions of civilized men, and then draw the queerest conclusions from it" (§194). Frazer's superstition then consists in having taken a routine, commonplace occurrence within a ritual complex and adding false excitement to it. We shall see what the source of this excitement is a little later. For now, I want to draw out a little more of what it means to think of ritual actions as expressions that are both set apart from the mundane and are yet commonplace. As Michael Lambek (2007) observes, religious utterances, although different from extraordinary utterances or everyday acts, are not extraordinary either since they entail nothing more than slight shifts and reframing of ordinary speech and ordinary acts. He suggests that we might regard such acts as parasitical on ordinary acts, producing what he calls the mystery of the ordinary in that it can produce this newness, this something other than itself.

Let me suggest here a slightly different inflection, taking an example from the conflict of interpretations around a simple ritual gesture for the fulfillment of a wish and the argument and counterargument that follows between the critics and defenders of the mīmāṃsā school of Indian philosophy (see Das 1983, 2016). The critics ridicule the proponents of mīmāṃsā for countless injunctions, such as the one in which someone desirous of sons should boil bits of gold, much as one boils grains of rice, as an offering to be made in the sacrificial ritual. The critics say that everyone knows that grains of rice can be boiled to cook them and they will satisfy hunger, but not pieces of gold. The reply from the defenders of the mīmāṃsā is a calm assertion that, indeed, that criticism holds true for action in the mundane world, but the injunction pertains to sacrificial action and thus has no relevance for action in the mundane world. What the defenders of the mīmāṃsā achieve here is to restore calm to what otherwise might have become an argument about the truth or falsity of such ritual actions. I suggest that though we know that the sacrificial arena is a bounded one in which actions and expressions are imbued with heightened intensity, they do not necessarily challenge the common background of our everyday lives.

Consider the following remark that Wittgenstein offers in his criticism of Frazer:

> I would like to say: nothing shows our kinship to those savages better than the fact that Frazer has at hand a word as familiar to us as "ghost" or "shade" to describe the views of these people.
>
> (For this surely is something different from what it would be if he were to describe, say, how the savages imagined that their heads would fall off when they have slain an enemy; in this case, *our description* would have nothing superstitious or magical about it.)
>
> Yes, the strangeness of this relates not only to the expressions "ghost" and "shade," and far too little is made of the fact that we count the

words "soul" [*Seele*] and "spirit" [*Geist*] into our own civilized vocabulary. Compared to this, it is a minor detail that we do not believe that our soul eats and drinks. (#23)[7]

What I take from this remark is that the familiar word *ghost* gestures to the fact that an understanding derived from the common background of our lives as humans is implicated in the description of "savage" customs. The fact that Frazer can use such words at hand as *ghosts* and *shade* connects our life to that of the so-called savages, gives us a footing in that life: their customs can be imagined within our form of life as a "human" form of life. If, on the other hand, someone had reported that the savage belief is that their own heads simply fall off the body when they kill an enemy (and are put back when the need arises), we would not know how to relate to such a description and would consider that we were, perhaps, not of the same flesh or that their ideas of what heads are and where they belong on the body are perhaps in need of a completely different description. The mīmāmsā scholars were able to preserve the integrity of the everyday when they desisted from saying that boiled pieces of gold were a perfect substitute for cooked rice for purposes of satisfying hunger than, say, for satisfying the ritual requirement of an offering in a particular kind of sacrifice. In that case, it would have been perfectly right to add excitement to what was commonplace in the way rituals were enacted. Let us take one more example of what Wittgenstein means by the harmony between language and the world and in what way Frazer seems to him to have violated a much more important aspect of what we might mean by thinking than simply to have committed an error by mistaking symbolic expressions for factual statements.

Consider: "The agreement, harmony, of thought and reality consists in this: if I say falsely that something is *red*, it nonetheless isn't *red*. And if I want to explain to someone the word 'red' in the sentence 'That isn't red,' I point to something red" (Wittgenstein [1953] 1968, §429; see Travis 2009 for a detailed discussion of this example). The point here is that the issue is not if the statement is *true* or *false* according to whether the thing pointed to is red or not but, rather, if it *could have* been red or not-red (Travis 2009). In other words, in speaking of shoes being red, there should be at least the possibility that they could be red. In this sense, the truth of a statement and the falseness of a statement are not states that completely exclude each other. Statements and facts, so to say, are not simply made for each other as gloves and hands are—as J. L. Austin (1950) said, there are different dimensions and degrees of success that statements achieve—part of this depends on whether a space has been prepared for a particular kind of statement. In the context of the fire festivals, Frank Cioffi ([1987] 1998) takes Wittgenstein to be saying that when we consider the sinister character attributed to these festivals in their contemporary enactment it is the space that the story finds already prepared for it that has to be scrutinized and not only the space that the events themselves might occupy.[8] So what Frazer fails to understand is not so much this or that fact about the fire festivals but the nature of the problem he is supposed to be resolving. (Consider also Wittgenstein's discussion of pain: "I have no pain in my arm," to ask, "In what sense does my present painless state contain the possibility of pain" (Wittgenstein [1953] 1968, §448)? Elsewhere he asks, "Does what is ordinary always make the impression of ordinariness?" (Wittgenstein [1953] 1968, §600). And now we can understand the importance Wittgenstein attributes to the fact that Frazer uses words like *ghost* or *shade*—words that might suggest the uncanny but in way that gestures to their already having a home in our language.)

A second important theme that makes a considerable impression on Wittgenstein is the deep (and sinister) character of magic. "What makes magic deep?" he asks. Why do we get the sensation of something deep and sinister in the contemplation of human sacrifice? For Frazer, the traces of human sacrifice are particularly clear and unequivocal in the Beltane Fire Festival, which involves the mock threat of burning a human victim selected arbitrarily by the ritual use of a cake prepared for this very purpose. For Wittgenstein, such an evocation of human sacrifice that is supposed to lie at the origin of the festival explains nothing in itself—in order to understand why a deep and sinister feeling is created we would have to look at present practices and not the putative origin of the offering in the fire festival. Similarly, the explanation that the priest-king must be "killed in his prime because according to the notion of the savages, his soul would not be kept fresh otherwise" (#1), which impresses Frazer, cannot be made to do much work here. As Thomas de Zengotita (1989, 392) says of this explanation, "What should be made of this? According to Wittgenstein, not much." Instead, we should ask what kind of experiences did such thoughts evoke in Frazer himself? Let us listen to Wittgenstein on Frazer once again:

What I want to say is this: what is sinister, deep [about all this] does not lie in how the history of this practice actually went, for perhaps it did not go that way at all; nor that it maybe or [even] probably went that way, but in what gives me reason to assume so. What makes human sacrifice so deep and sinister in the first place? For is it only the suffering of the victim that impress us thus? All manners of illnesses bring about just as much suffering, and yet do not evoke this impression. No, this deep and sinister aspect does not become self-evident just from our knowledge of the history of the external actions; rather, we impute it to them [reintroduce it into them] on the basis of an inner experience of our own. (#43)

I think there are two remarkable things Wittgenstein achieves here. First, he redefines depth not as vertical, inward depth (Zengotita 1989) but as spread out into the context. Second, he turns Frazer's interpretations to reflect on what these can tell us about English society through the various incipient rituals we construct every day, such as addressing our illness or hitting a rock to "punish" it. In other words, the reflexive gesture that many anthropologists made by asking what the interpretation of a ritual tells us about the discursive power or desire of the observer (see, for example, D. Scott 1994; Povinelli 2002) is evoked here not only to fault Frazer for his interpretation of these rituals but also to illuminate an aspect of our form of life as a human form of life.

Returning to the first point, take the concluding sentences of Remark #42 in *Remarks on Frazer*. Wittgenstein states:

The question is: Does this—shall we say—sinister character adhere to the custom of the Beltane fire in itself as it was practiced a hundred years ago, or only if the hypothesis of its origin were to be confirmed. I believe that what appears to us as sinister is the inner nature of the practice as performed in recent times, and the facts of human sacrifice as we know them only indicate the direction in which we ought to look at it. When I speak of the inner nature of the practice, I mean all of those circumstances in which it is carried out and that are not included in the report on such a festival, because they consist not so much in particular actions that characterize the festival than in what one might call the spirit of the festival that would be described, for example, if one were to describe the kind of people that take part in it, their usual way of behaving [on other occasions]—that is, their character—and the kind of games they play at other times. And then one would see that what is sinister lies in the character of these people themselves. (#42)

Wittgenstein assigns great importance of the dispersal of activities such that the context is not defined purely by activities that characterize the festival but also how people bring aspects of behavior (e.g., gestures, gait, ways of using words) into the scene of the festival. Note that Wittgenstein is not picking up only certain features of language (e.g., the use of indexicals) as connecting language to the world; instead, he is positing the character of worldliness or context-saturated character of language and a whole range of dispersed actions that he characterizes as the spirit of the festival (on the varied ways that language connects to the world see Moyal-Sharrock 2009). If further support was needed for this point, we could read *Philosophical Investigations*, in which Wittgenstein takes the sentence "He measured him with a hostile glance and said . . ." ([1953] 1968, §652) and asks how a reader of a narrative in which this sentence appears guesses at or supplies the meaning of this sentence. After all, the narrative might show the hostile glance later to be a pretense, or the reader may be kept in suspense about whether or not these words are pretense, so the reader is challenged to guess at a possible interpretation. "But then the main thing he guesses at is context." In other words, ordinarily we just take the words to mean what they say, but when planted with a doubt (were these two men friends or enemies?) what we have to guess is not the meaning of the words but their context. In order to discern why the fire festivals create a feeling of dread in their modern enactments, we would have to discern the spirit of the festival and not simply particular ritual gestures.

The second point regarding the similarity between our customs and theirs is well illustrated in the examples Wittgenstein gives of kissing a picture of the beloved not because we are in error in thinking that the picture *is* the loved one but because it satisfies a wish:

> Burning an effigy. Kissing the picture of a loved one. This is *obviously not* based on a belief that it will have a definite effect on the object that the picture represents. It aims at some satisfaction, and does achieve it, too. Or rather, it does not *aim* at anything; we act in this way and then feel satisfied. (#9)

I cannot pursue the theme of what "feeling satisfied" tells us about the relation between, say, a wish and its satisfaction, an expectation and its fulfillment, or an order and its execution, except to state that no further evidence as to the truth or falsity of such statements is asked for. Wittgenstein gives us a whole range of examples in which it would be absurd to say that an error was committed, since these are not, in the first place, matters of opinion and thus cannot be true of false. In drawing connections between our practices and those that Frazer evokes as evidence of primitive mentality, Wittgenstein's aim is to arrive at what he calls a perspicuous arrangement. He makes the case that "a perspicuous representation produces just that understanding which consists in 'seeing connexions.' Hence the importance of finding and inventing *intermediate* cases" ([1953] 1968, §122).

The effort that Wittgenstein makes in arranging the cases in a way that we can see connections (see also Sachs 1988) has the effect of taking away the excitement that superstition adds to what might be banal actions or those expressions produced through grammatical illusions. Moreover, his further achievement is to suggest that there is a background of common sense that we might identify as part of the human way of life, but we must pause and ask what notion of human informs him here. The best guide for making our way through this question is not the "universalism versus relativism" debate but the frequent references to the natural history of mankind, which are related equally to our being embodied creatures and creatures who have a life in language. Wittgenstein says, "Commanding, questioning, recounting, chatting, are as much a part of our natural history as walking, eating, drinking, playing" ([1953] 1968, §25). Thus, what we do as embodied creatures (walking, eating) and as creatures who have a life in language (recounting, questioning) are not laid along the axis of nature and culture but rather along the axis of a "natural history" of mankind.

Finally, consider one of the last three passages in *Philosophical Investigations*:

If the formation of concepts can be explained by facts of nature, should we not be interested, not in grammar, but rather in that in nature, which is the basis of grammar?—Our interest certainly includes the correspondence between concepts and very general facts of nature. (Such facts as mostly do not strike us because of their generality.) But our interest does not fall back upon these possible causes of the formation of concepts; we are not doing natural science; nor yet natural history—since we can also invent fictitious natural history for our purposes. ([1953] 1968, 230ᵉ)

The ideas here are of rightness, fitness, of our expressions carrying greater natural weight in a way that we might come to feel that our language and world are in harmony with each other. Thus, how we choose and value words is not about (or not only about) having a common framework for interpreting the meaning of what is said but what the person means in saying them—the sense in which one's words are an expression of what matters to one and of the rightness in relation to context. "The whirl of organism" to which Wittgenstein alludes in reference to forms of life refers in part to what Austin characterizes as made possible by our ordinary language: it "embodies all the distinctions men have found worth drawing and the connections they have found worth marking in the lifetimes of many generations" (Austin 1957, 8). It is also made possible partly because we share a sense of the natural, as in Austin's example that one cannot say, "I stepped on the baby inadvertently." It is not that the sentence is not grammatical in terms of linguistic rules or that the sentence does not make sense treated just as a sentence; it is that the sense of one's natural attitude to how your body is in relation to that of a baby lying on the floor or on the grass, perhaps, makes no sense when one uses the term "inadvertently" for it takes us to regions of life one does not normally inhabit (a person, we might say, does not *inadvertently* step on a baby). If one had instead said, "I stepped on the child accidentally," that would be a possible construction, for such accidents do happen. Here Austin shows the intimacy between language and the world by bringing expression in harmony with action that alludes to distinctions (inadvertently and accidentally) as natural to our way of being in the world. As Sandra Laugier (2018a) puts it, for Austin, the statement fits the facts in different ways, on different occasions, for different intents and purposes—"fits" does not carry any sense of correspondence or even correctness but, rather, it designates the character of the utterance in particular circumstances, for particular interests. Does this mean that there are no overarching norms for rightness of usage? The point is that such norms are context bound, and hence no general theory can be offered that would cover all situations.

My goal here has not been to give a chronological account of what I think are seminal concepts that link our understanding of different forms of life to our form of life as humans but instead to say that Frazer provided an important provocation to Wittgenstein as to how we might see other forms of life as both ours and theirs, much as our own forms of life fold the natural and the social, modes of living and modes of dying into each other. In my own remarks on specific paragraphs in *Remarks on Frazer*, I will try to say how attunement and absorption in the world through our agreements in our forms of life does not exclude the idea that we might have been otherwise than we are. This register of the subjunctive mood is particularly appropriate to think of the domains of rituals and myths (see Das 1998b).

## PART II: REMARKS ON FRAZER

I have given a very brief description of the project that brought different anthropologists together to comment on different parts of *Remarks on Frazer*, but one important aspect of this action was that I did not get to choose which remarks I would comment on because I simply delayed making my choices, but also because I depend upon contingent events to push my thought further and so wanted to see what fate would throw in my direction (see da Col and Palmié forthcoming). I was finally encouraged to comment on the following remarks: 27, 28, 29, 30, 32, and 34.[9] And though initially I felt a sense of panic because I could not get a handle on them, I found, to my surprise, that they opened up another region of Wittgenstein's thought that connected to the anthropological mode of thinking. However, it is important to note that these remarks seem to stand as reflections that show our familiarity with many of the rituals and highly formalized gestural languages in other forms of life. Yet they begin by asking, How might I make these actions significant to myself?

> I could imagine that I might have had to choose some being on earth as my soul's dwelling place, and that my spirit had chosen this unsightly creature as its seat and vantage point. Perhaps because the exception of a beautiful dwelling would repel him. Of course, for the spirit to do so, he would have to be very sure of himself. (#27)

*Commentary*: Zengotita (1989) makes the point that in suggesting that depth is not about inward depth but about connections, Wittgenstein spreads out subjectivity into context, which results in the radical move of dissolving the Protestant or Cartesian subject. Similar to the imagination that my pain could be in another body (Das 2007), Wittgenstein is also provoking us to imagine that the boundaries of our bodies are not the boundaries of our subjectivity for our existence is always capable of being more, or other, than its present realizations. For all our worldliness, then, we might never be fully at home in any particular world. Might one then think of ritual as one way of imagining, What if the world was otherwise? In my reading, this thought could morph into the deep skepticism that might destroy my everyday life or, conversely, it might show that the ability to imagine a different everyday (or eventual everyday) is part of the actual everyday.

How have anthropologists addressed this problem of the subjunctive mood? A promising move is made by Adam Seligman, Robert Weller, Michael Puett, and Bennett Simon (2008, 17–42), who start a substantive chapter titled "Ritual and the Subjunctive" by declaring that ritual creates a shared and conventional world of human sociality but that "such a world is always subjunctive, just one possible alternative" (17). An important example of such a subjunctive world that Seligman et al. give is that of creating certain social illusions by our everyday practices of politeness, for instance. Rituals of politeness, they suggest, posit a possible world of activity that pulls its practitioners outside the Hobbesian world of war of each against all. One problem with this interpretation is that the authors seem to posit the world of polite interactions as "illusory," since the sense of options created for a child who may be pleased to pass the salt in everyday domestic interactions is illusory—for cannot we *command* her to pass the salt or grab the salt cellar from her, making the "please" a fiction? However, the authors slip into a position in which they seem to implicitly attribute "reality" to the Hobbesian world of war of each against all rather than treating it as part of the mythical world of the state of nature, a fiction created to authorize a certain form of sovereignty. Then there are two forms of fiction circulating as part and parcel of the actual world, rather than the world created through ritual being illusory and the other world of conflict or power being real.

In Wittgenstein's account, possibility was the space prepared for a particular statement or story to find a footing, not simply an alternative to actuality. How might such a story as imagining a myth of origin for oneself, in which one's decaying or unsightly body was what one's spirit had chosen as the best picture or the best dwelling place for itself, find a footing in the world? Are the senses of the subjunctive different in Wittgenstein's "I could imagine" remark versus what Seligman et al. describe? Both accounts address the issue of how the inner and the outer are stitched together but take us in fairly different directions.

One could say "every view has its charm," but that would be wrong. What is correct is that every view is significant for whoever sees it so (but that does not mean one sees it as something other than it is). Indeed, in this sense every view is equally significant.

Yes, it is important that I must make my own even any one's contempt for me, as an essential and significant part of the world seen from my vantage point. (#28)

*Commentary*: The theme here relates to how one might make one's life significant to oneself or, in Stanley Cavell's signature idea, What is it to find one's voice in one's own culture? Laugier (2011) argues that whereas for Wittgenstein the central question was the common use of language, Cavell makes a new question arise from that problematic—the question of the relation between an individual speaker and the linguistic community. "For Cavell, this leads to a reintroduction of the voice into philosophy and to a redefinition of subjectivity in language precisely on the basis of the relationship of the individual voice to the linguistic community: the relation of a voice to voices" (Laugier 2011, 633). In Remark #28, the issue is not only establishing the relation of my body and my soul or the alignment between them alone but also seeing singularity within the domain of culture. Every view to be found in a given form of life acquires significance as it is made part of one's own disposition, or one's vantage point on one's culture (see Hage 2014), but not when seen as if in a catalogue of beliefs testifying to the internal pluralism or internal heterogeneity of a culture. What is at stake here is not a parabolic insistence on the significance of one's existence or the uniqueness of one's experience, as in Cavell's (1979) famous discussion: "But surely you cannot be having THIS pain," pointing to one's chest and thumping it. Rather, the insistence is on the work of making my voice *count*, on taking the facts of my existence upon myself. In saying that taking someone else's contempt for myself as part of how the world is for me, I attest to my singular vantage point on the world.

I am particularly interested here in pursuing the idea of what it means to take the facts of my existence upon myself through aligning myself to ritual performances, whether religious or secular. One way we could approach this question is by asking what it is for one to be attached to the words one utters, the gestures one makes, and thus taking an external performance as attesting to an internal state. Austin (1962) famously saw a promise as the outward and visible sign (initially read so for convenience or for some similar reason) that was read as indicative of an inward and spiritual act. From there, he said, it is a short step to assume that the outward utterance is a description, true or false, of the occurrence of an inward act. Thus, for instance, we begin to ask whether the person who promised to come back tomorrow meant his words. Austin's point, of course, was that at least as far as illocutionary force of an utterance was concerned, the officiating priest did not have to be sincere in declaring someone man and wife. The external performance was not stitched to an inner state of sincerity—if all the conventions were in place for the marriage to be accomplished, his words would accomplish it. If such utterances, such as making a promise, were to be regarded as the prototype of all ritual utterances, then collective performances do not have to be translated into any evidence of inner attachment. Then the kind of pressure Wittgenstein is putting on "making my own" the viewpoints I encounter would not carry weight. But matters are, of course, more complicated.

First, as Cavell (1994) brilliantly demonstrates, there are different moments in the performance of such ritual enactments as a marriage ritual. It may be sufficient for the presiding priest to utter the correct formulas without raising issues of sincerity or attachment to those words, but the man who says "I do" had better not be a bigamist who intends to cheat the bride of her inheritance. Thus, the issues of how one makes the collective words one's own; the relationship between the third-person statements of belief and the first-person statements of belief becomes an urgent issue. After all, I do not come to know my belief in the same way as I get to know the beliefs of others—nor do I have to examine myself to see if I am in pain. These are all matters that call for attention to our singular relations to the world and that cannot be derived from generalized descriptions.

An intriguing aspect of Wittgenstein's remarks is his insistence that my view of the world must also include the viewpoint of those who have contempt for me. It makes me think of the anthropological studies of certain castes or sects that were despised either for the lowly tasks they performed (Parry 1994) or for their transgressive practices (Suri and Pitchford 2010). Parry, for instance, describes how the Mahabrahmans, a caste of funeral priests who make their living on the funeral gifts they receive, feel that their work of absorbing the death pollution of others makes them open to misfortunes and feelings of ill-being. The ritual acts of eating the sins of others makes them wealthy but also makes their bodies heavy, slothful, unlike the bodies of those who earn their living with the sweat of their brow. The Aghoris, a sect known for its transgressive and even repulsive practices (such as eating corpses, living in cremation grounds), however, seem to convert their intimacy with death as life-giving to others, much as Lord Shiva made the gods immortal by taking poison that had emerged in the churning of the sea upon himself. Such research on the ways in which individuals might integrate the contempt of others into their own perspectives on the world still remains fragmentary, since anthropologists have not given sustained attention to the relation between the absorption of the third-person perspective on one's ritual role and the first-person account of how this provides a vantage point for singular individuals.[10]

> If a human being were free to choose to be born in a tree in the forest, then there would be some who would seek out the most beautiful or highest tree for themselves, some who would choose the smallest, and some who would choose an average or below-average tree, and I do not mean out of philistinism, but for just the reason, or the kind of reason for which someone else chose the highest. That the feeling we have for our life is comparable to that of a being that could choose its standpoint in the world has, I believe, its basis in the myth—or belief—that we choose our bodies before birth. (#29)

*Commentary*: My remark here is based on my somewhat shaky and intermittent understanding that Wittgenstein is using a philosophical allegory to contest the Cartesian allegory in which I am able to doubt if my body is mine but not if my mind is mine.[11] The fate of the human body in philosophy appears in many places in *Philosophical Investigations* and in *On Certainty*. I offer the suggestion that we could learn something about how Wittgenstein's remark about the human body being the best picture of the human soul (*PI*, 178ᵉ) might be illuminated through a comparison with the intimate relations he posits between a word and its meaning. Elsewhere, he speaks about imagining a language in which use of the idea of "soul" of the words plays no part. "In which, for example, we had no objection to replacing one word by another arbitrary one of our invention" (*PI*, §530). But this paragraph immediately draws comparison with Wittgenstein's evocation of a people who are "soul blind" and to Wittgenstein's pointing us to the feeling we have for the physiognomy of words. Our relation to our bodies, then, are not simply that of imagining them as an arbitrary relation any more than we can simply replace one word by another by consulting a dictionary, almost as if our words did not matter to us. What, then, shall we make of the last line of Remark #29? I believe what is being suggested here is that our feelings about the rightness of our bodies as somehow fitting for us is similar to our feelings for our lives as a whole—not simply the rightness of this or that action that we perform (see Das 2015c).

What about the fact, then, that in many cases techniques of the body are about our bodies being able to give expression to other bodies, such as bodies of animals or bodies of plants, as in many yoga postures (Alter 2004)? Or the fact that in Amerindian mythologies humans might make their home in human bodies or in animal bodies (Descola 1992, 2009; Vilaça 2005)? Of course, if our relation to our bodies might be that of having to contain or release the animal that is housed in them—as in all the talk of "animal spirits"—then there should be no difficulty in imagining that there are also humans in animal skins. What might distinguish a café skeptic's formulations on all these possibilities of human and animal bodies from the range of practices encountered, say, in the life of a yogi or a family with a jaguar brother-in-law is the fact that the feeling we have of our life as a whole comes not from one or another myth or item of belief but from the sense of what it is to live *this* life and not another. Of course, it is also true that one might not simply have the feel for the kind of life that one's culture requires of one, like the young head of a farm family in the Bocage who must learn to vanquish the claims of others on the land but may have no inclination for violence and hence must be brought into it through practices of, say, witchcraft (see Favret-Saada 2015).

Let's turn to the next remark that Wittgenstein makes on Frazer.

I believe the characteristic feature of primitive man is that he does not act on the basis of *opinions* (as Frazer thinks). (#30)

*Commentary*: I propose that we pair this remark with the following two paragraphs from *Philosophical Investigations*:

"So you are saying that human agreement decides what is true and what is false?"—It is what human beings say that is true and false; and they agree in the language they use. This is not agreement in language but in form of life. (*PI*, §241)

My attitude toward him is an attitude toward a soul. I am not of the *opinion* that he has a soul. (*PI*, §178)

Did Frazer think primitive man acted on the basis of opinions? I believe what Wittgenstein is identifying as "opinion" is the form of argumentation to which Frazer often resorts in which a custom is explained by citing a participant's view of what he or she is doing when following a custom. Thus, early on in *Golden Bough*, Frazer explains: "The notion that a person can influence a plant homeopathically by his act or condition comes out clearly in a remark made by a Malay woman. Being asked why she stripped the upper part of her body naked in reaping the rice, she explained that she did it to make the rice-husks thinner, as she was tired of pounding thick-husked rice. Clearly, she thought that the less clothing she wore the less husk there would be on the rice" (Frazer [1922] 2004, 32). In many ways, anthropology has moved far beyond this mode of "explaining" the meaning of a ritual with our advances in semiotic or hermeneutic interpretation of the ritual complex. Yet, Wittgenstein seems to me to discern an important question—namely, when and how do we know that what is being said is an indicative statement, an order, a proposition, the expression of a wish, or something else? It is the nature of our agreements that tell us the difference between these forms of talk, and yet this agreement is not simply over a particular speech act but over criteria grown within a form of life. The methodological imperative to bring context centrally into the analysis of speech acts by attention to metapragmatic signaling grew in response to some of these issues. However, it is worth asking how much the emphasis on what is formulaic (e.g., speech acts with illocutionary force) or what can be elicited in speech by way of explanation of what is happening orients our analysis toward certain objects of analysis (e.g., declarations of sovereign subjects in ritual, witchcraft accusations) as compared to other things (discursive and nondiscursive) that are going on both within a ritual or ceremonial occasion and outside it.[12]

> It could have been no insignificant reason—that is, no *reason* at all—for which certain races of man came to venerate the oak tree other than that they and the oak were united in a community of life, so that they came into being not by choice, but jointly, like the dog and the flea (were fleas to develop a ritual, it would relate to the dog).

One might say, it was not their union (of oak trees and humans) that occasioned these rites, but, in a certain sense, their separation.

For the awakening of intellect goes along with the separation from the original *soil*, the original ground of life. (The origin of *choice*.)

(The form of the awakening mind is veneration.) (#31)

*Commentary*: There are two thoughts here: one relates to the community of life and the second to the picture of thought. A community of *life*, suggests Wittgenstein, is a community made up of what sustains life. Here, rituals seem to relate not to arbitrary constructions but to expressions of this mutuality of human and nonhuman in making up the community of life. There is a whole trajectory of anthropological thought we could trace in this connection made between animals and totemic symbols and rites. Are animals chosen because they are good to eat (Radcliffe-Brown [1929] 1952)[13] or because they are good to think (Lévi-Strauss [1962] 1966)? Body or mind? Interestingly, we might go back to a classic such as Durkheim's ([1912] 1995) *Elementary Forms of Religious Life* and discover that while he says somewhat lamely that animals are chosen as totems because they are easy to represent, he also insists that the totemic sign has to be painfully inscribed on the body as a means of making future memory (Das 1995a).

And then there is that pretense of community as in sacrificial rituals, the illusions with which we cover our forms of cruelty. "You do not want to kill, O judges and sacrificers until the animal has nodded? Behold, the pale criminal has nodded: out of his eyes speaks the great contempt" (Nietzsche 1961, 35).

In the second part of Remark #32, Wittgenstein gives us a picture of thought that lies in the moment of our separation from the original ground: a picture that takes the moment of detachment as the sign of the awakening mind. This is resonant of how Michael Jackson (2015) formulates his own process of thinking. Yet it seems to me that later, in *Philosophical Investigations*, Wittgenstein has vastly complicated the relation between thinking and awakening of intellect. For example, Wittgenstein asks us to consider what relation solving a mathematical problem has to the context and ground of its formulation (*PI*, §334). And this is followed by the question as to what happens when we try to find the right expression for our thoughts. Does the thought exist before the expression? And if we say that thinking is an incorporeal process, that makes sense only when we are trying to distinguish thinking from eating; otherwise it is only the picture of things going on in our head that leads us to the idea that thinking can be separated from its context and its ground (see *PI*, §339). Awakening to my life, I suggest, has a different modality than that of thinking; here, it is helpful to be in company with Cavell on the difference between knowing and acknowledging and to be mindful of the horror that might come with the success of knowledge, as when reason itself becomes demonic (see Cavell 1969b; Das 2015c).

While I do not have the space to elaborate this distinction in greater detail, I point to the discussion on the fatality of the "success of knowledge" as Cavell discusses through the figure of Faust. "If there were a drama of pure knowledge, it seems that Faust must be its protagonist. But is Faust a tragic figure? Is he to be understood in terms of the light of skepticism? Skepticism, after all, has to do with the absolute *failure* of knowledge, whereas what Faust lived was the absolute *success* of knowledge. But apparently, what he is to have discovered about this success is that it is not humanly satisfying. He is the Midas of knowledge" (Cavell 1979, 455).

In other words, the success of knowledge is that if I allow myself to trust only that which I have come to know through the application of rational procedures, then I am bound to turn reason against itself much as Midas was bound to turn his golden touch against his own children. One instance of the application of the idea of reason turning demonic is that it blocks us from accepting such things as the humanity of the other on trust—demanding evidence where none should be needed—or it asks for proof for the love of my partner, or the fact (for a man) that my children are mine, or that the groan I hear is, indeed, an expression of pain. The point is not that such doubts might not arise in the weave of life but that they cannot be settled by the production of more and more evidence. The fatal consequences of the success of knowledge can only be mitigated by accepting the other in his or her concrete reality. Wittgenstein, in asking, "How can I prove the existence of the other?" is inclined to turn to the existence of the concrete other in such quotidian scenes as children playing in the street. From the perspective of the one demanding hard evidence such scenes are not enough to settle the problem of existence—for one who is willing to accept that our agreements are fragile but that these agreements are all we have, doubts are not absolutely extinguished but a way is found to live with them.

(In ancient times he was obliged to sit on the throne for some hours every morning, with the imperial crown on his head, but to sit altogether like a statue, without stirring either hands or feet, head or eyes, nor indeed any part of his body, because, by this means, it was thought that he could preserve peace and tranquility in his empire . . .)

When someone in our (or at least my) society laughs too much, I press my lips together in an almost involuntary fashion, as if I believed I could thereby keep his lips closed.[14] (#33)

*Commentary*: In order to interpret this remark, it is helpful to insert the earlier remark in which Wittgenstein says, "At a certain stage of early society the king or priest is often thought to be endowed with supernatural powers or to be an incarnation of a deity, and consistently with this belief the course of nature is supposed to be more or less under his control" (#32), and then goes on to remark, "It is of course not the case that the people believe that the ruler has these powers while the ruler himself very well knows that he does not have them, or does not know so only if he is an idiot or fool. Rather, the notion of his power is of course arranged in a way such that it corresponds with experience—his own and that of the people. That any kind of hypocrisy plays a role in this is only true to the extent that it suggests itself in most of that humans do anyway" (#33). The excitement around the idea that the king wrongly believes that sitting still like a statue will ensure peace and tranquility of the empire is taken away by juxtaposing it with the quotidian example of pressing your lips together to block the loud or vulgar laughter of someone in your vicinity, not because you *believe* that it will block this offensive laughter but because a response is drawn out of you. With this perspicuous arrangement, the excitement is removed, and one is tempted to say that disguised nonsense gives way to patent nonsense. That is, if we understand that in Wittgenstein's hands the reader has been taken to a place where she can see that the question with regard to nonsense was never that of being confronted with gibberish but with a discourse that had the air of being a perfectly sensible discourse but was revealed to disguising its lack of sense, when we reach the point of patent nonsense we have been educated to draw the boundaries between sense and nonsense in a new way.

## PART III: IN THE REALM OF ETHNOGRAPHY AGAIN

I have argued that Wittgenstein's *Remarks on Frazer* could be taken to ask two questions: First, what is it to be in the grip of a picture? Second, is it possible to imagine that one's life could be otherwise? In this final section, I wish to offer two ethnographic examples to show how these ideas might be productive to think of everyday encounters, on the one hand, and work done to bring about a different, one might say, eventual, everyday, on the other.

I first take an ethnographic scene in which the existence of the other is seen as a threat to the survival of one's own way of life and trace how the desire for the psychic annihilation of the other is expressed as a temptation to escape the everyday. I contrast this with a second scene in which a possibility for newness is created by taking a stance in which a discourse, somewhat foreign to the prevailing one, is absorbed by the metaphor of "overhearing," suggesting that even if one is not a direct addressee of the speech emanating from an elsewhere, one could still participate in it. What I am trying to do here is to release the potential contained in Wittgenstein's critique of Frazer to think of the moral issues that contemporary conditions of living with the other raise, both in terms of threat and promise.

Let us recall *PI*, §110, where Wittgenstein is emphatic that to be in a grip of a picture is not simply to be mistaken on some fact or the other but to be in a grip of a superstition: "'Language (or thought) is something unique'—this proves to be a superstition (*not* a mistake!), itself produced by grammatical illusions."

In her ethnographically rich book on fairness, class, and belonging in contemporary England, Katherine Smith (2012) tracks the sense of being excluded, discriminated, and even disenfranchised among English working-class members and how these feelings come to be expressed in relation to their imagination of what Muslim immigrants are able to "extract" from the government.[15] Smith's working-class respondents in Halleigh (in the vicinity of Manchester, UK) constantly evoked such expressions as "It's not fair" and "There is no free speech" in relation to the presence of Muslims in Britain and in their own local communities. Sometimes these expressions were used to express what they felt was preferential treatment given to the Muslims in such matters as bending institutional rules to accommodate their religious beliefs and at other times around an unease with the veiling of the face or not being able to share a sense of humor. On the question of veiling, one informant expressed his unease in the following way:

> When we see someone and we are speaking to them, we like to see their faces. It's our way of life here. But they don't respect that. We just have to respect them in our country. (Smith 2012, 94)

Smith describes a more dramatic form of "protest" when Aaron, a young man who wanted to assert his right to free speech, began to wear a balaclava every Sunday to various local pubs on the pretext that it was his "religion." When asked by the landlords to either remove the balaclava or leave, he would shout, "This is my religion." When asked why he was doing this, Aaron replied that he was carrying on a single-person protest against the fact that Jack Straw, member of parliament, had felt compelled to offer a public apology for remarks made when he was home secretary in 2006 pertaining to the discomfort he felt when talking to Muslim women who were wearing a niqab. Straw had asked them to remove it if they wanted to speak to him or else to choose to speak to a female member of his staff instead of him. In Aaron's words:

> I put on a balaclava. I thought, right, I'm going to make a statement. You know, what if I wore a balaclava on a Sunday. . . . It's my religion. . . . I have known the landlords in these pubs for years, but they have all come up to me and they would say, ". . . You've got to leave unless you want to take that off." I told them, "I'm not taking this off. It's my right to wear this. It's my religion." (Smith 2012, 93–94)

There are other instances Smith describes where informants, both male and female, felt that their sense of what is funny, when something is a joke and when an insult, is not shared with the Muslim migrants. Called "having a barter" the insults, quick-witted responses, and cultivating a disposition of "being not too sensitive" or "not taking it personally" were forms through which dyadic relations were maintained and exhibited in this working-class neighborhood. As one of the informants explained, "It isn't really insults. Well, it is, but we just like to have a laugh. We just wind each other up. No one gets offended or anything. We just all sort of know, it's just a laugh, you know?" (Smith 2012, 114).

We could call the remarks made of the importance of "seeing a face" or "sharing a sense of humor" as forms of quotidian racism through which Muslims are excluded from a shared life. But we might also focus on the way that talking about Muslims in this way also begins to make what would have been an everyday, unremarkable practice elsewhere a subject of great excitement—a sense of becoming disjointed with life in this part of working-class England, leading to feelings that there can be no space prepared within this form of life for Muslim others. In Aaron's actions in wearing the balaclava, and proclaiming it to be his religion, we can see that there is a parodying of the niqab—yet Aaron seems unable to see that his actions are in the nature of a flight from the everyday. Others, including the landlords of the pub, recognize this as the parody that it is and thus get him to leave.[16] Might it have been possible for these men and women to imagine a different form of interaction with their Muslim neighbors if they had tried to see what connections they might make with other things there are in their lives—maybe replacing the polarity within which they cast their relations with Muslims by analogies that might allow them to connect (M. D. Jackson 1987)? That such connections and analogies are regularly made and that certain words belonging to one tradition can be taken to be simply "words at hand" and used with different inflections across traditions is a common observation in many ethnographies on relations across different religious communities in India (Alam 2004; Chatterji 2012; Das 2010a, 2010c; Henn 2014). It is not that such possibilities of mutual engagement and recognition provide any guarantees against violence, but, as Singh (2015) argues, a mode of agonistic intimacy allows those who are locked in conflict at one threshold of life—say, in political contestations—to come together at another threshold of life—say, through practices of spirit possession. If we think of the everyday as holding the potential for continuous transfigurations, then we need to track how everyday slights, grudges, betrayals, and boredoms can turn into lethal conflicts. As I have shown in the case of one of the neighborhoods I worked in, years of small jealousies and grudges between members of two different religions and castes (Hindu Chamars and Sikh Siglikars) inhabiting two adjoining streets mutated into a violent orgy of killings as more powerful political actors converted this space into a theater of conflict for national-level political confrontations (see Das 2007, chap. 9). Or else, as Fassin (2013) notes for police patrols deployed to keep order in areas where Muslim migrants live in the suburbs of Paris, the boredom of nothing happening can convert into a kind of quotidian racism in which police end up throwing around random insults and completely inappropriate body searches that could in turn grow into violent riots. Cavell (2007) asks us, social scientists, to consider how these "little deaths of everyday life" might become magnified by standing sources of social enmity—racism, casteism, sexism, elitism. The counterpoint might be that it is in small acts of everyday repair that what looks like a standing possibility of violence can be contained. Singh's (2015) work alerts us to changing rhythms, to the waxing and waning intensities, through which this life of the other is engaged.

Wittgenstein's great insight into Frazer's *The Golden Bough* was that Frazer is unable to see that the feeling of dread that he attributes to the past dark crimes committed by savages is related to his own constricted imagination of the life of the other. This constricted imagination is apparent in Smith's informants who could not see that the Muslim neighbor does not have to fit fully into their lives as they imagine it in order to be part of that life. But there is a flight into fantasy that prevents her informants from seeing what is before their eyes. After all, none of the Muslim women who wore the niqab were likely to be hanging around with Aaron in the pub, so his imagination of the threats they posed to his way of being was more a result of what Wittgenstein thought of as "superstition." Smith cites Habermas (1995) on value disagreements, which, he argues, become deliberations about "who we are" and how we evaluate what is a good life. For Smith, Habermas's formulation that we cannot jump out of a particular life history or form of life in which we actually find ourselves—and with which our identities are irrevocably tied up—resonates with what her respondents stated about the anxieties about preserving their forms of life (Smith 2012, 91). But Wittgenstein would alert us to the fact that a harmony between our words and our worlds is also about being able to imagine the possibility that we could be other than we are (Jackson 2005, 2016).

I take Wittgenstein's comparison between our language (and thus our forms of life) to a city that is never finished as evidence of the open character of forms of life, though this open character does not mean it is infinitely stretchable:

> Our language can be seen as an ancient city; a maze of little streets and squares, of old and new houses, and of houses with additions from various periods; and this surrounded by a multitude of new boroughs with straight regular streets and uniform houses. (Wittgenstein [1953] 1968, §18)

## A SECOND EXAMPLE

Let me take a somewhat different example—that of how a new language of human rights is absorbed within a society that considers this language first to be alien but then opens itself to it through aligning its own conventions to the possibility of newness. Don Selby (2018), in his work on human rights in Thailand, traces the trauma in Thai society at the potential of violence within Buddhism that came to the surface in the brutal suppression and massacre of student demonstrations in 1976 in Bangkok in the course of the democracy movement. For many Buddhists, there was the further trauma of remembering that the killings had been justified by powerful Buddhist monks such as Kulliiowattho Bhikku, who argued that it was meritorious to kill Communists since they were the personifications of Mara, the evil incarnation in Buddhism, whose purpose is to destroy Buddhism. Are the teachings of Buddha then capable of generating such brutal violence? Social conventions did not permit open discussions, but Selby suggests that these anxieties were addressed through another language—that of human rights within the institutional spaces of the newly established National Human Rights Commission (NHRC), constitutionally mandated in 1997 and finally constituted in 2001. Selby tracks how initially the language of human rights was treated as something that was simply "overheard," as if the Thai people were not the direct addressees of this discourse but had come to participate in it through indirect means. However, as complaints from citizens began to pour in and were adjudicated, the language of human rights came to be treated as another potential contained within Buddhism (and not as coming from the West) as they thickened and gathered weight. The traditional institutional mechanisms, such as those of face work or of patronage relations, were bent and extended to do work for the NHRC (Selby 2018). This is a fascinating example of how a space of possibility for newness was created by reinterpretation of what Buddhism might mean in the context of aspirations for democracy. Selby comments that even without a proximal scene of devastation the event can occasion a turning back to the ordinary in novel ways (Selby 2014). He thus thickens the notion of the actual everyday by showing the potential of violence contained within it and tracking how newness might be absorbed within the scene of sameness to address moral disquiet. In Selby's stunning framing: "I argue that human rights appeared as if overheard, involving a consideration of understanding around a fragment, with the resources one has at hand rather than through a process of vernacularization" (Selby 2018). As Cavell would say it (and Selby cites him at various points in his book), "The practice of the ordinary may be thought of as an overcoming of iteration or replication or imitation by repetition, of counting by recounting, or calling by recalling. *It is the familiar invaded by another familiar*" (Cavell 1989, 45).

Of course, not all forms of newness might be absorbed in this way by extending the notion of tradition. Commenting on the aspirations expressed in what many call the Arab Spring, Talal Asad (2015) argues that traditions are plural and dynamic but that the events since 2011 in Egypt show that modern liberal states make it difficult or even impossible to permit certain experiments in the new direction within a particular tradition. Asad's analysis is complex and his conclusions about the possibility of a more just political formation in Egypt are pessimistic. The uprisings in Egypt, he says, expressed an aspiration that cannot be characterized as either "religious" or "secular" because people with religious and secular sensibilities were joined in their efforts to overthrow the old system and make a new beginning, to initiate a "democratic tradition" propelled by a desire that political obligation be founded on loyalty to the nation and not on fear of the state's violence. But as the later violent suppression of the movement, as well the internal dissensions that developed within the movement, showed, an aspiration is not a realization. As Asad summarizes these issues:

> Some years later, well after the July 3rd military coup, looking back at the January uprising, it becomes apparent that there never was a "revolution" because there was no new foundation. There was a moment of enthusiasm in the uprising, as in all major protests and rebellions, but the solidarity it generated was evanescent. A hopeful attempt at beginning a tradition never guarantees the hoped for future: clear aims, good judgment, patience, and willingness to learn a new language and how to inhabit a new body, are required to respond to the various dangers and opportunities that emerge from attempts to found a new political order. (Asad 2015, 8–9)

There are two important points that Asad is making. First, when one thinks of newness in terms of collective political action, it involves both tectonic shifts that might be in the nature of slow changes that are not on the surface as well as the energies that go into brining newness at the political level, but these energies are not always durable. Asad seems to acutely feel the failure of the Egyptian uprisings, noting that even among the Muslim intellectuals and leaders he interviewed there was less awareness of what learning a new language might entail such that it could be recognized as both new and Islamic or Egyptian. However, because Asad's essay occasionally collapses the notion of tradition with that of a form of life, he might have underestimated the importance of these moments of heightened intensities within the lifeworlds and their potential for generating something that might exist for now in the margins of consciousness but might later grow into something yet unthought (or not). Said otherwise, one might ask if even failed political projects leave residues in the form of potential or unfinished stories that might reappear later in new ethical sensibilities in our lives. Thinking, then, of the everyday in terms of the potential, the actual, and the eventual should free us from the default position that many scholars often unthinkingly fall into—viz., that the everyday is nothing other than the site for routine, repetition, and acquired habits. The implications for thinking about the stakes in the political to which Wittgenstein and Cavell open us are indeed staggering but not so obvious. For now, I leave this chapter with the idea that in learning what is the human rights discourse, or how to think differently of justice, the challenge is not to learn *a new language*, as if the very idea of language was "new," or to simply correct earlier erroneous understandings of concepts like "human" or "rights." We may, instead, learn from the analogy Wittgenstein makes with the child: "The child already has a language, only not this one" (*PI*, §32).

# 10

## CONCEPTS CRISSCROSSING

*Anthropology and Knowledge-Making*

Moving from Wittgenstein's *Remarks on Frazer* to the broader question of knowledge-making in anthropology, let us imagine this chapter as a conversation taking place over a period of time, interrupted by other demands and returning to the topic of concepts—without clear conclusions except for a willingness to submit oneself to being educated in public. *How* are concepts generated in anthropological thought? Instead of treating concepts as neutral intellectual tools that stand between theory as a network of connected propositions and empirical observations, what if we thought of the way anthropologists engage fieldwork and their respective intellectual milieus as constituting a form of life within which concepts arise? As for the specificity of anthropological concepts, are these specialized disciplinary currencies with which we carry out our commerce of making intelligible certain forms of life that we have immersed ourselves in during the phase of anthropological fieldwork? Intelligible for whom? And what relation do the anthropological concepts have to the vernacular concepts that we encounter in our field sites?

A common way of thinking of concepts places them as abstract objects of thought that organize our experience, which is rendered otherwise as inchoate, amorphous, and waiting to be given form. Posing the relation between concepts and experience in this manner appears somewhat unfortunate to me as it assumes that experience and concepts correspond to the distinction between concrete and abstract in unproblematic ways. Nor does this formulation dwell sufficiently on the questions of what kind of relation concepts bear to the pressures of the real. Is there a difference in the way that the semiotic apparatus of signs and symbols brings in the real—e.g., in terms of relations of revealing and concealing—and in the normative constraints put on concepts as they hook into a particular region of the real? Are there different pictures of reality that guide our thinking of the apparatus of signifying practices, on the one hand, and conceptual formations, on the other? When I speak of the normative constraints on concepts, I am not thinking so much of rules that determine how a concept should be applied but implicit understandings as well as judgments on what "seems right" or "fits the facts" brought within the purview of a concept, more or less. Austin's ordinary realism regarding claims to knowledge in his essay "Other Minds" is helpful in taking this thought forward. As he says, "Enough is enough: it doesn't mean everything. Enough means that (within reason and for the present intents and purposes) it can't be anything else, there is no room for an alternative competing description of it. It does *not* mean, e.g., enough to show it isn't a stuffed goldfinch" (Austin 1946, 156; [1961] 1979, 84).

In the above citation, we have an example of how we might restrict the proliferation of a concept since the limits of a concept can only be tested as it moves from one context to another. Similarly, its normativity as a more or less good fit determines how it might cover more than one thing or recognize similarity not on the basis of sameness but on the basis of which aspects of a situation count for determining what is an appropriate extension of a concept. We learn from Wittgenstein that when it comes to the kind of judgments about the rightness of a word in one context versus another, it is not rules but the way we experience the physiognomy of words that counts.

> How do we find the "right" word? How do I choose among words? Without doubt it is sometimes as if I were comparing them by fine differences of smell: *That* is too. . . . *that* is too. . . . —*this* is the right one. . . . It is possible—and this is important—to say a *great deal* about a fine aesthetic difference.—The first thing you say may, of course, be just: This word fits, that doesn't—or something of the kind. But then you can discuss all the extensive ramifications of the tie-up effected by each of the words. The first judgment is not the end of the matter, for it is the field of force of a word that is decisive. (Wittgenstein [1953] 1968, 218–19ᵉ)

Of course, words act sometimes as concepts and at other times as signs, but the important point here is that the normativity implied in the idea that this is right and that is not right is shown to be related to grains of experience (as if words had smells), to a force field rather than to any explicit rules about correct speech. One casts about for the right word until one reaches a feeling of satisfaction.[1] In Sandra Laugier's (2017) felicitous phrasing, to think of concepts in terms of their sensitivity to experience is to acknowledge that concepts with which we live are in this world and of the ordinary world. This is an insight that is lost in the process of thinking of normativity as meeting some kind of normative standards that are rule-bound and tools for determining what might be included or excluded within a class, as I hope to show in what follows.

Instead of addressing these questions in an abstract way, I will take a few concrete examples from the ethnography of two classic texts—Godfrey Lienhardt (1961) on the Dinka and E. E. Evans-Pritchard ([1956] 1970) on the Nuer—to set up the issues under discussion. I will follow this discussion with some queries on such issues as those of radical incommensurability as opposed to more gentle and flexible ontologies. Evans-Pritchard's views on the importance of the study of so-called primitive religions for understanding Christianity and his critiques of the distinctions between natural religions and revealed religions are well known and I am not going to revisit these questions. My interests, instead, lie in the details of the respective monographs of Lienhardt and Evans-Pritchard in which the experiences in the field, including discussions with informants who are asked to reflect on their own practices, are sought to be organized under such concepts as those of God, deities, spirits, sacrifice, offerings, libations, prayer, invocation, etc.—all terms that are treated as translatable for European readers yet pose difficult questions about existence and about reality.[2]

I will add one caveat right at the start of this discussion. Both Evans-Pritchard and Lienhardt were inclined to treat the societies they studied as isolated and hence available for thinking about religion in its elementary form after Durkheim ([1912] 1995); yet it is not as if the concepts they were encountering among the Nuer, the Azande, or the Dinka were entirely untouched by experiences of other religions. In fact, Arabic terms seeped into the religious vocabularies of the Nuer and the Dinka, and experiences with Christian missionaries left recognizable traces in the descriptions of events or in the explanations offered about various terms to the anthropologists. So, in some ways the reality these anthropologists describe is not raw sensory experiences that have not been already conceptualized; these have been conceptualized many times over. There is a crisscrossing of concepts from different domains of experience—spirits, government officials, cattle, kin—as well as an overlap between vernacular concepts and the conceptual repertoire that the anthropologists bring from their own experiences, as I hope to show. Stated in more general terms, I claim that it is not as if there is a network of vernacular concepts over which a second-order analysis is placed—as if what ordinary people make of their social world is a confused understanding of the real and the deployment of disciplinary theoretical concepts raises their concepts to a new level.[3] At the very least, to think of crisscrossing of vernacular concepts with anthropological ones rather than a hierarchical relation between them would suggest that words as appellation may point to specific objects but they do not cut up the real as if each concept had a domain over which it was master.[4] I will frequently return to this theme, allowing it to be expanded over the course of this chapter.

## THE CRISSCROSSING OF CONCEPTS

In some of my earlier work (Das 2015a, 2018), I examine the open texture of concepts, as well as the role our common background as humans plays in making concepts intelligible not only across different cultures but also within the same social world. Here I want to dwell on a different idea: that of concepts as they crisscross each other and, in a related vein, when they touch or overlap. In the process, I will ask how such overlaps or crisscrossing stimulate one to think of similarity and difference as the results rather than the conditions of such overlaps. As Wittgenstein's notion of family resemblances in *Philosophical Investigations* alerts us, we have to look and see.

Wittgenstein's famous formulation of family resemblances in *Philosophical Investigations* repudiates two important ideas related to concepts that had given him trouble earlier. The first is the notion that there could be a general form of a proposition of which the astonishing variety of propositions found in actual usage were simply examples. This is a project he turns away from after the *Tractatus*. The second idea that he questions is that everything we classify under a concept has to necessarily have something in common. Indeed, we do use criteria to determine what is similar, what is different, but these are not simply logical criteria; they are criteria grown within a form of life that rests less on a set of formalized rules (I do not deny that rules have some place) and more on customs, habits, manners[5]—in what philosophers such as Iris Murdoch, Cora Diamond, and Sandra Laugier call the "texture" of life. But I am running ahead of myself. Let me return to the crisscrossing and overlapping of concepts. Allow me to take parts of the discussion from remarks 65 to 70 in *Philosophical Investigations* to get into this discussion.

Remark 65 concedes that items we might gather as examples of a general concept might not have any one characteristic in common: "I am saying that these phenomena have no one thing in common which makes us use the same word for all,—but they are *related* to each other in many different ways" (§65).

Remark 66 takes examples from many different games and exhorts us that instead of saying there must be something common in everything we classify as a game, "*look and see* if there is anything common at all." When we do look and see what happens in board games, and in card games, and in the difference between the emphasis on winning and losing in ball games and in the game of the child throwing the ball against wall and catching it, we see how "similarities crop up and disappear." As the concluding two lines of §66 say, "And the result of the examination is: we see a complicated network of similarities overlapping and crisscrossing, sometimes overall similarities, sometimes similarities in detail."

In the next remark (§67), Wittgenstein provides his famous articulation of the concept of "family resemblance," for, similar to the various resemblances one finds among members of a family in terms of, say, physical traits, we find resemblances among different games "that overlap and crisscross in the same way."

I want to pause here and emphasize a few salient points, since the concept of family resemblance in a general way has been used by many anthropologists to great advantage but with the assumption that the resemblance Wittgenstein is talking about is exclusively the resemblance among different things classified under one name. Instead, I suggest that what is of equal importance in Wittgenstein is the idea that we *extend* our concepts not by notions of similarity that are already defined once and for all but rather by allowing a particular similarity to appear and disappear as we look and see what direct or indirect relation one member of the class (say, that of board games) has with another member of the class (say, outdoor games). He compares the procedure for extending concepts as that of spinning a thread— "And we extend our concept of number as in spinning a thread we twist fibre on fibre. And the strength of the thread does not reside in the fact that some one fibre runs through its whole length, but in the overlapping of many fibres" (§67). One important consequence of this mode of thinking of concepts is that Wittgenstein explicitly argues for concepts having blurred edges, and he means here something much more radical than simply pointing to cases that fall in the margins of any classification. He is, in fact, pointing to our everyday practices within which concepts are part of living a certain kind of life. If I may be allowed, I would like to cite one other paragraph from *Philosophical Investigations* that goes to the heart of the issue on the blurred boundaries of concepts and their relation to life.

> One might say that the concept "game" is a concept with blurred edges.—
> "But is a blurred concept a concept at all"—Is an indistinct photograph
> a picture of a person at all? Is it even always an advantage to replace an
> indistinct picture by a sharp one? Isn't the indistinct one often what we
> need?
>
> Frege compares a concept to an area and says that an area with vague
> boundaries cannot be called an area at all. This presumably means that
> we cannot do anything with it.—But is it senseless to say: "Stand roughly
> there"? Suppose I was standing with someone in a city square and said
> that. And as I say it I do not draw any kind of boundary, but perhaps point
> with my hand—as if I were indicating a particular *spot*. And this is just
> how one might explain to someone what a game is. One gives examples
> and intends them to be taken in a particular way.—I do not, however,
> mean by this that he is supposed to see in those examples that common
> thing which I for some reason—unable to express; but that he is now to
> *employ* those examples in a particular way. Here giving examples is not
> an indirect means of explaining—in default of a better. For any general
> definition can be misunderstood too. The point is that this is how we play
> the game. (I mean the language game with the word "game.") (§71)

There are many ways of interpreting these observations, but as I read them the salient points I want to take relate to the possible mishaps around anthropological concepts. First, how does a concept (vernacular or anthropological) get extended and how do we find a sense of the rightness or wrongness of a particular direction of extension? Said otherwise, if concepts have a normativity through which we (the people we study or the anthropologists) recognize the constraint imposed on a concept as to which region of reality or to which stretch of reality it applies, then from where does this feeling of rightness or wrongness derive? Second, is the possibility of the extension of a concept related to the way in which we learn not simply to classify according to similarities and differences but learn *what constitutes similarity or difference*—then might we go further and say that the possibilities opened up by crisscrossing and overlaps in concepts also open up forms of life to newness? Third, to what extent does it matter whether a concept parses out a region of the real in an indistinct or indeterminate way or whether it muscles down a region of reality to itself? Is this a matter of the kind of needs that particular concepts are made to serve in the flux of life?[6]

## OF GODS, SPIRITS, POWERS, IMAGES

Let us now take up the classic ethnographies of the Dinka and the Nuer to dwell on a set of terms roughly forming a group—translated by Lienhardt and Evans-Pritchard in their respective ethnographies as "God," "gods," "spirits," "powers," and "images." Could we use the idea of family resemblances to advantage in considering how these terms relate to each other—under which conditions they function as signs or as concepts? Let me begin with the Dinka.

The first word Lienhardt parses out for understanding Dinka religion is *nhialic*, the locative form of *nhial*, meaning "sky" or "of the above." His initial temptation is to translate this term as "God." The three attributes that would justify such a translation, in his eyes, are: first, *nhialic* is addressed and referred to as "creator" (*achiak*); second, as "my father" (*wa*); third, prayer and sacrifice are offered to it. What stops him from translating *nhialic* as "God" is that such a translation would raise metaphysical and semantic problems of "our own" for which, he says, there are no parallels for the Dinka. At first sight, this is a perfect example of the extension of a concept to a new situation—the possibility that the term *God* could be extended to cover the term *nhialic* and at the same time discovering that the normativity of the concept puts a constraint on its extension.

Let me give the full citation:

It would be easy, it is true, to translate *nhialic aciek* and *nhialic wa* as "God the creator" and "God (my) father," for the attributes of *nhialic* and God there closely coincide, as do many others—unity (of a kind), power, justice, "*nhialic* highness" for example. When, however, number of "spirits" later discussed are all said in Dinka to be *nhialic*, it would not make similar sense in English to say that they were "all God." The word *nhialic* is meaningful in relation to a number of Dinka terms with which our "God" has no such association. *Nhialic* is figured sometimes as a Being, a personal Supreme Being even, and sometimes as a *kind* of being and activity which sums up the activities of a multiplicity of beings, while the word "God" has no such extended meaning in our common speech." (Lienhardt 1961, 29–30)

Lienhardt overcomes this first difficulty of translation by opting for the term *Divinity*. Like the usage of the word *God*, he opts to write "Divinity" with a capital D and without definite or indefinite article. As he writes, "'Divinity' like *nhialic*, can be used to convey to the mind at once *a* being, a *kind* of nature or existence, and a quality of that kind of being; it can be made to appear more substantive or qualitative, more personal or general, in connotation, according to context, as is the word *nhialic*. It saves us, too, despite its occasional clumsiness, from shifting our attention from a Dinka word to undefined, yet for everyone fairly definite, conceptions of our own" (Lienhardt 1961, 30).

Going to another set of terms, Lienhardt talks of *yeeth*, which some might have rendered as "spirits" but he chooses to render as "Powers." "The Dinka claim that they encounter 'spirits' of various kinds, which they call generically *jok*. In this account, I call them 'Powers'" (Lienhardt 1961, 28). The term *yeeth*, he observes further, is a word that has singular and plural forms. "*Nhialic*, *Divinity*, has no plural; it is both singular and plural in intention. In some senses discussed later all the existences called *yeeth* may be equated with Divinity, and in account I have found it fitting to refer to them as *divinities*, thus written without the capital letter" (30).

Let us pause here to think of the implications. In considering the crisscrossing of concepts, the first question I posed was that of the extension of concepts and how we determine the rightness or wrongness of extensions. For Lienhardt, the major concern seems to be that in translating *nhialic* as "God" (with a capital G) he would be able to capture the similarities between "our" (read: Christian) conception of God (God the creator, God the father), but it would fail to take into account the extensions of the term *nhialic* to other deities. He thinks he gets out of this quandary by using the term *Divinity* yet reintroduces the Christian conceptions by the grammatical conventions of a capital D and absence of any definite or indefinite article as modifier. This grammatical device allows a background of the Christian debates on monotheism and the prohibition against associating any other god with the name of God to be read into the anthropological text. Thus, the normativity in the concept of god derives from Lienhardt's privileging of a particular Christian commonsensical perception of the direction in which the term could be extended. We might them say that the term *nhialic* now represents an overlap between the Christian concept of God (even as its limit) and the Dinka concept through the very grammatical conventions that Lienhardt uses. However, matters turn out to be a little more complicated in both directions. In the case of the Dinka, we are not sure how the presence of missionaries and government officials, as well as anthropologists, inflected their religious vocabulary with new shades of meaning and improvisations in such practices as those of prayer and sacrifice. We do have some evidence in the text, as, for instance, when a spirit is reprimanded by an elder as to why it had seized someone who is with a foreigner, and a government official at that. But except for fleeting descriptions this issue is not taken up in any detail in Lienhardt. Conversely, it is not clear as to why the long history of biblical translations of the term *God*, which tackled issues of equivalence between vernacular terms for god/s found in societies the missionaries encountered and the Christian God, does not come up for discussion in Lienhardt's account despite the active work done by missionaries in this region. Early in his discussion, Lienhardt cedes the authority to judge if the concept of *nhialic* could be translated by the term *God* to the theologians—"Perhaps the extent to which it would be permissible to translate *nhialic* by 'God' is something of which theologians might judge at the end of an account of Dinka religion" (29)—but theologians had been engaged in such discussions for a considerable period of time. It is of great interest, then, to see how the normativity of the concept of God gets articulated in the discipline of biblical translations when questions of how to convey the news of the Christian God to people of countries already populated with various gods and goddesses was at issue. I am drawing the next few paragraphs from debates that took place in India, where the mission projects had to deal with the question of how to fix the limits of the concept of God—perhaps the debates that took place in the context of African missions were different. Similarly, in regions in which the lines of division between people of the book and kafirs (or nonbelievers) were at issue, the question of translation would take on a different perspective.[7] Despite such differences, the question of the crisscrossing of concepts remains valid for all these situations.

The debates on locating Christian theological concepts within the rich theological and philosophical vocabulary of Hindu and Buddhist texts was engaged in full force in India since the latter half of the nineteenth century.[8] Let us briefly consider the kind of issues that arose in the process of identifying the correct term for translation of the concept of God. First, it must be remembered that the issue for the Christian missionaries was not that of finding a term that would ring true for the professional theologians alone but that of finding the best way to bring Christianity to a group of people who already had their own gods and goddesses and philosophical texts, recognized for their depth and sophistication. How could they be persuaded to adopt a new faith and, even after being persuaded of the rightness of the message, how were the converts to find the correct expressions with which the Christian God could be worshipped in prayer or in liturgy? There was the further question of diversity in vernacular languages and the authority of Sanskrit, as well as the diversity among Christian groups as regards the theological questions pertaining to Christology and the literal versus symbolic interpretations of the Eucharist. My aim is not to provide any comprehensive survey of these issues but to show that the concept of God or gods already represented a crisscrossing of different concepts regarding divine names, such that a different tradition resonated within the naming practices as well as in invocations and prayers.

One of the important differences in the Bible translations in the south and north of India was that the southern Bibles tended to use the term *deva* for God whereas in the north *īśvara* was the preferred term. One important question that the missionaries were faced with was whether the technical theological/philosophical renderings of these terms within Hindu texts and exegesis was to be taken into account in settling on a translation or whether the popular vernacular uses were to be treated as authoritative enough for Christian purposes. After all, their interest in the translation was strongly determined by the overarching interest of how to present the Christian God to the populations they were hoping to convert. The 1871 Union version of the Tamil Bible adopted *deva* as the standard translation for "God"; earlier versions had used *deva* but only within a compound word. Since *deva* was a Sanskrit-derived term, there was some effort to use the Tamil term *koda-*

*val* instead, but this usage did not catch on—perhaps because of the prestige of Sanskrit despite the currents of devotional movements that enshrined vernacular terms in their religious vocabulary. What were the arguments *for* and *against* the use of the term *deva*? It should be noted that there are several classes of beings who might be thought of as devas—for instance, in Vedic rituals, devas are simply the beings evoked within the parameters of sacrifice and who are brought into existence for the duration of the sacrifice, while in the mythological genealogies of the Puranas the devas are the lesser gods and the cousins of the demons. One can see that importing these characteristics into the Christian God posed many obstacles for the translators.

As far as the correct usage of the terms is concerned, the ontological questions about the existence and characteristics of deities in the sacrifice that concerned the various commentators in the mīmāmsā school (the hermeneutic school on ritual theory and language) were less in the nature of ontological questions and more in the nature of grammatical questions, although ontology could not be completely avoided.[9] It would take me too afar to pursue this question in the detail it deserves. However, it might suffice to point out that the frame of the discussion was provided by the question as to whether the Vedic injunctions specifying a deity in relation to an offering meant that the *devatā* (deity) was the *recipient* of the oblations offered in the sacrifice or if the mention of the name of a devata was simply a function of the requirement that a recipient be linguistically and grammatically specified in order for the offering to be made. How were boundaries drawn through grammar? Was a particular devatā invoked in the ritual to be mentioned in the accusative case or the dative case? And how did that determine the relation between the offering, the invocation, and the god (see Das 1983)? In many cases the gods were seen to be adjectival in character. As Francis Clooney, a Jesuit theologian and mīmāmsā scholar puts it: "It seems then that in Śabara's view, there is no essence to *devatā*, at least none that is relevant to the sacrifice; there is only a web of grammatical and act-oriented relations, whereby that which functions as a *devatā* is established" (Clooney 1997, 346; see also Clooney 2010).[10] Clearly, grammar does not consist here simply as rules for correct speech and writing indicates the intimacy between grammar and philosophy. Let us recall Wittgenstein: "Grammar tells us what kind of object anything is (Theology as grammar.)" (Wittgenstein [1953] 1968, §373).[11]

It would take me too far afield to go into the details here of different phil-osophical theories in India on how subjects and objects of ritual are cre-ated or how the variety of actions performed in a ritual are seen in relation to each other, but what is interesting is that the missionaries had to con-tend with these technicalities.[12] Debates continued on these matters—for in-stance, on the use of the word deva, Tiliander (1974) thinks that the choice of deva in the Tamil Union version was a retrograde step because of the poly-theistic taint attached to it. However, Israel (2011) thinks *deva* was a happy choice, because Hindus did not use it for the almighty, and in discussions on Tamil terminology the issue for the translators was to find an unfamil-iar term, not a familiar one. Similar debates took place with regard to the term īśwara, which was the word used in most North Indian languages. The historian of Christianity Julius Richter, writing in 1908, is of the opinion that the term *ishvara* had an advantage because it was common to all Indian languages—yet, because it was a technical expression for a phase of the lower Brahma in union with *avidyā* (lit. "that which knowledge is not"), referring to god as caught in *māyā* (illusion, contingent reality), the word was "useless" for Christian purposes (Richter 1908, 270). The competing term bhagwāna appears in some texts. Tiliander (1974) thinks that bhagwāna deserves a place in Christian vocabulary so as to be not seen as exclusive to devotees of Vishnu. Conversely, Rai (1992) considers it unsuitable be-cause of its close association with Rama and Krishna and also its sexual undertones.

My point in going into the discussion on divine names in the context of the translation of biblical notions of God is to emphasize that while vernac-ular translations of the Bible took for granted the general notions of trans-lation embedded in Protestant missionary movements, it is when we think of the particularity—*which* word had a feeling of rightness about it—that we see how context came to be embedded in the normativity of the concept. Here, extension of the concept is not peripheral but central to its definition and the debates on what seems right or wrong; the feeling of fitness shows that concepts of Hindu gods and Christian God crisscross each other in both directions. Thus, it is not only that the biblical God in India leads a life among the Hindu gods so that the latter secrete their meanings into the for-mer by crisscrossing of each with the other but also that in Hindu devo-tional practices and praise hymns, terms like bhagwāna and īśwara come to convey different inflections as Hindus confronted the presence of Christians among themselves.[13] This set of issues has some relevance for thinking about commensurability and incommensurability, but I will delay that discussion for a little longer.

Let me turn to Evans-Pritchard's rendering of the same issue pertaining to how a local term might be translated and the bearing it has on the understanding of anthropological concepts. Commenting on the rendering of vernacular concepts, William Hanks (2015) remarks: "At a very different level of description, ethnographers have also used the method of translation as a way of revealing and making sense of difference and, like Boas, the objective for anthropologists has usually been to make sense of the foreign language in its foreignness. For example, Evans-Pritchard ([1937] 1976, appendix 1) is scrupulous to make his translations into English strictly accountable to the coherence of Azande concepts *in their own cultural context*, a strategy also pursued in his classic study of Nuer religion ([1956] 1970)" (emphasis added).

In contrast to Hank's confident assertion that Evans-Pritchard's translation strictly cohered with Azande or Nuer concepts in their "own cultural context," Timothy Larsen (2014) orients us to *Nuer Religion* in a different way:

> One immediately knows what kind of book *Nuer Religion* is: on the very first page Evans-Pritchard discusses the term *kwoth*, ("spirit") in relation to the equivalents in what in traditional Catholic teaching are the three sacred languages: the Latin *spiritus*, the Greek *pneuma*, and the Hebrew *ruah*. In the preface, Evans-Pritchard asserted that Nuer and Dinka religions "have features that bring to mind the Hebrews of the Old Testament" and therefore he defiantly warned readers that the Bible would be a recurring point of reference. (107)

My concern here is not so much to trace the way Evans-Pritchard's notions of what was at stake in understanding what he saw as primitive religions change according to his personal biography (e.g., conversion to Catholicism) but to show that even someone as sophisticated a thinker as Hank, who criticizes other anthropologists for their simplistic views on context, ends up himself with an impoverished view of context, reducing it to the authentic Nuer or Dinka religion untouched by missionary activities, relations with Arab traders, or the activities of the government against Nuer and Dinka prophets. It is in this sense that we are obliged to think of "vernacular" concepts as crisscrossing with other concepts that seeped into Nuer or Dinka life and in the texts of the anthropologists. The defiant note on the recurrence of biblical references to which Larsen alludes becomes legible not only in relation to the newness that entered into Nuer concepts of gods and spirits but also in the light of missionary concerns as to whether primitive societies were ready to receive Christianity.

I give the following references from Evans-Pritchard's work on the Nuer and the Azande to show how pervasive the Christian concepts (not simply at the discursive level of words but in joining words and acts) are in his texts.[14] I am not arguing that the frequent references to the Old Testament imply that Nuer conceptions of God were not honed in relation to their material and social environment, but I make two further claims: first, that the social context of the Nuer or the Azande is difficult to comprehend independently of the colonial context (a point forcefully made by Talal Asad [1979] with regard to British social anthropology in this period); and second, that the analogies with figures in the Old Testament smuggled in normative standards consistent with certain Christian values to determine which religious figures would count as God and which as mere spirits. Incidentally, these procedures also set the standards for who the idealized reader of the text was, since familiarity with the Old Testament was assumed on the part of the reader as setting general standards for intelligibility. Here are some citations to remind the reader of what is at stake in these comparisons:

> But the commonest Nuer way of trying to express their idea of the nature of God is to say that he is like wind or air, a metaphor which seems appropriate because it is found throughout the hierological literature of the world and *we are particularly familiar with it in the Old Testament.* . . . Unlike the other spirits God has no prophets or sanctuaries or earthly forms. (Evans-Pritchard [1956] 1970, 4; emphasis added)

> It will be noted that he [Professor Westerman] has translated two different words, *cak* (chak) and *that* (thate), by "create," but they have not quite the same sense, for whereas *cak* means creation *ex nihilo* and in thought or imagination, *thate* means to make something out of something else already materially existing, as when a child moulds clay into the shape of an ox or a smith beats a spear out of iron. . . . The distinction is similar to that between "created" and "made" in the first chapter

of Genesis, "created" there being a translation of the Hebrew *br'* which can only be used for divine activity. (Evans-Pritchard [1956] 1970, 5)

> Nuer do not complain when misfortunes befall them. They say that it is God's will (*rwac kwoth*), that it is his world (*e ghaude*), and I have often heard Nuer say this in their sufferings—that he is good (*goagh*). . . . I cannot convey the Nuer attitude better than by quoting the book of Job: "the Lord gave, and the Lord hath taken away; blessed be the name of the Lord" (1.21). (Evans-Pritchard [1956] 1970, 13)

Next, I give some citations about the Azande to show how the contrast between the Nuer and the Azande is sought to be conveyed in which the standard for the comparison is provided by what is considered to be a proper *religious* attitude. Even though Evans-Pritchard does not assimilate Azande notions of witchcraft to superstition, this unspoken category hovers in the text much as the grammatical device of signaling the singularity of God is implicit in Lienhardt. Here are the relevant citations from Evans-Pritchard on the Azande:

> I have never been able to elicit any interest in, and have found that Azande are frankly bored by, questions about the Supreme Being. . . . The divine name was often voiced as a thoughtless expletive something not to be confused with a pious utterance. When a prince named his son "Mbori-has closed my lips," he was not testifying to the workings of divine providence in his life; the poor flummoxed father had simply responded when asked what they should call the child that he could not think of a name. (Evans-Pritchard 1936, 38)

> "Witches as the Azande describe them clearly cannot exist." (Evans-Pritchard [1937] 1976, 18)

## QUESTIONS OF COMMENSURABILITY AND TRANSLATION

At this point, I take a detour from the ethnographies to ask how the normativity of a concept that allows it to be extended in some directions and not in others is related to the different interests that a concept might serve. In what sense might we say that the concepts of divinity or of god across two different societal contexts are commensurate with each other? Does this question call for rethinking the notion of ontology itself as sometimes rigid and muscular but at other times gentle and flexible?

In a recent paper, Stephan Palmié (2018) asks some of these questions with reference to the manner in which anthropology dealt with the issue of so-called irrational beliefs (Hollis and Lukes 1982). Evans-Pritchard's ([1937] 1976) account of Azande witchcraft holds a special place in this discussion. For Evans-Pritchard, even though Azande beliefs about witchcraft were based upon false premises, they were logically coherent and thus, under a certain definition of rationality, could be held as rational. Recall the citation I gave earlier—"Witches as the Azande describe them clearly cannot exist." One could, of course, ask what makes the distinction between Nuer beliefs in the entity *kwoth* to be based on correct premises and that of the Azande on witches to be based on false premises. We have already seen that the question was settled by taking Christian concepts of God and its theological underpinning as providing the relevant criteria, but let us for the moment leave that question aside.[15] Evans-Pritchard demonstrates that, once subjected to true hermeneutics and using the principle of charity, one could say that the Azande witchcraft beliefs were rational because each strand was supported by another strand within a web of belief. The question of rationality moved from treating a proposition as true or false to asking if the web of beliefs could be treated as part of a symbolic system within which doubt arising at one level could be settled with reference to another strand within this web. Thus, what was seen as erroneous belief at the level of material causation was recast as meaningful at the level of symbolic signification. Palmié points out that what different arguments under the general rubric of the "ontological turn" in anthropology challenged was the very picture of reality that was sought to be explained by the use of the signifying apparatus bypassing the ontological question of existence. As Holbraad and Pedersen (2017) state, the challenge for anthropology was not that of recasting the statements from informants about witches or stones that are alive as symbolic statements but to take them at face value and ask what challenges these statements pose to the anthropologist's own conceptual apparatus and theoretical statements. If, in other words, one accepted that statements about, say, stones being living entities, or women being married to jaguars, were true, then we would have to accept the idea that what was at issue was the incommensurability and a radical otherness to such societies within which such statements were accepted as correct descriptions of the world. In some ways, the issue was similar to the older one of multiple worlds: what is not true in one world could be true in another world. However, as I argue elsewhere (along with my coeditors, see Das et al. 2014), the proponents of the ontological turn rarely went into the question of well-made versus badly made ontologies or demonstrated the tensions between different ontologies when different worlds touch or influence each other—something that the process of translation brings to the fore. One might say that the question of incommensurability is that of the rise of noncriterial differences that, in effect, make it impossible to imagine a future together, but this fate is not reserved only for encounters between societies that are distant from each other—such experiences can be part of one's everyday life when, for instance, one is faced with behavior that does not so much violate this or that norm but violates the very picture of human life that we may have even as we know that the limits of the human body or human voice are not knowable or even given in advance (Das 2007).

Palmié's intervention in this debate on incommensurability is to ask if an alternative to that of radical otherness and incommensurability might be proposed taking the same kind of facts that at first glance challenge our picture of the world and not just of one or the other item of belief in it. He goes on to offer two important corrections to the thesis of incommensurability and radical otherness. First, he asks what happens when we shift our gaze from the level of discursive statements that treat belief in propositional terms to the various ritual *acts* that have to be performed in order to make the idea of stones being or behaving like living beings. What we find when we make such a shift is that a series of actions have to be performed by human beings for some stones to become "living" stones. Using Bruno Latour's (2005) proposals of an actor-network theory, Palmié (2018, 795) states: "Many agents and actants must be mobilized in order for stones thrown in the river to become active indwelling deities." Second, Palmié argues that is because anthropologists make the mediators disappear in the excitement of encountering "radical alterity" that they contribute to the picture of self-enclosed ontologies that are always located at a distance. In fact, one of the puzzling things about the ontology debate is that it overlooks the possibility of encountering puzzling ontologies within our own neighborhoods—for example, as in the case of Muslim subjects in Delhi becoming possessed by Hindu ghosts rather than by jinns. The latter would have posed no major issues for the subject since the existence of jinns is testified to by the Qur'an, but my own Muslim informants in the streets of Delhi always puzzled about the fact that Muslim healing practices were stalled by the presence of Hindu ghosts in Muslim bodies. Often, they had to find a Hindu exorcist because the Muslim healers were apprehensive of falling into the snares of the devil or in the general realm of *kala ilm*—dark knowledge (see Das 2010b; 2015a, chap. 5). What role have anthropologists played in making the acts of mediation disappear in their own descriptions? How have they contributed to the picture of groups isolated in their worlds with little attention to the touching of different worlds or their intersections even within a multiple world picture?[16]

### A THOUGHT EXPERIMENT

Until now I have been concerned with the question of concepts of God as encapsulated in particular nominal terms, but as Wittgenstein taught us, a concept is not simply a replacement for a word—it entails a series of actions through which a region of reality is parsed out both for thinking and acting. Let us then consider the third characteristic of *nhial*—viz., that prayers and sacrifice are offered to him. My thought experiment here is to ask if a particularly Christian model of sacrifice and prayer had not been the vector through which Lienhardt or Evans-Pritchard came to understand what was entailed in the acts of slaughter of the animal, or of substitution as the defining model of sacrifice, how might the notion of gods or spirits been moved to a different register?

In 1980 I was privileged to give the Henry Myers Lecture at the Royal Anthropological Institute in London and I chose to speak on the language of sacrifice, partly to acknowledge the different ways in which the theme of religion, religious belief, and particularly sacrifice had been engaged in previous Myers lectures such as those delivered by Professors Radcliffe-Brown, Evans-Pritchard, Rodney Needham, and others. However, it was also the case that I had been studying the mīmāṃsā texts (for no particular reason)—to which I made a reference earlier—and had found that the dominant models of sacrifice as communication between men and gods through the transfer of offerings just did not work. In my lecture that was published in 1983 in the *Journal of the Royal Anthropological Institute*, I tried to lay out an alternative theory of sacrifice (Das 1983). Here I take the liberty of reproducing some of the claims that I then made; I hope to clarify why they still matter to me. My commentator Professor Adrian Meyer was a gracious host and managed to say some nice things about the lecture, but over the years it became clear to me that my views on taking Indian ritual theory as a competing theory and not merely as a laying out of vernacular concepts simply could not find a footing within anthropological or sociological theory. I say this not as a complaint or a lament but as an indication of the fact that there was nothing radically new in my interpretation. Many Indologists and scholars of Sanskrit had pointed to a complex network of relations among humans, objects, gods, utterances of words, and incantations and claimed that the center of gravity in the act of sacrifice as interpreted in mīmāmsā texts did not lie in the killing of the animal; rather, the dispersed acts that had to be performed—ranging from the preparation of the site, to the invocation of gods, to the different types of exchanges, to the substitutions that were made—provided the context for philosophical reflections on the nature of language, or of the liveliness of offerings, or on what exactly one is to understand by "creation." Most important, I had argued for the centrality of grammar in understanding ritual actions—for instance, the word for "deity," as I explained earlier, when declined in accusative case gave a different meaning to the ritual act (the offering as ransom) than when declined in the dative case (the offering as an act of honoring). The texts I was analyzing were not peripheral texts. Their importance is attested by many scholars in the fields of Indology, Indian philosophy, and even legal studies— yet, the kind of iron curtain that keeps anthropology of religion from responding to the pressures that texts from other traditions exert on their concepts remains something of a mystery to me.

Immodest though it may sound, I think it is important for me to reproduce some of the ideas on sacrifice that I had put forward in 1982, not because my understanding of these issues is still stuck at that point—indeed, as I have gone deeper into a whole body of related texts I am convinced that these texts offer many more challenges to anthropology of religion than I had anticipated then. Nevertheless, the point of recapitulating some of the issues I had raised is to point to other possibilities that might be released regarding the crisscrossing of different kinds of concepts pertaining to gods, spirits, or ritual.

For my purposes, I single out four important differences in canonical anthropological theories of sacrifice and the rendering of sacrifice in the mīmāmsā texts. Consider the different components of ritual actions within the sacrificial complex: preparation of the site, invocation, killing the animal, and consuming the remains of the slaughtered animal. Within anthropological theory, the main purpose of the sacrifice is seen in terms of cleansing the social body or averting a danger to the sacrificator through a logic of substitution. The mīmāmsā texts too incorporate these components in the sacrificial complex, but the interpretation placed on these is very different. First, the sacrificator (to use Hubert and Mauss's terminology) in the *Mīmāmsā Śāstra* is seen not as a bearer of pollution, sin, danger, or any other negative traits of which the slaughter of an animal or its expulsion would help to rid the social body—instead, the sacrificator is defined, first and foremost, as a bearer of desire. The governing injunction is "svargakāmah yajeta"—may he who has desire for heaven perform *yajña* (fire sacrifice). It is also important to note that the governing injunction is not expressed in the imperative mood but in the optative mood, the main aspect of which lies in its contingency—*if* the sacrificator has a desire, *then* he might perform the yajña. Yet desire is a complex category tied to creation, and much debate on these issues circles around the question as to whether heaven is an already given category or if it is produced through the actions that are undertaken in the sacrificial arena.

One major opposition that structures the character of any particular sacrifice in the mīmāmsā texts is the distinction between *purusārtha* (acts that are performed for the sake of the agent) and *kratvārtha* (acts in which the goal is the completion of the action).[17] In the former case, one might think of the sacrificator as agent who is standing *within* the action and in this case the desire for which he performs the sacrifice is desire for objects or outcomes specific to his desires (e.g., desire for a son, desire for revenge). In the second case, the agent stands *outside* the action. Thus, for instance, if the sacrificator in this kind of sacrifice were to die before the sacrifice is completed, the injunction is to fill the body of an antelope with his bones and to complete the sacrifice by this substitute sacrificator since the sacrifice is being performed not to gain specific objects or outcomes but to secure the order of the world—hence sacrifice is also called "the womb of the order of the world" (*ṛtasya yoni*). There are resonances with the two different ways actions are classified in grammar through the device of active voice (*atmanepada*—lit. "word for self") and the active voice (or *parasmaipada*—lit. "word for other"), which provided the overall classification of verbs in the main school of Panian grammar.[18]

There are two other points that are of some relevance. First, men and gods are seen to equally participate in the sacrifice—with fire as the priest of the gods bearing witness on their behalf and the human priests(s) as the officiants and witnesses on behalf of the sacrificator. I will not go into the technical aspects of the parallels between the killing of the soma (a plant) in the sacrifice, who is seen as sacrificially killed by the gods and revived by humans in the sacrificial arena, and the killing of the animal, on behalf of men, who then receives a new life from the gods, except to point out that the gods who are present in the sacrificial arena are not seen as primary; it is the offering that is seen as primary. Thus, if there is a discrepancy between the gods invoked and the offering stipulated, it is enjoined that these specific gods must be replaced by the other gods to bring the offering and the gods to whom it is offered in harmony with each other, and not the other way around (Das 1983).[19] In general, though, it is not permitted for the deity or the offering to be substituted, as that would change the character of the sacrifice.

Finally, the principle of substitution is central to the discussions of sacrifice but it is not simply that for want of an ox you settle for a cucumber as Lévi-Strauss (1963) thought; rather, the more profound notion is that only through substitutions might life and its recreation be possible. Thus, men and gods are engaged through sacrifice in recreating what is destroyed in one realm by creating it in another—just as desire for specific objects has to be educated, for the experience of desire as the impersonal (*apuruṣeya*) desire for heaven may become the source of the kratvārtha actions through which the world is being consistently renewed. I was bold enough in 1980 when I delivered the lecture to conclude it by saying: "Vedic sacrifice may be seen to constitute a global alternative to the Christian idea of sacrifice rather than being a restrictive form of sacrifice included in the inclusive symbol of the sacrifice of Christ" (1983, 460). Of course, my claim went unheeded, but it was never extinguished for me.

For now, it is time to turn to another strand of this thought experiment. I invite you to imagine that the concepts of gods are not primarily about their goodness and justice (though these might be evoked in praise hymns) but also about their capriciousness, sexual appetites, or divine deceptions. Within this framework, the question of the existence of God or gods is placed within a completely different framework in which what is of importance is the grammatical *aspect* of a deity that exists for the duration for which it is evoked.[20] Gods and goddesses are seen to be as ephemeral as other things that are eaten up by time. They can be as subject to temptation, violence, adoration, and hatred for these emotions are also not seen as eternal substances. Would the thesis of "radical otherness" have found any footing? Or would one have found different kinds of resonances? For example, in the process of translating texts from Sanskrit into Tibetan in which Kashmiri Pandits seem to have played an important role, how were encounters with such ideas rendered? Were the concerns of the Tibetan scholars different from those of Christian theologians when searching for equivalent terms for God in the Sanskrit vocabulary?

Jonathan Gold's (2007) study of a thirteenth-century Tibetan text, *Gateway to Learning* (*Mikha pa' jug p'ai sgo*) by the famed scholar Śākya Pandita, gives us the insight into what was at stake in translation since the scriptures of Tibetan Buddhism were essentially texts in translation taken from Sanskrit sources on Buddha's teachings. In Gold's words: "Śākya Pandita consequently reflects with greater depth than any other premodern Buddhist on the nature of translation, and on the challenges that *dharma* faces during its travels among diverse cultures and languages" (ix). Let us just take one of the issues that pertains to the present discussion on the different kinds of interests that led Śākya Pandita to identify errors in translation and the special name proper names of gods held in this discussion. It might be helpful to give the full citation on this point from Gold:

> Finally, as to proper names, Sa-pan mentions these as mistakes in translation—names that are mistranslated. But I count them as unexplained context because whether or not the names are correctly translated, they mean nothing without a knowledge of context. Sa-pan says that *Dāmodara* (*Dha mo da ra*), a name for Krishna gets translated as as khyab 'yug, the ordinary translation term for Vishnu. Damodara, which means "rope belly" is an epithet for Krishna because when he was a child Yashodha tied a rope around his belly. The Tibetan translators did not know the story, and so mistranslated the name. Sa-pan suggests *tha gu lto* ("rope belly") as a better translation. (34–35)

As Gold sees it, the mistranslation of a proper name posed very special problems since other errors—such as redundancy, concepts left unexplained, or use of obscure vocabulary—could be corrected by learned interpreters, but if the story around the shifts of name of the same deity is not known to the interpreter or teacher, he has no means of correcting his error. In the case of Damodara, for example, the story refers to the naughtiness of the child

Krishna and the "punishment" that Yashodha (his foster mother) gave him, which was that he was tied to a stone and told not to move. He did not himself move but he moved the heavy stone. This playful aspect of Krishna as the naughty child is quite distinct from the adult Krishna as a "friend" (*sakhā*) to Draupadi or the wise charioteer (*pārthasārthi*) to Arjuna in the battle of the Mahabharata who proclaimed the message of dispassionate action. What consequences this mistranslation had within the Tibetan Buddhist canon is difficult for me to assess. Gold does point out the importance of complete fidelity to the text shown, for instance, when the early teachers demonstrated their absolute mastery over both languages through back-translations that provided a perfect match between source and target languages.[21] The question of translation of proper names takes on a different kind of importance than would be assumed in a theory of proper names that thought of names as standing in an arbitrary relation to the person in terms of meaning but act as a rigid designator in terms of reference, in the sense that it designates the same object in all contexts.

I stop the story of my thought experiment at this point to suggest that it is helpful to think of the different ways in which the normativity of concepts is established in the crisscrossing I have described. The question whether the term *God* can be extended to *kwoth* or *nhial* assumed the monopoly of Christian theology as the mediating discourse for legitimate or not-so-legitimate extensions. In the case of India, the interests biblical scholars brought to bear on the question of translation of names of God into equivalent Sanskrit terms were different than, let us say, the interests of the thirteenth-century Tibetan Buddhist scholars. Questions of similarity, sameness, difference, commensurability, and incommensurability are *learned* in the context of living a life: although they are important components of cognitive models, those are not the exclusive domains of their operations.

I conclude this section with two citations from Wittgenstein: "Concepts lead us to make investigations, are the expression of our interest, and direct our interest" (Wittgenstein [1953] 1968, §570). "For we can avoid ineptness or emptiness in our assertions only by presenting the model as what it is, as an object of comparison—as, so speak, a measuring rod not as a preconceived idea to which reality *must* correspond" (Wittgenstein [1953] 1968, §131).

## BACK TO THE SPIRITS

Let us get back to the spirits in Dinkaland. Lienhardt shifts to four different terms in the process of describing different kinds of spirits and the roles they play in Dinka religion: spirits, divinities, Powers, and images. A close attention to the shifts of register in Lienhardt's discussion is important to see how he effects a series of substitutions through which he generates a new category of analysis—that of self-knowledge—and a measuring rod that judges the Dinka as somehow less capable of self-examination as compared to Europeans. The procedures through which this remarkable conclusion is reached are important to trace not only because they show how an evaluation is smuggled within a description but also because these procedures tell us something about the blind spots in anthropological knowledge within what were considered to be its canonical texts.[22]

First, consider "spirits" who are ubiquitous in Dinka life. Lienhardt says: "Within the single world known to them (for they dwell little upon fancies of any 'other world' of different constitution) the Dinka claim that they encounter 'spirits' of various kinds, which they call generically *jok*. In this account, I call them 'Powers'" (Lienhardt 1961, 28). There is no attempt here to explain as to why a translation of the term *jok* as "spirits" is not found adequate. However, from the descriptions that follow, one can decipher two reasons that might explain this substitution. First, Lienhardt argues that the Dinka "experience" the spirits, for they claim to actually encounter them especially in the context of illness and misfortune, but that this experience cannot be transmitted or made intelligible to the European who cannot find any corresponding experience of encounter with spirits. As he says, "Europeans may perhaps concede an objective reality of this order to Dinka Divinity, where it most resembles the 'God' of the universal religions; But no European actually encounters Deng, Gerang, or other Powers as the Dinka claim to do" (145). As we have seen earlier, the reality of God of universal religion is not in question for Lienhardt though for universal read religions of the Book. However, the Dinka experience of these encounters is not validated by European experience and so it cannot be "real."[23] This makes Lienhardt take the first step of substituting spirits with Powers. With this substitution Lienhardt makes a shift from the experience that Dinka have of spirits to that of representations—yet these are still, to his credit, *Dinka* representations. "Thus, even for Dinka themselves, a Power is not an immediate *datum* of experience of the same order as physical facts or events with which it is associated. To refer to the activity of a Power is to offer an interpretation, and not merely a description of experience" (148).

In opting for the term *Powers* (with a capital P), Lienhardt is aiming at a neutral interpretive term that might resonate with some Dinka ideas about how power is exercised by external agencies on a person that can also be made intelligible to Europeans, for the experience of being acted upon from the outside by some powers is not completely alien to Europeans. More importantly, my sense is that the move to treat spirits as the first level datum of experience and Powers as representations allows Lienhardt to avoid the question of how to treat a dissonance in the notion of reality itself and instead conjure a theory of Dinka self-knowledge that can account for their relations to spirits as a mechanism through which responsibility for self-knowledge is evaded.

If Dinka powers be representations, asks Lienhardt, what are they representations of? He then goes on to speak of Powers not as ultrahuman beings, as the Dinka speak of them, but as "images"—"or, as I prefer to call them, 'images'" (Lienhardt 1961, 147). Notice the shifts: from spirits to Powers, from Powers to images. At this point Lienhardt's discussion zeroes in on the question of self-knowledge to suggest that the Dinka are unable to take responsibility for their own transgressions and can come to terms with them only by projecting their negative emotions onto external spirits that then "image" the experiences—I am tempted to say they reflect back the experience—by providing an opportunity for the affected person to verbalize them through invocations and to take remedial action through the ritual of sacrifice.

Consider the following two formulations on self-knowledge in Lienhardt's text:

> The process of treating a sick man whose sickness is attributed to a Power is thus to isolate for the sufferer and his kin a particular Power which can be regarded as a subject of activity within him, from the self which is its object. . . . Hence, when a man is strongly possessed, it is held that it is no use speaking to him, as a human person, for what is acting is not the man but the Power. It is the process of making manifest what I have called an "image" corresponding to the affective state of the sufferer as cause to effect, which I now discuss. . . . It raises first a difficult question

of differences between Dinka and European self-knowledge which I can discuss only inadequately. The Dinka have no conception which at all closely corresponds to our popular modern conception of the "mind," as mediating and, as it were, storing up the experiences of the self. So it seems that what we should call in some cases the "memories" of experiences, and regard in some way as intrinsic and interior to the remembering person and modified in their effect upon him by that interiority, appear to the Dinka as exteriorly acting upon him, as were the sources from which they derived. (Lienhardt 1961, 148–49)

The fact that in the initial stages states of possession may be self-encouraged, or even counterfeited, is recognized by the Dinka, but unlike us they do not think that this voluntary co-operation of the conscious possession as coming from a source other than himself. Again, we see the difference between the underlying passivity of the Dinka in their relation to events, and the active construction we tend to place upon our own role in shaping them. (235)

We might now have arrived at a place where we can ask: First, what picture of experience does Lienhardt bring to the scene of the spirits? And, second, what is the notion of image that emerges from his analysis? As to the first point, it would seem that for Lienhardt experience is stored in something like an interior space that is transparent to a seeing self in the European case—the inner counterpart to a rational self that is publicly expressed in the figure of the Christian God. It is not that the Dinka lack the ability to aspire for justice and goodness as evidenced, Lienhardt says, in the expressions they use for Divinity. In that case, their religion aligns with the conceptions of God in revealed religions. What the Dinka lack, as far as Lienhardt is concerned, is the capacity for self-knowledge. However, could there be a different notion of self-knowledge that is at stake?

Wittgenstein's astute reflections on the question of first-person access and first-person authority are meant to loosen the grip of the picture of the self as oscillating between the moments of complete insertion in sensations and flux of experiences, on the one hand, and taking a third-person stance toward one's experiences, on the other hand. Instead, in the scenes he creates in *Philosophical Investigations*, one finds frequently that there is a hearer—that sometimes an act of reporting might be both about the state of affairs and about how things are with the one who is reporting. Let me loop back to the observations I made on first-person authority and access to experience in Chapter 4 (see page 135):

> Now one of the important dimensions in Wittgenstein's discussion on first-person authority is that he introduces a hearer: the first-person statement is not a private soliloquy—there is someone to whom my statement is addressed. For instance, "a report is not meant to inform *the hearer* about its subject matter but about the *person making the report.*" Without going into much greater detail, my argument is that presence of the second person here wards off the possibility that first-person statements are about experience that might be rendered as completely private. Or that talking to myself means that I have invented words and expressions that carry meaning only for me.

It seems to me that the Dinka notions of self-knowledge might be less about self-evasion and more about the shared character of experience. The ethnographic descriptions strongly suggest that the spirit that has come into the body of the afflicted person, as well as in the diviner, often brings to the fore the knowledge of past transgressions to be diffused within the local world of the afflicted person. I take two instances from the ethnography. The first is the case of Ajak, the young son of the master of the fishing-spear (a clan held high within clan hierarchy) who had left for the town at an early age, causing somewhat fraught relations between his father and him. Lienhardt describes three episodes of Ajak's becoming possessed—in two of the episodes he was with Lienhardt. It was not clear from the description if he was acting as Lienhardt's assistant, but everyone seems to have assumed a close association between them. What is most interesting in these episodes is the fact that the diviners who try to intervene on his behalf are unable to decipher who the spirit is and ultimately admonish the spirit for seizing Ajak when he is away from home and, moreover, with a foreigner who was also a government official.[24]

Lienhardt writes that a minor master of the fishing-spear came to help during the first episode of the possession, initially addressing the entity that had entered Ajak's body as "You, Power,"[25] "You, divinity," and "You ghost." Failing to get a response by the entity to declare itself and say how it had been wronged (if so) by Ajak, the master admonished it, saying, "You, Power (*jok*), why do you seize a man who is far away from home? Why do you not seize him there at home where the cattle are? What can he do it about it here?

He is travelling in a foreign place, and he is with this European. Why do you seize a man who works for the Government?" (Lienhardt 1961, 59). The master then also admonished Ajak, now as a man (and not as spirit), asking him to think of what secret harm he had done and why he was behaving in this way when he was away from home. After much casting about with different possibilities—his father's ghost, a neglected clan divinity, a free divinity—the matter was left unresolved. What is fascinating here is that it was assumed not only that had he been in his local surroundings he would have had cattle to offer in sacrifice in order to placate the troubling spirit but also that he would have been surrounded by people who would have more knowledge about which kind of transgressions he had to acknowledge. Acknowledgment here does not seem to be like coming to terms with one's own conscience, though that is the language Lienhardt falls into, but taking the help of the community to repair what might have been a relationship gone astray, including relationships with the dead. Instead of the vertical sense of the self as depth located in an interior part of the person, the self is here conceptualized as spread over relationships, much as experience is seen to be context saturated (see Chapter 9).

I now come to the second question I posed: what is the notion of image or imaging that Lienhardt is proposing? Since he does not provide any direct discussion of what he understands by "image," we must infer that from the observations he makes on Dinka self-knowledge where his preference for thinking of Powers not as representations but as images seems directly related to a certain kind of veiling of the real they perform. The reality obscured by the appearance of Powers as images is the reality of the self. In the entry on image in *Dictionary of Untranslatables*, Barbara Cassin and her collaborators (Cassin et al. 2014) point out the tension between a productive and a reproductive sense of "image." The former is signaled in the idea of image as fantasia—the ability to produce fictions—and the latter in the ideas in the vicinity of mimesis, or imitation. We might see in Lienhardt's discussion an idea that an imaging of experience is in the nature of a veiling, a production of something a little false that allows a conception of self-knowledge as happening in a scene of avoidance—a covering over of what Lienhardt thinks of as the pricking of the conscience by the powerful voice of the spirit. However, there is a related meaning of "image" derived from its close connection with vision—that is that an image can allow us to see another thing not through the act of representation but by treating it as the visible trace of something that is invisible or has become invisible. The idea of trace and absence are fundamental to grammar and aesthetics in many Sanskrit texts (see Filliozat 1991–1992; Freschi and Pontillo 2013), and I know that what I am going to suggest now is at the level of speculation, but thinking of image in this latter sense might illuminate some parts of the ethnography for which Lienhardt does not seem to be able to make a place within his schema. I take one example.

As in the case of the Nuer, in the case of the Dinka too there were very few prophets partly because of punitive actions taken against them by the colonial government.[26] Of the two prophets whose names were known in the area Lienhardt knew best, one had died after a long period of exile, following a patrol carried out against him by the government, and the other might have been alive but Lienhardt was told that he did not show any inclination to meet him. So, it does seem that there were disorders introduced by the colonial government, including interference with religious leaders, but Lienhardt does not create any place in his narrative for these kinds of disorders. I was struck by the one occasion when a different kind of prophet appears, of which Lienhardt gives a somewhat whimsical account. One day Lienhardt is told that a black goat, a prophet, has come to the village, and when he goes to see it he finds various gifts and special foods being offered to the "prophet." Women were performing dances in its honor. As I read the faintly ironic account of how the Dinka read the goat's reaction as indicative of its pleasure or of its disinterest and learn toward the end of the discussion that the goat was taken from one village to another and offered hospitality as the sign of the coming of the prophet to them, it occurred to me that Lienhardt does little by way of asking the villagers what made them think of the goat as a prophet. Now suppose we thought of this goat as the visible and remaining trace of the actual prophets who had been killed or imprisoned or exiled—would it be too fanciful? Perhaps my thoughts went into this direction because in Bengal a "white goat for Kali"[27] came to signify the killing of the Feringhees (white foreigners) who were said to have bled the country and angered the goddess as a 1905 article in the journal *Yugantar* tells us (see Kinsley 1975).[28] Obviously I am not suggesting that the black goat revered by the Dinka through what seem like accidents and contingencies had anything like the symbolic significance of the white goat for Kali, but I am struck by the poignancy of the situation in which the human prophets have been eliminated but the thought of how any traces of them might be left in Dinka life is not even at the horizon of Lienhardt's thought. In any case, there seems to be a studious avoidance of any discussion about the presence of the British in Dinkaland on Lienhardt's part, mirroring the avoidance of experience he attributes to the Dinka.

## CONCLUDING COMMENTS

As I indicated in the opening passage of this chapter, I did not start with a well-honed argument. Instead, I wanted to share a reading of two classics in anthropology following the lines and pathways that led to connections between the ethnography and the concepts in these texts without knowing where I would end up. I discovered how much Evans-Pritchard's and Lienhardt's ways of deploying anthropological concepts relied on their taken-for-granted assumptions of the universality of Christian concepts as measures and European experience as the touchstone for what counted as real. I want to now reflect back on what we might have learned about concepts. The tensions between signs and concepts appears occasionally within anthropological texts but has not been a subject of sustained reflection by anthropologists. Writing in 1962 in *La Pensée Savage* (*The Savage Mind*),[29] Lévi-Strauss talked of linguistic signs as providing a link between images and concepts and commented: "Signs resemble images in being concrete entities but they resemble concepts in their powers of reference. Neither concepts nor signs relate exclusively to themselves; either may be substituted for something else. Concepts, however, have an unlimited capacity in this respect, while signs have not" (18). He clarifies this difference with the help of the difference between the figures of the bricoleur and the engineer. For the bricoleur the possibilities of creation are constrained by the fact that she must use elements from an already existent set that had other uses and now must be reimagined within a different configuration. For example, the units of a myth already have a meaning in language: the bricoleur could choose one or another unit from the pregiven set, but each choice will lead to a reorganization of the whole. The engineer, however, while limited by constraints of resources or by her own knowledge, is not limited to using only materials that have already been defined by previous usage.[30] While acknowledging that the distinction between the bricoleur and the engineer is not an absolute one, Lévi-Strauss thinks that their difference is a real one: the engineer works by means of concepts and the bricoleur by means of signs.

"One way indeed in which signs can be opposed to concepts is that whereas concepts aim to be wholly transparent with respect to reality, signs allow and even require the interposing and incorporation of a certain amount of human culture into reality" (20).

Lévi-Strauss's acute formulation of this difference between concepts and signs goes to the heart of the matter (though his idealized picture of the engineer is quite inadequate). One might restate his position by saying that the range of signifying practices tends to show a variety of ways in which reality might be veiled—Lévi-Strauss thinks of that as some bits of human culture coming into reality. In contrast, the imagination of a concept is that it aims to be transparent—by which he means that it is essential to the definition of a concept that it seeks to pry open a region of reality, as essential for thought. From this perspective, I find it fascinating that the division between concepts and signs might be read into the analytical processes deployed by Lienhardt and Evans-Pritchard in which a prior commitment to a declaration of what is transparent with regard to the real (that which corresponds to the God of Christian tradition) and that which is false (spirits, witches) and hence veils different aspects of reality is built into the assumptions that allow for the conclusions about Dinka and Nuer religion. I am not suggesting that these authors go with the specific purpose of showing that the standard for a concept of God is to be found in Christian theology or in the European experience of religion; rather, I am suggesting that since thinking cannot be set apart from a form of life, their concepts end up crisscrossing and overlapping in ways that reveal their unspoken commitments and at the same time conceal from them what should have been evident, such as the presence of missionaries and the disorders in Nuer or Dinka life due to the colonial forms of control. Wittgenstein's famous formulation—"A picture held us captive. And we could not get outside it, for it lay in our language and language seemed to repeat it to us inexorably" (Wittgenstein [1953] 1968, §115)—is of some relevance here. I cannot say how much the explicit commitment to look at other models of god, or of sacrifice, or of prayer might have helped to remove the hold of this picture but it would be worth trying.

There are two final points with which I want to conclude: First, I want to reiterate Benoist's (2010) important point that concepts are not simply given in advance waiting to be employed; rather, the content of concepts depends upon how they are employed and what kind of interests lead one to deploy one rather than another concept. Second, there is a basic requirement of descriptiveness that alone can give life to our concepts, to flesh them out.[31] Thus, the description of events such as the admonishment to the spirit for seizing someone away from home or when he was with a foreigner, and a government official at that, in Lienhardt's book did not act simply as an example of a concept (e.g., of the spirit or of Powers) to which it remained external but as showing the swirl of affects, the importance of place, and the way the idea of what is appropriate in relation to government and what is not that showed how the concept might expand. Finally, a concept is not simply capturing what is there but might be thought of as roaming in the space of possibilities, and here it might establish intimate relations with images, which also trade in the relation between presence, absence, affirmation, and negation. My challenge in reading these texts was to see them not simply as procedures for applying concepts as intellectual tools to the concreteness of Nuer or Dinka religion but to see how one might capture the churning life with gods and spirits and goats (unfortunately, I had to leave out my notes on cattle) as providing challenges to the making of anthropological knowledge. The journey was important for me more than where I have reached. I agree that I have idled here and there and meandered on the way, especially in the way I brought in references to Sanskrit texts, but these were also my expressions of gila—a loving reproach—to my chosen interlocutors in anthropology.

# 11

## THE LIFE OF CONCEPTS

*In the Vicinity of Dying*

> If death interrupts all dialogues, it is only natural to write posthumous letters.
>
> —ANDRÉS NEUMAN, TALKING TO OURSELVES

After many years had passed, I returned to a short reflection that Stanley Cavell had written on an essay on pain that I had submitted to the journal *Daedalus* and to which he was invited by the editor to comment as the referees who had reviewed this essay had very mixed reactions to it. It perhaps speaks to the gentleness of academic culture twenty years ago or to sheer luck that Cavell, who could have had no intimation of who this obscure anthropologist from the University of Delhi was, nevertheless took the time to read this essay and to write a comment on it. His comment made a shift in the way I began to see the world and my place in it. How differently I was to discover only with each step I took to face up to what was important or what counted for me as important. Here is the opening passage of his comment:

> This essay leaves me with a sense not only of achieved depth but of inexhaustible tact, of simplicity and attention in the face of unencompassable devastations of spirit. With no thought of doing it justice, I will trace a line or two of Veena Das's more elusive thoughts, which readers of her essay may be having some difficulty with. The first sentence of her essay ends by confessing that she finds that the languages of pain "often elude

me." In what follows I will be guided by the thought that to understand her perplexity is the surest route to understanding her readers' perplexity. Veena Das's topic is pain, in a historical instance in which its "enormity . . . is not in question." Her problem presents itself to her as the lack of "languages of pain through which social sciences could gaze at, touch or become textual bodies on which this pain is written." This opening sentence fairly obviously enacts, in its open tolerance of obscurity, the absence of such standing or given languages for such pain. If the scientific intellect is silent on the issue, she who speaks scientifically, committed to making herself intelligible to others similarly committed, is going to have to beg, borrow, steal, and invent words and tones of words with which to break this silence. (Cavell 1996, 93)

In the last chapter, I was led into thinking of anthropological knowledge as somehow slipping into a kind of epistemic violence by the way concepts were generated through a blindness to what was before the eyes of observers. I am less interested in games of praise and blame and think that Cavell understood well that an open tolerance of obscurity is not easy for those who wish to speak from positions of authority. Could it then be that a different register of anthropological creativity opens up when we can find ways of acknowledging that we would have to beg, borrow, and steal words for no ready-made standing languages are available? I offer the thought that there are different routes by which an anthropologist awakens to the reality in which she is sometimes thrown, or sometimes drifts into; what we call fieldwork is perhaps better described as a mode of being-with. In my last book, *Affliction*, I employ modes of collecting data that pertain to the dimensionality of morbidity and yet interweave the findings of the intensive surveys on morbidity and mortality with descriptions of children's voices and of the feel of a neighborhood garnered through attention to fleeting conversations, roadside quarrels, or sudden words that surfaced as if from nowhere. Our concepts are not something we take to our fieldwork as parts of ready-made equipment even in such cases when we are writing to address policy-makers and global health specialists, not to speak of our fellow anthropologists, our friends, and our kin. Concepts may arise as we attend to patterns in statistical data but equally through experiences of the most quotidian kind. Hence, I want to think here of how concepts might be drawn out of us even as we deal with fine-grain experiences that slip below the more stable categories of a society. As anthropologists, we do not always know who we are when we are submerged in fieldwork. Perhaps being in the vicinity of death in these neighborhoods I studied might have been the doorway opened for me to be able to think of thinking itself as irretrievably tied with questions of death. I hope I will be able to describe something of that feeling in the course of this final chapter.

With something of this spirit, I come to a text on death, an experiment with what the author calls "anthropoetry." What I found remarkable in this text is the close embedding of the poems with a landscape (a field site, as the term goes) known through earlier fieldwork but rendered anew in the wake of a sudden traumatic loss.

The text in question is Renato Rosaldo's (2014) book, *The Day of Shelly's Death: The Poetry and Ethnography of Grief.* The book recreates the event of the tragic death of Shelly Rosaldo, Renato's wife, while they were both on a field trip to a remote mountainous region in northern Philippines, not far from where they had conducted their earlier fieldwork.[1] In an interview on how he came to write poetry, Rosaldo says:

> What happened was on September 26, 1996 I suffered a stroke, and within—I'd like to think within a week, but it must have been a little bit longer than that—within a short time, a couple of weeks, poems started coming to me and I was sitting there and these lines would start coming to me. I didn't know exactly what they were and so what I started doing was I started writing them down because I thought I should do that. . . . I had never written poetry before. I'd written a lot of prose with a lot of attention to writing, so I thought of myself as a writer and a teacher. . . . But the last thing I expected to do was for poems to start coming to me. . . . So, as I began healing my fantasy was that I would write a book of poems called "Healing Songs." Because I saw the poetry as healing, deeply healing for me, and it was just brightening my day. (Rosaldo, n.d.)

I think the poetry is healing not only for Rosaldo as the person who has suffered this grief but for anthropology itself, as I hope will become clear as we proceed. The weaving of the extraordinary and the ordinary—grieving his wife's sudden death and performing ordinary acts he must continue to perform, like feeding and bathing his two young children—run twined in each other within the swirl of emotions of grief and feelings of numbness.

The sense that the everyday will be returned but in a deformed way profoundly shapes how we think of the ordinary.

## THE DAY OF SHELLY'S DEATH:
## THE POETRY AND ETHNOGRAPHY OF GRIEF

On October 11, 1981, Michelle Rosaldo (Shelly), while on a trip to a new field site in a remote village in Northern Philippines, slipped and fell into a turbulent river and died. The poems recreating the event of Shelly's death are told through several voices: those of Rosaldo's two sons (one five years old and the other fourteen months old), along with the voices of several other people (priests, nuns, shopkeepers, a woman Catechist who was acting as their fieldwork guide, taxi drivers, a constable), as well as people Ronaldo and Shelly had both known from their earlier long-time fieldwork among the neighboring Ilongot people. Many of these voices are in the first person. They are not a representation of the event of Shelly's death, Rosaldo says, but rather are the event itself. When I first read these poems, I was struck by a curious feeling: the title that kept coming into my head, unbidden, was, "The Day Shelly Died," but, of course, "The Day of Shelly's Death" is what captures the event. It is not "the day Shelly died," which might gesture to a pastness, to a memory. "The day of Shelly's death" hits you with the force of a presence, for the day is everywhere, beyond and above the divisions of past, present, and future. That day was prefigured in the omens and forebodings that are scattered all over the text, as well as the hints within moments of her death that life will go on, that Renato will find love again, that the children will grow up, find other mothers, get married, find joy in their own children. Here one touches the uncanniness of ethnographic writing: one conveys that past from a point in one's life when one is already in another time, a future present.[2] So in reading these poems, one occupies this double time—"Shelly's death will happen / Shelly's death has happened."

As many literary critics note, Rosaldo's poems are stunning in their simplicity. For me, they render what it is to be faced with inordinate knowledge— knowledge that overwhelms us. Words shimmer through this mesh of poetry and prose much as words sometimes surface during fieldwork that are not in the service of an explicit narrative but burst forth as signs of other regions or thresholds of life to which the ethnographer is invited or instigated to enter. I will try to capture here the force of such words, but first allow me to give two lengthy quotations, one in Rosaldo's voice and the other from the foreword by professor of literature Jean Franco.

> The subject of this collection of poetry is an event, the death of Michelle Zimbalist Rosaldo in the Philippines. This event erupted into my life but also into a number of other lives in the village of Munayang and the nearby towns of Lagawe and Kiangan. This collection attempts to capture that eruption and its reverberations through the medium of poetry. (Rosaldo 2014, 101)

And then:

> Rosaldo's "anthropoetry" reaches beyond the narrative of personal loss and gives voice to a chorus of villagers, officials, priests, nuns; and their children; and it is through their oblique view that the singular becomes plural, that the personal loss does not occur in isolation but within a social network reimagined by the poet so that the villagers of Mungyang whom they had scarcely got to know and the people Renato meets on the arduous journey back to Manila become the chorus and the places he and Shelly had traveled together, stages in the bureaucracy of death. Not for nothing did the ancients envisage death as a journey. (Franco 2014, xvi)

These are good enough descriptions as are various references to the "intersubjective" dimension of experience, but they do not capture the uncanny character of time or the sense that in encountering the voicing through which the characters in these poems speak, we hear ghostly voices that convey the menace and dangers that lurk in everyday life without yet becoming full-fledged tragedies. I take two aspects of this atmosphere of menace: one is the forebodings and omens that are scattered throughout the poems and the second is the accusations, spoken and unspoken, that crystallize in the person of the soldier but also in the speech and actions of the children and some of the adults who just accidentally happen to be around. Indeed, the poems are, as Rosaldo describes them, the poetry and ethnography of grief. They are also about the way grief opens the path to rage—a signature theme of Rosaldo's writing. But almost without any overt recognition of this aspect, what creeps into the poems is the sense of menace that stalks the couple right from their arrival in Ilongot country, to their departure from Mungayan where they had hoped to settle for a new fieldwork project. The menace is realized tragically in the dead body of Shelly.

## PREMONITIONS

Let us eschew a chronological order—either the order of the event or the order of telling—but instead take three characters standing in very different relations to Renato and Shelly. I would caution that we do not know in advance how Rosaldo's voice will echo within the voices of these characters. The poems were written twenty-eight years after Shelly's death, and the characters themselves are real people—all except one have appeared in Rosaldo's earlier ethnography of headhunting (Rosaldo 1980)—and their concrete presence during the second fieldwork is alluded to in the time line Rosaldo gives (whose house they stopped in to sleep, where they eat, who gave advice). Yet they are also poetic creations. I was reminded powerfully of Jakobson writing on Mayakovsky's poetry: "Just as the creative ego of the poet is not coextensive with the actual existing self, so conversely the latter does not take in all of the former. . . . The terrible 'double' of the poet is his conventional and commonplace 'self'" (Jakobson 1985, 116). One might extend this argument to say that the actual event of Shelly's slipping and falling to her death is refracted in all directions in many microevents—so the boundaries of what constituted her death are not given once and for all—her death creates these doubles.

The existence of Midalya—one among the nine persons from their earlier fieldwork among the Ilongots who speaks in the first person as do all others in this group—is marked not only by her own name but also through the places and times given in maps and time lines at which she said something that lingers in the different poems. Midalya is among nine others who are kin of one sort or another, present and marked with a time stamp—September 1981—the fragments of speech and gestures that are in the poems happen before the family goes to Ifugao country. A month before Shelly's death on October 11, 1981.

In his broader reflections on those who people these poems, Rosaldo speaks of some as standing within "an accidental field of relations" and others as part of the infrastructure of research—people who offer hospitality in the field, those who cook and clean for us, act as nannies and ayahs, providing physical care that enable anthropologists to do their work. Midalya was the woman who worked as a "maid" during their first field trip, and they stayed in her house for a whole year. In this poem, they meet her before they take off for their new field site.

Shelly and I, Renato, live in their house for a year.
I say,

> We're the same as you.
>> We eat your food.
>>> Sleep on your floor.

Midalya says

> I keep your house
>> Cook your food
>>> I am your maid

Midalya's words have weight
Spoken as matter of fact.
I cannot but accept their truth.

On our visit of 1981 Midalya huddles
Shelly and me in a dark corner by the hearth.
She weeps, saying farewell, urging
Us to be careful, her premonition insisting
what she divines and I as yet do not know. (Rosaldo 2014, 33)

In this poem, the premonition is marked. Renato, though, will learn only too late what she, Midalya already divines; look at the phrase—*I as yet do not know*. There are other omens; sometimes a small event that seems comic actually presages the tragedy to come. At other times the disaster that awaits them is already present in the precariousness all around them. In early September, Renato, Shelly, and the children partake of a feast in their honor in Lakay's home. After they ate, Sam, their older son, "dropped to the rattan floor of the house and began writhing. At first our hosts were upset but when he smiled and went back to twisting on the floor they shrieked with delight. They understood he was imitating the chicken's last moments" (Rosaldo 2014, 11). The child had just seen a chicken being slaughtered but, as yet with no genuine sense of what the extinction of another life in another body means, it is comic for him. At least in that September before he encounters his own mother's death. But then too one cannot decipher what "knowing" is for him.

I put Sam on my shoulders, tell him his mom is dead.
He wants to know when he will get a new one. (53)

Then there are the numerous falls before the fatal fall of Shelly:

> Nena our Ifugao language teacher and new friend, said she would come with us to Kiangan, but the night before our departure she said she could not travel because her nephew of four had just fallen from a stone wall. I forget Nena's exact words, but remember shuddering as I pictured a boy falling, upside-down, arms flailing. (39)

> At St. Joseph's church in Kiangen, Sister Doris tells us to meet Father Joe who, like her, has been in Kiangan for many years. . . . She expresses great concern for our safety, then says a suitable fieldwork site might be Mungayang where a woman named Conchita Camaldi is the catechist. Conchita can be trusted. (39)

Or, consider how a premonition of danger merges with the unspoken menace of the landscape—expressed now through Christian imagery. In the words of a Belgian nun:

> The same, the very spot where I fell. I told Shelly and Renato seven years ago when we met at the Beyer Lodge in Banawe, I told them. Heathen spirits cackled, mocking my crucifix. These spirits follow whims, not my will. (8)

### ACCUSATIONS: THE SCENE OF SUSPICION

The police officer who has summoned Rosaldo to investigate "chief suspect/ her husband" speaks first in a tone of accusation but is soon transported to a moment of his own past. Here the description is both in the first and third person, the inside and outside are joined, so to say—the landscape is ominous "not yet Christian"—yet the grief of this broken man somehow gets through to the investigating officer.

> Kiangan, not yet Christian,
> Guerrilla cadres, New People's Army
> To them my ears cut off
> As much a trophy as my Armalite

> American woman dead, investigate
> Possible homicide. Chief suspect
> her husband. . . .

Was there foul play? I ask.
No, he says, *it was an accident.*

He's pale, trembling, trudging,
With him two sons, a little boy and a baby.
In him I see
the same
ashen face
knotted shoulders
automaton walk my father had the day my mother died. The same.

I tell the pale, trembling man
Investigation's over
No reason to linger. (70)

There is much else that could be said here, the accusations unvoiced but living in the material objects: the shoes Renato had bought for Shelly and Sam and which she was wearing when she slipped, thinking them to be reliable; the checkpoints in which bodies, mutilated and tortured, of those rumored to be terrorists are produced; the riverbed where the river deposits the dead bodies of the tortured—the men know where the river will deposit the dead body of Shelly too. And then there is the figure of Conchita, trusted by both sides in the war, whose *I shall be the one* echoes across the pages. The one who is fated to preside over Shelly's death? The one who will absolve Renato?

I hope you can see how the landscape and its dangers color the biography of individuals in the poems. But it is Shelly's death that almost forces what was diffused in the landscape to become concentrated, to turn into the multimirrored surface on which all the earlier smaller events—the fall of the Belgian nun, and that of the Ifugao teacher's nephew from the stone wall, and Sam's comic writhing and twisting in mimicking the last moments of a chicken being slaughtered—find flashing recognitions, anticipations of something terrible about to happen.[3] It is then to the relation between ethnography and biography that I finally turn, tracing some of the characters who appear in the poems back to the earlier text of Rosaldo's ethnographic work on headhunting (Rosaldo 1980), before his famous essay "Grief and a Headhunter's Rage" (Rosaldo 1984), written four years after Shelly's death, appeared as a commentary on his earlier work, explaining how it was only after Shelly's death that some understanding of what the Ilongot meant when they said headhunting was a way of dealing with grief dawned on him. But the poems go further, much further, in explicating the relations between biography and ethnography.

## ETHNOGRAPHY AND BIOGRAPHY

The essay "Grief and a Headhunter's Rage" by Rosaldo, which first appeared in 1984, describes how the dominance of exchange as a model for feud had made Rosaldo somewhat insensible to the deeper meaning of several statements made by older Ilongot men as to why they went on headhunting missions (Rosaldo 1984). "If you ask an older Ilongot man of northern Luzon, Philippines, why he cuts off human heads, his answer is a one-liner . . . : he says that rage, born of grief, impels him to kill his fellow human beings" (Rosaldo 2014, 118). It was only after the passage of fourteen years following Shelly's death that Rosaldo began to grasp the meaning of this statement. Recalling how he was led to Shelly's body, Rosaldo says he found himself overcome not only by grief but also rage. "How could she abandon me? How could she have been so stupid as to fall? I tried to cry, I sobbed, but rage blocked the tears" (124). It is not that he did not feel the deep cutting pain of sorrow or the cold realization of the finality of death, but he says he simply did not have the experience (despite the death by suicide of his younger brother earlier) that would have allowed him to decipher what the Ilongot meant when they said that bereavement was the source of their desire to take heads—at least he could not earlier understand the full weight of this line of thought. So, Shelly's death is not only a grave injury on his psyche—it is also a cognitive opening. This opening, I suggest, finds a route to the statements on grief leading to rage that had eluded him earlier; it is also a way for him to acknowledge that his complete absorption in the narratives of headhunting and everything related to this form of warfare had created an ignorance of other stories. He lets Taru's voice make this criticism in a muffled voice.

> I never figure in men's talk
> . . .
> Nato and Seli, our names for Renato and Shelly, listen
> To my half-brother Tubkaw, neglect me, never ask for my stories

Years of coughing blood have made me gaunt.
Death has come close and three times I've recuperated. (17)

Here is a figure who is stalked by disease rather than by the prospect of
death in headhunting expeditions that are seen to mark the hero in the cultural milieu of the Ilongot and, thus, Rosaldo almost misses him in his
earlier work. It is not that tuberculosis does not figure in Rosaldo's work on
the history of Ilongot headhunting, but those who have tuberculosis—their
deaths and their frailties—are subsumed within the capacities or incapaci-
ties of men to wage headhunting expeditions. Thus, tuberculosis is mentioned once in the context of a feud between the Butag-Rumpad bands
between 1923 and 1956. Rosaldo gives an account of the arrests of all the able-
bodied men of the Rumpad group by the troops (rumored to be instigated
by someone in the Betag group) to avenge an earlier insult but mentions only
as an aside that two men who were infirm and debilitated by tuberculosis
escaped the arrests since they were seen as ineffectual for any headhunting
raids (Rosaldo 1980, 72). The dramatic quality of the deaths through behead-
ing is the subject of stories that are remembered and circulated in the oratory of Tubkaw, the half-brother of Taru. As Taru says in the poem cited
earlier, "Nato" and "Seli" listen to those stories but not to the stories of sores
on the body and the coughing of blood. In Taru's complaint we have the first
indication that Rosaldo is aware or is made aware after Shelly's death that
surrounding the dramatic deaths that he researched meticulously, there are
other deaths that were also part of the milieu but were left out in the ethnographic telling because they did not fit the orientation of the ethnography
toward the history and anthropology of headhunting. Like the minor characters who often escape the ethnographer's attention, and toward whom Rosaldo becomes much more attuned after all the incidental interactions
brought about by the bureaucratic demands and the demands of caring his
two sons need immediately after their mother's death, there are also minor
stories that never make it into the ethnography. Such minor currents of stories, of accidental encounters in the field, of words blurted out that derange
the context, are precisely what make up the texture of the ordinary in the
present book. Rosaldo's genius lies in the fact that he absorbs these as part
of the milieu even when they were absent in the initial ethnography. This
almost unmarked absorption is evident in the voice he gives to the accidental

and minor figures (though not only to them) through his poetry, making the intersection of ethnography and biography into anthropoetry.

Taru does not figure in the earlier book on headhunting (Rosaldo 1980), but others who speak through these poems do—thus Tukbaw is the great orator and the "Ilongot brother" of Rosaldo and his oratory figures prominently in both Renato's and Michelle Rosaldo's respective ethnographies. In the poem on Tubkaw, Rosaldo lets Tubkaw evoke their closeness as he speaks of a hospital visit to Bambang with "Nato," who sleeps in the hospital with Tubkaw rather than going to a more comfortable hotel to spend the night there. Thus, "I say that, like a brother, he didn't abandon me" (Rosaldo 2014, 21). Yet in the eyes of Tubkaw's wife, Wagat, whose complicated web of relations and their grudges and betrayals are woven into the dramatic structure of the feuds in the earlier book, "Tubkaw proudly tells Nato the story of his life/nothing in it for me" (19). Tubkaw contests the characterization of his oratory as just fancy speech. This small squabble points to the tensions that mark not only the relations between feuding bands but also the threads of grudges and betrayals that run through the most intimate of relations within a tightly knit kinship unit. Is it important to move from here to a moment of abstraction to baptize these currents and crosscurrents as the "negative" dimension of kinship (e.g., Sahlins 2013)? Or is thought already embedded in the descriptions and the examples that help us conceive of texture as laying of fiber upon fiber rather than to search for a single thread that runs through the form of life we may name as kinship or relatedness or being-together?

The poems then achieve something remarkable: they are occasioned by Shelly's death but they show that faced with traumatic injury, Renato does what being an anthropologist will make him do, which is turn to the worlds he has inhabited through his ethnographic work. This aspect of one's being as an anthropologist was not transparent to me until I found myself in a seminar at the Czech Academy of Sciences in February 2018 with David Mosse, known for his brilliant work on the anthropology of development. David spoke of how he was learning to engage with the world again almost six or seven years after his twenty-three-year-old son had tragically taken his own life. David was now almost compulsively drawn toward fieldwork among survivor groups and support groups related to suicide all over London. Someone from the audience asked him why *that* was the mode of engagement he chose. I do not remember the question very well but I remember David's answer with crystal clarity. He said, "That is because I am an anthropologist—and this is what anthropologists do. If I were a carpenter I am sure I would have done something different." I was stunned because this was a definition of "doing anthropology" that simply rang true for me. I had encountered this kind of impulse earlier—say, in Janet Carsten's writings on house memories that captured the lives of her Jewish parents in Berlin, a way of life lost and rebuilt again in London (Carsten 2004, 2018). Or the fragments of the work of Clara Han and Andrew Brandel on how to render the reverberations of war, fascist camps, displacement, and the violence of refugee life that marked relations within their respective families—all this through the eyes of the child and the grandchild who grew up to be anthropologists (Han forthcoming; Han and Brandel 2019). Again, I am not saying that David's answer can be generalized, or that a carpenter's way of re-engaging the world is at a lower level than, say, that of an artist or a philosopher, or even that one is not simultaneously many of these fragments; rather, I am suggesting that anthropology perhaps teaches us how to reinhabit a broken world more than it teaches anything else. Its concepts, then, do not and cannot live in some rarefied, frictionless space of pure thought.

The poetic impulse that Rosaldo brings to the event of Shelly's death does not take him to a realm we might call imaginary in contrast to the world that we might call real. The poetic voice he finds is anchored in maps of the area, the marking of the exact spot where Shelly slipped, names of towns and villages, description of actual rivers unnamed because the Ilongot do not name rivers, photographs of the people from Ilongot country who figure in the poems and to whom Rosaldo lends his voice even against himself. Reality here is deeply contextual—one has neither a frontal view of reality as if it were before our eyes nor a relativist view as if death could be conceptualized and grasped rather than being the searing singular event the book portrays. I weave the theme of what it means to speak of a struggle to make living and thinking commensurable to each other in various chapters of this book, but here is one passage from Wittgenstein that guides me in thinking of context. Wittgenstein is speaking of experiencing a word, such that a word uttered to oneself brings to mind a whole scenario, or a person, "as if the word were a portrait of the whole thing" (Wittgenstein [1953] 1968, 226$^e$, §264).

But wouldn't these words too be only a *germ*? They must surely belong to a language and to a context, in order really to be the expression of the thought *of* that man. (Wittgenstein [1953] 1968, 228ᵉ, §283)

And now a shift of mood as I go to another account taken from a recent essay I published in response to a question posed by Morten Nielsen and Nigel Rapport on how one comes to compose a particular text (Nielsen and Rapport 2018). Several anthropologists responded to this provocation, but almost all took this to be a question of methods (say, of collaboration or of storing and accessing data) or writing experiments they had undertaken. To my surprise, I was led into writing a different kind of essay and imagine that this must have been so because I had spent that whole summer reading Jocelyn Benoist's (2010) book on concepts and so the issues swirling in my mind were triggered by ideas about particularity but also by his intriguing remark that a particular invitation from a student to think about Africa as a concept had given him back his taste for life. How does life being breathed into words relate to our own ability to breathe again? Perhaps this is what connects or creates a circuit of connections that are the conditions for thinking.

I had written a short commentary, entitled "The Grains of Experience," that was published in the online journal *Somatosphere* on Nayanika Mookherjee's (2015) powerful book *The Spectral Wound*, which I had read and admired greatly. Yet some half-formed questions niggled at me. I asked myself whether one can come to the understanding of concepts through some other routes than the classical one of assuming that concepts are about the intellectual procedures of comparing, abstracting, and moving from the particular to the general. I had been claiming in much of my writing (apart from what appears in this book) that there was no sharp boundary between experience and concepts—that experience clings to concepts rather than being eliminated in the process of generating purity of thought. I had been invoking a number of passages from Wittgenstein and the devastating counterexamples he gives against the idea that concepts have a bounded definitional structure. I will not repeat my earlier observations on the relation between open texture, flexible or vague boundaries, or language games and resemblance between concepts. In Mookherjee's book, I had before me a delicate rendering of the experience of a number of women who were raped by soldiers of the Pakistani army during the 1971 war in Bangladesh. Mookherjee's descriptions were subtle and sensitive to the texture of life (and death)—the voices of the women had not been deadened by repeated recitals before human rights organizations or truth commissions. There was also the contrast Mookherjee made between the figure of the *birangona* (war heroine) that had emerged in the national discourse in Bangladesh that tried to situate these women not as stigmatized, impure women to be shunned but as heroines to be embraced. Their violation was rendered on the model of heroic sacrifice, putting them on par with the sacrifices made by the male freedom fighters. Mookherjee thought of their presence in the national media and in left-liberal discourse as "spectral," locating this concept within Derrida's notion of "the trace." The experience of real women, she wrote, had to be evacuated in order for the birangona to function as a national figure. I asked myself: Is there an underlying assumption here that in the cases of women in the village of Enayatpur, who had only been able to speak in fragments, we are witnessing *the flow of lived experience*, while in the discourse on the birangonas valorized in the national media *experience had been evacuated* to generate a purified representation? Was the first capturing "lived experience" and the latter "concept formation"?

In my original commentary on Mookherjee's book, I formulated my puzzle as follows: "In debates on testimony and trauma the discussion ranges around the polemics of speech and silence but how about the specificity of the grains of experience?" (Das 2017, 40). The expression "grains of experience" had stuck with me from Gareth Evans's (1982) posthumous book *Varieties of Reference*, as well as from its delicate elaboration on concepts by Benoist (2010). The problem of reference had become engrossing because, while I had a healthy distrust of correspondence theories of truth, I could not simply turn away from such issues as *what it is for our words to be worldbound*. Nor could distinctions between the sign and the index suffice, for even when context was not linguistically marked, I took from Wittgenstein the idea that the whole of our language is context-bound and yet our access to context can be easily lost, putting a world itself in jeopardy. As I wrote in Chapter 9, Wittgenstein's remarks on the harmony between thought and reality (Wittgenstein [1953], 1968, §29, §30)[4] brought the question of possibility as an essential feature of the real. If I might loop back to my own words, I wrote that harmony between thought and reality did not lie in correctly specifying the referent of a concept but rather in understanding that possibility may well provide the footing within which actuality can be realized. There are other places where the intimate connection between concepts and the place of possibility is discussed in *PI*, but I will take only one example—that of the discussion on how we come to speak of machines "having" or "possessing" the possibilities of movement (Wittgenstein [1953], 1968, §194). In deciphering what we could mean by the *possibility* of movement, Wittgenstein tempts us to think that we might be describing the empirical conditions (play between socket and pin) or we might assume that the possibility of movement is like the shadow of the movement itself but subsequently reestablishes the ordinariness by asking if we might let these waves of question on question subside as soon as we ask ourselves: how do we use the phrase "possibility of movement" when we talk of a *given* machine. After all, the washing machine does not quite move in the same way as a bicycle—it cannot transport me somewhere.

I want to summarize these points by saying that Wittgenstein is cautioning us that there is a difference between what Kant called merely logical possibility and real possibility—hence between evoking such figures as the flowers grown in the sky as discussions on logic in Sanskrit texts repeatedly drew attention to, and to think of the possibility of the pot being contained in the clay. We shall see that the figures of thought that came unbidden to women who had been raped during the war of independence in Bangladesh attach to concrete objects (rice, cloth) and are embedded in their understanding of what their relations were within which the unfolding of this event is imagined.

For now, the point is that as I read and reread Mookherjee's book over a stretch of time, I felt I was ready to tackle an issue that Evans had articulated. I knew I would need to keep returning to this issue, but the very limits within which a commentary is written gave me the incentive to put my swirling thoughts and emotions on paper—in some way to control my own wildness. In the commentary, my observations now took the following shape:

> In his highly influential work on concepts, Gareth Evans (1982) proposed that the content of experience is non-conceptual—only when one has shifted from experience to *judgment* based on that experience has one moved from the non-conceptual to the conceptual content of experience. Taking his example from colors, (to stand in for other kinds of percep-

tual experience) Evans argued that the conceptual ability to recognize colors, as when we know what is red, green, or burnt sienna, is not enough since this naming and the capacity it represents is coarser in grain than the finer shades and details of our color experience. Thus, for Evans, there is something in experience that evades description in terms of conceptual content. This notion of the non-conceptual content of experience is tied to two different thoughts that might be interrogated. The first is that concepts are by definition abstract entities rather than concrete or empirical ones. (Despite the grudging acknowledgement by philosophers of "empirical concepts," these are placed at lower levels of thought than say, "categories of understanding.") Second, it could be questioned if a concept is embodied *in a word*, rather than in everything that goes on in the world with that word and others like it. (Das 2017, 40)

I then went on to take examples from Mookherjee's account of the fragments of testimony that came out in the course of everyday activities during her interactions with the women. I wrote:

At another time Kajoli recalled how even as she was being raped by the military, she was thinking about whether she would lose her entitlements to rice and clothes in her conjugal home—a theme repeated in a number of other accounts in which unbidden thoughts about future losses come looming even as a woman is being violated and perhaps is even facing death. Rashida recounted that "When I was being raped I thought my life was over. . . . I thought that I had been married for just a year, so my husband may not keep me at home, may not give me rice and clothes" (Mookherjee 2015, 111). In these statements, we find years of experiences of women: the rendering of the precariousness of a woman's life in her natal and conjugal home due to fights between co-wives, the hostility of in-laws, stories of abandonment and the importance of sexual chastity, becoming distilled in that episode of the specific violation. (Das 2017)

Consider the sentence: "Even as she was being raped by the military, Kajoli was *thinking*." Here, thought is not something done in the atmosphere of a philosophy lesson but within the thick of experience. It is accounts such as these that have led me to acknowledge that there is something terribly wrong in assuming that there are distinct moments to experience: some in which we simply live and feel and others in which we think. There is a wonderful way in which Jocelyn Benoist summarizes this view: "goûtez ou pensez."

In my own work on sexual violation during the massive violence of the Partition of India, I describe stories as acquiring a footing in the real through being embedded within a field of force made up of swirling words, other stories, gestures, and much else (Das 2007). But there is also one particular experience that might stand as my personal tribunal through which I can put to the test the idea that *feeling and thinking are not separated*. Many years ago, a man, probably in the midst of a psychotic episode, broke into my house when I was alone and tried to strangle me. I talked him out of it but all along my one compelling thought was that I did not want to die groveling and begging for mercy. Thus, when Kajoli and Rashida speak of the way thoughts came unbidden even as they were facing such terrible violation, I feel that they offer an insight into the nature of experiential concepts that could sometimes perhaps be garnered from thought experiments in philosophy but that carries far greater weight for me coming from the mouths of women who were offering their "extreme history" (*chorom itihas*) to Mookherjee, the anthropologist and the one they could affectionately address as "ma" (lit. "mother" but used in Bengal for little girls too).

Yet it remains that I cannot say if I am able to decipher how experience clings to thought in these accounts because I had puzzled over these questions in Wittgenstein and Evans or whether Wittgenstein and Evans began to make sense in the light of the realization that such issues appear outside textbooks too—they are not simply academic games. I do know that my confidence in my response was greatly strengthened by reading what women like Kajoli and Rashida were able to articulate.

But let us now say that I have been able to find some peace on the question that concepts do not have, or for the most part do not have, a definitional structure. Of course, I do know that under certain circumstances placing a boundary around a concept might be required—for example, in a court of law that might simply decree that a pigeon is a predatory bird, treating pigeons as purely legal objects (as Bruno Latour [2010] mentions in his book on law), or in a Euclidian space when we can say without any ambiguity that the shortest distance between two points is a straight line. But this "muscling down" of concepts to a region of the real—whether this real is related to legal spaces or mathematical ones—holds true only for that region. Outside the French administrative courts, the pigeon is not treated as a predatory bird; similarly, if the concept of distance itself changes, say, in a non-Euclidian space, then the definition of the straight line too disappears. Thus, despite the tendency of many anthropologists to demand definitive definitions as a condition for building theory, we know that these classical notions of concepts have been put under considerable pressure for several decades now. Worries that now haunted me, after writing the Mookherjee commentary, were of a new kind. Let me elaborate.

In my graduate classes, and in some recent writing, I evoke Cora Diamond's (2006) compelling reading of J. M. Coetzee's fictional character Mrs. Costello, who is wounded by the thought of people eating animals—animals she can imagine as companions. Diamond calls this the "difficulty of reality" and the "difficulty of philosophy." The rawness Mrs. Costello feels, what she is not able to comprehend, is how people could go about their ordinary lives as if nothing were amiss. I think there is a strong formulation here that it is not our concepts that help us overcome what is recalcitrant in reality but rather such simple things as the exchange of glances in which the other is recognized. The issue for Mrs. Costello, after all, is not that of the rights of animals as a generic category but rather that she can imagine some animals as her companions. In some of her other work, Diamond argues that literature (rather than philosophy or social science) captures much better such questions as the depth of our denial or recognition of the other. As she says, "I cannot choose what weight it shall have that I fail you or betray you, or that I on some occasion look at you but with a look that leaves you a mere circumstance and not a human being. Levi and Tolstoy show us, then, the shape of certain possibilities in human life" (Diamond 1988, 265).

So, if concepts are entities that wander around in the uncultivated gardens of possibility, then I wonder if the kinds of thoughts I admire in Diamond, and also in the writing of Cavell, are a critique of concepts under a certain picture of thinking that assumes a detached view in which all steps from basic premise to conclusion are laid out in the structure of arguments? Wittgenstein includes in his examples of concepts the entire repertoire of words, gestures, and sounds through which the entire unstated background of our lives is evoked. He calls this the natural history of mankind, a history that might be expressed in such ordinary expressions as that we have "things at hand" (because we are the kinds of creatures who have hands), "seeing red" (because our color concepts make us think of emotions as having color), and so on. So, then, the challenge for me is to see that even when concepts seem very crystalline as they become embodied in words—"honor," "shame," "proper name"—they belong to thought because they are mobile, can move from one context to another, stitching and patching disparate contexts, and not because they have abstracted some general properties of the entities under examination. Yet, because a concept cannot be stretched indefinitely, the process of mastering it is also the process of mastering where its limits lie. Some concepts (like some rules) will tolerate much flexibility and others will not—but that is precisely how we learn to live with concepts, not just use them in some rarefied processes of "organizing our experience." These issues are the swirling thoughts and emotions that went into my writing this text and, in turn, generated new questions that are not likely to be resolved anytime soon, if ever, but in relation to which I took some steps forward in my own thinking.

It also happens that I am an avid reader of Sanskrit texts, both for the immense pleasure they give me and for an ambition I nurture to make them appear as offering modes of reasoning within our contemporary anthropological or philosophical concerns. Yet, if I take two steps forward in these directions, I seem to move back several steps every time. In Chapter 10, some of these concerns of what is "sameness," what is "substitution," and what is to understand the figures of grammar as both aesthetic and logical figures came out.[5] But I shrink back from more systematic rendering of the importance for anthropologists of engaging concepts from these traditions, intimidated by the astonishing scholarship of some of the Sanskrit scholars not only in English and French but also in Hindi and Bangla (languages with which I am reasonably comfortable). But what I cannot do at the level of general theoretical discussions because of my limits, I can perhaps do through examples. Mookherjee's examination of the birangona and her critique made me think that perhaps I could bring in my reading of the Bangla and Sanskrit texts to bear on the question of the raped or abducted woman.

This is how the issue found expression in my commentary on Mookherjee's book. An instance is when Kajoli was shouting across the field one day to tell her ten-year-old son to come home because of a brewing storm. As Mookherjee (2015, 134) describes it, she suddenly said: "I was caught in a *toofan* (cyclone) and *apnar bhai* . . . (referring to her husband) . . . wasn't even at home during the event" (2015, 110). Mookherjee glosses this reference to the storm as a weather metaphor ("Kajoli let a reference to the rape and her husband's absence that day trickle out through a weather metaphor"). But what seems to me to be significant here is the long aesthetic tradition in Sanskrit and Bangla of rendering sensory experience of dread, foreboding, and fear as openness to impressions from the world in the form of the sounds of thunder, lightning, and rumbling of clouds.[6] It seems possible, at least, for one to think that what Kajoli is telling is not simply a "lived experience" (though it is that too) but an experience that contains a conceptual content that is concrete, empirical, and yet belongs as much to thought as to what the body has come to forcefully know. I am not suggesting that the use of the weather imagery makes Kajoli consciously put her experience in terms of the aesthetics through which the scene of abduction was rendered in poetry in Sanskrit or Bangla but that what she does with this experience finds a footing in the world through imagery that she can evoke.

Swayam Bagaria (2017), in a brilliant commentary on the way references to the storm and to a boat surface in Kajoli's account and in a fragment of poetry recalled by Mookherjee, writes:

> They are both a result of the cachet of the oral-folkloric, one acquired through phenomenal deliberation and the other inherited through poetic canon. But rather than emphasizing their traditional and customary status as tropes that reemphasizes the depth of language, I want to suggest here that their inclusion in their contexts also make these readily available resources of language into concepts, literal concepts that show the textualization of the bodies of these women as bodies thus making any easy passing on of the message embedded in these figurations difficult or even impossible. This is not what can be called the region of language that can be translatable into any form of publicly recognizable form of memory; rather I want to think of it as a peculiar variation of lingual memory that implicates the history of the language, rather than institutions and people, in the sedimentation of memory. (Bagaria 2017)

Borrowing the notion of lingual memory from Alton Becker (1995), Bagaria suggests here that particular words can swell up and bear the weight of a memory that is not embedded within any coherent discourse or narrative: it is not that the boat and the storm simply recall earlier usages but that they both allow expressivity and block the passing of the memory of rape and humiliation into easily tradable public goods. There is an interesting discussion to be had on how the words become concepts here not by repetition but by conveying the singularity of a searing experience.

Mookherjee draws on a large visual archive, as well as public performances and discussions in media, to make a persuasive case for the argument that within a logic of representation, the imagery of the birangona at the national level manages to "remember" the war heroine as a national figure on condition that she can be disappeared through death, suicide, insanity, or departure for India in the case of Hindu women. In her words: "The real person of the *birangona* thus having exited, the account brings back her haunted specter to feed the national imaginary" (Mookherjee 2015, 182). Without denying the power of this argument, I was interested in a side question: From where did the affective imagery of the birangona emerge?

Again, by sheer happenstance, in my early teens I had been quite interested in Hindi and Bangla literature (and continue to be so). Though I had not read the nineteenth-century poetry and plays produced on the birangona within the national fervor of an anticolonial movement, I had read and often recited the heroic poetry produced by women poets such as Subhadra Kumari Chauhan and was very attached to the figures of Rani Laxmi Bai and Begum Hazrat Mahal, who were the inspirations for the later emergence of the figure of the birangona. These memories surged, making me look again at the poems of Michael Madhusudan Dutt and to formulate the idea that even though the figure of the birangona gets transformed from the heroic to the abject, there is a background in the kavya tradition that gives the figure affective force. Would Diamond's notion that sometimes our concepts are simply not in line with our experiences—because the background conditions under which they made sense at one time have disappeared but the language continues—apply to the resurrection of this figure in the Bengali media in the newly independent Bangladesh? The lines that concluded these kinds of thoughts read as follows in my commentary:

> It might perhaps be interesting to see its [the birangona's] double edged character—it claims a footing into the aesthetic tradition in Bengal even as it evacuates the particularity of the experiences of women who end up bearing the burdens of having been muscled into becoming its referents. (Das 2017)

I end this movement, then, with the tentative suggestion that amounts to accepting Mookherjee's analysis and critique of the figure of the birangona and hoping that in the future scholars might look more closely toward concepts of aesthetic emotion as elaborated in Sanskrit or vernacular languages, which show that whole narratives, fragments of stories, sentences, words, and even particles of grammar can bear the weight of memory, parsing the real in different modes of revealing and concealing. The disquiet in the figure of the birangona as Mookherjee portrays it is that it seeks to *typ-ify* the experience of being raped and thus occludes the singularity of such figures. Some of the kavya literature does that too, as many classical anthropological texts did as they rendered the particularity of experience through very coarse general concepts. In the best expressions of the kavya theories of emotion, however, the typification is almost always peeled away. Thus, although a figure like Rama, the protagonist of the epic Ramayana, is often seen as an exemplar whose fate it is to be reinterpreted over and over again— the twelfth-century dramatist Bhava-bhuti's Rama expresses his love for Sita, the wife he abandoned, in one way while the great poet Kalidas expresses it in quite another way—no one would confuse Bhava-bhuti's Rama with that of Kalidas. It is this difference that allows *the grains of experience to be retained in the character* so that, despite bearing the same proper name and following the same plot line, these two figures could never be merged into one.

There are many conversations of this kind that I have in my head from the milieu of my early teens, when we could spend hours debating if Rama really loved Sita or just followed the script of a dutiful husband. Recently, I was amused to see Gary Tubb, a Sanskritist of exquisite sensibility,[7] pose the same question for Kalidas's Rama ("Does his Rama love Sita?"). Tubb writes:

> But what is more striking in the Raghuvamsa is that the affection shown by these kings toward their wives, and depicted so movingly in such verses as Aja's lament for Indumati, is almost totally absent in Kalidas's treatment of Rama, a character who in the hands of other Sanskrit poets such as Bhavabhuti is credited with the most elaborate and vocal yearnings for his missing Sita. (Tubb 2014, 81)

I felt I wanted to reassure Tubb that while Kalidas's Rama does not cry and lament his losses, or faint at the memory of Sita, as many other poets will make him do, the following verse from Raghuvamsam (which I write from memory) should be proof enough of his love. This is the verse that comes when Lakshmana (Rama's younger brother) comes back from the forest after abandoning Sita there and recounts to Rama how Sita had cried aloud like the *chakrandi* bird separated from her mate when she thought Lakshmana was now out of the range of the sounds of the forest:

*babhūva rāma sahasā savāshpah tuṣāravarshīva sahasra chandrah*
*kaulīnabhītena grhāninrastā nā tena vaidehasutā manastah*

Suddenly Rama was with tears much as the moon is
that rains down the hail
For fear of scandal,
by him, she was banished
from home
the daughter of Videha
(who) from the heart, could not be expelled (my translation)

If I were to interpret this verse well, I would reflect on the analogy with the moon that becomes itself covered with the snowy sheen it rains down (my teacher Mrs. Sundari interpreted this analogy to mean that his eyes were brimming with tears that remained unshed) and also on the fact that Rama dared not take the name of Sita anymore but could only evoke her as Videha's daughter, and again that nowhere is agency ascribed to Rama, for in using the instrumental case for him, Kalidas makes the expulsion of Sita simply a cowardly act taken by a man who is driven by fear rather than as the act of a righteous king. There was certainly some resonance that I found in these scenes of abduction and expulsion and the accounts in Mookherjee's book of husbands caught between the fear of ignominy and their love for their wives who had faced such brutality.

These thoughts on aesthetics and grammar are not new to me—they inform my writing in all kinds of devious ways—but I cannot get enough of a grasp on these thoughts that are like sediments of memories of a time when the pleasure of the text was everything.

Nor can I offer any tight connections between what goes on in one's life when one writes or reads and the kinds of writing or reading it produces. But I do know that my sense of the affective as it clings to concepts comes from those longings that go beyond a particular text or a piece of writing. As does my conviction that the issue is not whether our concepts grasp or touch a region of reality *correctly*; the important thing is to realize that concepts must be led to a place where they are at home, there alone it makes sense to even ask if a concept works. Wittgenstein's formulation that our task is to "lead words home" reveals how a notion like the birangona might become spectral but also how in making their everyday life people struggle to move out of the grip of the ghostly into that which can give the concept a ground on which to stand.

Although I provide references to the books that I have cited, these texts functioned for me in different ways than a scholarly apparatus would if the enterprise of writing was a purely rational undertaking with no emotional content. Yet much remains and must remain unsaid.

> It's not the mirror that is draped, but
> What remains unspoken between us.

Forrest Gander

The last reflection comes from a recent discussion in class. The question before us was to interrogate the notion that the limits of the human body or the human voice were not knowable in advance. I had made the point that I did not think that different cultures provided instantiations of something universal called "the human condition," and yet it was very important to be attentive to the way that the notion of something (some sign, some expression, some sudden exclamation), not knowable in advance, might be evoked as a sign of a form of life being a human form of life.

A particular question assigned for a response on which we were hovering was: "Compare Charles Taylor's suggestion that radically alternative practices found in cultures other than our own can be explained and evaluated by, and only by, developing a 'language of perspicuous contrast' within which both others' ways of life and ours can be described as 'alternative possibilities in relation to some human constants at work in both.'"

I somehow drifted into a discussion on how this question of alterity was made so much easier to address because the radically alternative practices were sought in an elsewhere. I had been trying to write about the case of Kh, the eight-year-old girl who was abducted and repeatedly and brutally raped (see Chapter 8). What completely threw me off in this case was not just the cruelty but that this cruelty was perpetrated on the child in the same single room from which the man was plying his trade, cohabiting with his two wives, and that they were living there with their two small children.

I evoked Cavell's notion of horror as the possibility that human identity could be dissolved but still could not explain why for me, even if I can see myself talking to this man or being in some ordinary interaction with him, I cannot conceive of the possibility that we are of the same flesh. And how is this to be distinguished (if it can be so distinguished) from the fourteen-year-old girl in Baltimore reflecting on her early childhood, saying in a meditative mood, "But, except for the sex part, my stepfather was a very good dad." Is this the "difficulty of reality"? Should thought stop here?

# ACKNOWLEDGMENTS

It is a great pleasure to express my grateful thanks to Clara Han and Bhrigu-pati Singh for including this book in their remarkably innovative series "Thinking from Elsewhere" for Fordham University Press and for the close attention and critical comments they have given me throughout the period of writing. Their friendship and trust in me are two of the most precious gifts that animate my intellectual life. I was also very fortunate to receive detailed comments on different chapters from Charlie Hallisey, Michael Jackson, Piergiorgio Donatelli, Richard Rechtman, Paola Marrati, Michael Lambek, Lotte Segal, Julia Eckert, Nayanika Mookherjee, and Didier Fassin. These comments helped me in getting a perspective and a grip on what I was trying to do. My friendship with Roma Chatterji, Sangeeta Chattoo, Deepak Mehta, Rita Brara, Yasmeen Arif, Pratiksha Baxi, Shalini Randeria, and Aditya Bharadwaj—all from D'School days—has sustained me intellectually and spiritually, as they all know. I am grateful for the op-portunities to collaborate with Naveeda Khan, whose discussions in class can make the driest of topics shimmer with fun and laughter, and Deborah Poole, whose resolute reading of texts I truly admire. I was able to spend two weeks of sheer bliss with a group of scholars in Lausanne as they que-ried me with the greatest of attention on the minutest points in my writing. Thank you, Yves Erard, Marco Motta, Joséphine Stebler, Claude Welscher, and Danielle Robert—it is a rare privilege to find readers with your impec-cable judgment. Also, for their intellectual sympathies and support over the years, I thank Arthur Kleinman, Talal Asad, James Laidlaw, Marilyn Strath-ern, Caroline Humphrey, and Claude Imbert.

To my graduate students, many of whom are now professors with award-winning books and teachers who find the same kind of joy I find in teaching, I hope that how much I have learned from you is reflected in the book and that echoes of our discussions over all these years reverberate in the text. Megha, Aditi, Pooja, Vaibhav, Maya, Sameena, Aaron, Richard, Don, Young-gyung, Sylvain, Andrew Bush, Neena, Fouad, Onder, Bhrigu, Amrita, Sid, Serra, Ghazal, Sruti, Mariam, Greg might stand here for all the others whose work I have learned much from and whose astonishing, diverse ways of thinking inspire me. I am also very grateful to Thomas Lay, who knew the right direction in which to steer the book and to tell me exactly when to stop, and to Eric Newman and Ziggy Snow for their editorial contributions.

Over the last year, as I was completing the book, I was blessed to be with six remarkable companions who had the gift to be able to anticipate unerringly when I needed a push, when a citation, when a cartoon, when a poem, when a song, and when a stringent criticism. To these six—Sandra Laugier, Andrew Brandel, Swayam Bagaria, Marco Motta, Michael Puett, and Kunal Joshi—I have only one thing to say: I do not know what I could have ever done, and in which previous life, to deserve such generosity from you, but I can say that I have worked really hard to meet your expectations and to keep your trust.

It should go without saying but I will nevertheless say it: it is only the loyalty and steadfastness of all members of ISERDD—especially Charu, Rajan, Purshottam, and Gita—that sustains the work we do. To all of them and to the families who continue to open their homes and hearths to us, I am truly grateful.

I know I could not have sustained an academic life without the kind of family I have in which ideas really matter. Saumya, Jishnu, and Sanmay have engaged in vigorous conversations over what knowledge is for us; and Ranen has been woken up at all odd hours to listen to a puzzle or to help catch a fleeting thought. It is now more than fifty years when you left, Dev, but not a single day has passed without something or other coming back from our life together and sprouting a hope. It is perhaps also time that I acknowledge my open debt of survival and what I might have learned from *beeji* and *pitaji* even though it resides in some deep layers of forgotten times.

My debt to Stanley Cavell for giving me voice would be palpable in my writing—less obvious might be my intuition that the love for philosophy or literature or music has already taken root in the generations to come—my evidence being that the first full word Nathaniel uttered was "WOW."

In that spirit, it is a privilege to be able to thank Anish Kapoor for permission to reproduce his image *White Dark IV* and Maarten Ottens for the beautiful design of the cover.

And to ma who taught me how to breathe under water—*namasteyastu mahamaye.*

नमस्तेऽस्तु महामाये

The following chapters were published earlier, and I gratefully acknowledge editors and publishers for the permission given to reproduce revised versions of these papers.

Chapter 1 was previously published as "Wittgenstein and Anthropology," *Annual Review of Anthropology* 27 (1998): 171–95.

Chapter 3 was published as "Ordinary Ethics," in *A Companion to Moral Anthropology,* edited by Didier Fassin, 133–49 (West Sussex: Wiley-Blackwell, 2012).

Chapter 4 was published as "Ethics, Self-Knowledge, and Life Taken as a Whole," *HAU: Journal of Ethnographic Theory* 8, no. 3 (2018): 537–49.

Chapter 5 was published as "Engaging the Life of the Other: Love and Everyday Life," in *Ordinary Ethics: Anthropology, Language, and Action,* edited by Michael Lambek, 376–99 (New York: Fordham University Press, 2010).

Chapter 6 was published as "The Boundaries of the 'We': Cruelty, Responsibility, and Forms of Life," *Critical Horizons: A Journal of Philosophy and Social Theory* 7, no. 2 (2016): 168–85.

Chapter 7 was published as "A Child Disappears: Law in the Courts, Law in the Interstices of Everyday Life," *Contributions to Indian Sociology* 53, no. 1 (2019): 97–132.

# NOTES

**PREFACE**

1. In thinking of the philosophy of collecting, Stanley Cavell (2005e) discusses several authors who have taken collecting as an activity relating to things, as ways of rearranging the world. More crucially for me, though, are his remarks on collecting as a procedure for doing philosophy: "If Heidegger is a philosopher of collecting, Wittgenstein composes his *Investigations* in such a way as to suggest that philosophy is, or has become for him, a procedure of collecting. . . . In his preface he calls the book, *'really only an album.'* For some, me among them, this feature of Wittgenstein's presentation of his thought, is part of their attraction" (Cavell 2005e, 244).

2. The play, of course, has the story of Rama as related in the Ramayana composed by Valmiki in the background but in the Indian imagination of texts, these are written after the event but at the same time, might unfold along with the event or even presage the event. As Karnad says of this feature, "In fact, as the action of the play unfolds in front of us, we are continuously made conscious that the epic is being composed and developing in the background. Valmiki is invisible till the last few minutes of the play but we are aware of his creative presence in the wings right through" (Karnad 2007, 21).

3. I am powerfully reminded of my son Jishnu's stories at about age five: when the plot and characters became too tangled, he would suddenly stop and write: "*phir toofan aaya aur sab mar gaye*" (then came a storm and everyone died). The ruse did not always work with Mrs. Gauba, his brilliant, loving, and, in her own way, stern teacher at Shiv Niketan. It made me think of the naturalness of leaving things in the middle.

4. I have given detailed descriptions of these areas in earlier publications and so will not repeat them here. Please consult Das (2007, 2015a) in particular, but also see Das (2011a) and Das and Walton (2015).

5. I do not provide any discussion of anthropology's absorption of Wittgenstein because I find that though Wittgenstein is often evoked in the writings of Clifford Geertz on the North American side or sometimes by Pierre Bourdieu on the side of French sociology, the discussion remains confined to a very general level. However, see Clément (1996) and Salgues (2008) for an especially informed discussion on this topic.

## INTRODUCTION

1. In the revised third edition of *Philosophical Investigations* (Wittgenstein 2001), P. M. S. Hacker and Joachim Schulte translate the third line in §109 as "The pneumatic conception of thought," but in earlier editions Elizabeth Anscombe (Wittgenstein [1953] 1968) translates it as "The conception of thought in a gaseous medium." See Schulte (2006), who argues that the pneumatic conception can be traced to Wittgenstein's earlier and middle period work and that in the rest of §109 Wittgenstein is alluding to both helpful and misleading features of his earlier thought. This is probably correct and "gaseous" may be misleading, but there is de-licious irony in the term *gaseous*. The Urban Dictionary defines *pneumatic* as a clever way to call someone an airhead (playing off the traditional meaning of *pneu-matic*, which is "pertaining to or filled with air"; gaseous, in other words) (Urban Dictionary, s.v. "pneumatic," by itcomesandgoes, May 11, 2010, http://www .urbandictionary.com/define.php?term=pneumatic).

2. In his stringent criticism of Malinowski's theory of magic, which took recourse to the notion that magic was deployed in risky situations that caused anxiety, Lévi-Strauss (1964) writes: "As affectivity is the most obscure side of man, there has been a constant temptation to resort to it." (69). Radcliffe-Brown ([1929] 1952, 149) simi-larly argues, "Thus, while one anthropological theory is that magic and religion give men confidence, comfort, and a sense of security, it could equally well be argued that they give men fears and anxieties from which they would otherwise be free." I cite these authors not necessarily because I place intellect above affect but to make the methodological point that our explanations sometimes cover up with high-sounding concepts what we do not understand.

3. Detailed descriptions of my field sites—the first among a network of families displaced by the Partition of India in 1947, as well as among the survivors of the violence against Sikhs in Delhi in 1984, and the second in several low-income neigh-borhoods in Delhi—are described respectively in two earlier books: *Life and Words: Violence and the Descent into the Ordinary*, published in 2007, and *Afflic-tion: Health, Disease, Poverty*, published in 2015. All the examples, scenes, and cases that are described in the present book are taken from my latter fieldwork from 1999 to 2017. These are juxtaposed with analysis of certain literary texts as well as the reading of a philosophical autobiography. Such juxtapositions are common in an-

thropological writing but are often done to embellish or enliven their accounts (see Brandel 2018 for an account of this tendency). As the reader will see, these juxtapositions are integral to the development of my thought. Also, the anthropologist as one who completes fieldwork and moves on to the academy to write has been complicated by the much longer-term contacts enabled not only by the ease of travel but also by the ability to communicate through letters, email, WhatsApp, and other media (see Day 2018; M. D. Jackson 2009).

4. ISERDD is the abbreviation for the Institute of Socio-economic Research on Development and Democracy, a research and advocacy organization of which I am a founding member. The organization recruits and trains men and women from low-income areas as fieldworkers and researchers and has collaborated in many research projects on the themes of health and citizenship.

5. Today with the advent of big data and computational analysis the "scientific" method has itself been put into question as philosophers debate if the new developments in data sciences announce an end to the need for theory (see Anderson 2018; Kitchin 2014).

6. In his book, *The Claim of Reason*, Cavell (1979, 403) eloquently describes what it is to have "a voice in [one's] own history" and how one might be denied that voice in philosophy and politics. He says, memorably to my ears, "Do I respect the doll? I may respect its feelings, lay it comfortably in a nice box before storing it for another generation. But it has no say, for example, about whether it is comfortable. It has no *voice in its own history.*"

7. See further my argument on parts and wholes in my book *Affliction* (Das 2015a). As a problem of partial ordering in mathematical reasoning, one might take recourse to the three processes of transitivity, reflexivity, and antisymmetry, but obviously in other domains, such as those of theology and anthropology, these questions become different—e.g., in what way is God contained in the trinity or how might we think of persons as fractal as in Wagner (1991)?

8. It might appear as a diversion to take up such a detailed discussion (even more could have been done) of a book whose theme does not bear directly on the issues, but I do so as testimony that for all that is dead and pretentious in anthropology, there are sparkling jewels that show how descent into the darkness might recover genuine thought. As the *Īśāvāsyopaniṣad* (one of my beloved texts) prays: "Remove the golden lid (of blinding light) for me, the one desirous of beholding the truth" (Hiriyanna [1911] 1972). Rosaldo's perspective is not that of the detached observer of the Upanishad—his searing poems grow out of grief——but I was struck by the resonance with figures of light and darkness and the dangers of a fully lighted world.

9. Here is an excerpt from the chapter in which he appears: "A local leader in Delhi, where I was working, once asked me in jest, 'If you fly high, where will you fall?' I replied, as I was expected to, 'On the earth.' He laughed, nodded, and said, 'So our friendship should be with the earth, no?'" (see Chapter 2).

10. See the special issue of *MLN* (December 2011) on the occasion of the publication of Cavell's philosophical autobiography, *Little Did I Know*, and especially the papers by Donatelli, Laugier, and Marrati. See also Chapter 9 for the theme of the ways a child learns to bear inordinate knowledge about the relations between his parents that I take from this autobiography and Das (2011b) for an early reflection on time in the same special issue.

11. "What is your aim in philosophy?—To show the fly the way out of the flybottle" (*PI*, §309).

12. See Cavell (1987) for a full discussion on how the problematic of skepticism is inherited in Shakespeare's plays, and thus how literature gives expression to the problem of skepticism. I have argued that the sense of everyday as also a scene of trance and illusion comes in many forms in the anthropological literature (Das 1998b, 2007, 2014)—a theme that I carry forward in this book.

13. द्वा सुपर्णासयुजा सखाया समानं वृक्षं परिषस्वजाते।
तयोरन्यः पिप्पलं स्वाद्त्त्यनश्नन्नन्यो अभिचाकशीति

## 1. WITTGENSTEIN AND ANTHROPOLOGY: ANTICIPATIONS

1. This point is discussed in greater detail in Chapter 3, "Ordinary Ethics."

2. In her insightful remarks on rule-following in Wittgenstein, Laugier (2001) makes the point that for Kripke the basic question is when do we know that the rule is correctly applied, whereas for Wittgenstein what counts is the place that rules occupy in a form of life (see also Diamond 1989). When Wittgenstein refers to the mythological as a way of speaking, Laugier asks, What is the mythological opposed to? She argues that in the ordinary conception of rules, one might naturally slip into "speaking mythologically" without negating the practical, everyday place of rules in our lives.

3. What seems to have outraged Cavell (2005a, 69) in Rogin's descriptions—"Even for a thumbnail sketch, this contains too many errors to pass by"—is his lack of attention to particulars. Thus, for instance, Rogin's reference to the dance as "black *tap*"—"while this homage is to black dancing in some form, it is explicitly enough, not to black *tap*" (69).

4. This theme in general and Manjit's case in particular was to become an important anchor for my subsequent writings (see Das 2007) and figures again in Chapter 3, "Ordinary Ethics."

5. James Conant (2005) gives a nice diagnostic reading of Williams's (mis)reading of Cavell by pointing out that for Williams the problem is that a sentence might be meaningful but the context in which it is used makes it weird or unintelligible. We know what the utterance means but we do not know what the one who speaks means by asserting it. Conant's incisive criticism here is that it is not as if there is first a meaningful utterance and then its use—rather meaning and use cannot be

made to come apart. The meaning of a sentence is not a property that the sentence already has independent of the concrete claims made by the speaker—hence context is not external to meaning but internal to it. The answer to the skeptic's anxiety that one can never know with certainty what someone else means by what they say is not to search for complete transparency of meaning but to persuade him to give up the desire for complete transparency of meaning.

6. The issue of philosophical grammar will come up frequently in the following chapters. Here what I want to point out is that what Wittgenstein calls "grammar" is not simply a grid of rules for determining correct ways of following its prescriptions—rather, grammar is what allows us to determine what an object is. I might signal here the fact that this conception of grammar is much closer to discussions of grammar in Indian philosophy, a theme I am actively exploring for my next work, of which an early draft was presented in a seminar on detail in Paris (see Das 2019).

## 2. A POLITICS OF THE ORDINARY: ACTION, EXPRESSION, AND EVERYDAY LIFE

1. I was inclined to say "cure for such violence" in earlier versions of this chapter to contest the idea that an escape to some higher realm of morality would halt such violence. I realized in rereading this chapter that I would need to explain my notion of what constituted "cure" or "healing," for when I use these words I do not mean to suggest a return to normality as if there was no remainder with which to contend. Hence this slight shift of emphasis where I speak of an interruption that is sometimes all one can hope for.

2. Butler's argument is not exhausted by the reference to infrastructure for she is equally interested in wresting resistance out of the vulnerability of the human body in the exposure of the body to power. Of course, for me, this particular formulation is precisely what the technique of satyagraha in Gandhi entailed, but for Gandhi the performance of vulnerability of the body as a means of awakening the conscience of the perpetrator required the joining of the private and the public through techniques of discipline and self-making in the private and everyday life of the satyagrahi. Gandhi finds a single line in Butler's essay—"The deliberate exposure to harm was crucial to Gandhi's notion of non-violent civil disobedience" (Butler 2016, 20)—which is fine as far as it goes but completely misses the point that for Gandhi the emphasis was not on *disobedience* as in "civil disobedience" but on truth as in *satyagraha*, the insistence on truth. This is why he experimented with different terms to describe what was entailed in the body's exposure to harm, going from "truth-force," "soul-force," and "passive resistance" (M. K. Gandhi 1909) to "civil disobedience," to "civil resistance" (M. K. Gandhi 1935) before settling finally on "satyagraha" (M. K. Gandhi 1920).

3. For those who might be tempted to think of such situations as "exceptional," I point out that almost 70 percent of Delhi's population lives in "unplanned settlements" that include slums, shanty settlements, and the "unauthorized" colonies. The land on which shanties or houses are built in these areas (with the exception of designated slums) are all in zones of ambiguity as far as legal rights over such occupied lands are concerned (see Das 2011a; Das and Walton 2015; Datta 2012).

4. See Berlant (2007) for the concept of nonsovereign agency. I agree with Berlant that the coupling of sovereignty of the individual with individual autonomy leads to a melodramatic view of agency centered on the decision event and appreciate her attempts to lay bare the contours of everyday life as her notion of "slow death" unfolds. However, I find much more in the lives of the poor I study than the exhausting pressures of reproduction of life. The vulnerability of the poor is not in question for me, but I do not find it easy to say that they stay attached to lives that "do not work" as in Berlant (2011).

5. The unequal distribution of life chances is a compelling question for Fassin (2018), but while he comes to it by drawing a line of separation between biopolitics as the government of populations and the politics of life, I argue that how populations are governed does not fall into a neutral technological issue of management but is central to the politics of life (see Das 2011a; Das and Walton 2015). Further, the medical infrastructure itself can have a huge impact on quality of medical care and life chances as some of us show in the case of tuberculosis in India (see Kwan et al. 2018; Satyanarayana et al. 2015) and thus might be better seen as an essential component of the politics of life.

6. The reference to thoughts and feelings makes the deciphering of the inner within performative utterances a complex undertaking. For instance, in a (Christian) marriage ceremony, the bride and groom must presumably have the inner feelings appropriate for a couple undertaking to love and honor each other, but I do not know what inner feelings and thoughts the priest is expected to have. In a Hindu ceremony, it is the performance of the ritual with the fire as witness (though not in secondary marriages) that accomplishes the act. There are no "promises" made or consent taken. Thus, conventions also determine what thoughts and feeling are stipulated—yet, in the natural history of the human, thoughts and feeling must surely go in many directions.

7. The cutting it down to size must be appreciated in the context of the weighty discussions on truth, probability, and partial beliefs within epistemology in the writings of Frank Ramsey and Bertrand Russell in the atmosphere of philosophical discussions at Oxford and Cambridge that must have surrounded Austin.

8. Although the distinction between misfires and abuse as two ways in which a performative utterance may fail or be infelicitous applies primarily to utterances, the term *misfires* could be applied to a whole procedure as when the performance of a marriage ritual misfires. In medical jurisprudence, there is a distinction made

between an error committed by a surgeon and a surgery misfiring because of factors beyond the control of the surgeon. Another way to say this is that all performative utterances might fail either because the inner feelings and sentiments that Austin talks about are absent (I never intended to keep my promise) or because the world has a say in it (I could not keep my promise because of an accident). However, as Cavell notes, failure in the case of utterances with illocutionary force are characteristically reparable; passionate statements when they go astray are much more difficult to repair.

9. Erard (2019) makes the brilliant point that the essay on passionate statements could be read profitably as the mirror opposite of the succeeding essay, "The Wittgensteinian Event," in the same book (Cavell 2005c) as demonstrating two different routes of return to the ordinary between Austin and Wittgenstein.

10. For instance, take Austin's example, that you cannot say that "I inadvertently stepped on the baby" but I can say in such an extreme circumstance that "I accidentally stepped on the baby" (I was blinded in an impending stroke, for instance). What is at stake is not rules of linguistic grammar but something like Wittgenstein's notion of philosophical grammar that assumes that criteria grow out of the mutual absorption of the natural and the social in any human form of life.

11. See Khan (2012) for an insightful ethnography of belonging and disappointment.

12. I note that even when our attention might be completely caught up in documenting catastrophic events, as was the case in Sri Lanka during the brutal civil war, the adjacent smaller-level events, such as beautification drives and demolition of illegal housing colonies, constitute a politics of another kind (see Amarasuriya and Spencer 2015).

13. According to the Delhi government records, the current number of unauthorized colonies is 1,639. Provisional certificates of regularization were given to these colonies in 2010, but subsequently certificates for 73 colonies were revoked because of fraud by the building mafia (Department of Urban Development 2006).

14. In addition to the fascinating work of historians on the origin of mapping for governing the Empire, anthropologists have done impressive work on how mapmaking as a technique comes to be absorbed within the indigenous-activist collaborations for control of resources or determination of property rights in collaboration or contest with state actors and corporations (see Chapin, Lamb, and Threlkeld 2005). While the labor of having a map recognized as an agreed representation of a locality and its residents bears some similarity to exercises of countermapping, it is important to pay attention to the differences when the contests are in crowded slums and the goal is to get a stamp of bureaucratic approval through political maneuvers at every step of the way. In this sense, the question is different from indigenous geography (e.g., Larson and Johnson 2012) and pertains more to stabilizing and "making legal" what is not in the legal record.

15. Although the period of emergency is remembered mostly for the coercive practices of sterilization and forcible relocation of the poor, it was also a period when self-propelled massive movements of the poor to peripheral or otherwise uninhabitable spaces within the city occurred because of their search for assets (see especially Tarlo 2003).

16. I am trying to put together the history of different segments of the neighborhood, but it seems like work for another lifetime. For now, the point I would emphasize is that though this task is a bit like putting together the history of a rock with different sediments, the political work of securing the infrastructure first of all requires that the Delhi State recognizes the neighborhood as an authorized colony. Here I show how this imperative is both pursued and evaded by the collaborations that evolve between the representatives of the neighborhood, the bureaucrats working in government and the private sector, and the local politicians.

17. All personal names in the chapter, except that of Sanjeev Gupta, are pseudonyms. *Vidyut* means "electricity" and is my affectionate pun on his name.

18. The juxtaposition of a personal name with the honorific "Sir" is a common mode of showing respect to officials—in contrast, politicians are sometimes honored by the addition of the Hindi particle "ji," which is also used in contexts of kinship.

19. Elsewhere I describe the processes by which houses came to have more than one address that were either self-assigned or given by different authorities—thus C6 might also carry the address P123 and, in any case, might be next to another house with the number D21. Similarly, houses with the same letter might be dispersed over several different streets (see Das 2012b).

20. I can only point to, without being able to elaborate on, the complex genres of storytelling in Indian aesthetics, distinguished by multiple framing devices at the beginning and end of the story. To give just one example: storytelling in the genre of *kahani* indicates that the characters of the story disappear in their own world of stories at the end, while *katha* indicates the telling of a sacred story in which the listener is taken into the world of mythological personages whose presence transforms ordinary space into a mythic one, and *kissa*, a Farsi word, is used to convey a story that does not end at the conclusion of the narration. That characters of stories might have other lives that are not revealed to the listener is a common assumption of narrative traditions in India (Chatterji 1986, 2012).

21. See Hansen (2008) for an excellent account of the way in which the notion of aura was narrowed in time to refer primarily to aesthetic objects, whereas initially it could be the property of all objects.

22. I have in mind the contrast one could make with a statement such as "I name the ship Queen Elizabeth" (Austin 1962, 5).

23. J. O. Urmson wrote in 1977 that the attempt to create a performative-constative dichotomy is "viscous," arguing that the constative is merely one variety of speech

act, governed primarily by linguistic conventions, while the performative is primarily the conventional acts governed primarily by nonlinguistic conventions. After offering several examples of sentences in which the word "hereby" would be mistakenly applied, he concludes: "But the true performative should not be classed as a speech-act at all since performative utterances make use of conventions of language to make clear the character and content of the act, it is non-linguistic convention that determines that the utterance of these words, with the meaning that they have constitutes the conventional act" (Urmson 1977, 127).

While I think there is something interesting in separating the performance aspect from the action aspect, it is the knitting together of action and expression that helps us appreciate the social dimension of both performative and constative utterances.

24. See Chapter 4 for further elaboration on the question of addressing and the grammatical person.

25. Each street in these neighborhoods has a somewhat different character depending on how close it is to the main road, whether it is wide or narrow, and whether it functions more as a female space that extends the home or primarily as a male one, often a little away from the houses as in corners where main streets and side streets meet. Butler's picture of the street as the ground on which people might assemble is a very limited notion of the street but nor are classic pictures of the flaneur, the aimless stroller, the connoisseur of the street, easy to picture here. Of recent ethnographies of the street, Ajay Gandhi (2015) gives a nice account of the sociality that develops in the streets of old Delhi, and Andrew Brandel (2016) shows how the figure of the flaneur emerges in Berlin through the work of journalists and artists who excavate the hidden memories of violence and expulsion of the Nazi past.

26. The urge to comment on the events of 9/11 in different vernacular mediums is captured nicely by Roma Chatterji (2012) in her analysis of the bin Laden scrolls that emerged among the folk painters of Bengal.

27. The Hindi phrase "*seva mein nivedan hai*" (lit. "in your service it is stated") is rendered in the bureaucratic formula used in applications—Respectfully, I wish to submit. The concluding salutation "Your humble servant" is also routinely used, though the Hindi term *sevak* connotes "one who serves" and can also be translated as "devotee" to be distinguished from *naukar* or "someone who is paid for his service" or "a mercenary."

28. I say this on the basis of the fact that all Sheela's descriptions, offered in scattered fragments, referred to other acts but not to actual sexual intercourse. This might have been an aspect of her reticence, but my sense was that she was subjected to many small acts of sexual humiliation—not unknown in cases of domestic abuse.

29. This is the extent to which she could speak—condensed renderings of what the acts of abuse were.

30. The reference to psychoanalysis was not a ruse on my part to get her to talk. She had asked me if abuse of girls happened in America too and I had replied that

there were doctors who specialized in treating depression resulting from such abuse—the English word *depression* is often used by people in this area along with *tension*, something I note in Das and Das (2007).

31. The term *banda* literally means "God's creature" when used by a Muslim. For Hindus, it is simply a word at hand and does not carry any special connotations. For a discussion of how words from different theological contexts seep into ordinary vocabulary see Das (2011a).

32. Consider also the difference of tonality when Michael D. Jackson (2011) talks of life within limits, Kleinman, Weiming, and Zhang (2011) of adequate life, Singh (2012) of thresholds of life, and Fassin (2007) of the different way that a love of life is bequeathed to surviving relatives by patients dying of AIDS in South Africa.

## 3. ORDINARY ETHICS: TAKE ONE

1. In his famous passage on the notion of adequation, Austin writes: "Enough is enough: it doesn't mean everything. Enough means enough to show that (within reason, and for present intents and purposes) it 'can't' be anything else, there is no room for an alternative, competing, description of it. It does not mean, e.g. enough to show it isn't a stuffed goldfinch" (Austin 1946, 156; [1961] 1979, 84).

2. The metaphor of reading is used in Urdu poetry and in everyday life almost as if reading has nothing to do with literacy. For instance, the famous Sufi poet Bulleh Shah's (eighteenth-century) Punjabi poem *"padh padh aalim te fazal hoya, kadey aapne aap nu padya hi nahin"* (reading and reading [books] to become a man of knowledge, you never read yourself) is one of the most popular poems in this genre.

3. As I argue in the last chapter, there is an important difference between the view that ethical life is best understood as a leap that takes us from a particular perspective to a universal one and the view that the ethical might be better understood as the work one does on the actual everyday that generates the eventual everyday. To cast this kind of ordinary work performed on the everyday as itself ethical is not to relinquish political action or acquiesce to the idea of a quietism in the face of injustice but to commit oneself to repeated, ongoing work in the register of the ordinary.

4. I have not observed this gesture among the slum populations that I now study, which might either be related to ethnic differences between the Punjabi families I studied earlier and the families from Bihar and Uttar Pradesh who form the bulk of the populations in the slum populations I worked with more recently. However, it could also be a result of small changes in the use of domestic objects. It is difficult for me to say anything more on this issue.

5. In a classic paper on money, Jonathan Parry (1989) argues that the suspicion of money as a sign of modernity that many have assumed to be widespread in traditional societies does not hold fast for India, where it is the gift that is imbued with ambiguity.

6. I am making a limited point with regard to Badiou's notion of the ethical as a leap away from the everyday—without taking on any of the other strands in his thinking.

7. Clara Han (2014) touches on this register of the ethical in her delicate description of acts of neighbors among the poor in Santiago, Chile: when they pretend to have cooked too much food, for instance, simply so that a neighbor who is running very short of food can take the "leftovers" without any loss of face. Han brings out a new dimension of pretending in relation to what she calls "critical moments" in the lives of families that are deciphered by caring neighbors without the family having to declare its small crises that are corroding the ability to feed the children or ward off another kind of domestic emergency.

8. Writing these lines also gave me the further insight into my reasons for the feeling of profound estrangement from university administrators and colleagues who emphasize to students that they must be pragmatic in their choice of topics for research: not all topics, they say (rightly), sell in the academic market; or that it is our duty as teachers to curtail early on the unreasonable love some students have for pursuit of an education that they see as doomed if not directed to the pragmatics of job markets. My own teachers, in contrast (I think of professors M. N. Srinivas, A. M. Shah, André Béteille, and J. P. S. Uberoi), taught me that it was a privilege to have some years where I could read the books I wanted and write on things that I loved for their own sake. If I ended up teaching in a school or a small college, this was, I thought, honorable and lovable work. My point is not that other ways of aspiring to a future are not valid life projects but that, as Diamond says of our desires, they have the power to threaten morality but for that reason should not be put under the constraint of morality of universal rules or pragmatics of the market right at the start. As Sandra Laugier repeatedly writes, the importance of what is important to *us*, in both aesthetics and ethics, is a complex undertaking; I have tried to learn that lesson—well or poorly, I cannot say.

## 4. ETHICS, SELF-KNOWLEDGE, AND WORDS NOT AT HOME: THE EPHEMERAL AND THE DURABLE

1. Although I intend to elaborate this point later in the chapter, I want to give an indication of how the importance of judgment from a third-person point of view might be contrasted with the idea of what is *important for me* from a first-person perspective. The latter provides a way to think of our ability to relate to the concreteness of the other. Thus, in Wittgenstein's discussion on what it is for me to be certain that someone else is really glad to see me, it becomes clear that what is at stake is not some metaphysical question about how I can know the other, or the accuracy of my judgment regarding whether I was right *in general* about being able to read the meaning of a smile, but rather about my comfort when "*this* person (with

*this* past etc.) behaves in *this* way" (Wittgenstein 1992, 84a). Later we shall see how such considerations lead us to think of the specificity of the second person as distinct from the impersonality of the third-person perspective. For a close reading of this passage, see Canfield (2004).

2. For a first-level formulation, being-with might be seen in Heidegger's ([1927] 1967) terms as "dwelling alongside." For an anthropological formulation of how we might think of ethics as a mode of being-with, see Mohammad (2010). Later I engage with this modality of being-with in relation to the specific reference to kinship as in Sahlins (2013). However, I think of being-with as a verb, a mode of doing things rather than a state of being.

3. Although it deserves a fuller discussion than I can provide here, my understanding of the ordinary and of forms of life takes very different turns from that of Didier Fassin (2018) despite our similarities of aspiration. To take one key metaphor in Fassin, he thinks of his writing as solving a jigsaw puzzle in which each part has a definable place within a whole (since it was cut, I might add, from a coherent whole in the first place). Contrasting my attraction for a rich mosaic with his attraction for the "modesty" of a jigsaw puzzle, "whose few pieces adjust to each other and complement one another to form a coherent picture," Fassin fails to appreciate the dangers of such coherence as the condition for critique. See also Donatelli (2019) for a picture of critique that emerges from the messiness of life, though I agree that sometimes when speaking to policy makers or petitioning a court of law, I too have had to give more coherence to my arguments. This requirement from our academic work should, however, be a major topic for further reflection.

4. In an intensive and extremely helpful discussion of my work at the Centre for Ethics at the University of Pardubice, I was urged to clarify my notion of imagination. I think this is an important task since I do not engage how a Cavell-inspired idea of the imagination of the everyday as domestic, for instance, differs from the place of imagination in the Lacanian tripartite structure of the imaginary, the symbolic, and the real. I will content myself for now by saying that what imagining is doing here is challenging the idea of the everyday as something obvious. At some later stage, I hope to show how this idea of imagining in relation to presence and absence informs some of the figures of absence in Sanskrit grammar and linguistics (see Filliozat 1991–1992), which have been important resources for thinking for me.

5. In this context, see Wittgenstein's discussion on the relation between symptom and criteria in the *Blue Book* where he shows that a deciphering of symptom is akin to testing a hypothesis, while offering objective criteria is another way of simply naming the disease (Wittgenstein 1958, 25).

6. Although not strictly parallel, there is a resonance between this notion of significance offered here and Foucault's idea about the truth sky and the truth thunderbolt that I allude to in the Introduction.

7. Since my acquaintance with these families goes back to the early seventies, she was talking to a much younger version of this ethnographer than the one who is writing now.

8. "Homemade biscuits" refers to a common practice then of sending raw ingredients to a shop to have it baked into biscuits, but tastes were already changing as packaged biscuits became much more popular even among the poor.

9. I am not sure how to understand my actions. In my mind I was doing what she might have wanted me to do—sensitivities honed through a very long relation to her as her daughter-in-law. What is more intriguing is that I find myself doing similar things in the course of fieldwork and many such instances appear in Das (2007).

10. Rendering the vocabulary used in discussions of the occult (outside the specialized vocabulary of tantra) is difficult because naming the entities risks bringing them into existence. I have used the generic term "dark forces" because the emphasis in defining such terms is on verbs rather than nouns. Verbs of forcible possession, dispossession, and actions performed in trance describe better what it is to be in the grip of a ghostly existence than nouns—corresponding to the idea that words have force (not just meaning) as in Austin (1962).

11. Cora Diamond offers an important modification to the general understanding of Anscombe on the first person. She says, "She [Anscombe] is usually read as arguing that 'I' is not a referring expression. But a better formulation of her conclusion is her own: 'I' is neither a name nor another kind of expression whose logical role is to make a reference *at all*" (cited in Diamond 2019, 238). The issue, as I understand it, is as follows: "I" as a referring expression makes no sense unless we know what "referring" alludes to here. But we cannot have a clear conception of what "referring" *could* mean here. Further, whatever its use we may arrive at—proper name, demonstrative pronoun—the "I" does not fit into those. Hence, if we continued on that path of reasoning, we would end up being caught in the game of inventing referents, as Anscombe's thought experiment on "I" seen simultaneously as first person and as third person further shows. (I discuss this experiment in Das 2015c.)

12. The philosopher Stephen Darwall (2006) defines the second-person standpoint as the perspective you take in relation to me when we make and acknowledge claims on each other's conduct and will. His concern is to examine the conditions under which I will find the claims you make on me to be justified either because we share a space of reasons or because one can count on some emotion such as sympathy to accept that the other has claims over one. I think that Darwall's moves are very interesting in that they blur the boundary between the authority given to the first person on grounds of avowal and third person on grounds of impersonal and cool appraisal. Yet the pressure of immediacy and embodied interactions in the relation between first person and second person is very muted in this discussion. In earlier work, I discuss Darwall's contributions in relation to the idea of the triadic structure in Indian poetics that explicitly defines the second person as the one who

is addressed (see Das 2015c; for a profound understanding of the grammatical person in Indian poetics see Bäumer 2008).

13. Much of the discussion takes the form "X has a belief that P" where $P$ is something about the state of the world that manages to create a sharp divide in first-person statements between parts that are world-oriented and parts that are self-oriented. However, consider the wonderful example Wittgenstein gives in *Culture and Value*. He says, "Suppose some were a believer and said: 'I believe in Last Judgment' and I said; 'Well I am not so sure. Possibly.' You would say that there was an enormous gulf between us. If he said, 'There is a German airplane overhead,' and I said, 'Possibly, I am not sure,' you would say, we were fairly near. It isn't a question of my being anywhere near him, but on an entirely different plane" (Wittgenstein 1980, 53). Said otherwise, the discussion on belief when using the forms of the proposition does not make any room for such phenomena as intensities, waxing and waning of belief, and the affects that go with these. Ethnographic accounts do much better here than thought experiments for revealing this aspect of belief (see the marvelous description of waxing and waning religious intensities in Singh 2015).

14. It is not my case that Moran makes the link between responsibility and culpability in any direct way, but the examples he gives seem to me to indicate that I am responsible for changing my beliefs because they are shown to be false or controlling my desires because they are either disruptive or in some ways stand in need of correction.

15. In some ways, Cavell's singling out the "you" in passionate statements, as I discuss in Chapter 2, might be seen as the point at which the second person as addressee comes into dramatic relief, but what he says about passionate statements might in many ordinary circumstances be simply the case for the second person.

16. The question of biology continues reappearing in different guises, so it is only with a particular picture of biology as forming the basis of kinship that one would quarrel (see Han and Das 2015).

17. As early as 1940, R. G. Collingwood drew on Whitehead to explain that being and doing were not distinct states. "According to modern physics, Whitehead explains, there is no distinction between events that happen and the bodies to which they happen. Being and doing, where doing includes undergoing, are not distinguishable. The modern physicist cannot say: 'If this event were not happening to this body, this body would not of course be doing what it now is doing, but it would still be what it now is.' Or put it this way: at a given instant, where there are no events there are no bodies" (Collingwood [1940] 2014, 267).

## 5. DISORDERS OF DESIRE OR MORAL STRIVING? ENGAGING THE LIFE OF THE OTHER

1. Sometimes what looks like a traditional route of fulfilling kinship obligations might be a cover for new ways of inhabiting traditional norms. In his riveting study

of transnational marriages in the shadow of war in Sri Lanka, Maunaguru (2019) shows how the obligation to marry a cross-cousin, for instance, could be mobilized in the completely new context of contracting marriages across continents to be able to escape the terrible conditions of war.

2. I take the liberty of repeating what §219 of *Philosophical Investigations* states: "'All the steps are already taken' means: I no longer have a choice. . . . But if something of this sort really were the case, how would it help? No; my description only made sense if it was understood symbolically.—I should have said: This is how it strikes me."

3. Foucault is worth citing in some detail here. He says that eventalization "means making visible a *singularity* at places where there is a temptation to evoke a historical constant, an immediate anthropological trait or an obviousness that imposes itself uniformly on all. . . . As a way of lightening the weight of causality, 'eventalization' thus works by constructing around a singular event analyzed as a process a 'polygon' or rather a 'polyhedron' of intelligibility, the number of whose faces is not given in advance and can never properly be taken as finite" (Foucault 1996, 277). However, the notion of eventalization also comes to have a different weight when seen within the neoliberal dispositif in which what Povinelli (2011) calls quasi-events that are strewn in everyday life have to be elevated to the level of an event through mediatization in order for them to receive critical attention.

4. Among my interlocutors, this aspect of speech was compared to an arrow that once having left the bow cannot be taken back—"*ek bar baan dhanush se nikal gaya to vapis nahin liya ja sakta*." Although such references were often evoked to explain ongoing hurt, enmity, or inability to forget, and are different from the sense of something having been revealed that I emphasized in the last chapter, there is a whole philosophy of what it is for words to remain in the world through the mechanism of involuntary memory.

5. The question of dissolving a marriage in which one spouse has converted to Islam has received considerable attention in law, though at the level of adjudication rather than legislation. Thus, for instance, Basu (1949) discusses the landmark cases from the 1920s on this issue. The legislative acts formulated to address the question of forcible abduction of women during the Partition brought a whole range of anxieties, fears, and fantasies into being around the issue of Hindu-Muslim marriages in the public domain (Das 2007).

6. The work of the historian Prem Chowdhry establishes that the tolerance of intercommunity marriages has declined in modernity, at least in north India, though reliance on cases that come up in caste panchayats, or courts, predisposes one to ignore those who continue to live in the recesses of everyday life. See Chowdhry (1997a, 1997b). In fact, Ravinder Kaur (2004) argues that there are long-established traditions in certain parts of Haryana in which wives were brought from regions as far away as Bengal and Assam, though the pressure of a declining sex ratio has increased the demand for wives from outside in Punjab and Haryana

and so we cannot judge how much these new demographics create the conditions for acceptance of such marriages in larger numbers.

7. I am grateful to Pratiksha Baxi for sending me some supplementary material pertaining to this controversy.

8. See Shahan Sha A v. State of Kerala, B.A. No. 52888 (2009).

9. Details of the various episodes, including the court hearings, can be found in *Indian Muslim*, October 27, 2009. Downloaded from http://twocircles.net.

10. Last year, in March 2018, there was much discussion of a case of a Hindu-Muslim marriage that had come up to the Supreme Court as a result of an appeal against the judgment of the Kerala High Court that had annulled the marriage of a Hindu girl who had converted to Islam. In its inquiry in this case on the basis of a case filed by the girl's father, the Kerala High Court had accepted the findings of the National Investigation Agency (NIA) that there was a vast network of "love jihad" activists that conspired to lure "innocent" Hindu girls to the Islamic fold to use them in terrorist operations. While the Supreme Court set aside the judgment of the High Court, it allowed the investigations by the NIA to continue. See "'Love Jihad' Case: SC Sets Aside High Court Order that Annulled Hadiya's Marriage," *Times of India*, March 8, 2018. Incidentally, the NIA ended its probe on love jihad in October 2018, saying there was "love but no jihad."

11. It is common in north India for English-speaking persons to speak of someone as "communal" or "secular," or even to insert these English words within Hindi sentences, as in "*Voh admi bahut secular hai*" (That man is very secular). I am afraid that my own writing might have imbibed these modes of speaking, and I thank Michael Lambek for gently pointing out those errors.

12. RSS refers to the Rashtriya Swayamsevak Sangh, a Hindu nationalist organization affiliated with the BJP and generally hostile to the rights granted to Muslims in the Indian polity. On the local level, branches of the RSS are often involved in preventing cross-religious marriages by intimidation.

13. *Urs* (lit. "nuptial ceremony") refers to the celebration of the death anniversaries of various pirs, celebrated at the sites of their tombs. The saints, far from dying, are believed to reach the zenith of their spiritual life on this occasion. The biography of the pir is recited or sung on this and other occasions. It has a standard plot structure, which involves a journey on the occasion of the pir's marriage that is interrupted to offer help to an oppressed figure and in the course of which the pir meets a heroic death.

14. The idea that true love is difficult to sustain and one is tested in one's love by the pressures of society is, on the one hand, a deeply cherished notion honed within a mythological imagination of relationships and, on the other hand, often derided as unrealistic, unachievable, and the stuff of films and of madness.

15. I note a further thought here, though I cannot develop it fully for lack of space. The expression Saba used has some resonance with the upper-caste Hindu notion,

popularized by Hindi cinema and television serials, that a chaste woman falls in love only once and that true love is to be found only once in a lifetime.

16. Many new opportunities have opened up in recent years that allow couples and others to discuss their problems and seek advice. See, for instance, the *Times of India* column "Ask the Expert," https://timesofindia.indiatimes.com/life-style /relationships/ask-the-expert.

17. *Namaz* (in Urdu) refers to the five prayers offered by Muslims to Allah by reading prescribed sections from the Qur'an and is considered to be one of the five pillars of Islam.

18. *Saṃskāra* refers to the impressions formed on one's being from the intimate environment in which one grows up; the term also refers in more specific way to rites of passage.

19. The rules for prostration and correct forms of worship are laid out in the sura of the Qur'an entitled "As-Sajda." Instruction on correct procedures are also the subject of many fatwas issued by the Darul Uloom and by local muftis.

20. The honorific *mian* is often added to Allah among South Asian Muslims. The term *Bismillah* is an abbreviation of the longer phrase "bismillahirrahmanirrahim"— "In the name of God, most gracious, most merciful." It is recited before every sura of the Qur'an except the ninth sura, which includes the famous sword verse, according to which Muslims are exhorted to kill any *kafir* (nonbeliever) they encounter; though it must be remembered that the command was given in the context of the Battle of Tabuk, as my Muslim friends in this neighborhood never tire of reminding me. The fact that Kuldip's grandfather could dream of the ayats of the Qur'an but could not say "Bismillah" because of the command of the goddess could mean several things. It could mean that, though he recites the verses, he does not do so with full allegiance to Islam. It could have the darker meaning that the verses he recites are the verses, or are seen as similar to the verses, in the ninth sura, in which God's anger against kafirs is most evident and that he uses these verses by trapping the anger that lies in the words to overcome the disease or perhaps to perform harmful magic. This point was somewhat dangerous to pursue; hence, Saba takes leave of the interpretation by referring to the mysterious ways of Allah.

21. In addition to well-known regional shrines of pirs, there are numerous other shrines that remain unknown outside the small *kasbas*, or urban neighborhoods. Sometimes the pir is known both by a Hindu name and by a Muslim name and may have functionaries from both communities. At other times, as in this case, either a Muslim family or a Hindu one might officiate as the main ritual functionary at the shrine. See Saheb (1998).

22. The analogy of the watermark is mine. He used the term *mandir ka saaya jaisa*, "as if there were the shadow of a temple." His gesture of moving his hands in slow motion from one side to another as he talked of this scene reminded me of a watermark.

23. Their son had not yet been circumcised. However, among many Indian Muslim communities, the ritual of circumcision is customarily performed when the child is a bit older. Mehta (2000) describes how the ritual of circumcision called *Musalmani* ("making a Muslim") among the Ansaris includes a verbal statement addressed to the child to the effect that until that day he was a Hindu and now he is going to become a Muslim. The fascinating account shows how the social memory of conversion might thus be encoded in ritual language.

24. Although compromise is not legal in the case of rape, and thus court records do not ever state that a compromise was reached, Baxi (2014), in her remarkable work on the adjudication of rape in the district courts in Gujarat, notes that the courts regularly arrived at this solution, partly in recognition of the fact that parents will sometimes register criminal charges of abduction and rape against a man, even if their daughter has left voluntarily with him, in order to "punish" the girl and her lover. In such cases, courts are aware that the courtroom is being used to avenge the honor of the family rather than to seek justice. Alternatively, the courts recognize that parents might have already "recovered" the girl, who, because of the long time it takes for a case to be adjudicated in court, might now be married to someone else and settled in her conjugal home. This is not to deny that a settlement might be the result of pressure put on the courts by men in power, especially if the girl comes from a lower-status family that does not have the means to make court appearances over such a long period of time.

25. See also the special issue "Love and Desire in Pre-modern Persian Poetry and Prose," *Iranian Studies* 42, no. 5 (2009).

## 6. PSYCHIATRIC POWER, MENTAL ILLNESS, AND THE CLAIM TO THE REAL: FOUCAULT IN THE SLUMS OF DELHI

1. In his wonderful formulation on the ubiquity and treatment of addiction on similar low-income neighborhoods Singh (2019) asks, Can a neighborhood be sick? It is becoming increasingly clear that shifting the scene of madness from an elusive emphasis on the clinic in which the patient is the bearer or location of disease to the network of relations within which madness psychiatric illness spreads out is crucial for the understanding of who is the patient. Thus, Anne Lovell (2014) argues that the failures to which all human relations are prone, such as missed connections or the difficulty of alignment with and attunement to others, make it difficult for arriving at an agreed-upon definition of the situation. Further, the behavior of the nonmad toward the mad—how family members, neighbors, police, or psychiatrists participate in these interactions—has an unpredictability that makes it difficult to get an appreciation of the situation for the person designated as mad. I am not proposing that madness is entirely socially constructed but that it is placed within a social field that comes to encompass the mad and the nonmad into pre-

carity. In her courageous work with torture victims, Segal (2018) shows that family members of the tortured person often find that their own experiences become framed entirely through the experience of the family member who has experienced torture—thus drawing boundaries between the one and the other becomes very difficult in therapy and in everyday life.

2. For a detailed depiction of the heterogeneity of the medical infrastructure in such neighborhoods, see Das 2015a.

3. A reviewer asked with some impatience: Is madness a refusal of normativity or does it creep up on us unbidden? My answer is: both. It is a refusal of the normativity that asks a person from a low-income neighborhood to curb his ambitions for an education right at the start as unrealizable, hence maddening, and it also comes unbidden as one does not know why some are able to "accommodate" or "adapt" by giving up on their desires while others arrive at madness as one gets into the tempo of skepticism. It is not for me to judge who is right and who is wrong, but I feel my prose should be able to make some room for such expressions of desire. As the reviewer correctly observed, "Swapan lost his world but I doubt he lost it deliberately." Indeed, one's world is not something one might just accidentally lay aside. Nor is it simply psychiatric illness in itself but what is made of it in *this* milieu, *these lives*, that accounts for the way his world comes to be lost.

4. I add as a pointer that the discussion shifts in the following years—for instance, in *Security, Territory, Population* (Foucault 2007), as Foucault now thinks of normalization through the security apparatus and becomes more attuned to the distribution of normalities in the plural.

5. Canguilhem appears again in *Security, Territory, Population* when the notion of milieu finds elaboration: "What one tries to reach through this milieu, is precisely the conjunction of a series of events produced by these individuals, populations, and groups, and quasi natural events which occur around them" (Foucault 2007, 26).

6. "Of course, the motiveless crime becomes a problem for the law because a change from the arithmetic relation between crime and punishment has given way to a different notion of punishment as requiring absolute conviction on the part of the judge" (Foucault 2003, 7). However, as I describe in Chapter 9, motive is not a very important category in determining responsibility in the criminal law in India—intention is. It would be interesting to see why Foucault thinks that motiveless crime became such a legal impasse in the cases he identifies.

7. This story appears again next year in the first volume of *The History of Sexuality* and has generated a fair amount of discussion in feminist studies, especially with regard to Foucault's evocation of a lost innocence and the pastoral quality of life that makes him feel authorized to "read" the child Sophie's subjectivity, as in his claim that the child herself did not feel much and went off to buy some roasted almonds. That sexual abuse leaves children bewildered or frightened about what the

nature of the experience was is not something one can read from single acts like that of going off to buy roasted almonds. Acting normally to cover up a devastating confusion is not easily discernable in the texts of the archive. However, that the story plays a different role in *The History of Sexuality* seems indicated by the framing sentences in Foucault's discussion as if the issue was not what happened to the child but what philosophical story we can tell through this episode. As an example of this approach, see Spencer Jackson (2010, 39) who states: "The introduction of the story of Jouy in the first volume of *The History of Sexuality* marks a shift from Foucault's generally scholarly discourse into the language of a fairy tale. The first line of the tale, 'One day in 1867,' abruptly resituates the ensuing paragraph within the ambiguous realm of a fictional representation of a presumably real historical event within a philosophical text. . . . With the traditional opening of a fairy tale, Foucault immediately distinguishes his written portrait of Jouy from the one that he offers in a lecture less than a year earlier." Jackson goes on to discuss the implications for a philosophical understanding of an absolute outside in the ontology of the in-itself.

8. Compare Durkheim (1982, 101) in the discussion on the normal and the pathological: "Nothing is good indefinitely and to an unlimited extent. The authority which the moral conscience enjoys must not be excessive; otherwise no one would dare criticize it, and it would too easily congeal into an immutable form. To make progress, individual originality must be able to express itself. In order that the originality of the idealist whose dreams transcend his century may find expression, it is necessary that the originality of the criminal, who is below the level of his time, shall also be possible. One does not occur without the other."

9. It should be clear that I am not proposing a shift from Wittgenstein to Foucault as if the former is discarded in favor of the latter. Rather, it seems interesting to me to think of the way different aspects of the case come to light and, hence, deepen the question of how anthropology addresses philosophy.

10. For a detailed account, see Das (2015a).

11. It is possible in Hindi to use the phrase expressing absence of agreement without necessarily a specific object on which agreement is sought.

12. This form of talk in which a grievous hurt is not put into exact words but left to the other in a conversational turn is a form of eliding that is commonly practiced.

13. There were a few scattered examples of some young people managing to realize these promises in these neighborhoods—for example, one of the boys had been admitted to a medical college through caste-based reservations. But for every person who could be held up as an example of the value of hard work and education, there were scores of others who registered for a degree in distance education in one of the local universities and then found that the reading materials never arrived and promised contact hours with a teacher never materialized. The luckier ones were

able to afford private tuition and sometimes get a job as a bus conductor or a shop assistant that certainly raised family incomes but were far below what Swapan aspired to become.

14. "Big Men" referred to a category of person in Melanesian politics whose powers derived from new kinds of opportunities and a managed circulation of accumulated wealth. In contrast, great men, to which the category of big men was opposed, emerged through balanced exchanges in marriage and warfare. Subsequently, the idea behind this typology came to be used not to characterize whole societies but to show different kinds of power strategies under conditions of rapid change.

15. That the relation with the police goes further than policing of families is clear in the analysis of the lettres de cachet offered by Farge and Foucault (2014) in which they give the primary documents from the archives at Bastille showing how the police were trusted to respond to requests for the incarceration of family members (wives, sons, daughters) who were seen as dangerous to the family. See also Quétel (2011) for viewing the different arrangements of policing in Paris and the provinces as also the reasoning deployed to refuse requests for incarceration of certain family members.

16. Since it is essential to the modality of sovereign power that it is episodic rather than consistent, there are other cases in which the police can be brutal, but in general in the conditions of the slums the local police are much more tied into the financial arrangements of bribery, regular but illegal extractions of money, and work more through the local mediations of politicians and "big men" than by standing apart. It is standard practice to bring in a police force from other precincts if a police operation to demolish any part of the illegal occupations or to settle other "law and order" issues has to be mounted.

17. The condition in institutions for treatment of psychiatric patients was indeed dismal until a number of public interest litigations led to the Supreme Court's injunctions on improvements in these institutions. The best description of changes in law and the various interventions made by the courts for improving conditions in asylums is to be found in Dhanda (2000).

18. Please note that a simple statement indicative of the outcome (e.g., "He was admitted to the hospital for treatment of mental illness") would elide a whole swirl of microdecisions and actions (e.g., finding someone who had contacts so as to get past the emergency ward, arranging for money, finding someone to take the patient to the hospital) that had to be completed in order to create the conditions of possibility for such an outcome. These microactions tell us equally about the phenomena under consideration as does the outcome.

19. This is a standard form of address to parents and elders.

20. For an account of the average time a provider in a low-income neighborhood spends on patients and the quality of care, see Das and Hammer (2004).

21. The authors state that "since the end of the Second World War, and taking here only the example of health, a range of powerful agencies within states and a range of transnational bodies have taken on a new importance. So have a host of bioethics commissions, regulatory agencies and professional organizations: a whole 'bioethical complex,' in which the power of medical agents to 'let die' at the end of life, the start of life or in reproduction, are simultaneously enhanced by medical technology and regulated by other authorities as never before" (Rabinow and Rose 2006, 203). The "letting die" is much more pervasive through mechanisms other than those imagined by Rabinow and Rose. On other registers, both Biehl (2013) and Povinelli (2011) consider abandonment of the vulnerable as a form of "letting die," but as Han (2012) and Pinto (2014) show, families do a lot of work on care before they reach the point at which a vulnerable relative is abandoned.

## 7. THE BOUNDARIES OF THE "WE": CRUELTY, RESPONSIBILITY, AND FORMS OF LIFE

1. The question that haunted me in Swapan's story as it meshed into the story of his neighborhood was this: is the pathological normativity I describe in the case of Swapan not the general condition of our lives? After all, what is normativity when at the edges of our consciousness we know that the democratic societies in which we live participate in long-distance wars through the supply of weapons and allow famines to devastate whole regions of the world when some of this destruction could have been halted. At the end of the *Mahabharata*, Gandhari (the mother of the Kauravas, who have all been slaughtered in a war for which they were themselves partly responsible) turns to Krishna and blames him saying, "You could have prevented the war," and Krishna accepts this guilt of having enabled the devastating violence (see Das 2012c). I am in the process of developing the idea that ethics in general is not possible, but that leaves us to think of how to live ethical lives to the extent possible within these conditions of pathological normativity—*Kali Yuga* as the Hindus would name it.

2. For a more detailed discussion, see Han and Das (2015, 1–31).

3. The proposition that we suffer deprivation of imagination under conditions of injustice might need more discussion, for one could easily cite counterexamples in which the concrete experience of injustice is what leads to political protest. However, I think Lear is referring to a complete destruction of a form of life rather than simply injustice that can cover a very wide variety of experiences.

4. I thank Akio Tanabe for this astute point. I think this characterization of life also marks the way my own ethnography on violence is conducted, which is why I do not think that the difference between ethnography and literature can be characterized as the difference between "real lives and "true lives" as in Didier Fassin (2014). I agree with Fassin that the ethnographer cannot invent events—she must

retain fidelity to what actually happened or what she was told. My difficulty in this formulation is that what is told to the anthropologist often has an element of fantasy. Further, the meaning or significance of what you are observing during fieldwork is not self-evident. Indeed, if everyday life is laced with fantasy and skepticism, the question of arriving at the real in ethnographic accounts is more problematic than suggested by Fassin even as I agree that ethnography's anchoring in the real is different from a novel's anchoring in the real.

## 8. A CHILD DISAPPEARS: LAW IN THE COURTS, LAW IN THE INTERSTICES OF EVERYDAY LIFE

1. The treatment of a case as a bounded entity is beginning to be seriously interrogated in recent scholarship. In the case of land disputes, Chaganti (2018) argues that case generates other linked cases over conflicting claims; Sehdev (2018) argues that in matrimonial disputes, criminal and civil case are simultaneously litigated; and Ibrahim (2013), Mulla (2014), and Satyogi (2016) show how police procedures, forensic medicine, and the pull of relationships are entangled in decisions of whether to take a case further for prosecution.

2. There is some confusion in the court documents as to whether Rita was his ex-wife or is still married to him. A witness appeared as her present husband but cases of three-cornered relationships known in the neighborhoods as "settlements" are not uncommon. Because of the complexities of this case it was not feasible for me to contact any of the accused in the case. Mostly, I followed the trail of the public documents.

3. Pursuing the history of each kind of document in terms of its admissibility provides very interesting insights into the way legal mechanisms are thought to work not only in the court but also outside it. For instance, are police diaries reliable records of the procedures followed by police? The Provision of Section 172 of the Code of Criminal Procedure states that any criminal court may send for the police diaries not as evidence in the case but to aid it in an inquiry. The court may use the special diary not as evidence of any date, fact, or statement referred to in it but as containing indications of sources and lines of inquiry and as suggesting the names of persons whose evidence may be material for the purpose of doing justice between the State and the accused. This provision and its amendments could only have grown out of the suspicion with which courts themselves have had to make judgments on police procedures in view of media exposures of police corruption.

4. In the present case, responsibility is assigned to the accused and his accomplices on the basis of *samanya aashay*—lit. "common intention." Common intention is defined in Section 34 of the Indian Penal Code and is distinguished from same or similar intention since it must show the existence of an agreed-upon plan (*State v. Sajdu Khan and Others*, 1950). In *Shyamal Ghosh v. State of West Bengal*, it

was stated that the test of common intention was that "each of the persons is liable for the act in the same manner as if it were done by him alone." The presiding judge calls this a necessary "legal fiction." In rape cases, the question of common intention when more than one person is said to have acted in collusion raises further questions as to how liable others are if only one of them committed the rape. In *Jitender v. State* (2009), the Supreme Court upheld the appeal of the petitioner Jitender to disallow the attempt of the prosecution to charge him with rape in an ongoing case in which three men (including Jitender) had forcibly taken a schoolgirl to an empty house but only one of them (Mukesh) had raped her. The reasoning offered by the two sides is important to consider since it was argued on the one side that since rape was committed only by one person, common intention to commit gang rape should not be assumed. The other side argued that even if only one person had committed the actual rape, there was sufficient material to show that the other accused were members of the group that acted in concert to commit the rape. In the present case regarding Kh, the judge established common intention by enumerating their participation in the injuries inflicted and the fact that the two women stayed at the same place when rape was being committed while turning their faces away. These heinous actions, the judge stated, showed their previous agreed-upon plan as a meeting of minds (*mastishk milap*) and thus as proving common intention.

5. I try as far as possible to maintain the syntax of the Hindi grammar in my translations, but it makes for awkward sentences. Except for the medical reports and citations from High Court judgments that are in English, all other material is in Hindi and all translations are mine.

6. Legal judgments in India, especially from the higher courts, seem to have a large portion dedicated to remarks made as obiter dicta—opinions expressed by the judge "by the way," which are not essential to the decision—in comparison to the ratio decidendi—the legal principle that underlies the decision in that particular case.

7. For example, in *State v. Mahmood Farooqui* (2018), the Supreme Court recently acquitted the accused on the ground that where the accused and the victim were in a relationship, consent or its lack were very difficult to establish despite the woman having stated that she did not consent to a particular sexual act.

8. The ubiquitous use of the passive voice is a pervasive feature of legal language (Bhatia 1993). Other grammatical features are the abundant use of subordinate clauses and the repetition of noun phrases and verb phrases.

9. Recall that police documents such as the special diary cannot be used as evidence of dates, times, etc., in criminal proceedings—these can only be used to indicate the procedures followed in making inquiries.

10. While I cannot take the theme of intertextuality in the judgments and in police documents, I want to indicate that many forms of talk in the everyday interactions in the neighborhoods reproduce dialogues from Hindi films. These ways

of talking also make their way into police documents. Thus, Sudhanshu's speech is resonant with melodramatic forms of villainous talk in films. Terms such as *dabang* (man wielding power and terror) and *screen shot* (in English) to describe an incident (*"screen shot ye tha,"* this was the screen shot) show how much forms of talk incorporate imaginaries from Hindi films. Please see Chatterji and Mehta (2007) for more examples.

11. Powell, Hlavka, and Mulla (2017) show the importance of intersectionality of race and gender in the determination of credibility of the child's testimony in US courts.

12. Judges presiding over cases in sessions courts tend to give copious citations from higher courts since they anticipate cases going further on appeal and citations serve as shields against criticisms from higher courts.

13. While I do not have the space to develop the point in any detail here, the imperative to show motive in rape cases engages courts primarily in cases of gang rape—for instance, the motif of "punishment" of lower-caste women by upper-caste Gujjar landlords appeared in the infamous Bhanwari Devi case (Dutta and Sircar 2013; see also Oberman 1994 for a case of gang rape where the rape of girls was part of a game of scoring points). On the dimension of class in gang rapes, see Mehta (2019).

Establishment of common intention is of far greater concern in criminal proceedings in cases involving more than one accused than establishment of motive. In general, courts have maintained that where direct evidence of the crime is available, establishment of motive is not important, whereas if evidence was only circumstantial motive would play a greater role. This does not mean that motive is not evoked but that "motiveless crime" does not constitute the crisis of intelligibility that it seems to have evoked in French courts as in the notorious case of Henriette Cornier (Foucault 2003). This factor might be also attributed to the considerably smaller role of criminal psychiatry in India. However, motive nonetheless haunts the discussion of the case as in the defense's claims that there was a motive (earlier enmities, revenge) on the part of Kh's mother to implicate the accused in false charges and in the speculations expressed by the parents in their earlier dispositions that the girl might have seen something pointing to a trafficking episode and was kidnapped to prevent revelations of other criminal actions on the part of neighbors.

14. I should state clearly that I am not proposing a comparison between the cases discussed by Sabean and the case under consideration here in terms of any substantive issues. I am more interested in exploring how the method for the analysis of judicial records might be exported to contexts other than that of eighteenth-century Germany.

15. I am aware of the risks of speaking of "the law," which I use as a shorthand term to describe what kind of discursive statements and local practices are generated

in these neighborhoods under the sign of law. I take my cue here from Foucault's method of studying the state not as a stable institution recognizable by a definite predicate but as coming into being through the processes he calls "statizations," which include governmentalizing of the state apparatus and addressing impasses in law by supplementing its authority in making a place for disciplines to address these blockages (see especially Foucault 2003, 2007). The difference is that whereas Foucault is relying on the archive of expert discourses and court judgments, I am taking the ordinary, everyday talk as part of our understanding of the legal apparatus, including the discursive forms it generates.

16. The feminine gender marker is missing here, probably due to the fact that the petition was typed by a man who slipped into the use of masculine gender.

17. It might help to get a feel for these leaders who rise and fall rapidly if I narrate an instance from 2012. The candidate contesting on the Congress ticket was to pass this shanty cluster in a tour of the area. Our local leader, flush with excitement, had gathered two dozen followers who were waiting by the roadside with garlands of marigold and rose petals to be showered on the candidate. There was much hope that the Congress candidate would alight from his decorated vehicle and greet the people gathered there. After four hours' wait in the scorching hot sun, the procession arrived, and the car slowed down but did not halt. People were rushing toward it with the heavy garlands, but the candidate did not alight. Instead, one of his minions gestured that the garlands could be thrown toward the car and as people began to flip the garlands in that direction, he expertly caught them and put them in the vehicle. The candidate, with his hands folded in a gesture of thanks, passed by and the crowd dispersed with a very dejected-looking leader in tow. The official candidate was a CEO of a private hospital and the only solace was that he lost. But the winning candidate was also the CEO of another private hospital who had announced free treatment for the jhuggi dwellers, and it did materialize for some.

18. See the earlier discussion in Chapter 6 where Donatelli offers a subtle critique of Elizabeth Povinelli's (2011) impulse to detect the venue of negative critique in the disquieting presence of otherness, such as in the corroding lifeforms of indigenous communities that are seen as already extinguished under the pressure of modern forms of governance under late liberalism.

## 9. OF MISTAKES, ERRORS, AND SUPERSTITION: READING WITTGENSTEIN'S REMARKS ON FRAZER

1. The desire to philosophically and anthropologically arrive at an idea of reality from which the human is made absent has stimulated some very interesting work, but I am not engaging it here. I do not imagine that the question of a human form of life necessarily commits one to any superior claims for the human over and above, say, claims accorded to animals or to the planet. Interestingly, much writing on the

nonhuman often smuggles in the discussion an idea of reality as meaningful by the very signifying apparatuses that are marshalled to say that nonhuman or nonsentient entities nevertheless engage in meaningful actions. For me the question of meaningful or meaningless simply does not apply to reality, nor do I think of the real as if it were frontally before us.

2. I have used the 1976 version translated by Peter Winch.

3. I am fascinated by the ongoing debates on continuity versus discontinuity between early and later Wittgenstein—the standard reading of the *Tractatus* and the austere reading—and although I have learned much from these debates, especially on the importance of the theme of nonsense in Wittgenstein, my point here is limited to a related but different register in his thought—namely, the place of superstition versus simple mistake in the context of his comments on Frazer.

4. I leave, for the moment, the intriguing discussion of nonsense that would take us to the difficult questions of not only sense and reference but also whether meaning resides in words or sentences, and the distinction between nonsense as gibberish versus nonsense that is illuminating. In the latter case—as, for instance, when a sentence is not a syntactic mess—it looks as if it could make sense but on close examination is revealed to be nonsense. We need to examine each sentence for its alignment with the world in a different way than in cases of pure gibberish (see Conant and Diamond [2004] and Meredith Williams [2004] for a very interesting debate on the status of nonsense in the *Tractatus*). I elsewhere (see Das 2016) examine how the question of words in and out of sentences is engaged in grammatical and ritual theory in Sanskrit; the echoes of some of that discussion resonate here.

5. The distinction between disguised nonsense and patent nonsense is interesting because Frazer's sentences are not quite gibberish, so finding why they make no sense is a task one sets oneself. It is not obvious.

6. One could make finer distinctions—for instance, error refers to opinions whereas mistakes might be made because of misunderstandings or because, in the case of language, one is not master of one's expressions. See the distinction J. L. Austin makes between abuses and misfires (Austin 1962, 16, 18) as two different ways in which a performative utterance can fail. See also the discussion in Chapter 2.

7. I am following the convention in Wittgenstein's *Remarks on Frazer* to refer to the remarks using the "#" sign. Numbered remarks are more an editorial convenience in this text because it was reconstructed from fragments after Wittgenstein's death. Numbering of paragraphs does not carry the weight it did in *Philosophical Investigations*.

8. Frank Cioffi's (1990) later discussion "Wittgenstein and Obscurantism" charges Wittgenstein with methodological obscurantism, for passing his epistemic preference for a methodological one in refusing to entertain any historical explanation for the feeling of dread that the contemplation of the fire festival evokes. Speaking up for the relevance of such explanations, Cioffi states that Catholic confession, for

instance, can be explained by Catholic dogma, but in a counterargument one may say, surely, Catholic dogmas about apostolic succession, priestly ordination, and the power to absolve the sinner belong to the same practice of confession, the conditions of its emergence within this form of life; they are not "explanations" of the confessional practices (see Hacker 1992).

9. The numbers correspond to the numbers in da Col and Palmié (forthcoming). I have commented on the parts of these remarks that were significant for my analysis.

10. Although the theme of religion and emotion has received attention in the work of Saba Mahmood (2005) and Charles Hirschkind (2006), exemplary for some purposes, these authors take subjectivity to be the same as the process of subjectivation—hence, the individuals cited in their accounts all speak as generalized subjects representing "typical experiences" rather than as singular ones. For an account of the general theme of religion and emotion, see François Berthomé and Michael Houseman (2010).

11. In characterizing the scene of Cartesian doubt as an allegory of philosophy's refusal of the ordinary, I am following Cavell (1989) when he thinks of the builders' language or the weird scene of choosing a red apple by first assembling all red things and then selecting an apple from them rather than the other way around as "allegories"—philosophical enactments of a thought at war with itself. The sense of life and its ruins that these allegories enact is best captured for me in in this passage from "Declining Decline": "Now take all this, the events of the *Investigations*— from the scenes and consequences of inheritance and instruction and fascination, and the request for an apple, and the building of what might seem the first building, to the possibility of the loss of attachment as such to the inheritance, and these moments are tracked by the struggle for philosophy with itself, with the losing and turning one's way, and the chronic breakdowns of madness and conceive it as a complete sophisticated culture, or say, a way of life, ours" (Cavell 1989, 64–65). These are dramatic philosophical enactments of philosophy's refusal of the ordinary; they are not symbolic representations of this refusal.

12. For an acute criticism of the tendency in Anglo-American anthropology to settle on, say, witchcraft accusations as the most important component in the understanding of witchcraft because these have the appearance of facts that can be immediately grasped, see Jeanne Favret-Saada (2015).

13. The sharp opposition between "good to eat" and "good to think" that Claude Lévi-Strauss proposes might be, as he himself acknowledges, softened by tracing what he calls the "evolution" in Radcliffe-Brown's thought. The functionalist explanation, which Lévi-Strauss refers to as his first theory, is summarized as follows: "According to Radcliffe-Brown's first theory, as for Malinowski, an animal only becomes 'totemic' because it is 'good to eat'" (Lévi-Strauss 1964, 62). However, he also acknowledges that for Radcliffe-Brown, as for Durkheim, the problem of totemism

was to be placed within the larger issue of the way in which nature was incorporated within the social. See also Milton Singer (1984).

14. Surprisingly, Peter Hacker (1992) takes this involuntary action as an example of an instrumental, albeit naturalized, action. He misses the "as if" and also the fact that an expression may be simply drawn out of us!

15. See also Das (2000) and Hage (1998) for discussions on how violence against the other might be shot through with an experience of vulnerability of one's own life.

16. I am not making the point that revealing the trancelike character of his fears will persuade Aaron that his form of life is not under threat by Muslims, for it is within the structure of skepticism about the other that it makes it hard to awaken from such a trance. I do want to note, though, that others within his own social world find Aaron to be behaving in a weird fashion, showing that a different sense of what it is to live with these others is also part of the milieu, as Smith's ethnography also shows.

## 10. CONCEPTS CRISSCROSSING: ANTHROPOLOGY AND KNOWLEDGE-MAKING

1. The feel for correctness is arrived at in a different way in the grammarian Panini's notions of when a rule is necessary and when we can leave it to experience. Thus, the term *bhrātr* in Sanskrit could, strictly speaking, mean both brother and sister, but in commentaries on Panini, he is not faulted for the absence of a limiting rule here for when in common parlance one says *bhrātr*, the commentator says, one expects the brother to be indicated for all practical purposes and not the sister (see Candotti and Pontillo 2013, 111).

2. I wish to add here that I have read these texts many times over since 1964. These were formative texts in my training at the Delhi School of Economics under the headship of Professor M. N. Srinivas and part of the syllabi I later taught. So, when I started to reread them for this chapter, I did not know where I would end up.

3. This hierarchical relation between anthropological or sociological concepts and the concepts entailed in so-called indigenous thought is often taken for granted. As an example, consider Lévi-Strauss's (1950) exhortation that sociology would be set on a dangerous path and "ethnography would dissolve into a verbose phenomenology" if social reality were "reduced to the conception that man has of it."

Now it would be no one's position that reality is transparent either to the people or to the anthropologist, but what is at stake here is the status of description in relation to the object of description: Is that object an opinion that might be expressed in the form of a proposition? Is it a thing with identifiable characteristics? Or is the object of description a form of life? If the last, then a surplus of description is essential to the task at hand. (For a brilliant exposition on an anthropological tonality in description, see Laugier forthcoming.)

4. The recent work of Myhre (2018) of making vernacular concepts count without being subjected to second-order "analytical" concepts is a very important and interesting experiment of seeing how concepts may grow within forms of life, though I feel that it also demonstrates how strong the hold is of the Christian underpinning of anthropological concepts such as that of sacrifice and pure gift. See my comments on the book (Das 2019).

5. I do not take up the discussion here of what a rule is. This was a question that pervades the thought of the school of grammarians, ritual hermeneutics, and proponents of law in the Sanskrit texts I have studied and on which I hope to write in much more detail in a book in collaboration with Naveeda Khan. However, see Freschi and Pontillo (2013) and Candotti and Pontillo (2013) for learned discussions on the nature of rules with regard to extensions and with reference to the conceptual geography of rules governing absence that touch on issues different from the zero degree in structural linguistics, including that of signs that are imperceptible and characterized as entities between existence and nonexistence or, better stated, as between existence and inexistence.

6. One question that I must postpone for another occasion relates to the importance of examples especially when concepts are seen to defy a definitional structure. I have been very intrigued by the stipulation in the Nyāya school of Indian philosophy that the category of example is a fundamental epistemological category but that every argument requires one to produce both a concordant example and a discordant one. Nāgārjuna's refutation of this argument rests in part on the etymology of the Sanskrit word for "example," which is *drishtānta*—that which is seen at the end. Nagarjuna argues that since the beginning and middle of the argument is not possible to stipulate, the end is also not visible (Nagarjuna 2018, verses 25–31). I think these points might have some relevance for ethnographic descriptions used as examples or instantiations, but I am not able to work my way around these issues at this juncture.

7. There is a copious literature on the question of divine names and their translation—for instance, whether the term *Allah* can be used in the Bible to refer to God and whether *Allah* is a pre-Islamic term (see K. J. Thomas 2001). In the case of India, with its vast proliferation of languages and dialects, we can find enough discussion on divine names in each language in which the Bible was translated. In addition, there are questions of how terms for the Islamic prophet and for Jesus were incorporated within Hindu texts, including the well-known *Bhaviṣya Purāṇa*—a complicated text written within the genre of Puranic texts but clearly incorporating accretions from various periods right up to the experience of the British rule (Pargiter 1913; see also Das 2010c).

8. I find it interesting that in arguing for a robust relation between anthropology and theology, as in the important work of Joel Robbins (2006), theology is assumed to be exclusively Christian. It is as if the challenges that, say, Hindu

conceptions of god or of ritual to Christian conceptions of God were by definition outside the frame of any discussion on the topic of anthropology and theology.

9. My discussion here is limited to the discussions in the mīmāmsā because I am not offering a comprehensive discussion about Hindu gods but showing how even thinking of one strand within discussions in this tradition complicates the simple common sense that Lienhardt and Evans-Pritchard evoke.

10. There is a massive literature on the mīmāmsā, including translations and commentaries on individual texts. I have relied on Jaimini's (1970–1976) *Mīmāmsādarśanam*, which includes commentaries by Śabara and Kumārilla Bhatta. My aim here is a limited one: to show that there is nothing obvious about the idea that some overarching questions about belief, devotion, or spirituality would be intrinsic to the idea of deity, god, or gods.

11. That grammatical concepts were about much more than learning to speak in a refined way was recognized by Louis Renou as early as 1942 (see Renou 1941–1942). One of the most prominent scholars to open up the discussion of the relation between grammatical concepts and philosophical reflection in Indian philosophy, including Buddhist texts, is Kamaleswar Bhattacharya. As one example, he shows how Nagarjuna's intriguing passage "The road that is being traveled at present is not being traveled at present" is not a reiteration of Zeno's paradox about time but is based on a grammatical reading of the *nominative case* and its relation to action, despite the apparent reference to the past, present, and future in the full verse (see Bhattacharya 1985).

12. I am not going into the question here of earlier debates on whether the Bible should be translated in vernacular languages that took place in Europe, since these issues had been long settled, but see Hill (2006) and Smalley (1991).

13. There is a whole history to be unearthed here, including the prominence given to generic terms over proper names in invocations in the reform sects such as the Arya Samaj. Consider also the different affects that come to mark the commentaries on the mīmāmsā as they come under pressure from the rise of devotional movements, as is evident in later commentaries such as that of Khandadeva (mid-seventeenth century) who, having concluded that the *devatā* is nothing more than the word (*shabdamātram devatā*), qualifies his statement by adding: "All of the preceding is Jaimini's view; just to repeat it soils my tongue. My only refuge is remembering Hari (Krishna)" (as cited in Clooney 1997, 354).

14. If I might be permitted a personal anecdote, I recall the following conversation with my teacher, Professor M. N. Srinivas. Srinivas (known to his friends as Chamu) had completed his dissertation, "Religion and Society among the Coorgs of South India," under Evans-Pritchard's supervision at Oxford. Evans-Pritchard and he were deep in conversation by the fireside when, as Srinivas recalled, Evans-Pritchard suddenly said, "Chamu, how can you have a book on religion without even one chapter on God? I think you should add a chapter on God"; to which Chamu

replied, "Either the book goes to the press or it goes into the fire now." The absence of an overarching God in this classic anthropological text on Hinduism owed much to Srinivas's earthy sensibilities on what he called the "field view" of Indian society.

15. In their discussion of the theory and practice of translation as it pertains to biblical translations, Nida and Taber (2003) discuss the normative standards through which different components of the word *God* might be distinguished from the word *gods*. An issue they discuss is how a strict monotheism under which there were no other gods except God was to be distinguished from that in which the one God was superior to all other gods. This difficulty is addressed in different ways in the discussion on the rival terms used in India: the Jesuits, for instance, have incorporated such ritual gestures as the waving of the lamp or celebration of Hindu festivals associated with particular gods such as Rama and Krishna on the grounds that these are cultural festivals and commit them to no strict ontology regarding the existence of one or many gods.

16. Edmund Leach (1989–1990) somewhat belatedly comes to the realization that in their search for authentic primitive societies, anthropologists, including himself, had completely ignored the colonial officials or the missionaries who were very much present but made to disappear. About the monographs on the Nuer and the Dinka, he says, "At that period the area was under heavy colonial administration and densely populated with Catholic missionaries. The books of both authors are generously illustrated with photographs. No European appears in any of these photographs; nearly all the Nuer and Dinka are naked" (48). Leach then goes on to contrast these pictures with those that appear in the writings of Francis Mading Den—born in 1938, son of a paramount chief of the Ngok Dinka—who got his doctorate degree at Yale and whose photographs include that of the first car that came to Ngok territory and, as Leach notes with heavy irony, all the characters in his photographs appear to be fully clothed.

17. The term *puruṣārtha* here is different from the term used to indicate the four aims of human life. The primary term *kratu* in the compound work *kratvārtha* (for the sake of action) is used sometimes and the term *kriyā* (verb) at other times.

18. As Benveniste (1971a) notes, the middle voice did not arise as a mediating term between active and passive voice—rather, it is the disappearance of the middle voice that led to the main view of action as either active or passive. For an application of this distinction in legal judgments, see Chapter 8.

19. I would like to clarify that a tension developed within Brahmanism in the first millennia as some gods began to be personalized. The growth of devotional cults in the bhakti movement in the medieval period led to a different set of tensions as minute differences came to characterize the different relations between the devotees and their chosen gods. However, elements of the idea that the names of gods refer to different aspects that cannot be simply assimilated into one aggregate inform many important debates.

20. Briefly, the issue is that of crossing over of existence and nonexistence with affirmation and negation. Different inflections of the fourfold possibility of "exists," "does not exist," "exists *and* does not exist," "either exists or does not exist" might be found in different philosophical discussions with a further possibility of "perhaps" added to each within Jainism. The problem of negation is not unique to texts from the Indic traditions, but the varied practices around these complex issues is quite stunning, as is the idea that sounds in a word subjected to erasure and substitution become nonperceptible (*adarśanam*) but not nonexistent. Ontologically, such grammatical erasure of sounds makes them entities that are seen as lying between existence and nonexistence (see Freschi and Pontillo 2013).

21. It is also the case that some Sanskrit original texts that were lost have been reconstructed from manuscripts found in Tibet.

22. We owe the brilliant insight to Laugier (2018a) that description entails not simply the act of describing what we *see* from a distance but also what is raked from leaves of memory, for instance. In this sense, description involves some violence.

23. Although I cannot expand on this point here, there are other ethnographies in which anthropologists (foreign or native) might concede that the experience of living with informants who encounter spirits makes the "reality" of the spirits a much more complex question than Lienhardt's or Evans-Pritchard's understanding of experience as entirely locked into the individual makes it out to be. See especially Favret-Saada (1980, 2012), Lambek (2014), and Motta (2016, 2017, 2019).

24. Lienhardt explains that the Dinka tend to think of any foreigner who is not a trader or a missionary to be some kind of government official.

25. I am not certain, but it seems that the term *Power* here is Lienhardt's translation of what would literally be "You Spirit."

26. In the case of the Nuer, while drawing attention to the difficult conditions of fieldwork and Evans-Pritchard's disagreements with the way colonial policy was being implemented by the then-governor of Upper Nile Province, C. A. Willis, Johnson (1982) notes the punitive expeditions against the prophets and the fact that some violent events initiated by the government happened in the vicinity of Evans-Pritchard's field sites. Johnson writes: "The Lou had already made their resentment of Evans-Pritchard known because of his association with the Government which had bombed them, burnt their villages, seized their cattle, took prisoners, herded them in 'concentration areas,' killed their prophet Guek and had blown up and desecrated the Mound of his father Ngun Deng, their greatest prophet" (236). The excellent archival work done by Johnson leaves no room for thinking that Evans-Pritchard was not fully aware of what was going on—this does not take away the importance of Evans-Pritchard's work unless one is totally oblivious to the contaminated nature of all knowledge, nor is there room for moral high ground as if we anthropologists now embody a purer life.

27. The normal sacrificial offering to the goddess Kali in Bengal is a black goat.

28. Writing in 1910, Valentine Chirol, a British diplomat and writer, had this to say: "It is not surprising that among extremists one of the favorite euphemisms applied to the killing of an Englishman is 'sacrificing a white goat to Kali.' . . . In 1906 I was visiting one of the Hindu temples in Benaras and found in the courtyard a number of young students, who had come on an excursion from Bengal. I got into conversation with them, and they soon began to air, for my benefit, their political views which were decidedly 'advanced.' They were, however, quite civil and friendly and they invited me to come up to the temple door and see them sacrifice to Kali a poor bleating kid they had brought with them. When I declined one of them . . . came forward and pressed me, and said if I would accompany them they would not mind even sacrificing a white goat. There was a general shout of laughter at what was evidently regarded by others as a huge joke. I turned away, though I did not understand the grim humour as I understand it now" (Chirol [1910] 2010, 86–87).

29. The mistranslation of the title, including the puns on *pensée* and *pansy*, have been numerous, so I will refrain from any comments.

30. Here Lévi-Strauss's understanding of concepts seems different from that of Wittgenstein who thinks of concepts as building on usages or practices that are already embedded in life. Consider the following observation from Wittgenstein: "How does one teach a child (say in arithmetic) 'Now take *these* things together!' or 'Now *these* go together'? Clearly 'taking together' and 'going together' must originally have had another meaning for him than that of seeing in this way or that.— And this is a remark about concepts, not about teaching methods" (Wittgenstein [1953] 1968, 208$^e$).

31. Wittgenstein says in connection with analyzing a concept in terms of the use of words that it is different from Nominalism: "Nominalists make the mistake of interpreting all words as names, and so of not really describing their use, but only, so to speak, giving a paper draft on such a description" (Wittgenstein [1953] 1968, §383).

## 11. THE LIFE OF CONCEPTS: IN THE VICINITY OF DYING

1. I want to register my deep-felt gratitude to the author for his generosity in allowing the tragic events that overtook his life, and his reflections on them, to become available to readers. I apologize for any infelicities I might have inadvertently committed in writing on them.

2. In his notes in the *Brown Book*, Wittgenstein (1958) asks whether a feeling of pastness distinguishes memory images from other images. Yet when the anthropologist is writing up her text, the question of who she was at that time when the event she is describing "happened" is a difficult question to answer. In her nuanced interweaving of her own experience of a disastrous love affair with experiences she is recording of women with mental illness, Sarah Pinto conveys both the texture of

the present when she is in the field and the sense that the fieldwork experiences already belong to the past—a typical way time is experienced as we move between fieldwork and writing. I offer the full quotation for its exquisite rendering of this experience of coevalness: "I will not know yet that time will bring, at first, less articulation and more dissolution, and then, not until years later, a new love who will offer kindness and sanity, overturning—easily, gracefully—everything that I have come to fear is true about love and home, and much of what I write here" (Pinto 2014, 152). The future present of the narration performs the function of dispersing the narrator over a stretch of time different from that of the spectral present.

3. Roma Chatterji's work speaks most clearly to the character of reverberations and reflections when she describes how the smallest of marks in the folk paintings by the Chitrakars of Bengal she has been studying can allude to an earlier myth or a story within the myth or story being related now (Chatterji 2012). The painter Akbar Padamsee speaks of the impact that the *bimba-pratibimba* school of Indian philosophy—the idea that a reflection is not so much a reflection of a reality but of another reflection—had on the way in which he arranged different parts of a landscape into a metascape (see Das 2010d). Similarly, each poem here is a reflection not only of Shelly's death but also of every other poem in the text.

4. This is the remark that provided the inspiration for my comments on Wittgenstein's *Remarks on Frazer* in Chapter 9.

5. I leave for now the expression "figures of grammar" without further explanation, but in the *kavya* texts, as also in texts on hermeneutics and logic, grammar provides figures of thought.

6. I am bracketing for now a discussion of how aesthetic genres moved between Sanskrit, Persian, and vernacular languages in the early modern period.

7. Though as I revisited a couple of his essays, I felt some crudeness in his translation of *ha dhik* or *dhik* as "hell with" rather than the old-fashioned "woe to." The physiognomy of "hell with" is just not in tune with that of *ha dhik*.

# REFERENCES

Adams, Vincanne. 2013. *Markets of Sorrow, Labors of Faith: New Orleans in the Wake of Katrina*. Durham, N.C.: Duke University Press.

Agamben, Giorgio. 1998. *Homo Sacer: Sovereign Power and Bare Life*. Translated by Daniel Heller-Roazen. Stanford, Calif.: Stanford University Press.

Alam, Muzaffar. 2004. *The Languages of Political Islam: India 1200–1800*. Chicago: University of Chicago Press.

Alter, Joseph S. 2004. *Yoga in Modern India: The Body between Science and Philosophy*. Princeton, N.J.: Princeton University Press.

Amarasuriya, Harini, and Jonathan Spencer. 2015. "'With That, Discipline Will Also Come to Them': The Politics of the Urban Poor in Postwar Colombo." *Current Anthropology* 56 (S11): S66–S75.

Améry, Jean. 1980. *At the Mind's Limits*. Translated by Sidney Rosenfeld and Stella P. Rosenfeld. Bloomington: Indiana University Press.

Amin, Shahid. 2015. *Conquest and Community: The Afterlife of Warrior Saint Ghazi Miyan*. New Delhi: Orient Blackswan.

Amy, Lori E. 2010. *The Wars We Inherit: Military Life, Gender Violence and Memory*. Philadelphia: Temple University Press.

Anderson, Chris. 2018. "The End of Theory: The Data Deluge Makes the Scientific Method Obsolete." *Wired*, June 23, 2008. https://www.wired.com/2008/06/pb-theory/.

Anscombe, Gertrude Elizabeth M. 1975. "The First Person." In *Mind and Language: Wolfson College Lectures, 1974*, edited by Samuel Guttenplan, 45–64. Oxford: Clarendon.

———. 1981. "The First Person." In *Metaphysics and Philosophy of Mind*. Vol. 2 of *Collected Philosophical Papers*, 21–37. Oxford: Basil Blackwell.

Apel, Dora. 2005. "Torture Culture: Lynching Photographs and the Images of Abu Ghraib." *Art Journal* 64 (2): 88–100.

Appadurai, Arjun. 1996. *Modernity at Large: Cultural Dimensions of Globalization*. Minneapolis: University of Minnesota Press.

Arendt, Hannah. 1963. *Eichmann in Jerusalem: A Report on the Banality of Evil*. New York: Penguin.

Asad, Talal. 1979. "Anthropology and the Colonial Encounter." In *The Politics of Anthropology: From Colonialism and Sexism toward a View from Below*, edited by Gerrit Huezer and Bruce Manheim, 85–94. The Hague: Mouton Publishers.

———. 1990. "The Concept of Cultural Translation in British Social Anthropology." In *Genealogies of Religion: Discipline and Reasons of Power in Christianity and Islam*, 171–200. Baltimore, Md.: Johns Hopkins University Press.

———. 2000. "What Do Human Rights Do? An Anthropological Enquiry." *Theory and Event* 4 (4).

———. 2015. "Thinking about Tradition, Religion, and Politics in Egypt Today." *Critical Inquiry* 42 (Autumn): 166–214.

Aucouturier, Valérie. 2015. "The Grammar of Sensation." In *Normativity in Perception*, edited by Maxime Doyon and Thiemo Breyer, 208–25. London: Palgrave Macmillan UK.

Austin, John Langshaw. 1946. "Other Minds." *Proceedings of the Aristotelian Society* S20: 148–87.

———. 1950. "Truth." *Aristotelian Society* S24 (1): S111–28.

———. 1957. "A Plea for Excuses: The Presidential Address." *Proceedings of the Aristotelian Society* 57: 1–30.

———. (1961) 1979. *Philosophical Papers*. Edited by J. O. Urmson and G. J. Warnock. Oxford: Oxford University Press.

———. 1962. *How to Do Things with Words*. Cambridge, Mass.: Harvard University Press.

———. 1979a. "A Plea for Excuses." In *Philosophical Papers*, edited by J. O. Urmson and G. J. Warnock, 175–204. Oxford: Oxford University Press.

———. 1979b. "Pretending." In *Philosophical Papers*, edited by J. O. Urmson and G. J. Warnock, 253–71. Oxford: Oxford University Press.

Badiou, Alain. 1994. "Being by Numbers: Lauren Sedofsky Talks with Alain Badiou." *Artforum* (October).

———. 2001. *Ethics: An Essay on the Understanding of Evil*. Translated by Peter Hallward. London: Verso.

Bagaria, Swayam. 2017. "Interiorities of Memory." *Somatosphere*, February 10, 2017. http://somatosphere.net/forumpost/interiorities-of-memory.

Baker, J. P., and P. M. S. Hacker. 1980. *Wittgenstein: Meaning and Understanding*. Vol. 1. Oxford: Blackwell.

Basu, K. K. 1949. "Hindu-Muslim Marriages." *Indian Law Review*: 24–36.

Bäumer, Bettina. 2008. "The Three Grammatical Persons and Trika." In *Linguistic Traditions of Kashmir: Essays in Memory of Pandit Dinanath Yaksh*, edited by

Mrinal Kaul and Ashok Aklujkar, 206–22. New Delhi: DK Printworld, the Harabhatta Shastri Indological Research Institute.

Baxi, Pratiksha. 2014. *Public Secrets of Law: Rape Trials in India.* New Delhi: Oxford University Press.

Bearn, Gordon C. F. 1977. *Waking to Wonder: Wittgenstein's Existential Investigations.* New York: State University of New York Press.

Becker, Alton. 1995. *Beyond Translation: Essays towards a Modern Philology.* Ann Arbor: University of Michigan Press.

Becker, Peter, and William Clark. 2001. Introduction to *Little Tools of Knowledge: Historical Essays on Academic and Bureaucratic Practices,* edited by Peter Becker and William Clark, 1–29. Ann Arbor: University of Michigan Press.

Benjamin, Walter. 1969. "The Work of Art in the Age of Mechanical Reproduction." In *Illuminations,* edited by Hannah Arendt, translated by Harry Zahn, 217–51. New York: Random House.

———. 2008. *The Work of Art in the Age of Its Technical Reproducibility and Other Writings on Media.* Edited by Michael W. Jennings, Brigid Doherty, and Thomas Y. Levin. Cambridge, Mass.: Harvard University Press.

Bennett, Lynn. 1983. *Dangerous Wives and Sacred Sisters: Social and Symbolic Roles of High-Caste Women in Nepal.* New York: Columbia University Press.

Benoist, Jocelyn. 2010. *Concepts: Introduction à l'analyse.* Paris: Les éditions CERF.

———. 2018. "How Social Are Our Concepts?" Paper presented at the Seminar on Concepts, Harvard University, April 3–4, 2018.

Benveniste, Emile. 1971a. "Active and Middle Voice in the Verb." In *Problems in General Linguistics,* 145–52. Miami, Fl.: University of Miami Press.

———. 1971b. "The Nature of Pronouns." In *Problems in General Linguistics,* 217–22. Miami, Fl.: University of Miami Press.

Bergson, Henri. 1911. *Laughter: An Essay on the Meaning of the Comic.* London: Macmillan.

———. 1990. *Matter and Memory.* Translated by N. M. Paul and W. S. Palmer. New York: Zone Books.

Berlant, Lauren. 2007. "Slow Death (Sovereignty, Obesity, Lateral Agency)." *Critical Inquiry* 33 (4): 754–80.

———. 2011. *Cruel Optimism.* Durham, N.C.: Duke University Press.

Bersani, Leo. 2008. "The Power of Evil and the Power of Love." In *Intimacies,* edited by Leo Bersani and Adam Philips, 57–89. Chicago: University of Chicago Press.

Berthomé, François, and Michael Houseman. 2010. "Ritual and Emotions: Moving Relations, Patterned Effusions." *Religion and Society* 1: 57–75.

Bhabha, Homi K. 1995. "By Bread Alone: Signs of Violence in the Mid-nineteenth Century." In *Location of Culture,* 198–212. London: Routledge.

Bhatia, Vijay Kumar. 1993. *Analysing Genre: Language Use in Professional Settings.* New York: Longman.

Bhattacharya, Kamaleswar. 1985. "Nagarjuna's Arguments against Motion." *Journal of the International Association of Buddhist Studies* 8 (1): 7–16.

Bhava-bhuti. 2007. *Rama's Last Act (Uttararamacharita).* Translated by Sheldon Pollock. New York: New York University Press.

Biehl, João. 2013. *Vita: Life in a Zone of Social Abandonment.* Berkeley: University of California Press.

Bloch, Maurice. 2013. "What Kind of 'Is' Is Sahlins' 'Is'?" *HAU: Journal of Ethnographic Theory* 3 (2): 253–57.

Bourdieu, Pierre. 1984. *Distinction: A Social Critique of the Judgment of Taste.* Translated by Richard Nice. Cambridge, Mass.: Harvard University Press.

———. 1990. *The Logic of Practice.* Cambridge: Polity.

Bouveresse, Jacque. 2008. "Wittgenstein's Critique of Frazer." In *Wittgenstein and Reason*, edited by John Preston, 1–21. Oxford: Blackwell Publishing.

Brandel, Andrew. 2016. "City of Letters: The Making of Literary Life in Berlin." PhD diss., Johns Hopkins University.

———. 2018. "A Poet in the Field: The Companionship of Literature and Anthropology." *Anthropology of This Century* 21.

Brandom, Robert. 2008. *Making It Explicit: Reasoning, Representing and Discursive Commitment.* Cambridge, Mass.: Harvard University Press.

Braudel, Fernand. 1979. *The Structure of Everyday Life.* Vol. 1 of *Civilization and Capitalism, 15th–18th Century.* Translated by Sten Reynolds. Berkeley: University of California Press.

Bush, J. Andrew. Forthcoming. *Islam and Intimacy in Kurdistan.* Stanford, Calif.: Stanford University Press.

Butler, Judith. 2016. "Rethinking Vulnerability and Resistance." In *Vulnerability in Resistance*, edited by Judith Butler, Zenep Gambetti, and Laticia Sabsay, 12–27. Durham, N.C.: Duke University Press.

Cameron, Sharon. 2007. "Representing Grief: Emerson's 'Experience.'" In *Impersonality: Seven Essays*, 53–79. Chicago: University of Chicago Press.

Candotti, Maria Piera, and Tiziana Pontillo. 2013. "The Earlier Pāṇinian Tradition on the Imperceptible Sign." In *Signless Signification in Ancient India and Beyond*, edited by Tiziana Pontillo and Maria Piera Candotti, 99–154. London: Anthem Press.

Canfield, Jon. 2004. "Pretence and the Inner." In *The Third Wittgenstein: The Post-Investigations Works*, edited by Danièle Moyal-Sharrock, D. Z. Phillips, and Mario von der Ruhr, 168–83. London: Routledge.

Canguilhem, Georges. 1991. *The Normal and the Pathological.* Translated by Carolyn R. Fawcett. New York: Zone Books.

Carsten, Janet. 2004. *After Kinship.* Cambridge: Cambridge University Press.

———. 2013. "What Kinship Does—and How." *HAU: Journal of Ethnographic Theory* 3 (2): 245–51.

———. 2018. "House-Lives as Ethnography/Biography." *Social Anthropology* 26 (1): 103–14.

Cassin, Barbara, Emily Apter, Jacques Lezra, and Michael Wood, eds. 2014. *Dictionary of Untranslatables: A Philosophical Lexicon.* Princeton, N.J.: Princeton University Press.

Caton, Steven. 1986. "'Salam Tahiyah': Greetings from the Highlands of Yemen." *American Ethnologist* 13 (2): 290–308.

———. 2006. *Yemen Chronicle: An Anthropology of War and Mediation.* New York: Hill and Wang.

———. 2010. "Abu Ghraib and the Problem of Evil." In *Ordinary Ethics: Anthropology, Language and Action*, edited by Michael Lambek, 165–87. New York: Fordham University Press.

Cavell, Stanley. 1962. "The Availability of Wittgenstein's Later Philosophy." *Philosophical Review* 71 (1): 71–93.

———. 1969a. "Ending the Waiting Game: A Reading of Beckett's *Endgame*." In *Must We Mean What We Say? A Book of Essays*, 115–62. Oxford: Oxford University Press.

———. 1969b. *Must We Mean What We Say? A Book of Essays.* Oxford: Oxford University Press.

———. 1979. *The Claim of Reason: Wittgenstein, Skepticism, Morality, and Tragedy.* Oxford: Oxford University Press.

———. 1981. *Pursuits of Happiness: The Hollywood Comedy of Remarriage.* Cambridge, Mass.: Harvard University Press.

———. 1984. "Existentialism and Analytical Philosophy." In *Themes Out of School: Effects and Causes*, 195–234. San Francisco: North Point.

———. 1987. *Disowning Knowledge: In Seven Plays of Shakespeare.* Cambridge: Cambridge University Press.

———. 1988a. "Being Odd, Getting Even: Descartes, Emerson, Poe." In *In Quest of the Ordinary: Lines of Skepticism and Romanticism.* Chicago: University of University Press.

———. 1988b. "The Uncanniness of the Ordinary." In *In Quest of the Ordinary: Lines of Skepticism and Romanticism.* Chicago: University of Chicago Press.

———. 1989. "Declining Decline: Wittgenstein as a Philosopher of Culture." In *This New Yet Unapproachable America: Lectures after Emerson after Wittgenstein*, 29–77. Chicago: University of Chicago Press.

———. 1990a. "The Argument of the Ordinary: Scenes of Instruction in Wittgenstein and in Kripke." In *Conditions Handsome and Unhandsome: The Constitution of Emersonian Perfectionism*, 64–101. Chicago: University of Chicago Press.

———. 1990b. *Conditions Handsome and Unhandsome: The Constitution of Emersonian Perfectionism*. Chicago: University of Chicago Press.

———. 1992. *The Senses of Walden*. Chicago: University of Chicago Press.

———. 1994. *A Pitch of Philosophy: Autobiographical Exercises*. Cambridge, Mass.: Harvard University Press.

———. 1995. "Notes and Afterthoughts on the Opening of Wittgenstein's *Investigations*." In *Philosophical Passages: Wittgenstein, Emerson, Austin, Derrida*, 125–87. Oxford: Blackwell.

———. 1996. *Contesting Tears: The Hollywood Melodrama of the Unknown Woman*. Chicago: University of Chicago Press.

———. 1997. "Comments on Veena Das's Essay 'Language and Body: Transactions in the Construction of Pain.'" *Daedalus* 125 (1): 93–99.

———. 2003. "Finding and Founding: Taking Steps in Emerson's 'Experience.'" In *Emerson's Transcendental Etudes*, 110–41. Stanford, Calif.: Stanford University Press.

———. 2005a. "Fred Astaire Asserts the Right to Praise." In *Philosophy the Day after Tomorrow*, 61–82. Cambridge, Mass.: Harvard University Press.

———. 2005b. "Performative and Passionate Utterance." In *Philosophy the Day after Tomorrow*, 155–92. Cambridge, Mass.: Harvard University Press.

———. 2005c. *Philosophy the Day after Tomorrow*. Cambridge, Mass.: Harvard University Press.

———. 2005d. "Thoreau Thinks of Ponds, Heidegger of Rivers." In *Philosophy the Day after Tomorrow*, 215–36. Cambridge, Mass.: Harvard University Press.

———. 2005e. "The World as Things." In *Philosophy the Day after Tomorrow*. Cambridge, Mass.: Harvard University Press.

———. 2007. Foreword to *Life and Words: Violence and the Descent into the Ordinary*, by Veena Das, ix–xvi. Berkeley: University of California Press.

———. 2010. *Little Did I Know: Excerpts from Memory*. Palo Alto, Calif.: Stanford University Press.

Chaganti, Sruti. 2018. "Norm, Concept, and Materiality of Land: Case Law on Land Acquisition." Unpublished manuscript.

Chakrabarti, Arindam. 2013. "Now Kali, I Shall Eat You Up: On the Logic of the Vocative." In *Ramchandra Gandhi: The Man and His Philosophy*, edited by A. Raghuramaraj, 194–207. New Delhi: Routledge.

Chapin, Mac, Zachary Lamb, and Bill Threlkeld. 2005. "Mapping Indigenous Lands." *Annual Review of Anthropology* 34: 610–38.

Chatterji, Roma. 1986. "The Voyage of the Hero: The Self and the Other in One Narrative Tradition of Purulia." *Contributions to Indian Sociology* 19: 95–114.

———. 2012. *Speaking with Pictures: Folk Art and the Narrative Tradition in India*. New Delhi: Routledge.

Chatterji, Roma, and Deepak Mehta. 1995. "A Case Study of a Communal Riot in Dharavi, Bombay." *Religion and Society* 42 (4): 5–26.

———. 2007. *Living with Violence: An Anthropology of Events and Everyday Life.* New Delhi: Routledge.

Chaturvedi, R. 1998. "Witchcraft and Other Minds." M.Phil. diss., University of Delhi.

Chauviré, Christiane, and Jérôme Sackur. 2003. *Le vocabulaire de Wittgenstein.* Paris: Ellipses.

Chirol, Valentine Ignatius. (1910) 2010. *Indian Unrest.* Droid ebooks.

Chowdhry, Prem. 1997a. *Contentious Marriages, Eloping Couples.* New Delhi: Oxford University Press.

———. 1997b. "Enforcing Cultural Codes: Gender and Violence in Northern India." *Economic and Political Weekly* 32 (19): 1019–28.

Cioffi, Frank. (1987) 1998. "Wittgenstein and the Fire Festivals." In *Wittgenstein on Freud and Frazer,* by Frank Cioffi, 80–106. Cambridge: Cambridge University Press.

———. 1990. "The Inaugural Address: Wittgenstein and Obscurantism." *Proceedings of the Aristotelian Society* S64: S1–23.

Clasteres, Pierre. 1974. *Societe contre l'etat.* Paris Les Editions Minuit.

Clément, Fabrice. 1996. "Une nouvelle 'forme de vie' pour les sciences sociales." *Revue européenne des sciences sociales* 34 (106): 156–68.

Clifford, James. 1990. "On Ethnographic Allegory." In *Writing Culture: The Poetics and Politics of Ethnography,* edited by James Clifford and George E. Marcus, 98–122. New Delhi: Oxford University Press.

Clooney, Francis X. 1997. "What's a God? The Quest for the Right Understanding of Devatā in Brāhmaṅical Ritual Theory (Mīmāṃsā)." *International Journal of Hindu Studies* 1 (2): 337–85.

———. 2010. *Hindu God, Christian God: How Reason Helps Break Down the Boundaries between Religions.* London: Oxford University Press.

Coetzee, John Maxwell. 1982. *Waiting for the Barbarians.* London: Penguin.

———. 2007. *Diary of a Bad Year.* London: Penguin.

Collingwood, R. G. (1940) 2014. *An Essay on Metaphysics.* New York: Oxford University Press.

Collins, Daryl, Jonathan Murduch, Stuart Rutherford, and Orlanda Ruthven. 2009. *Portfolios of the Poor: How the World's Poor Live on $2 a Day.* Princeton, N.J.: Princeton University Press.

Conant, James. 2005. "Stanley Cavell's Wittgenstein." *Harvard Review of Philosophy* 13 (1): 51–65.

Conant, James, and Cora Diamond. 2004. "On Reading the Tractatus Resolutely: Reply to Meredith Williams and Peter Sullivan." In *Wittgenstein's Lasting Significance,* edited by Max Kolbel and Bernhard Weiss, 46–99. London: Routledge.

Crapanzano, Vincent. 1985. *Waiting: The Whites of South Africa*. New York: Random House.

Crary, Alice. 2000. "Wittgenstein's Philosophy in Relation to Political Thought." In *The New Wittgenstein*, edited by Alice Crary and Rupert Read, 128–56. London: Routledge.

———. 2007. *Beyond Moral Judgment*. Cambridge, Mass.: Harvard University Press.

Critchley, Simon. 2005. "Cavell's 'Romanticism' and Cavell's Romanticism." In *Contending with Stanley Cavell*, edited by Russell B. Goodman, 37–54. New York: Oxford University Press.

da Col, Giovanni, and Stephan Palmié, ed. Forthcoming. *The Mythology in Our Language: Remarks on Frazer's "Golden Bough."* Translated by Stephan Palmié. Chicago: HAU Books.

Daniel, E. Valentine. 1996. *Charred Lullabies: Chapters in an Anthropography of Violence*. Princeton, N.J.: Princeton University Press.

Darwall, Stephen. 2006. *The Second-Person Standpoint: Morality, Respect, and Accountability*. Cambridge, Mass.: Harvard University Press.

Das, Jishnu, and Jeffrey Hammer. 2004. "Strained Mercy: Quality of Medical Care in Delhi." *Economic and Political Weekly* 39 (9): 951–61.

Das, Veena. 1976. "Masks and Faces: An Essay on Punjabi Kinship." *Contributions to Indian Sociology* 10 (1): 1–30.

———. 1977. *Structure and Cognition: Aspects of Hindu Caste and Ritual*. New Delhi: Oxford University Press.

———. 1983. "Language of Sacrifice." *Man* 18 (3): 445–62.

———. 1990a. *Mirrors of Violence: Communities, Riots and Survivors in South Asia*. New Delhi: Oxford University Press.

———. 1990b. "Our Work to Cry: Your Work to Listen." In *Mirrors of Violence: Communities, Riots and Survivors in South Asia*, 345–99. New Delhi: Oxford University Press.

———. 1990c. "Voices of Children." In "Another India." Special issue, *Daedalus*: 48–65

———. 1995a. *Critical Events: An Anthropological Perspective on Contemporary India*. New Delhi: Oxford University Press.

———. 1995b. "Voice as Birth of Culture." *Ethnos* 60 (3–4): 159–81.

———. 1996a. "Sexual Violence, Discursive Formations and the State." *Economic and Political Weekly* 31 (35/37): 2411–23.

———. 1996b. "Violence and the Work of Time." Presented at Plenary Session on Violence. University of Edinburgh, Edinburgh, Scotland.

———. 1997. "Language and Body: Transactions in the Construction of Pain." In *Social Suffering*, edited by Arthur Kleinman, Veena Das, and Margaret Lock, 67–92. Berkeley: University of California Press.

———. 1998a. "Specificities: Official Narratives, Rumour, and the Social Production of Hate." *Social Identities* 4 (1): 1–23.

———. 1998b. "Wittgenstein and Anthropology." *Annual Review of Anthropology* 27: 171–95.

———. 2000. "The Act of Witnessing: Violence, Poisonous Knowledge, and Subjectivity." In *Violence and Subjectivity*, edited by Veena Das, Arthur Kleinman, Mamphela Ramphele, and Pamela Reynolds, 205–25. Berkeley: University of California Press.

———. 2004. "The Signature of the State: The Paradox of Illegibility." In *Anthropology in the Margins of the State: Comparative Ethnographies*, edited by Veena Das and Deborah Poole, 225–52. Santa Fe: SAR Press.

———. 2007. *Life and Words: Violence and the Descent into the Ordinary*. Berkeley: University of California Press.

———. 2008. "Violence, Gender and Subjectivity." *Annual Review of Anthropology* 37: 283–99.

———. 2009. "Two Plaits and a Step into the World: A Childhood Remembered." In *Remembered Childhood: Essays in Honour of Andrè Bèteille*. Edited by Malavika Karlekar and Rudrangshu Mukherjee, 196–206. New Delhi: Oxford University Press.

———. 2010a. "Engaging the Life of the Other: Love and Everyday Life." In *Ordinary Ethics: Anthropology, Language and Action*, edited by Michael Lambek, 376–400. New York: Fordham University Press.

———. 2010b. "The Life of Humans and the Life of Roaming Spirits." In *Rethinking the Human*, edited by Michelle Molina and Donald K. Swearer, 31–51. Cambridge, Mass.: Harvard University Press.

———. 2010c. "Moral and Spiritual Striving in the Everyday: To Be a Muslim in Contemporary India." In *Ethical Life in South Asia*, edited by Anand Pandian and Daud Ali, 232–53. Bloomington: Indiana University Press.

———. 2010d. "On the Play of Mirrors." In *Akbar Padamsee: Work in Language*, edited by B. Padamsee and A. Gerimella, 254–65. Mumbai: Marg.

———. 2011a. "State, Citizenship, and the Urban Poor." *Citizenship Studies* 15 (3): 319–33.

———. 2011b. "Time is a Trickster and Other Fleeting Thoughts on Cavell, His Life, His Work." *MLN* 126 (5): 943–53.

———. 2012a. "Ordinary Ethics." In *A Companion to Moral Anthropology*, edited by Didier Fassin, 133–49. Malden, Mass.: Wiley-Blackwell.

———. 2012b. "The Poor in Political Theory." Paper presented at the conference on Political Modernity in the Twenty-First Century. Barcelona, February 20–22.

———. 2012c. "Violence and Nonviolence at the Heart of Hindu Ethics." In *The Oxford Handbook of Religion and Violence*, edited by Mark Jurgensmeyer, Margo Kitts, and Michael Jerryson, 15–40. New York: Oxford University Press.

———. 2014. "Action, Expression, and Everyday Life: Recounting Household Events." In *The Ground Between: Anthropologists Engage Philosophy*, edited by Veena Das, Michael Jackson, Arthur Kleinman, and Bhrigupati Singh, 279–306. Durham, N.C.: Duke University Press.

———. 2015a. *Affliction: Health, Disease, Poverty*. New York: Fordham University Press.

———. 2015b. "Naming beyond Pointing: Singularity, Relatedness, and the Foreshadowing of Death." In "On Names in South Asia: Iteration, (Im)propriety, and Dissimulation," edited by Joseph Campbell and Veena Das. Special issue, *SAMAJ*: http://samaj.revues.org/3985.

———. 2015c. "What Does Ordinary Ethics Look Like?" In *Four Lectures on Ethics: Anthropological Perspectives*, edited by Michael Lambek, Veena Das, Didier Fassin, and Webb Keane, 53–126. Chicago: HAU Books.

———. 2016. "Ritual Action and Grammatical Action: Life Lived in Language." Invited public lecture, March 24, 2016, Amherst College, Amherst, Mass.

———. 2017. "The Grains of Experience." *Somatosphere*, February 10, 2017. http://somatosphere.net/forumpost/the-grains-of-experience.

———. 2018. "Ethics, Self-Knowledge, and Life Taken as a Whole." *HAU: Journal of Ethnographic Theory* 8 (3): 537–49.

———. 2019. "Vernacular Concepts and the Physiognomy of Words." In "First Book Symposium on Returning Life: Language, Life Force and History in Kilimanjaro," edited by Knut Christian Myhre. Special issue, *Social Analysis* 63 (1): 103–22.

Das, Veena, and R. S. Bajwa. 1994. "Community and Violence in Contemporary Punjab." In "Violences et Non-Violences en Inde," edited by D. Vidal, G. Tarabout, and E. Mayer. Special issue, *Purushartha* 16: 245–59.

Das, Veena, and Ranendra Das. 2007. "How the Body Speaks." In *Subjectivity: Ethnographic Investigations*, edited by João Biehl, Byron Good, and Arthur Kleinman, 66–98. Berkeley: University of California Press.

Das, Veena, Michael Jackson, Arthur Kleinman, and Bhrigupati Singh. 2014. "Experiments between Anthropology and Philosophy: Affinities and Antagonisms." Introduction to *The Ground Between: Anthropologists Engage Philosophy*, edited by Veena Das, Michael Jackson, Arthur Kleinman, and Bhrigupati Singh, 1–26. Durham, N.C.: Duke University Press.

Das, Veena, and Deborah Poole. 2004. "State and Its Margins: Comparative Ethnographies." In *Anthropology in the Margins of the State*, edited by Veena Das and Deborah Poole, 225–52. Santa Fe: SAR Press.

Das, Veena, and Shalini Randeria. 2015. "Politics of the Urban Poor: Aesthetics, Ethics, Volatility, Precarity: An Introduction to Supplement 11." *Current Anthropology* 56 (S11): S3–S14.

Das, Veena, and Michael Walton. 2015. "Political Leadership and the Urban Poor." *Current Anthropology* 56 (S11): S44–S54.

Datta, Ayone. 2012. *The Illegal City: Spaces, Law, and Gender in a Delhi Squatter Settlement*. London: Ashgate.

Davis, Richard H. 1997. *Lives of Indian Images*. Princeton, N.J.: Princeton University Press.

Day, Sophie. 2018. "An Experiment in Story-Telling: Reassembling the House in Ladakh." *Social Anthropology* 26 (1): 88–102.

De Certeau, Michel. 1984. *The Practice of Everyday Life*. Translated by Steven Rendall (Berkeley: University of California Press).

DelConte, Matt. 2007. "A Further Study of Present Tense Narration: The Absentee Narratee and Four-Wall Present Tense in Coetzee's *Waiting for the Barbarians* and *Disgrace*." *Journal of Narrative Theory* 37 (3): 427–46.

Department of Urban Development. 2006. *City Development Plan*. Delhi: Government of Delhi.

Descola, Philippe. 1992. "Societies of Nature and the Nature of Society." In *Conceptualizing Society*, edited by Adam Kuper, 107–26. New York: Routledge.

———. 2009. "Human Natures." *Social Anthropology* 17 (2): 145–57.

de Vries, Hent. 2001. "Of Miracles and Special Effects." *Issues in Contemporary Philosophy of Religion* 50 (1–3): 41–56.

Dewey, John. 1922. *Human Nature and Conduct*. New York: Henry Holt.

Dhanda, Amita. 2000. *Legal Order and Mental Disorder*. New Delhi: Sage Publications.

Diamond, Cora, ed. 1976. *Wittgenstein's Lectures on the Foundations of Mathematics, Cambridge 1939*. Ithaca, N.Y.: Cornell University Press.

———. 1983. "Having a Rough Story about What Moral Philosophy Is." *New Literary History* 15 (1): 155–69.

———. 1988a. "Losing Your Concepts." *Ethics* 98 (2): 255–77.

———. 1988b. "Throwing Away the Ladder." *Philosophy* 63 (243): 5–27.

———. 1989. "Rules: Looking in the Right Place." In *Wittgenstein: Attention to Particulars*, edited by D. Z. Philips and Peter Winch, 12–35. New York: St. Martin's Press.

———. 1996. "'We Are Perpetually Moralists': Iris Murdoch, Fact and Value in Moral Philosophy." In *Iris Murdoch and the Search for Human Goodness*, edited by Maria Antonaccio and William Schweiker, 79–110. Chicago: University of Chicago Press.

———. 1997. "Moral Differences and Distances: Some Questions." In *Commonality and Particularity in Ethics*, edited by Lillia Alanen, Sara Heinämaa, and Thomas Wallgren, 197–234. New York: St. Martin's Press.

———. 2000. "Ethics, Imagination and the Method of Wittgenstein's *Tractatus*." In *The New Wittgenstein*, edited by Alice Crary and Rupert Read, 149–73. London: Routledge.

———. 2004. "Crisscross Philosophy." In *Wittgenstein at Work: Method in Philosophical Investigations*, edited by Erick Ammaler and Eugene Fischer, 201–20. New York: Routledge.

———. 2006. "The Difficulty of Reality and the Difficulty of Philosophy." In *Reading Cavell*, edited by Alice Crary and Sanford Shieh, 98–118. London: Routledge.

———. 2019. *Reading Wittgenstein with Anscombe, Going on to Ethics.* Cambridge, Mass.: Harvard University Press.

Donatelli, Piergiorgio. 2015. "Perfectionist Returns to the Ordinary." *MLN* 130 (5): 1023–39.

———. 2019. "The Social and the Ordinary." *Iride* 32 (86): 41–55.

Dumont, Louis. (1969) 1980. *Homo Hierarchicus: The Caste System and Its Implications.* Chicago: University of Chicago Press.

———. 1992. *Essays on Individualism: Modern Ideology in Anthropological Perspective.* Chicago: University of Chicago Press.

Durkheim, Émile. (1912) 1995. *The Elementary Forms of Religious Life.* Translated by Karen E. Fields. London: Oxford University Press.

———. 1982. *The Rules of Sociological Method and Selected Texts on Sociology and Its Method.* Edited by Steven Lukes. Translated by W. D. Halls. New York: Macmillan.

Dutta, Debolina, and Oishik Sircar. 2013. "India's Winter of Discontent: Some Feminist Dilemmas in the Wake of a Rape." *Feminist Studies* 39 (1): 293–306.

Eckert, Julia. 2006. "From Subjects to Citizens: Legalism from Below and the Homogenization of the Legal Sphere." *Journal of Legal Pluralism and Unofficial Law* 53–54: 45–57.

Emerson, Ralph W. (1844) 1969. "Experience." In *Essays: Second Series; Facsimile of First Editions*, 49–86. Columbus, Ohio: Charles E. Merrill Publishing Company.

Erard, Yves. 2019. "Quand exprime se faire: Les énoncés passionnés de Cavell, une expression entre Austin et Wittgenstein." Unpublished manuscript. 15 pages.

Erasmus. 1560. *The Civility of Childhood.* London. (Translation from Latin of *De cilitate morum puerilium.*)

Evans, Gareth. 1982. *The Varieties of Reference.* Edited by John Mc Dowell. London: Clarendon Press.

Evans-Pritchard, Edward Evan. 1936. "Zande theology." In *Sudan Notes and Records* 1: 5–46.

———. (1937) 1976. *Witchcraft, Oracles and Magic among the Azande.* Oxford: Clarendon.

———. 1940. *The Nuer: A Description of the Modes of Livelihood and Political Institutions of a Nilotic People.* Oxford: Clarendon.

———. (1956) 1970. *Nuer Religion.* Oxford: Clarendon.

Farge, Arlette, and Michel Foucault. 2014. *Le Dèsordre des Families: Lettres de Cachet des Archives de la Bastille au XVIII^e siècle*. Paris: Gallimard.

Fassin, Didier. 2007. *When Bodies Remember: Experiences and Politics of AIDS in South Africa*. Berkeley: University of California Press.

———. 2010. "Ethics of Survival: A Democratic Approach to the Politics of Life." *Humanity: An International Journal of Human Rights* 1 (1): 81–95.

———. 2013. *Enforcing Order: An Ethnography of Urban Policing*. New York: Polity.

———. 2014. "True Life, Real Lives: Revisiting the Boundaries between Ethnography and Fiction." *American Ethnologist* 4 (1): 40–55.

———. 2018. *Life: A Critical User's Manual*. London: Polity.

Faubion, James D. 2011. *An Anthropology of Ethics*. Cambridge: Cambridge University Press.

Favret-Saada, Jeanne. 1977. *Les mots, Ia mort, les sorts*. Paris: Gallimard.

———. 1980. *Deadly Words: Witchcraft in the Bocage*. Translated by Catherine Cullen. Cambridge: Cambridge University Press.

———. 2012. "Being Affected." *HAU: Journal of Ethnographic Theory* 2 (1): 435–45.

———. 2015. *The Anti-witch*. Translated by Matthew Carey. Chicago: HAU Books.

Filliozat, Pierre-Sylvain. 1991–1992. "Ellipsis, Lopa and Anuvrtti." *Annals of the Bhandarkar Oriental Research Institute* 72/73 (1/4): 675–87.

Floyd, Juliet. 2018. "Lebensformen: Living Logic." In *Language, Form(s) of Life and Logic*, edited by Christian Martin. Boston: Walter de Gruyer GmbH.

Foucault, Michel. 1988. *Madness and Civilization: A History of Insanity in the Age of Reason*. Translated by Richard Howard. New York: Vintage Books.

———. 1996. *Foucault Live: Interviews, 1966–84*. Edited by Sylvère Lotringer. Cambridge: MIT Press.

———. 1997. *Ethics, Subjectivity and Truth*. Edited by Paul Rabinow. New York: New Press.

———. 2003. *Abnormal: Lectures at the Collège de France, 1974–1975*. Edited by Valerio Marchetti and Antonella Salomoni. Translated by Graham Burchell. New York: Picador.

———. 2005. *The Hermeneutics of the Subject: Lectures at the College de France, 1981–1982*. Edited and translated by Frédéric Gros. New York: Picador.

———. 2006. *Psychiatric Power: Lectures at the College de France, 1973–1974*. Edited by Lagrange Macmillan. Translated by Graham Burchell. New York: Palgrave Macmillan.

———. 2007. *Security, Territory, Population: Lectures at the Collège de France, 1977–1978*. Edited by Michel Senellart. Translated by Graham Burchell. New York: Picador.

Franco, Jean. 2014. Foreword to *The Day of Shelly's Death: The Poetry and Ethnography of Grief*, xv–xvi. Durham, N.C.: Duke University Press.

Frazer, James. (1922) 2004. *The Golden Bough*. Sioux Falls, S.D.: NuVision Publications.

Freschi, Elisa, and Tiziana Pontillo. 2013. "When One Thing Applies More Than Once: Tantra and Prasaṅga in Śrautasūtra, Mīmāṃsā and Grammar." In *Signless Signification in Ancient India and Beyond*, edited by Tiziana Pontillo and Maria Piera Candotti, 33–98. London: Anthem Press.

Friedander, Eli. 2012. *Walter Benjamin: A Philosophical Portrait*. Cambridge, Mass.: Harvard University Press.

Gandhi, Ajay. 2015. "The Postcolonial Street: Patterns, Modes and Forms." In *Cities in South Asia*, edited by Crispin Bates and Minoru Mio, 265–82. London: Routledge.

Gandhi, Mohandas Karamchand. 1909. *Hind Swaraj*. Vol. 10 of *The Collected Works of Mahatma Gandhi*. New Delhi: Government of India.

———. 1920. "The Practice of Satyagraha." In *Young India*, Vol. 3. Ahmedabad: Navajiwan Publishing House. https://www.mkgandhi.org/swmgandhi/chap03.htm.

———. 1935. *Letter to P. Kodanda Rao*. Vol. 67 of *The Collected Works of Mahatma Gandhi*. New Delhi: Government of India.

Gardiner, Michael. 2000. *Critiques of Everyday Life*. New York: Routledge.

Gellner, Ernest. 1959. *Words and Things: A Critical Account of Linguistic Philosophy and a Study in Ideology*. London: Victor Gollanz.

———. 1970. "Concepts and Society." In *Rationality*, edited by B. R. Wilson, 18–49. Oxford: Blackwell.

Giddens, Anthony. 1992. *The Transformation of Intimacy: Sexuality, Love and Eroticism in Modern Societies*. Cambridge: Polity.

Gilsenan, Michael. 1996. *Lords of the Lebanese Marches: Violence and Narrative in an Arab Society*. Berkeley: University of California Press.

Godelier, Maurice, and Marilyn Strathern. 1991. *Big Men and Great Men: Personifications of Power in Melanesia*. Cambridge: Cambridge University Press.

Goffman, Erving. 1974. *Frame Analysis: An Essay on the Organization of Experience*. New York: Harper and Row.

Gold, Jonathan C. 2007. *The Dharma's Gatekeepers: Sakya Pandita on Buddhist Scholarship in Tibet*. New York: SUNY Press.

Good, M. J. D., P. E. Brodwin, B. Good, and A. Kleinman, eds. 1992. *Pain as Human Experience: An Anthropological Perspective*. Berkeley: University of California Press.

Guha, Ranajit. 1983. *Elementary Aspects of Peasant Insurgency in Colonial India*. New Delhi: Oxford University Press.

Gupta, Akhil. 2012. *Red Tape: Bureaucracy, Structural Violence, and Poverty in India*. Durham, N.C.: Duke University Press.

Habermas, Jurgen. 1995. *Moral Consciousness and Communicative Action.* Translated by Christian Lenhardt and Shierry Weber Nicholsen. Cambridge, Mass.: MIT Press.

Hacker, Peter. M. S. 1992. "Developmental Hypotheses and Perspicuous Representations: Wittgenstein on Frazer's 'Golden Bough.'" *Iyyun: The Jerusalem Philosophical Quarterly* 41: 277–99.

Hadot, Pierre. 1995. *Philosophy as a Way of Life.* Edited by Arnold I. Davidson. Oxford: Blackwell.

———. 2009. *The Present Alone Is Our Happiness: Conversations with Jeannie Carlier and Arnold I. Davidson.* Stanford, Calif.: Stanford University Press.

Hage, Ghassan. 1998. *White Nation: Fantasies of White Supremacy in a Multicultural Society.* New York: Routledge.

———. 2009. "Waiting Out the Crisis: On Stuckedness and Governmentality." In *Waiting,* edited by Ghassan Hage, 97–106. Carlton, Victoria, Australia: Melbourne University Press.

———. 2014. "Eavesdropping on Bourdieu's Philosophers." In *The Ground Between: Anthropologists Engage Philosophy,* edited by Veena Das, Michael Jackson, Arthur Kleinman, and Bhrigupati Singh, 138–58. Durham, N.C.: Duke University Press.

Hakyemez, Serra. 2016. "Lives and Times of Militancy." PhD diss., Johns Hopkins University.

———. 2017. "Margins of the Archive: Torture, Heroism, and the Ordinary in Prison No. 5, Turkey." *Anthropological Quarterly* 90 (1): 107–38.

Hallisey, Charles. 2010. "Between Intuition and Judgment: Moral Creativity in Theravada Buddhist Ethics." In *Ethical Life in South Asia,* edited by Anand Pandian and Daud Ali, 141–53. Bloomington: Indiana University Press.

Han, Clara. 2012. *Life in Debt: Times of Care and Violence in Neoliberal Chile.* Berkeley: University of California Press.

———. 2014. "The Difficulty of Kindness: Boundaries, Time, and the Ordinary." In *The Ground Between: Anthropologists Engage Philosophy,* edited by Veena Das, Michael Jackson, Arthur Kleinman, and Bhrigupati Singh, 71–93. Durham, N.C.: Duke University Press.

———. 2015. "Echoes of Death: Violence, Endurance, and Experience of Loss." *Living and Dying in the Contemporary World: A Compendium,* edited by Veena Das and Clara Han, 493–509. Berkeley: University of California Press.

———. 2018. "Echoes of Death and the Life History Method." Paper presented at the Panel on Kindred Concepts and Family Resemblance, American Ethnological Society Meetings, Philadelphia, Penn., March 18, 2018.

———. Forthcoming. *Seeing Like a Child.* New York: Fordham University Press.

Han, Clara, and Andrew Brandel. 2019. "Genres of Witnessing: Narrative, Violence, Generations." *Ethnos* 1: 1–18.

Han, Clara, and Veena Das. 2015. "Introduction: A Concept Note." In *Living and Dying in the Contemporary World: A Compendium*, edited by Veena Das and Clara Han, 1–38. Berkeley: University of California Press.

Hanks, William F. 2015. "The Space of Translation." In *Translating Worlds: The Epistemological Space of Translation*, edited by Carlo Severi and William F. Hanks, 21–50. Chicago: HAU Books.

Hansen, Miriam B. 2008. "Benjamin's Aura." *Critical Inquiry* 14: 336–75.

Heckel, Emily. 2010. "A Wittgensteinian Defense of Cultural Relativism." *Macalester Journal of Philosophy* 19 (1): Article 3.

Heidegger, Martin. (1927) 1967. *Being and Time*. Translated by J. Macquarrie and E. Robinson. Oxford: Blackwell.

Henn, Alexander. 2014. *Hindu-Catholic Encounters in Goa: Religion, Colonialism, and Modernity*. Bloomington: Indiana University Press.

Highmore, Benjamin. 2002. *Everyday Life and Cultural Theory: An Introduction*. New York: Routledge.

Hill, Harriet. 2006. "The Vernacular Treasure: A Century of Mother-Tongue Bible Translation." *International Bulletin of Missionary Research* 30 (2): 82–88.

Hinton, Alexander Laban. 2013. "The Paradox of Perpetration: A View from the Cambodian Genocide." In *Human Rights at the Crossroads*, edited by Mark Goodale, 153–62. New York: Oxford University Press.

Hiriyanna, Mysore. (1911) 1972. *Īśāvāsyopaniṣad*. With a commentary by Śankarācārya in Sanskrit. Mysore: Kavyalaya Publishers.

Hirschkind, Charles. 2006. *The Ethical Soundscape: Cassette Sermons and Islamic Counterpublics*. New York: Columbia University Press.

Holbraad, Martin, and Morten Axel Pedersen. 2017. *The Ontological Turn: An Anthropological Exposition*. Cambridge: Cambridge University Press.

Hollis, Martin, and Steven Lukes. 1982. *Rationality and Relativism*. Cambridge, Mass.: MIT Press.

Hollywood, Amy. 2002. "Performativity, Citationality, Ritualization." *History of Religions* 42 (2): 93–115.

Houtsma, Martjin, Thomas A. J. Wetsnik, E. Lévi Provençal, and H. A. R. Gibb. 1993. *E. J. Brill's First Encyclopedia of Islam, 1913–1936*. Leiden: Brill.

Hughes, Robert. 2007. "Riven: Badiou's Ethical Subject and the Event of Art as Trauma." *Postmodern Culture* 27 (3): 1–36.

Hull, Matthew. 2012. *Government of Paper: The Materiality of Bureaucracy in Urban Pakistan*. Berkeley: University of California Press.

Humphrey, Caroline, and James Laidlaw. 1994. *The Archetypal Actions of Ritual: A Theory of Ritual Illustrated by the Jain Act of Worship*. Oxford: Clarendon.

Ibrahim, Amrita. 2013 "'Who Is a Bigger Terrorist than the Police?' Photography as a Politics of Encounter in Delhi's Batla House." *South Asian Popular Culture* 11 (2): 133–44.

Israel, Hephzibah. 2011. *Religious Traditions in Colonial South India: Language, Translation and the Making of Protestant Identity*. Palgrave Studies in Cultural and Intellectual History. New York: Palgrave Macmillan.

Jackson, Michael D. 1987. "On Ethnographic Truth." *Canberra Anthropology* 10 (2): 1–31.

———. 1998. *Minima Ethnographica: Intersubjectivity and the Anthropological Project*. Chicago: University of Chicago Press.

———. 2005. *Existential Anthropology: Events, Exigencies and Effects*. New York: Berghahn.

———. 2009. *The Palm at the End of the Mind: Relatedness, Religiosity, and the Real*. Durham, N.C.: Duke University Press.

———. 2011. *Life within Limits: Well-Being in a World of Want*. Durham, N.C.: Duke University Press.

———. 2015. "Ajala's Heads: Reflections on Anthropology and Philosophy in a West African Setting." In *The Ground Between: Anthropologists Engage Philosophy*, edited by Veena Das, Michael Jackson, Arthur Kleinman, and Bhrigupati Singh, 27–50. Durham, N.C.: Duke University Press.

Jackson, Spencer. 2010. "The Subject of Time in Foucault's Tale of Jouy." *Sub-Stance* 39 (2): 39–51.

Jaimini. 1970–1976. *Mīmāṃsādarśanam, with the Bhāsya of Śabara and the Tantravārttika [1.2–3.8] and Tuptīkāi [4–12] of Kumārila Bhatta*. Edited by K. V. Abhyankar and G. A. Joshi. Trivandrum, India: University of Travancore.

Jakobson, Roman. 1985. *Verbal Art, Verbal Sign, Verbal Time*. Edited by Krystyna Pomorska and Stephen Rudy. Minneapolis: University of Minnesota Press.

James, William. 1890. *Habit*. New York: H. Holt.

Jeffery, Patricia, and Roger Jeffery. 1996. *Don't Marry Me to a Plowman! Women's Everyday Lives in Rural North India*. Boulder, Colo.: Westview Press.

Joas, Hans. 1996. *The Creativity of Action*. Translated by J. Gaines and P. Keast. Chicago: University of Chicago Press.

Johnson, Douglas H. 1982. "Evans-Pritchard, the Nuer, and the Sudan Political Service." *African Affairs* 81 (323): 231–46.

Johnston, Paul. 1993. *Wittgenstein: Rethinking the Inner*. New York: Routledge.

Kapferer, Bruce. 2016. "Comment." *Journal of the Royal Anthropological Institute* 22: 790–95.

Karnad, Girish. 2007. Foreword to *Rama's Last Act (Uttarramacharita)*. Translated by Sheldon Pollock. New York: New York University Press.

Kaur, Ravinder. 2004. "Across Region Marriages: Poverty, Female Migration, and the Sex Ratio." *Economic and Political Weekly* 39 (25): 2595–603.

Kelly, Kristin A. 2003. *Domestic Violence and the Politics of Privacy*. Ithaca, N.Y.: Cornell University Press.

Khan, Naveeda. 2006. "Of Children and Jinn: An Inquiry into an Unexpected Friendship during Uncertain Times." *Cultural Anthropology* 21 (2): 234–64.

———. 2012. *Muslim Becoming: Aspiration and Skepticism in Pakistan*. Durham, N.C.: Duke University Press.

Khare, Ravindra S. 1976. *The Hindu Hearth and Home*. Durham, N.C.: Carolina Academic Press.

Kinsley, David. 1975. *The Sword and the Flute: Kali and Krsna: Dark Visions of the Terrible and the Sublime in Hindu Mythology*. Berkeley: University of California Press.

Kitchin, Rob. 2014. "Big Data, New Epistemologies and Paradigm Shifts." *Big Data & Society* 1 (1): 1–12.

Kleinman, Arthur. 2006. *What Really Matters: Living a Moral Life amidst Uncertainty and Danger*. New York: Oxford University Press.

Kleinman, Arthur, Tu Weiming, and Everett Zhang. 2011. *Governance of Life in Chinese Moral Experiences: The Quest for an Adequate Life*. New York: Routledge.

Kohn, Eduardo. 2013. *How Forests Think: Toward an Anthropology beyond the Human*. Berkeley: University of California Press.

Kolsky, Elizabeth. 2010. "'The Body Evidencing the Crime': Rape on Trial in Colonial India, 1860–1947." *Gender & History* 22 (1): 109–30.

Korsgaard, Christine M. 1996. "The Authority of Reflection." In *The Sources of Normativity*, edited by Onora O'Neill, 90–130. Cambridge: Cambridge University Press.

Kripke, Saul. 1982. *Wittgenstein on Rules and Private Language*. London: Oxford University Press.

Kwan, A., B. Daniels, V. Saria, S. Satyanarayana, R. Subbaraman, A. McDowell, S. Bergkvist et al. 2018. "Variations in the Quality of Tuberculosis Care in Urban India: A Cross-Sectional, Standardized Patient Study in Two Cities." *PLoS Medicine* 15 (9): e1002653.

Kwon, Heonik. 2008. *Ghosts of War in Vietnam*. Cambridge: Cambridge University Press.

———. 2010. "The Ghosts of War and the Ethics of Memory." In *Ordinary Ethics: Anthropology, Language and Action*, edited by Michael Lambek, 400–15. New York: Fordham University Press.

Laidlaw, James. 2013. *The Subject of Virtue: An Anthropology of Ethics and Freedom*. Cambridge: Cambridge University Press.

Lambek, Michael. 2007. "On Catching Up with Oneself: Learning to Know That One Means What One Does." In *Learning Religion: Anthropological Approaches*, edited by David Berliner and Ramon Sarró, 65–82. Oxford: Berghahn.

———. 2010. "Toward an Ethics of the Act." In *Ordinary Ethics: Anthropology, Language and Action*, edited by Michael Lambek, 1–39. New York: Fordham University Press.

———. 2014. "The Interpretation of Lives or Life as Interpretation: Cohabiting with Spirits in the Malagasy World." *American Ethnologist* 41 (3): 491–50.

Lambek, Michael, Veena Das, Didier Fassin, and Webb Keane, eds. 2015. *Four Lectures on Ethics: Anthropological Perspectives*. Chicago: HAU Books.

Langer, Lawrence T. 1991. *Holocaust Testimonies: The Ruins of Memory*. New Haven, Conn.: Yale University Press.

———. 1997. "The Alarmed Vision: Social Suffering and Holocaust Atrocity." In *Social Suffering*, edited by Arthur Kleinman, Veena Das, and Margaret Lock, 47–67. Berkeley: University of California Press.

Larsen, Timothy. 2014. *The Slain God: Anthropologists and the Christian Faith*. Oxford: Oxford University Press.

Larsen, Soren C., and Jay T. Johnson. 2012. "In Between Worlds: Place, Experience, and Research in Indigenous Geography." *Journal of Cultural Geography* 29 (1): 1–13.

Latour, Bruno. 2005. *Reassembling the Social: An Introduction to Actor-Network Theory*. Oxford: Oxford University Press.

———. 2010. *The Making of Law: An Ethnography of the Conseil d'État*. London: Polity.

Laugier, Sandra. 2001. "Óu se trouvent les règles." *Archives de Philosophie* 64: 505–24.

———. 2011. "Introduction to the French Edition of *Must We Mean What We Say?*" *Critical Inquiry* 37 (4): 627–51.

———. 2015. "Voice as Form of Life and Life Form." In "Wittgenstein and Forms of Life." Special issue, *Nordic Wittgenstein Review* (October): 63–82.

———. 2016. "Politics of Vulnerability and Responsibility for Ordinary Others." *Critical Horizons* 17 (2): 207–23.

———. 2017. "Concepts of the Ordinary." Paper presented at Panel on Concepts, Experience and the Claims to the Real, American Anthropological Association, Washington, D.C., November 30, 2017.

———. 2018a. "The Vulnerability of Reality: Austin, Normativity, and Excuses." In *Interpreting J. L. Austin: Critical Essays*, edited by Savas Tsohatzidis, 119–41. Cambridge: Cambridge University Press.

———. 2018b. "What Matters: The Ethics and Aesthetics of Importance." In *Stanley Cavell on Aesthetic Understanding: Philosophers in Depth*, edited by G. L. Hagberg, 167–95. London: Palgrave Macmillan.

———. Forthcoming. "Afterword: On an Anthropological Tone in Philosophy." Translated by Daniela Ginzburg. In *The Mythology in Our Language: Remarks* on *Frazer*, edited by Giovanni Da Col and Stephan Palmié, 207–25. Chicago: HAU Books.

Lawrence, Patricia. 1995. "Work of Oracles: Overcoming Political Silences in Mattakalapu." Paper presented at Fifth Srilankan Conference, Indiana.

Leach, Edmund. 1989–1990. "Masquerade: The Presentation of the Self in Holi-day Life." *Cambridge Journal of Anthropology* 13 (3): 47–69.

Lear, Jonathan. 2008. "The Ethical Thought of J. M. Coetzee." *Raritan* 1 (28): 68–97.

———. 2015. "Waiting with Coetzee." *Raritan* 34 (4): 1–26.

Le Bon, Gustave. (1895) 1960. *The Crowd: A Study of the Popular Mind*. New York: Viking.

Lee, Benjamin. 1997. *Talking Heads: Language, Metalanguage and the Semiotics of Subjectivity*. Durham, N.C.: Duke University Press.

Lévi-Strauss, Claude. 1950. *Introduction à l'oeuvre de Marcel Mauss*. Paris: Presses Universitaires de France.

———. (1962) 1966. *The Savage Mind*. Chicago: University of Chicago Press.

———. 1963. *Structural Anthropology*. Translated by Claire Jacobson and Brooke Grundfest Schoepf. New York: Doubleday Anchor Books.

———. 1964. *Totemism*. Translated by Rodney Needham. London: Merlin Press.

———. (1964) 1969. *The Raw and the Cooked: Introduction to a Science of Mythology*, Vol. 1. New York: Harper and Row.

Lienhardt, Godfrey. 1961. *Divinity and Experience: The Religion of the Dinka*. Oxford: Clarendon.

Lovell, Anne M. 2013. "Tending to the Unseen in Extraordinary Circumstances: On Arendt's Natality and Severe Mental Illness after Hurricane Katrina." *Iride* 26 (3): 563–80.

———. 2014. "What Is Born of Humiliation? A Transmission across the Poverty-Mental-Illness Nexus." Paper presented in the session "Who Is the Subject of Illness? A Discussion of Affliction by Veena Das (Part I)" at the Annual Meetings of the American Anthropological Association, Washington, D.C., December 4, 2014.

Lukes, Steven. 1977. "Some Problems about Rationality." In *Essay in Social Theory*, 122–74. London: Macmillan.

Lutgendorf, Philip. 1997. "Monkey in the Middle: The Status of Hanuman in Popular Hinduism." *Religion* 27 (4): 311–32.

Lutz, Catherine A., and Lila Abu-Lughod, eds. 1990. *Language and the Politics of Emotion*. Cambridge: Cambridge University Press.

Lutz, Catherine A., and Geoffrey M. White. 1986. "The Anthropology of Emotions." *Annual Review Anthropology* 15: 405–36.

Mahmood, Saba. 2005. *Politics of Piety: The Islamic Revival and the Feminist Subject*. Princeton, N.J.: Princeton University Press.

Makine, Andreï. 2013. *Brief Loves that Live Forever: A Novel.* Minneapolis: Graywolf Press.

Malik, Aditya. 2015. "The Darbar of Goludev: Possession, Petitions, and Modernity." In *The Law of Possession: Ritual, Healing, and the Secular State,* edited by William Sax and Helene Basu, 193–225. New York: Oxford University Press.

Mankekar, Purnima. 1997. "'To Whom Does Ameena Belong?' Towards a Feminist Analysis of Childhood and Nationhood in Contemporary India." *Feminist Review* 56 (1): 26–60.

Marrati, Paola. 2011. "Childhood and Philosophy." *MLN* 126 (5): 954–61.

Mathur, Nayanika. 2016. *Paper Tiger: The Everyday Life of the State in the Indian Himalaya.* Cambridge: Cambridge University Press.

Maunaguru, Sidharthan. 2019. *Marrying for a Future: Transnational Srilankan Tamil Marriages in the Shadow of War.* Seattle: University of Seattle Press.

McDowell, John Henry. 1996. *Mind and World.* Cambridge, Mass.: Harvard University Press.

———. 1998. *Meaning, Knowledge and Reality.* Cambridge, Mass.: Harvard University Press.

———. 2000. "Non-cognitivism and Rule-Following." In *The New Wittgenstein,* edited by Alice Crary and Rupert Read, 38–51. London: Routledge.

Mehta, Deepak. 2000. "Circumcision, Body, Masculinity: The Ritual Wound and Collective Violence." In *Violence and Subjectivity,* edited by Veena Das, Arthur Kleinman, Mamphela Ramphele, and Pamela Reynolds, 79–102. Berkeley: University of California Press.

———. 2010. "Words that Wound: Archiving Hate in the Making of Hindu-Indian and Muslim-Pakistan in Bombay." In *Beyond Crisis: Re-evaluating Pakistan,* edited by Naveeda Khan, 315–44. New Delhi: Routledge.

———. 2015. "The Ayodhya Dispute: The Absent Mosque, State of Emergency and the Jural Deity." *Journal of Material Culture* 20 (4): 397–414.

———. 2019. "Crowds, Mob and the Law: The Delhi Rape Case." *Contributions to Indian Sociology* 53 (1): 158–83.

Mody, Perveez. 2008. *The Intimate State: Love Marriage and the Law in Delhi.* New Delhi: Routledge.

Mohammad, Hayder Al-. 2010. "Towards an Ethics of Being-With: Intertwinements of Life in Post-Invasion Basra." *Ethnos: Journal of Anthropology* 75 (4): 425–46.

Mookherjee, Nayanika. 2015. *The Spectral Wound. Sexual Violence, Public Memories, and the Bangladesh War of 1971.* Durham, N.C.: Duke University Press.

Moran, Richard. 2001. *Authority and Estrangement: An Essay on Self-knowledge.* Cambridge, Mass.: Harvard University Press.

Motta, Marco. 2016. "Jouer les esprits. Vivre au rythme de Yuganga à Zanzibar." PhD diss., Université de Lausanne, Faculté des sciences sociales et politiques.

———. 2017. "L'esprit qui ne dit pas son nom. Un rituel de possession laborieux à Zanzibar [focus]." *Terrain: Anthropologie & sciences humaines* 68: 108–13.

———. 2019. *Esprits fragiles. Réparer les liens ordinaires à Zanzibar.* Lausanne, Switzerland: BSN Press.

Moyal-Sharrock, Danièle, ed. 2004. *The Third Wittgenstein: The Post Investigations Works.* Aldershot, U.K.: Ashgate Wittgensteinian Studies.

———. 2009. "Introduction." *Philosophia* 37 (4): 557–62.

Mulla, Sameena. 2014. *The Violence of Care: Rape Victims, Forensic Nurses, and Sexual Assault Intervention.* New York: New York University Press.

Murata, Sachiko, and William C. Chittick. 1994. *The Vision of Islam.* New York: Paragon Press.

Murdoch, Iris. 1956. "Vision and Choice in Morality." *Proceedings of the Aristotelian Society* 30 (supp.): 35–58.

Myhre, Knut Christian. 2018. *Returning Life: Language, Life Force, and History in Kilimanjaro.* Oxford: Berghann.

Nagar, Amrit Lal. 2011. *Seth Bankemal.* [In Hindi.] New Delhi: Rajkamal and Sons.

Nagarjuna. 2018. *Crushing the Categories (Vaidalyaprakarana).* Introduction, translation, and commentary by Jan Westerhoff. New York and Sommerville, Mass.: Columbia University and Wisdom Publications.

Nandy, Ashis. 1990. "The Politics of Secularism and the Recovery of Religious Tolerance." In *Mirrors of Violence: Communities, Riots and Survivors*, edited by Veena Das, 69–93. New Delhi: Oxford University Press.

Needham, Rodney. 1972. *Belief, Language, and Experience.* Oxford: Blackwell.

Nida, Eugene Albert, and Charles Russell Taber. 2003. *The Theory and Practice of Translation.* Leiden, Netherlands: Brill.

Nielsen, Morton, and Nigel Rapport, eds. 2018. *The Composition of Anthropology: How Anthropological Texts Are Written.* New York: Routledge.

Nietzsche, Friedrich. 1961. *Thus Spoke Zarathustra: A Book for Everyone and No One.* Translated by R. Hollingdale. London: Penguin Classics.

Nieuwenhuys, Olga. 1996. "The Paradox of Child Labor and Anthropology." *Annual Review of Anthropology* 25: 237–51.

Oberman, Michelle. 1994. "Turning Girls into Women: Re-evaluating Modern Statutory Rape Law." *Journal of Criminal Law & Criminology* 85 (1): 15–79.

Palmié, Stephan. 2018. "When Is a Thing? Transduction and Immediacy in Afro-Cuban Ritual; or, ANT in Matanzas, Cuba, Summer of 1948." *Comparative Studies in Society and History* 60 (4): 786–809.

———. Forthcoming. "Translation is Not Explanation: Remarks on the Intellectual History and Context of Wittgenstein's Remarks on Frazer." In *The Mythology in Our Language: Remarks on Frazer's Golden Bough*, edited by

Giovanni da Col and Stephan Palmié, translated by Stephan Palmié, 1–27. Chicago: HAU Books.

Pandolfo, Stefania. 2018. *Knot of the Soul: Madness, Psychoanalysis, Islam.* Chicago: University of Chicago Press.

Pargiter, Frederick E., ed. 1913. *The Purana Text of the Dynasties of the Kali Age.* Oxford: Oxford University Press.

Parry, Jonathan. 1989. "On the Moral Perils of Exchange." In *Money and the Morality of Exchange,* edited by Jonathan Parry and Maurice Bloch, 64–94. Cambridge: Cambridge University Press.

———. 1994. *Death in Banaras.* Cambridge: Cambridge University Press.

———. 2001. "Ankalui's Errant Wife: Sex, Marriage, and Industry in Contemporary Chhattisgarh." *Modern Asian Studies Review* 35 (4): 783–820.

Peletz, Michael G. 2001. "Ambivalence in Kinship Since the 1940s." In *Relative Values: Reconfiguring Kinship Studies,* edited by Sarah Franklin and Susan McKinnon, 413–44. Durham, N.C.: Duke University Press.

Perdigon, Sylvain. 2011. "Between the Womb and the Hour: Ethics and Semiotics of Relatedness amongst Palestinian Refugees in Tyre, Lebanon." PhD diss., Johns Hopkins University.

———. 2015. "'For Us It Is Otherwise': Three Sketches on Making Poverty Sensible in the Palestinian Refugee Camps of Lebanon." *Current Anthropology* 56 (S11): S88–S96.

Pinto, Sarah. 2014. *Daughters of Parvati: Women and Madness in Contemporary India.* Philadelphia: University of Pennsylvania Press.

Poe, Edgar Allan. 1843. "The Black Cat." *Saturday Evening Post,* August 19, 1843.

Pollard, Bill. 2008. *Habits in Action: A Corrective to the Neglect of Habits in Contemporary Philosophy of Action.* Saarbrücken, Germany: Dr. Muller.

———. 2010. "Habitual Actions." In *A Companion to Philosophy of Action,* edited by Timothy O'Connor and Constantine Sandis, 74–81. Oxford: Wiley-Blackwell.

Povinelli, Elizabeth A. 2002. *The Cunning of Recognition: Indigenous Alterities and the Making of Australian Multiculturalism.* Durham, N.C.: Duke University Press.

———. 2011. *Economies of Abandonment: Social Belonging and Endurance in Late Liberalism.* Durham, N.C.: Duke University Press.

Powell, Amber Joy, Heather R. Hlavka, and Sameena Mulla. 2017. "Intersectionality and Credibility in Child Sexual Assault Trials." *Gender & Society* 31 (4): 457–80.

Prasad, Leela. 2007. *Poetics of Conduct: Oral Narrative and Moral Being in a South Indian Town.* New York: Columbia University Press.

———. 2010. "Ethical Subjects: Time, Timing and Reliability." In *Ethical Life in South Asia,* edited by Anand Pandian and Daud Ali, 174–92. Bloomington: Indiana University Press.

Price, Joshua M. 2002. "The Apotheosis of Home and Maintenance of Spaces of Violence." *Hypatia* 17 (4): 39–70.

Procupez, Valeria. 2015. "The Need for Patience: The Politics of Housing Emergency in Buenos Aires." *Current Anthropology* 56: S55–S65.

Puar, Jasbir K. 2004. "Abu Ghraib: Arguing against Exceptionalism." *Feminist Studies* 30 (2): 522–34.

Puett, Michael. 2014. "Ritual Disjunctions: Ghosts, Philosophy, and Anthropology." In *The Ground Between: Anthropologists Engage Philosophy*, edited by Veena Das, Michael Jackson, Arthur Kleinman, and Bhrigupati Singh, 218–32. Durham, N.C.: Duke University Press.

———. 2015. "Ritual and Ritual Obligations: Perspectives on Normativity from Classical China." *Journal of Value Inquiry* 49: 543–50.

Pugh, Jonathan. Forthcoming. "Resilience." In *Words and Worlds: A Lexicon for Dark Times*, edited by Veena Das and Didier Fassin. Durham, N.C.: Duke University Press.

Quétel, Claude. 2011. *Les Lettres de Cachet: Une Légende Noire*. Paris: Perrin.

Rabinow, Paul, and Nikolas Rose. 2006. "Biopower Today." *BioSocieties* 1 (2): 195–217.

Radcliffe-Brown, A. R. (1929) 1952. "The Sociological Theory of Totemism." In *Structure and Function in Primitive Society*, 117–33. London: Cohen & West.

Rai, Benjamin. 1992. "What Is His Name: Translation of Divine Names in Some Major North Indian Languages." *Bible Translator* 43 (4): 443–46.

Rajan, Rajeshwari Sundar. 2003. *The Scandal of the State: Women, Law, and Citizenship in Postcolonial India*. Durham, N.C.: Duke University Press.

Read, Rupert. 2005. "IV—Throwing Away 'The Bedrock.'" *Proceedings of the Aristotelian Society* 105 (1): 81–98.

Reader, Soran. 2007. "The Other Side of Agency." *Philosophy* 82 (4): 579–604.

———. 2010. "Agency, Patency and Personhood." In *A Companion to Philosophy of Action*, edited by Timothy O'Connor and Constantine Sandis, 200–7. Oxford: Wiley-Blackwell.

Rechtman, Richard. 2006. "The Survivor's Paradox: Psychological Consequences of the Khmer Rouge Rhetoric of Extermination." *Anthropology and Medicine* 13 (1): 1–11.

———. 2017. "From an Ethnography of the Everyday to Writing Echoes of Suffering." *Medicine Anthropology Theory* 4 (3): 130–42.

Rejali, Daius. 2007. *Torture and Democracy*. Princeton, N.J.: Princeton University Press.

Renou, Louis. 1941–1942. "Les connexions entre le ritual et la grammaire en Sanscrit." *Journal Asitique*: 105–65.

Reynolds, Pamela. 1995. "'Not Known Because Not Looked For': Ethnographers Listening to the Young in Southern Africa." *Ethnos* 60 (3–4): 159–81.

Richards, David A. J. 1971. *A Theory of Reasons for Action*. Oxford: Oxford University Press.

Richter, Julius. 1908. *A History of Missions in India*. Translated by Sydney H. Moore. Chicago: Fleming H. Revell Company.

Ricoeur, Paul. 1966. *Freedom and Nature: The Voluntary and the Involuntary*. Translated by Erazim Kohák. Evanston, Ill.: Northwestern University Press.

———. 1994. *Oneself as Another*. Chicago: University of Chicago Press.

Robbins, Joel. 2006. "Social Thought and Commentary: Anthropology and Theology: An Awkward Relationship?" *Anthropological Quarterly* 79 (2): 285–94.

Rosaldo, Renato. 1980. *Ilongot Headhunting, 1883–1973: A Study in Society and History*. Stanford, Calif.: Stanford University Press.

———. 1984. "Grief and a Headhunter's Rage: On the Cultural Force of Emotions." In *Text, Play, and Story: The Construction and Reconstruction of Self and Society*, edited by Edward M. Bruner, 178–95. Washington, D.C.: American Ethnological Society.

———. 2014. *The Day of Shelly's Death: The Poetry and Ethnography of Grief*. Durham, N.C.: Duke University Press.

———. n.d. How I Write—Conversation Transcript. https://web.stanford.edu /group/howiwrite/Transcripts/Rosaldo_transcript.html.

Rudé, George. 1959. *The Crowd in the French Revolution*. Oxford: Clarendon.

———. 1964. *The Crowd in History, 1730–1848*. New York: Wiley.

Sabean, David. 2001. "Peasant Voices and Bureaucratic Texts: Narrative Structure in Early Modern German Protocols." *Little Tools of Knowledge: Historical Essays on Academic and Bureaucratic Practices*, edited by Peter Becker and William Clark, 67–94. Ann Arbor: University of Michigan Press.

Sachs, David. 1988. "On Wittgenstein's *Remarks on Frazer's Golden Bough*." *Philosophical Investigations* 11 (2): 147–50.

Saheb, Shaik Abdul Azeez. 1998. "A Festival of Flags: Hindu and Sacralising of Localism at the Shrine of Nagar-e-Sharif in Tamil Nadu." In *Embodying Charisma: Modernity, Locality, and Performing of Emotions in Sufi Shrines*, edited by Pnina Weber and Helene Basu, 51–62. London: Routledge.

Sahlins, Marshall. 2013. *What Kinship Is—And Is Not*. Chicago: University of Chicago Press.

Sainsbury, R. Mark. 1996. "Concepts without Boundaries." In *Vagueness: A Reader*, edited by Rosanna Keefe and Peter Smith, 251–64. Cambridge, Mass.: MIT Press.

Salgues, Camille. 2008. "Un nouveau Wittgenstein encore inapprochable. Le rôle et la place du philosophe dans l'anthropologie." *L'Homme* 3–4 (187–88): 201–22.

Satyanarayana, S., R. Subbaraman, P. Shete, G. Gore, J. Das, A. Cattamanchi, K. Mayer et al. 2015. "Quality of Tuberculosis Care in India: A Systematic Review." *International Journal of Tuberculosis and Lung Disease*, 19 (7): 751–63.

Satyogi, Pooja. 2016. "Intimate Public Spaces: Policing 'Domestic Cruelty' in Police Cells in Delhi." PhD diss., Johns Hopkins University.

———. 2019. "Law, Police and 'Domestic Cruelty': Assembling Written Complaints from Oral Narratives." *Contributions to Indian Sociology* 53 (1): 46–71.

Scheper-Hughes, Nancy. 1992. *Death without Weeping: The Violence of Everyday Life in Brazil.* Berkeley: University of California Press.

Schulte, Joachim. 1993. *Experience and Expression: Wittgenstein's Philosophy of Psychology.* Oxford: Clarendon.

———. 2006. "The Pneumatic Conception of Thought." *Grazer Philosophiche Studien* 71 (1): 39–55.

Schutz, Alfred. 1970. *On Phenomenology and Social Relations: Selected Writings,* edited by H. R. Wagner. Chicago: University of Chicago Press.

Scott, David. 1994. *Formations of Ritual: Colonial and Anthropological Discourses on the Sinhala Yaktovil.* Minneapolis: University of Minnesota Press.

Scott, James C. 1985. *Weapons of the Weak.* New Haven, Conn.: Yale University Press.

———. 1990. *Domination and the Arts of Resistance: Hidden Transcripts.* New Haven, Conn.: Yale University Press.

Searle, John R. 1969. *Speech Acts.* Cambridge: Cambridge University Press.

Segal, Lotte Buch. 2018. "Tattered Textures of Kinship: The Effects of Torture among Iraqi Families in Denmark." *Medical Anthropology: Cross Cultural Studies in Health and Illness* 37 (7): 553–67, https://doi.org/10.1080/01459740.2018.1462807.

Sehdev, Megha Sharma. 2018. "Interim Artifacts of Law: Interruption and Absorption in Indian Domestic Violence Cases." PhD diss., Johns Hopkins University.

Selby, Don. 2014. "Experiments with Fate: Buddhist Morality and Human Rights in Thailand." In *Wording the World: Veena Das and Scenes of Inheritance,* edited by Roma Chatterji, 128–53. New York: Fordham University Press.

———. 2018. *Human Rights in Thailand.* Philadelphia: University of Pennsylvania Press.

Seligman, Adam B., Robert P. Weller, Michael J. Puett, and Bennett Simon. 2008. *Ritual and Its Consequences: An Essay on the Limits of Sincerity.* New York: Oxford University Press.

Severi, Carlo. (2007) 2015. *The Chimera Principle: An Anthropology of Memory and Imagination.* Translated by Janet Lloyd. Foreword by David Graeber. Chicago: HAU Books.

Sheringham, Michael. 2008. *Everyday Life: Theories and Practices from Surrealism to the Present.* Oxford: Oxford University Press.

Simone, Abdou Maliqalim. 2004 "People as Infrastructure: Intersecting Fragments in Johannesburg." *Public Culture* 16 (3): 407–29.

Singer, Milton. 1984. "A Neglected Source of Structuralism: Radcliffe-Brown, Russell, and Whitehead." *Semiotica* 48 (1–2): 11–96.

Singh, Bhrigupati. 2009. "Of Gods and Grains: Lives of Desire in Rural Central India." PhD diss., Johns Hopkins University.

———. 2012. "The Headless Horseman of Central India: Sovereignty at Varying Thresholds of Life." *Cultural Anthropology* 27 (2): 383–407.

———. 2015. *Poverty and the Quest for Life: Spiritual and Material Striving in Rural India.* Chicago: University of Chicago Press.

———. 2019. "Can a Neighborhood Fall Sick?" Unpublished manuscript.

Smalley, William A. 1991. *Translation as Mission: Bible Translation in the Modern Missionary Movement.* Macon, Ga.: Mercer University Press.

Smith, Katherine. 2012. *Fairness, Class and Belonging in Contemporary England.* New York: Palgrave.

Steinberg, Jonah. 2019. *A Garland of Bones: Child Runaways in India.* New Haven, Conn.: Yale University Press.

Stewart, Kathleen. 2007. *Ordinary Affects.* Durham, N.C.: Duke University Press.

Strathern, Marilyn. 1988. *The Gender of the Gift: Problems with Women and the Problems with Societies in Melanesia.* Berkeley: University of California Press.

Sundaram, Vivan. 2008. *Trash.* New Delhi: Photoink.

———. 2012. *Gagawaka: Making Strange.* New Delhi: Vadehra Art Gallery.

Suresh, Mayur. 2016. "The File as Hypertext: Documents, Files, and the Many Worlds of the Paper State." In *Law, Memory, Violence: Uncovering the Counter-Archive,* edited by Stewart Motha and Honni van Rijswijk, 97–115. London: Routledge.

Suri, Rochelle, and Daniel B. Pitchford. 2010. "The Gift of Life: Death as Teacher in the Aghori Sect." *Transpersonal Studies* 29 (1): 128–33.

Talebi, Shahla. 2011. *Ghosts of Revolution: Rekindled Memories of Imprisonment in Iran.* Stanford, Calif.: Stanford University Press.

Tambiah, Stanley J. 1996. *Leveling Crowds: Ethnonationalist Conflicts and Collective Violence in South Asia.* Berkeley: University of California Press.

Taneja, Anand Vivek. 2013. "Jinnealogy: Everyday Life and Islamic Theology in Post-Partition Delhi." *HAU: Journal of Ethnographic Theory* 3 (3): 139–65.

Tarlo, Emma. 2003. *Unsettling Memories: Narratives of the Emergency in Delhi.* Berkeley: University of California Press.

Taussig, Michael. 1992. "Reification and the Consciousness of the Patient." In *The Nervous System,* 83–111. New York: Routledge.

Taylor, Charles. 1996. "Iris Murdoch and Moral Philosophy." In *Iris Murdoch and the Search for Human Goodness,* edited by Maria Antonaccio and William Schweiker, 1–39. Chicago: University of Chicago Press.

Thomas, Kenneth J. 2001. "Allah in Translations of the Bible." *Bible Translator* 52 (3): 301–6.

Thomas, Yan. 2011. *Les opérations du droit*. Paris: EHESS.

Thompson, E. P. 1971. "The Moral Economy of the English Crowd in the Eighteenth Century." *Past Present* 50: 76–126.

Thoreau, Henry David. 1849. *On the Duty of Civil Disobedience*. Elegant Ebooks. https://www.ibiblio.org/ebooks/Thoreau/Civil%20Disobedience.pdf (accessed March 25, 2019).

Thrift, Nigel. 2007. *Non-representational Theory*. London: Routledge.

Tiliander, Bror. 1974. *Christian and Hindu Terminology: A Study in Their Mutual Relations with Special Reference to the Tamil Area*. Vol. 12. Uppsala, Sweden: Almqvist och Wiksell.

Trautman, Thomas. 1981. *Dravidian Kinship*. Cambridge: Cambridge University Press.

———. 2000. "India and the Study of Kinship Terminologies." *L'Homme. Question de parenté* 154/155: 559–72.

Travis, Charles. 2001. *Unshadowed Thought: Representations in Thought and Language*. Cambridge, Mass.: Harvard University Press.

———. 2009. *Thought's Footing: A Theme in Wittgenstein's Philosophical Investigations*. Oxford: Oxford University Press.

Trawick, Margaret. 1990. *Notes on Love in a Tamil Family*. Stanford: University of California Press.

Tsohatzidis, Savas L. 2018. "Performativity and the 'True/ False Fetish.'" In *Interpreting J. L. Austin: Critical Essays*, edited by Savas Tsohatzidis, 96–118. Cambridge: Cambridge University Press.

Tubb, Gary. 2014. "Baking Uma." In *Innovations and Turning Points: Towards a History of Kavya Literature*, edited by Yigal Bronner and David Shulman, 71–82. New Delhi: Oxford University Press.

Tylor, E. B. (1878) 1974. *Primitive Culture*. New York: Gordon.

Urmson, J. O. 1977. "Performative Utterances." *Midwest Studies in Philosophy* 11: 120–27.

van der Veer, Peter. 1994. *Religious Nationalism: Hindus and Muslims in India*. Berkeley: University of California Press.

Vilaça, Aparecida. 2005. "Chronically Unstable Bodies: Reflections on Amazonian Corporealities." *Journal of the Royal Anthropological Institute* 11 (3): 445–64.

Vismann, Cornelia. 2008. *Files: Law and Media Technology*. Translated by Geoffrey Winthrop-Young. Stanford, Calif.: Stanford University Press.

———. 2013. "Cultural Techniques and Sovereignty." *Theory, Culture, and Society* 30 (6): 83–93.

Viveiros de Castro, Eduardo. 1992. *From the Enemy's Point of View: Humanity and Divinity in an Amazonian Society*. Chicago: University of Chicago Press.

Vogel, Shane. 2009. "By the Light of What Comes After: Eventologies of the Ordinary." *Women & Performance: A Journal of Feminist Theory* 19 (2): 247–60, doi: 10.1080/07407700903034204.

Wagner, Roy. 1991. "The Fractal Person." *Big Men and Great Men: Personifications of Power in Melanesia*, edited by Maurice Godelier and Marilyn Strathern, 159–73. Cambridge: Cambridge University Press.

Weber, Max. 1978. *Economy and Society*. Vol. 1. Translated by Guenther Roth and Clauss Wittish. Berkeley: University of California Press.

Werbner, Pnina, and Helene Basu, eds. 1998. *Embodying Charisma: Modernity, Locality, and Performing of Emotions in Sufi Shrines*. London: Routledge.

Williams, Bernard. 1981. "Persons, Character, and Morality." In *Moral Luck: Philosophical Papers 1973–1980*. Cambridge: Cambridge University Press.

Williams, Meredith. 2004. "Nonsense and Cosmic Exile: The Austere Reading of the Tractatus." In *Wittgenstein's Lasting Significance*, edited by Max Kolbel and Bernhard Weiss, 6–31. London: Routledge.

Williams, Michael. 1996. *Unnatural Doubts*. Princeton, N.J.: Princeton University Press.

———. 2007. "Why (Wittgensteinian) Contextualism Is Not Relativism." *Episteme* 4 (1): 93–114.

Wittgenstein, Ludwig. (1953) 1968. *Philosophical Investigations*. Translated by G. E. M. Anscombe. London: Macmillan Publishing Company.

———. 1958. *The Blue and Brown Books*. Oxford: Blackwell.

———. 1969. *On Certainty*. Edited by G. E. M. Anscombe and G. H. von Wright. Translated by Denis Paul and G. E. M. Anscombe. Oxford: Basil Blackwell.

——— 1976. "Cause and Effect: Intuitive Awareness." Edited by Rush Rhees. Translated by Peter Winch. *Philosophia* 6 (3): 409–25.

———. 1980. *Culture and Value*. Edited by G. H. von Wright. Translated by Peter Winch. Oxford: Blackwell.

———. 1992. *Last Writings on the Philosophy of Psychology*, vol. 2. Edited by G. H. von Wright and H. Nyman. Translated by C. G. Luckhardt and M. A. E. Aue. Oxford: Blackwell.

———. 1993. "Ursache und Wirkung: Intuitives Erfassen / Cause and Effect: Intuitive Awareness." In *Ludwig Wittgenstein: Philosophical Occasions, 1912–1951*, edited by James C. Klagge and Alfred Nordmann, 370–405. Indianapolis/Cambridge: Hackett.

———. 2001. *Philosophical Investigations*. 3rd ed. Edited by P. M. S. Hacker and Joachim Schulte. Translated by G. E. M. Anscombe, P. M. S. Hacker and Joachim Schulte. Oxford: Blackwell Publishing.

Zengotita, Thomas de. 1989. "On Wittgenstein's *Remarks on Frazer's Golden Bough*." *Cultural Anthropology* 4 (4): 390–98.

## LEGAL CASES CITED

Government of India v. Sudhanshu and Others (2011)

Jitender v. State, Crl. M.C. 438/2009 S.C. (2009)

Om Prakash v. State of U.P., C.I.R.L.J, S.C. (2006)

Shahan Sha A v. State of Kerala, Bail Appl. No. 5288 (2009)

Smt. Bhanwari Devi v. State of Rajasthan (2) WLN 387 (1996)

State of A.P. v. Ganguli S Murthy (1977)

State v. Mahmood Farooqui (2018)

State v. Sajdu Khan and Others (1950)

## APPELLATE COURT JUDGMENTS CITED IN THE JUDGMENT OF *GOVERNMENT OF INDIA V. SUDHANSHU AND OTHERS* (2011)

Alagupandi v. State of Tamil Nadu, CRI. L.J. 3363 (2012)

Bhoganbhai-Hirjibhai v. State of Gujarat, AIR S.C. 735 (1983)

Darbara Singh v. State of Punjab, KI. L. J. 4757 (2012)

Dinesh v. Rajasthan, C.R.L.J. 1679 (2006)

Dinesh v. State of Rajasthan, C.R.L.J. 681 S.C. (2006)

Krishna Mochi v. State of Bihar (KaIMS) 230 S.C. (2002)

Krishna Pillai Shiv Kumar v. Kerala A/R S.C. 1237, M/S Siyaram and Others v.
    M.P. 2009; C.R.L.J. 2071 (1981)

Mahesh v. U.P. State All. High Court (D,B,) A.C.R. (3) P 30 (Hindi J) (2006)

Moh. Alam v. State Adm. City of Delhi, CRI., App. 431/99 (2006)

Munesh, CIR. L.J. 194 (2013)

Narendra Kumar v. N.C.T, CRI. L.J. 3032 (2012)

Om Prakash v. State of Uttar Pradesh, C.I.R.L.J., S.C., 2913 (2006)

State of A.P. v. Ganguli S. Murthy, CRI.L.J. 774 S.C. (1977)

State of Punjab v. Gurumit Singh, A.I.R., S.C., 1393 (1996)

Vishnu v. Maharashtra, C.R.L.J. 303 (2006)

West Bengal v. Meer Mad. Umar (3) A.C.R. 2200 S.C. (2000)

# INDEX

*Abnormal*, 22, 175, 180, 181–84
abuse, 62, 88–90, 92, 241, 342n8,
  345nn28,29,30, 355n19, 363n6
access, first person, 133, 149, 300–1; to context,
  19, 49, 321; to reality, 179; to water and
  electricity, 19, 20, 67, 221
action, 11, 16, 19, 35, 45, 69–70, 105–18,
  119–21, 140, 149, 179, 219; and expressions,
  21, 58, 60, 62, 64, 66, 72, 73, 78, 79, 92, 95,
  96, 150, 344n23; in grammar, 226, 228, 231,
  238, 244, 367n11, 368n18; and karma, 82–85;
  machine like, mechanical, 33, 108, 124, 125,
  154; moral/ethical, 63, 80, 105, 120–21;
  political, 27, 58, 59, 62, 186; ritual, 38,
  72, 80, 250, 251, 293, 29; types of, 38, 59,
  249, 365n14; vulnerability of, 10, 60;
  *See also* Austin; habit; performance;
  rules
aesthetics, 18, 37, 81, 88, 127, 138, 154, 204, 303,
  327, 330, 344n20, 347n8
affect, 24, 49, 95, 133, 144–45, 150, 154, 185,
  204–5, 239, 306, 338n2, 350n13, 367n13
agreement, 8, 186, 252, 321, 356n11; and
  consent, 13, 102, 206, 263; in forms
  of life, 13, 29, 35–36, 86, 102, 200–1,
  258, 263–64, 266. *See also* Cavell;
  Wittgenstein
Anscombe, G. E. M., 338n1; on the first
  person, 91, 134, 349n1; and philosophy, 1,
  10, 16, 18–19, 25, 29–30, 56–57, 60, 63, 67,
  90, 95, 97, 121–22, 125, 138, 145, 199, 245,
  246, 249, 264, 279, 288, 290, 293, 304,
  306, 309, 317–19
Arendt, Hannah, 59, 112
Asad, Talal, 31, 53, 97, 273, 288
Aspiration, 144, 149, 150, 152, 170, 186, 197,
  272–73, 348n3

Austin, J. L., 96, 100, 168, 253, 257, 260, 292,
  342n7, 343nn8–10, 344n22, 346n1; action
  and expression, 20, 60, 62, 95, 257; context,
  20, 257; excuses, 62, 64, 96, 112; felicity/
  infelicity, 20, 61–63, 87; illocutionary
  force, 20, 49, 63–64, 72, 79, 80, 107, 261, 264,
  343n8; performative utterances, 20, 61–62,
  342–43n8, 363n6; perlocutionary effect,
  20, 48, 49, 63–64, 72, 79; pretending,
  62–63, 105, 112; speech acts, 61, 264;
  truth, 61–62, 96, 342nn7–8

Baxi, Pratiksha, 218, 227–28, 333, 352n7,
  354n24
Beckett, Samuel, 60, 145, 146; *Endgame*, xii,
  145, 147
body, 54, 129, 273; decaying of, 259, 317;
  Foucault on, 17, 176, 184; givenness of, 5;
  human, 263, 291, 331, 341n2; individual, 31;
  and mind, 262, 265; and pain, 56, 258; as
  picture of the soul, 54, 260, 262; reading,
  55–56, 109, 110; social, 22, 177, 184, 294;
  and spirit, 301
belief, 17, 25, 31, 47, 51–54, 56, 125, 133–35,
  137, 147, 161, 220, 252, 255, 260–63,
  267–68, 290–92, 342n7, 350nn13,14,
  367n10
belonging, 10, 15, 19, 43, 66–67, 82, 155, 168,
  238, 268, 270, 343n11
Benoist, Jocelyn, 18, 247, 305, on concepts,
  10, 305, 320–21, 324; on reality, 12
Benveniste, Émile, 79, 225–26, 368n18
Berlant, Lauren, 93–95, 342
boundaries, 3, 66, 68–69, 80–81, 121, 136, 175,
  190, 258, 267, 280, 285, 312, 320, 324
Bourdieu, Pierre, 93, 102, 338n5
Bouveresse, Jacques, 248

Brandel, Andrew, 319, 339n3, 345n25
Butler, Judith, 59, 341, 345n25

Canguilhem, Georges, 22, 181–83, 189, 197, 355n5
case, psychiatry/psychiatric, 84, 150, 152, 158, 168, 174, 216–23, 225–27, 229–33, 235–45, 249
Caton, Steve, 102, 111–12, 114
Cavell, Stanley, xii, xiii, 1, 13, 16, 132, 145–46, 261, 307–8, 337n1, 364n11; on agreement, 40, 199; on the child, 31, 48; on everyday, 6, 7, 8, 12, 87, 100, 122, 125, 149, 200, 348n4; on expression, 137; on forms of life, 40, 149; on gender, 87; on the human, 18, 96, 123, 169, 206; on knowledge, 266; knowing and acknowledging, 53, 56, 266; on ordinary, 7, 9, 15, 343n9; on other/s, 10, 149; on pain, 55; on passionate utterances, 20, 63, 64, 86, 91, 343n8; on perlocutionary effect, 91; on politics, 12, 41; on private language, 136; on projection, 65, 86, 87; on rules, 35, 65; on skepticism, 17, 49, 50, 87, 356n12; on transfiguration, 42; on voice, 4, 5, 17, 123, 199, 260, 339n6
Chatterji, Roma, 33, 67, 270
child, 9, 14, 17, 24, 31–37, 63, 88, 91–92, 106, 133, 139–40, 150, 227–29, 250, 319
Christianity, 277, 284, 286, 288
citizen/citizenship, 67, 79, 151, 156, 198, 205, 211, 272, 339n4
Coetzee, John Maxwell, 23–4, 198–99, 201, 203–15, 325; *Diary of a Bad Year*, 23, 198, 202, 209, 212, 214; *Waiting for the Barbarians*, 23, 198, 201–2, 204–5, 207, 210
coevalness, 371n2. *See also* duration
color, 81, 322–23, 325–26. *See also* experience, fine grains of
community, 34–37, 116, 137, 151, 161, 163, 166, 170, 184, 200, 209, 211; community of life, 264–65; political community, 12–13, 23–24; not-community, 151
concepts, 52, 121, 181, 207, 246, 249, 276, 278–80, 320–25, 328–29, 331, 365n3, 366n4, 367n11, 370nn30–31; anthropological, 25, 26, 246, 247, 275, 278, 283, 287, 304, 308, 326, 329, 365n3; and context, 3, 12, 276, 292, 297, 326; crisscrossing of, 25, 174, 277–79, 281–82, 285–86, 288, 293, 297, 305; and experience, 8, 9, 275, 277, 320–23, 327, 329; of God/gods, 26, 247, 277, 281, 281–86, 294, 305; normativity of, 276, 280, 281, 283, 286, 289, 297; projection/extension of, 8,

34, 149, 280, 281, 286, 289, 306, 326; and reality, xiii, 4, 8–10, 277, 280, 281, 297, 302, 305, 322, 324, 325, 330; in relation to sign/image, 276, 281, 302, 305–6, 321, 366n4
concreteness, 195, 306, 347. *See also* rightness
consent, 12–14, 23, 41, 66, 151, 198, 218, 223, 232, 342n6
context, 3, 9, 12, 17–18, 20, 35, 40, 63–65, 86–87, 250, 254–55, 257–58, 264, 266, 272, 276, 287, 296–97, 302, 319–20, 321, 326, 341n5
convention, 12, 40, 47, 49, 60–64, 92, 205–6, 210, 259, 261, 271–72, 283, 312, 342n6
corruption, 75, 119, 239–41, 244, 359n3
Crary, Alice, 12, 18, 98
crisis, 179–80, 186–87, 189, 193, 196, 204, 241, 361
critique, 12, 41–42, 66, 93–94, 100, 245, 348
cruelty, 4, 110, 113, 216, 234, 247, 265, 331
culture, 3–33, 35, 39, 41–43, 51–52, 57, 66, 100, 173, 200, 260, 263, 278, 305, 331, 364n11; counter-culture, 19, 44, 57; nature and culture, 256; popular culture, 243
customs, 35, 38, 40, 99, 106, 108, 200, 252, 255, 278

Dalit, 74–75, 82
death: -bed statement, 21, 89, 126, 130, 137, 140, 148; *Day of Shelly's Death*, 6, 309–19; rituals, 130, 261–62; slow death, 94, 342n4
Delhi, Xiii, 1–2, 19, 21–24, 59, 67–69, 71–72, 77, 83–85, 87, 100, 109–10, 127, 149, 151, 157, 162, 167, 173, 186, 216, 229, 239, 291, 307, 338n3, 339n9, 342n3, 343n13, 344n16, 345n25
desire, 20, 63–64, 79, 82, 92, 100, 115, 129, 187, 195, 208–12, 214, 225, 254, 268, 273, 294–95, 347n8, 350n14, 353n3; disorders of, 21, 148, 151, 154, 173
detail, 2, 39, 60, 93–94, 119, 124, 196, 235–36, 238, 243, 247, 323, 341n5
Diamond, Cora, 7, 17–18, 26, 30, 97, 101, 117–19, 121–22, 148, 278, 325, 328, 340n2, 347n8, 349n11, 363n4
Dinka, 25–26, 277, 281–83, 287–88, 298–305, 368n16
domestic, 12–15, 42–45, 116, 123, 125, 138, 148, 259, 346n4, 347n7, 348n4; violence, 101, 110, 345n28
Donatelli, Piergiorgio, 6–8, 18, 174, 245, 340n10, 348n3, 362n18
dreams, 15, 160–61, 165–67, 169, 209–10, 212–13, 353n20

madness, 14, 22, 42, 45, 57, 114, 123, 173–75, 178–80, 185–89, 195–97, 354n1, 355n3, 364n11

map, 3, 20, 68, 74, 77, 312–19, 343n13

marriage, 49, 123, 144, 357n14; intercommunity, 149, 151–52, 155, 157, 161–63, 167–69, 171, 351nn5,6, 352nn10,12; as a picture of the everyday, 15, 66, 123; ritual, 49, 126, 261, 342nn6,8, 351n1

masculinity, 43, 120

McDowell, John, 79, 107

meaning, 3, 5, 12, 35, 40, 44, 48, 54, 65, 136, 145, 250, 255, 257, 262, 301, 340n5, 349n10, 363n4

media, 59, 93–94, 111, 235, 242, 321, 328, 339n3, 359n3

Mehta, Deepak, 33, 67, 86, 151, 220, 354n23, 361nn10,13

*mīmāṃsa*, 26, 39, 251–52, 285, 292–94, 367nn9,10,13

Mookerjee, Nayanika, 27, 320

moral, 119, 121, 148–50, 168–72, 214, 234, 246, 356n8; and ethical, 80, 97–100; philosophy, 17–18, 115, 117, 121, 171, 201, 347n8

Moran, Richard, 135, 137, 350n14

Mosse, David, 318

Muslim, 171–72, 184, 194, 268–71, 273, 291–92, 352n12, 353nn17,20,21, 354n23, 365n16; Muslim-Hindu marriages, 149, 151–52, 155, 157, 161–63, 167–69, 171, 351nn5,6, 352nn10,12. *See also* Islam

myth, 258–59, 263, 304, 371n3

mythology, 126, 263, 285, 344n20, 354n14; Wittgenstein on, 36, 149, 259, 262, 340n2

Nāgārjuna, 366n6, 367n11

name, 3, 61, 219, 213, 319, 344n22; changing one's, 163–64, 166–67; divine, 283–85, 289, 296, 366n7, 367n13, 368n19; in Hindu rituals, 130; husband's, 3, 90, 146; not naming, 89–91, 330; in Sanskrit grammar, 81; of streets, 69, 74; Wittgenstein on, 11, 31, 248, 279, 370n31

narration; ethics of, 101, 118

natural: as absorbed in the social, 40, 60, 65–66, 125, 257, 343n10; background of the human, 25, 43, 53, 207, 247, 256, 325, 342n6

newness, 22, 169, 170, 183, 251, 268, 270–73, 281, 288

nonsense, 3, 8, 61, 250, 267, 363nn3,4,5

normal, 109, 111, 140, 142, 188–89; and abnormal, 175; of concepts, 276–67, 281, 283, 286, 288–89, 297, 368n15; normatively normal, pathologically

normal, 182; pathological, 23, 182, 189, 197–98, 356n8, 358n1

*Normal and the Pathological,* 181, 356n8

norms, 22, 97, 108, 133, 140, 143–44, 257, 291, 350n11; internalization of, 175, 177, 181–83; new, 152, 182–83, 185, 189

Nuer, 26, 36, 52, 277, 281, 287–90, 303, 305–6, 368n16, 369n26

omens, 7, 11, 27, 166, 237, 241, 310–11, 313

ordinary: ethics, 99, 101–2, 105, 111–12, 116–17, 122, 124, 214; realism, 24, 125, 197, 243, 276

other, 10, 349n12; concrete, 10, 21, 93, 101, 131, 137–38, 200, 266, 347n1; skepticism and the, 17, 44, 50, 266, 268, 365n16

otherness, 37, 290–91, 296, 362n18

pain, 16, 41, 51, 54–56, 87, 98, 116, 131, 133, 247, 253, 258, 260–61, 265–66, 307–8

pathological. *See* normal

Parry, Jonathan, 129, 152–54, 170, 261, 346n5

partition of India, 2, 4, 42–43, 58, 88–89, 116, 137, 160, 208, 325, 338n3, 351n5

Perdigon, Sylvain, 100, 123

performance, xii, 20, 39, 61, 78–79, 82, 87, 154, 179, 244, 328, 341n2; ritual, 21, 109, 130, 166, 179, 249, 260–61, 342nn6,8

performatives, 20, 43, 48–49, 60–64, 72, 79, 91, 342nn6,8, 344n23, 363n6

person, grammatical (first, second, third), 5, 21, 51, 55, 64, 79, 90–91, 121, 124, 127, 131–37, 139, 149, 170, 244, 261–62, 300, 310, 312, 314, 347n1, 349n12, 350n13

Pinto, Sarah, 358n21, 370n2

*pir* (saint), 160, 166, 352n13, 353n21

police: diaries, 217, 220–22, 231–32, 235, 237, 359n3, 360n9, 361n10; harassment, 15, 24, 73, 75, 79, 162, 238–40, 245, 357n15; informer, 219–21, 232, 238, 243; procedure, 112, 151, 223, 229, 238, 240, 245, 359nn1,3

political community, 12–13, 23–24, 198, 202, 209, 211

politics, 5, 12, 59, 67, 93, 95, 171, 186, 221, 339n6, 342n5, 343n12; care as, 13, 14, 125; and consent, 12, 13, 14, 41, 214; of the ordinary, 19, 20, 58, 76, 92, 112

possible/possibility, 12, 20, 23, 39, 56, 64, 67, 87, 94, 99, 108, 111, 124, 135, 152, 170, 175, 203, 206, 207, 208, 215, 245, 253, 268, 281–91, 322, 332, 369n20; conditions of, 9, 80, 171, 219, 357n18; financial lives of the, 15, 104–5, 347n7; and footing, 252, 259, 322; imagination of, 12; of newness, 170, 268,

**Veena Das** is Krieger-Eisenhower Professor of Anthropology and adjunct professor of humanities at the Department of Comparative Thought and Literature at the Johns Hopkins University. Her most recent books are *Life and Words: Violence and the Descent into the Ordinary* (2007), *Affliction: Health, Disease, Poverty* (2015), and *Four Lectures on Ethics* (coauthored, 2015). She has also edited or coedited several books on social suffering, living and dying in the contemporary world, and the relation between philosophy and anthropology. Das is a Fellow of the American Academy of Arts and Sciences, the Academy of Scientists from Developing Societies, and Corresponding Fellow of the British Academy. She has received honorary doctorates from the University of Chicago, University of Edinburgh, University of Bern, and from Durham University. In 2015, she received the Nessim Habib Prize from the University of Geneva.

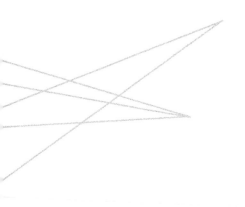

## Thinking from Elsewhere

Lightning Source UK Ltd.
Milton Keynes UK
UKHW012223140620
364850UK00003B/233